Theatre Under Deconstruction?
A Question of Approach

Studies in Modern Drama, volume 2
Garland Reference Library of the Humanities (vol. 1605)

Studies in Modern Drama
General Editor, Kimball King

Theatre Under Deconstruction?
A Question of Approach

Stratos E. Constantinidis

GARLAND PUBLISHING, INC. • NEW YORK & LONDON
1993

Library of Congress Cataloging-in-Publication Data

Constantinidis, Stratos E.
    Theatre under deconstruction? : A question of approach / by
Stratos E. Constantinidis.
        p.   cm. — (Studies in modern drama ; v. 2) (Garland
reference library of the humanities ; vol. 1605)
    Includes bibliographical refrences and index.
    ISBN 0–8153–0872–8
    1. Theater—Production and direction. 2. Drama—History and
criticism. 3. Deconstruction. I. Title. II. Series. III. Series:
Garland reference library of the humanities ; vol. 1605.
PN2053.C62   1993
792'.015—dc20   92–24320
                                                                      CIP

Printed on acid-free, 250-year-life paper
Manufactured in the United States of America

To Sharon and Sven

Contents

General Editor's Note

Theatre Under Deconstruction is the first publication of Garland Publishing's Studies in Modern Drama. The success of Casebooks on Modern Drama, which are collections of original essays on contemporary playwrights, has revealed that many scholars and general readers are deeply interested in current issues affecting the interpretation of dramatic literature. It seemed logical to permit a single author to express his or her views about a playwright or group of playwrights or to explore general topics related to the stage.

The present volume offers the reader interested in live performances a first encounter with deconstruction and suggests some ways in which deconstruction can be applied to practical and theoretical concerns. It begins with four controversial assumptions: that deconstruction can be defined; that it can be reduced to any analytical approach; that it can be simplified for general use; and that it can be applied to the work of playwrights, designers, directors, actors, audiences, and critics.

Stratos E. Constantinidis critically analyzes a wide range of texts that reveal popular misperceptions about deconstruction in the field of theatre. He investigates the charge that deconstruction is irresponsible and anti-historical and moves beyond the writings of major or minor theorists of deconstruction, as well as beyond the canon of traditional or radical theorists of the theater.

While most books on theatrical production only show that production styles—such as realism or expressionism—can be made manifest on stage, this book shows that the various analytical approaches—such as deconstruction, structuralism, and formalism—leave an impact on theatrical production. It suggests that deconstruction corrodes many of the assumptions of other approaches which regulate the production of plays.

Professor Constantinidis is currently teaching dramatic theory and criticism in the Department of Theater at Ohio State University and also serves as Director of Graduate Studies in that department. He has contributed articles to professional journals such as *Comparative Drama, Code/Kodikas: Ars Semeiotica,* the *Journal of Modern Greek Studies,* the *New Theatre Quarterly,* the *Journal of Dramatic Theory and Criticism, Poetics Today, Theater Studies, and World Literature Today.* He has translated and adapted into English the modern Greek comedy *Tale without Title,* by Iakovos Kambanellis, and has contributed "An Annotated Bibliography of Greek Dramatic Literature, History, and Criticism from 1824 to 1989" to the *Annotated Bibliography on Modern Greece.* He is presently working on a book entitled *Theatre in Communication Studies.*

In the near future, Garland studies of Joe Orton, Harold Pinter, and Peter Barnes, as well as topics of a more general nature, will provide sustained analyses of texts and ideas. Some of these studies will reflect their authors' mastery of contemporary theory, while others will be grounded in more traditional critical approaches. It is intended that, considered together, the Casebook series and the Studies series will provide a major resource for further research and appreciation of recent achievements in the theater.

Kimball King

List of Illustrations

Prologue

Well, if you ingenious scholars want high art in the theatre, please read the very learned Robortello of Udine. You will see in what he says about Aristotle and especially in what he writes about low art in theatre—which is scattered throughout many books— that today everything is in a state of confusion. However, if you wish to have my opinion on low art in the theatre, which now has the upper hand, and why it is necessary that audience demand should maintain the vulgar fad of those monstrous shows, then I will tell you what I think, please forgive me, because I must obey that audience which has the power to command me.

Lope de Vega, *The New Art of Writing Plays in this Age* (1609)

I think the theatre must be reformed in its plays, its speaking, its acting, and its scenery. That is to say, I think there is nothing good about it at present. First, we have to write or find plays that will make the theatre a place of intellectual excitment. . . . Second, we must make speech even more important than gesture upon the stage. . . . Third, we must simplify acting, especially in poetical drama, and in prose drama that is remote from real life. . . . Fourth, just as it is necessary to simplify gesture that it may accompany speech without being its rival, it is necessary to simplify both the form and colour of scenery and costume.

William Butler Yeats, *The Reform of the Theatre* (1903)

This book offers the advanced reader of drama, who is interested in live performances, a first encounter with deconstruction in the context of other analytical approaches in the field of theatre (such as structuralism and formalism), and it suggests some ways in which deconstruction might be applied to practical and theoretical concerns of theatre professionals. I begin with four controversial assumptions: that deconstruction can be defined; that it can be reduced to an analytical approach; that it can be simplified for general use; and that it can be applied to the work of playwrights, designers, directors, actors, audiences, and critics. These assumptions often make my narrative acquire a tone of assurance which sometimes creates the impression that I lack a self-awareness about my own critical position. I hope that this impression will stimulate my readers to rethink the issues that I discuss.

I wrote the book for two reasons: I wanted to understand some recurring problems in twentieth-century theatre theory and practice; and I wished to test the validity of deconstruction, as an "analytical approach," by applying it to a series of supposedly "great" (i.e., canonized) books authored by seminal theatre artists. I read critically a wide range of texts in order to discuss assumptions and inconsistencies in apparently seamless theories practiced by many of the most influential architects of the modern theatre. I also suggest strategies for future research in the areas of playwriting, design, directing, and acting.

There is a need to review and revise popular misperceptions about deconstruction in the field of theatre. Challenges such as John Ellis' *Against Deconstruction* (Princeton University Press, 1989) made me re-examine the "irresponsible" playfulness of several quasi-deconstructive theatrical experiments in the 1970s and the 1980s. In doing so, my primary goal was to investigate the charge that deconstruction is irresponsible and ahistorical. I discovered that once authorship is decentered during theatrical production, it is extended to empower with responsibility all those involved in the historical production of a play.

My secondary goal was to move, whenever possible, beyond the writings of "major" or "minor" theorists of deconstruction as well as to move beyond the canon of the "traditional" or "radical" theorists of the theatre. My intention was not to take my readers back to the "original" deconstruction of, say, Jacques Derrida or Paul de Man. Nor did I wish to take my readers back to the theories and practices of someone like Peter Brook or Jerzi Grotowski. The reader may realize that some of the theatre theorists whom I discuss had a "marginal" understanding of the issues involved. However, these theorists played a central, influential role in the theatre. Therefore, they provided the ground for my discussions, but by no means the foundation of my critical position.

There is also a pressing need for readable texts on the theory and practice of deconstruction in the theatre. Aside from Derrida's three essays on Antonin Artaud, most deconstructors have not dealt with theatre theory or practice. Likewise, most (post)structuralist drama critics, such as Herbert Blau, have touched upon deconstruction in an indirect manner. In addition, professional artists and graduate students often feel confused about critical concepts and issues because many "seminal" writers—from Antonin Artaud to Jacques Derrida—have discussed theatre in an obscure language while the humanists and social scientists, who have contributed to the study of theatre, often used forbidding methodological tools and jargon. In order to motivate the reader to move through a difficult issue, I have adopted a humorous tone, very defined arguments in order to show the practical side of a theoretical issue.

While most books on theatrical production only show how production styles—such as realism or expressionism—can be made manifest on stage, this book shows how the various analytical approaches—such as deconstruction, structuralism, or formalism—have an impact on theatrical production. I explored how deconstruction corrodes many of the assumptions of the other approaches which regulate the production of plays and how structure, meaning, and order, once dismantled, historically re-emerged in different, but equally repressive, forms. Readers from fields other than drama may find this book useful because the case of theatre offers clear and accessible examples of quasi-deconstructive theory and practice.

I have discussed issues which stimulated the formation of courses in the graduate curriculum, of panels in national conferences, and of special issues in reputable professional journals. I analyzed the problems by investigating specific examples of artistic and critical "malpractice." In doing so, I have tried to show the importance of methodologies—however diverse—in solving recurrent problems in theatrical production. Although I have focused on deconstruction, I attempt to place my discussion in the context of the principal findings of relevant quantitative studies from areas which are generally unknown to the average theatre artist, student, and teacher. Finally, I have illustrated how the many threads that make up and support a dominant theory for many consecutive decades have often been woven over arguments which conceal and suppress any opposing evidence.

My intention has been to expose the ideas of several "sacred cows" on the landscape of Western theatre—including luminaries such as Konstantin Stanislavsky, Antonin Artaud, Harold Clurman,

Jerzi Grotowski, Peter Brook, Richard Schechner, Joseph Chaikin, Johan Huizinga, Edmond Jones, Gordon Craig, Bertolt Brecht, Umberto Eco, Erwin Goffman, Lee Simonson, Mordecai Gorelik, Keir Elam, and Sam Shepard. My main objective was to help my readers become competent problem solvers by encouraging them to see around the corners of popular and influential theories in theatrical production.

This method has revealed that Derrida's concept of reversing and recasting binary oppositions is applicable to the world of theatre. However, this method has also exposed my own bias: that all analytical approaches are important and yet limited because no single one of them is "value-free" and "innocent." Those theatre practitioners and theorists (such as Peter Brook and Richard Schechner) who strove for "natural" responses and "scientific" objectivity were only misleading themselves and others.

I have focused on the poetics of theatre rather than on the thematics of drama, examining the medial transformations that a playtext undergoes in the hands of designers, directors, and actors until it meets the public eye. It is during these medial transformations that the influence of deconstruction is significant and promises far-reaching results.

Most introductory accounts of deconstruction—such as Christopher Norris's *Deconstruction: Theory and Practice* (Methuen, 1982) and Terry Eagleton's *Literary Theory* (University of Minnesota Press, 1983)—present some analytical approaches in a questionable historical sequence and do not concern themselves with dramatic literature or theatrical production. They begin with formalism (the Russian or the Anglo-American version), pass through phenomenology, structuralism, or semiotics, and conclude with deconstruction. They survey major critics, concepts, or theories discursively without describing (1) how and why these major critics generated questions which led to "major" answers and (2) how and why they answered them the way they did.

For this reason, I have abandoned the survey format in this book. Instead, I appeal to the spirit of inquiry in my readers by confronting them with several major problems which puzzle me— making *aporia* a necessary condition before attempting to solve anything. These motivating problems have helped me review answers which today appear sound or viable. I have not presented any theory, argument, or example without weaving it into this pervasive theme of problem solving.

Computer technology reopens the question of viable professional and artistic alternatives for theatre professionals. The advent of computer graphics in theatre design programs is also changing the way in which plays will be written and produced in the next century—as computer technology becomes more accessible to theatre artists. New technological inventions call for a re-examination of any established theories which control current theatrical practice. This is another way of saying that theory and practice can be distinguished, but cannot be separated.

What alternatives and benefits, if any, have resulted when "deconstructive" theatre artists have attempted to reform the structure of functions in theatrical production? I examined the work of actors, directors, designers, and playwrights, examining the innovative or renovative value of deconstruction in regard to the artistic and economic viability of theatre as a progressive institution. My intention has been "constructive" despite my focus on deconstruction. As I detail recent advances in the field and discuss future developments, I do not expect all my readers to share my views. In fact, I hope that this book will become a point of reference for dissent and fruitful debate.

The book has an introduction, three parts, and an epilogue that examine and discuss key problems in theatrical production and experience. Each part opens with a conversation among three friends who hardly agree on anything. These friends introduce the major topics that each chapter will deal with, and their arguments—interspersed with bibliographical references—provide the reader with the necessary background to situate the discussion within its broader historical context.

In the first part, I have investigated the domain of playwriting. In the context of speech and writing, I describe how the playwright's narrative (voice) has ordained the structure and the meaning of most Western theatrical productions. This state of affairs has sporadically been challenged by the advocates of a new aesthetic who argued that the production and perception of meaning in the theatre is a shared process. It changes as soon as the nature and structure of the interactive contact among playwrights, designers, directors, actors, spectators, and critics changes. I have also tried to explain why some of the challengers failed to introduce a new aesthetic as an alternative to logocentrism.

In the second part, I have examined the domain of designing and directing. I described how new technological inventions—such as computer-aided design—and new analytical tools—such as semiotics—are gradually changing research methods and production methods in the theatre, shifting the power structure for those who control the agents or the means of artistic production. I have also tried to explain why high technology, which facilitates the deconstructive work of some designers, if properly manipulated, may prevent them from altering the authoritarian framework of Western theatrical production.

In the third part, I have explored the domain of acting. I have described how the variety of theatrical experiences that a community of theatregoers can enjoy depends on the variety of production styles available to its theatre artists, and how, historically, different production styles lead to different methods of acting. Each novel method of acting affects the traditional structure of theatrical production by creating yet another type of theatre—say, Brecht's "epic theatre" or Brook's "holy theatre." I have also tried to explain why old and new methods of acting vary from one another only by the quantity (degree) of the self-involvement that actors and spectators experience rather than by the quality (kind) of verity that actors and spectators experience in realistic theatre or epic theatre.

No chapter tells a linear story of deconstruction in the field of theatre. Instead, each chapter reviews the most relevant literature within its focus and examines the various analytical approaches which have dealt with a problem. All chapters attempt to present consistent arguments, offer useful explanations, and dig up old and new scholarship by way of confronting several prevalent beliefs in the theory and practice of theatre. Although some readers may disagree with my emphasis, they may agree to reconsider many current theories which set the tenor for artistic work and research in theatre today.

Stratos E. Constantinidis

Acknowledgments

I am grateful to the following editors and publishers for various permissions: Methuen for permission to reprint one figure from page 37 of *Brecht on Theatre*, edited and translated by John Willett (London, 1978). Routledge, Chapman and Hall for permission to reprint one figure from page 72 of *Performance Theory*, revised and expanded by Richard Schechner (New York, 1988). *The Drama Review* for permission to reprint one figure from pages 8, 9, and 13 of the article "Drama, Script, Theatre, Performance" by Richard Schechner (New York, 1973). Brockhaus for permission to reprint Plate 36 (182B) of *Der Tell Halaf* by Max von Oppenheim (Leipzig, 1931). Messidor/Editions sociales for permission to reprint one figure from page 16 of *Lire le théâtre* by Anne Ubersfeld (Paris, 1977). The Macmillan Publishing Company and the University of Alabama Department of Theatre for permission to reprint one figure from pages 202, 203, and 204 of *The Director in the Theatre* by Marian Gallaway (New York, 1963). Routledge, Chapman and Hall for permission to reprint plates 4, 5, and 6 of *On the Art of Theatre* by Gordon Craig (London, 1911). Plenum Press for permission to reprint one figure from page 447 of *Advanced Computer Graphics*, edited by R. Parslow and R. Green (London, 1971). Plenum Press for permission to reprint one figure from page 64 of *Computer Graphics: Techniques and Applications* edited by R. Parslow et al. (London, 1969). *IEEE Computer Graphics and Applications* for permission to reprint one figure from pages 46 and 48 of "Aspects of Kinematic Simulation of Human Movement" (Los Alamitos, 1982). The Katonah Gallery and Mrs. Aronson for permission to reprint one figure on page 6 of *Stage Design As Visual Metaphor* by Boris Aronson, edited by Frank Rich (New York, 1989). Viking Press for permission to reprint one figure from page 92 of *Orghast at Persepolis* by Anthony Smith (New York, 1972). The *Journal of Dramatic Theory and Criticism* for permission to reprint my essay "Is Theatre Under Deconstruction" in a revised form as an introduction for this book (Lawrence, 1989). Gunter Narr and *Kodikas/Code: Ars Semeiotica* for permission to reprint my essay "Prompt-copy as a Subsystem: From Glossopoeia to Computer Graphics" in a revised form as the second chapter in Part Two of this book (Tübingen, 1987). Cambridge University Press and *The New Theatre Quarterly* for permission to reprint my article "Rehearsal as a Subsystem: Transactional Analysis and Role Research" in a revised form as the second chapter in Part Three of this book (Cambridge, 1988). Israel Science Publishers, Duke University Press and *Poetics Today* for permission to reprint my essay "Illusion in Theatre: The Sign/Stimulus Equivalence" in a revised form as the fourth chapter in Part Three of this book (Tel Aviv, 1988).

What Is Deconstruction?

Hebraism and Hellenism—between these two points of influence moves our world. At one time it feels more powerfully the attraction of one of them, at another time of the other.
Matthew Arnold, *Culture and Anarchy* (1869)

Are we Jews? Are we Greeks? We live in the difference between the Jew and the Greek, which is perhaps the unity of what is called history. We live in and of difference, that is, in hypocrisy.
Jacques Derrida, *Writing and Difference* (1967)

CHAPTER ONE

Destructive Solecisms

L ike all Western theatre artists, I have two good friends, a logocentrist and a deconstructor, who are not very kind to each other: John, the logocentrist, works in a theatre on Broadway while Jon, the deconstructor, in a theatre off Broadway. When they lived in London a couple of years ago, John was employed in a theatre on the West End; Jon in a theatre on the "Fringe." In fact, John always occupied the center of theatrical activity and Jon the periphery in every capital of the Western world that they worked. So, I think I understand why Jon is cross and wants to displace John from the center.

What I do not understand, when my two friends argue at my dinner table, is why they insist that their difference is fundamentally a linguistic problem. John argues that the Greco-Christian theatrical tradition has been logocentric: *that is, theatrical production always starts with a playtext which, no matter how sketchy and improvisational, is written by someone who functions as "playwright"; then, the director, the designers, and the actors develop this playtext into a performance.*

This is true up to a point, agrees Jon; behind the playtext, however, lurks the voice of the playwright, which is obeyed by directors, designers, and actors. Therefore, the Greco-Christian theatrical tradition has always been phonocentric: *that is, it always begins with interpreting not the playtext but the playwright's voice and intention by emphasizing speech over writing.*

Jon emphasizes writing, of course. The playtext, he claims, precedes both speech and the natural world. In plain English, the manuscript of any playwright comes before the "speech acts" and concurrent environment of any reader. Even the playwright is a reader to his own finished playtext; therefore, a playwright can learn about the world and his playtext by listening to the interpretations and glosses of drama scholars. Theatrical production proceeds through an interpretation of a playtext—of the written words that comprise it, to be precise.

According to John, logos *meant a rational, ordering principle in Classical Greek; it did not mean "speech." In Hellenistic Greek, under the influence of Christianity, this ordering principle came to mean a divine revelation* (theophany). *This revelation manifested itself primarily in visible terms in the New Testament through the incarnation of Jesus Christ. In fact, the Greco-Christian god—call him Dionysus or Jesus—is both visible and audible. It is the Hebrew god who reveals himself only as voice through speech in the Old Testament. The christianized* logos *transcends language—both speech and writing—through incarnation. Being lies beyond language. Being is known from itself, not from language. By way of analogy, the playtext comes alive in performance through the voice and body of the actors in the Greco-Christian theatrical tradition. The Hebrew tradition resents this* presence *because the Hebrew language does not have any form of the verb "to be" in the present tense; therefore, in John's opinion, the Hebrew tradition exalts the playtext because the written word does not require a presence (Atkins 1980:773). On the other hand, Greek language and logic concentrate on the relation between subject and predicate. The copula "is" requires an audio and/or visual presence. Presence in theatrical production means performance; it means live actors interacting with live spectators "here" and "now."*

Jon argues back that the Whorfian hypothesis has not been settled yet and that the Hebrew god does not reveal himself only as a voice; he actually led the children of Israel by a "pillar of cloud" during the day and by a "pillar of fire" at night (Exodus 13:21–22). Besides, the central theatrical act is the endless interpretation of a playtext, not the "incarnation" of a performance. Performance ends interpretation because it materializes the signs of a playtext and imposes ontology to textuality (Boman 1960:68, 151). This "idolatrous" Greek image-making views language as a system of audible and/or visible signs which represent reality through the use of metaphors. In metaphors, the figurative meanings replace the literal meanings, but even Aristotle knew that the literal meanings can cancel out the figurative meanings. Being, indeed, lies behind language, but being determines literal meaning because it allows this entire system of words and things to function.

This literal/figurative transfer of meanings through metaphors is hooked on the Platonic tradition. Plato's metaphysics, in Jon's opinion, transfers the mind from the visible and audible world to the invisible and inaudible world. These relationships have dominated the metaphysical explorations of Western theatre artists of pseudo-Oriental tastes from Euripides' "dionysiac" theatre to Brook's "holy" theatre. In the work of such theatre artists, it appears as if the Greco-Christian theatrical tradition implicitly adopts the Hebrew notion that the metaphysical exists only on the metaphorical plain of language where meaning "is" and "is not" at the same time. This metaphorical transfer that is accomplished through language, makes the "presence" of meaning ambivalent.

John finds these statements to be misleading generalizations which defy history. Plato indeed belittled writing in relationship to memory in Phaedrus, *but Plato banished playwrights and theatrical performances from his* Republic. *In fact, classical Greek drama developed and flourished before the days of Plato and Aristotle. Greek drama at its best was neither Platonic nor Aristotelian; it was Dionysiac! As for the medieval theatre, it was founded in the spirit of Christ, the little Dionysus, well before the Western scholars injected neo-Platonic, neo-Aristotelian, and neoclassical reformulations into Western drama. John believes that the endless interpretation and commentary that drama scholars have imposed on playtexts have displaced the real thing, the true "being" which only an open performance can introduce.*

The Hebrew tradition, in the opinion of John, sticks to the signs of inanimate words on a page and ignores the fulfilling presence of whatever these signs refer to on stage for one basic reason: the performance is the death of the playtext! A performance reifies signs, renders presence, and eternalizes significance "here" and "now." On the other hand, the game of scholarly interpretations mediates, equivocates, and displaces being by refusing to posit referents which fulfill a sign and stabilize it. In short, philological interpretations prevent the fulfilling presence of a performance.

For Jon, it is precisely this endless record of textual interpretations which testifies that a performance cannot exhaust the multiple interpretations that the various readings of a playtext make available. For example, the unreconciled glosses of a Greek or an Elizabethan playtext exist in a state of difference and displacement which prevents unity and fulfillment. This is the reason, according to Jon, that the Western theatrical tradition is

"disrespectful" to playtexts, updating and adapting their glosses for
stage presentation. This tradition believes that performance restores
being; that performance becomes a referent beyond language; that
performance stabilizes meaning by collapsing difference, promoting
direct identification and union.

The less patient my two friends grow with each other, the
more confusing their arguments become. Their linguistic metaphysics
upset my understanding of logos. I think that they are both wrong
because—whether they argue for or against—they do not regard
performance as one more text (a performance-text) which renders
presence and being on the stage quite ambivalent. I also think that
they limit their perspective when they discuss metaphors in the
narrow context of playtexts or performance-texts. If a logocentric
or deconstructive stance on metaphors can have any "cash" value
for the artistic and economic viability of theatre as a progressive
institution in society, this cannot be achieved by playtext analysis
or performance-text analysis alone.

Simply put, I see deconstruction as a method of analysis
and action which subverts the traditional ways of theatrical
production. It questions established definitions of "text," "author,"
and "reader" in Western theatrical tradition. Which "text" is most
vital in the theatrical experience: the playtext, the performance-
text, the prompt-copy, or the rehearsal-text? Who is the "author"
of the most vital text: the playwright, the dramaturge, the director,
the designer, the actor, the spectator, the general reader, the critic,
or the editor? Who is the most vital "reader" of the text: the scholar,
the critic, the general reader, the spectator, the actor, the director,
the designer, or the playwright? These questions of "textuality,"
"voice," and "interpretation" are based on value judgments and
have influenced—for better or worse—the structure of theatrical
production in Western societies over the years. In mainstream
theatrical production, they have created a hierarchy of priorities
and a chain of command which control behavior and arouse
expectations from the playwright right down to the audience.

This chain of command seems logical. At the one end of the
communication line stands the playwright. Who stands on the other
end of the line is conditional. It depends on the medium—say,
page or stage—by which the "text" is transmitted and subsequently
interpreted. The chain of command is also well ordered in

mainstream Western theatrical production. The playtext moves from hand to hand: from the playwright to the director; from the director to the designers and actors; and from the actors to the audience. The "word" is saved and retained from the playwright's pen to the actor's mouth and limbs.

Deconstruction proceeds to upset this itinerary in the play-production system of most Western theatre companies. Deconstruction first reverses the hierarchy in the system and then it dislodges the dominant unit in the system. In other words, deconstruction, as a method of action, proceeds by reversal and displacement. The logocentric systems of Western play production operate under two dominant spacial metaphors: the metaphor of the production line and the metaphor of the market ellipse.

Any theatre company that operates under the metaphor of the production line adopts a structured, hierarchical order of production which proceeds from playtexts to performance-texts through such intermediate, "subordinate" texts as the "prompt-copy" and the "rehearsal-text" (Figure 1). Under the metaphor of the market ellipse, the theatre companies of a country look like planets rotating around a sun. For example, the Broadway group of companies occupy the center while the Off-Broadway, the Off-Off-Broadway, and the regional theatre companies are displaced in the periphery of theatrical activity in the U.S.A. (Figure 2).

The companies on the outer rings generally repeat (rehash) the shows and the production structure of the companies in the center, even though (1) they have been pushed to the "margin" under such indicative names as "off," "off-off," "regional," "fringe," etc., and (2) they are in economic competition and artistic (both aesthetic and ideological) opposition with the companies of the center. This paradox shows the strength of the metaphor in shaping perceptions and in "fixing" behavioral and professional habits which reinforce the economic forces that keep these companies in artistic and economic exile or displacement. The eyes and ears of theatre artists, critics, and audiences have been fixed on a group of about 35 companies at the "center," although the so-called "regional" theatre in the U.S.A. covers an area of 3,000 miles from New York to California and has had well over 1,000 operating theatre companies in postwar years.

Even today, a show that originates in the regional theatre gravitates toward the "center." The trip of the show from the outer rings to New York City is still considered a test of excellence. The

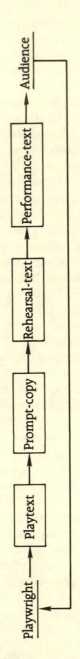

FIGURE 1. The Metaphor of the Production Line.

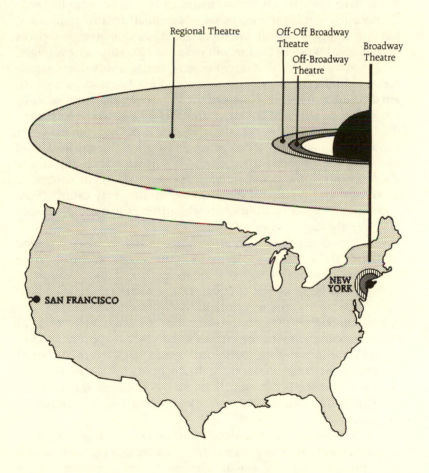

FIGURE 2. The Metaphor of the Market Ellipse.

closer the show travels to the "starlit" center, the more it gains in economic, professional, and artistic status. These logocentric theatre companies, however, are not the only companies in the theatre market of a country. The efforts of artistically opposed theatre companies to "de-center" Broadway production in the 1950s and 1960s have been largely unsuccessful so far. Those who flirt with deconstruction ally themselves with "marginal" theatre companies, but they do not delude themselves that the two dominant metaphors of traditional Western theatre will evaporate into thin air overnight.

On the one hand, history keeps repeating a very discouraging message under the present economic and artistic conditions which are dictated by the value system of the metropolis: the more radically the activity of a theatre company antagonizes the two "metaphors," the further out to the margin the company is pushed. On the other hand, the economic recessions which endanger the art and livelihood of the theatre professionals send out a warning signal: any abrupt displacement of the dominant value system, which has controlled centrifugal and centripetal forces in the theatre, may cause severe economic, professional, and artistic disturbances that could possibly ruin live theatre at large.

Consequently, deconstruction is not an activity which is geared to destroy the logocentric play-production system on Broadway or elsewhere abruptly. Gradual displacement and the creation of multiple centers of gravity of equal status—such as those attempted by the educational and repertory theatre companies in the U.S.A.—seems, although it may not prove to be, efficacious. However, as I will show in the following chapters, the gradual appropriation of unsettling trends by the traditional mode of Western theatrical production may spare the world of theatre from unpleasant economic or artistic shocks, but eventually it may not change the structure of play production decisively. The alternative, of course, is revolution.

Deconstruction contests two fundamental positions in traditional Western play production: (1) it unsettles the "law" which gives priority to the voice of an authoritative consciousness—be it the voice of a playwright, a designer, a director, an actor, or a critic; and (2) it undermines the value system that provides ideological justification for relations of power in the two dominant metaphors of Western theatrical tradition. Under deconstruction, displacement has been turned into a metonymic operation (Jakobson 1971:255) which expresses the repressed consciousness of all "authors" in theatrical production—not just of the playwright. A deconstructor sees no essential continuity and preservation of value or meaning between a playtext and its subsequent performance-texts. The idea of "textual" displacements suggests that the inflections of a playtext are limitless.

Displacement has an effect similar to that of shooting pool because it introduces a violent intervention intended to shake the established modes of play production and interpretation. The first ball sets off a new game and new combinations of meaning. Through displacement, deconstruction reverses the hierarchical order, and then proceeds to eliminate all existing oppositions. For example, the age-old tension between speech and writing in play production has been initially restructured. Speech, instead of becoming silence or disappearing in Artaud's "theatre of cruelty," has simply occupied a diminished place, and it continues to have a function within the new reordering of the system.

In other words, the deconstructive reversal displaces speech from a high point of dominance to a low point of subordination, introducing a new relationship "that could never be included in the previous regime" (Derrida 1981:42). The new relationship stands outside the previous binary opposition of dominance and subordination. Speech is severed from its authoritarian, metaphysical grounding and becomes just another aspect of the performance-text. The theatre artists are liberated from the "playwright-god" and his text; they are no longer the instruments who will re-present in their performance a "present" that exists elsewhere and prior to their performance (Artaud 1958:106–107; Derrida 1978:236).

The ideological impact of deconstruction in the politics of theatrical production is apparent. Deconstruction involves a "strategic" operation which wants to transform the field of theatre. A deconstructor incises the lines of possible rupture in the play-production system where the logocentric discourse is vulnerable. He stresses endless transformation at every step of the play-production process. Despite all deconstructive reinscriptions, however, logocentrism still dominates the traditional theatrical production mainly because hierarchies of dual oppositions quickly re-establish themselves. For example, experimental theatre companies got rid of the "playwright-god," but now they have the "director-guru" controlling the creativity of the other theatre artists.

Deconstruction offers no programs of revelations and innovations. Instead, it offers a continuous, scrupulous analysis that can undermine a hierarchical structure of binary oppositions. Of course, hierarchies and structures of domination persist in the theatre. The deconstructors unsettle the old and the new hierarchies by working within the system of Western theatrical production. They know that there are no final solutions, but they fend off the restoration of structures of domination and the myth of presence which still haunt theatre.

CHAPTER TWO

Revealing Oppressive Reversals

A popular solecism has been the association of deconstruction with images of "death" and "rebirth"—from Friedrich Nietzsche's dionysiac revival (*Birth of Tragedy*, 1872) to Antonin Artaud's bubonic plague (*Theatre and Its Double*, 1938). Those theatre artists, who recognized the relationship between author and authority, questioned the possibility of reconciling a playwright's authority with the artistic creativity of a director, a designer, or an actor in the context of a theatrical production. The critique of authority, which re-emerged in Europe and the U.S.A. in the late 1960s, shook up once again the traditional mode of theatrical production. Although deconstruction is not a mere critique of authority, several directors, designers, and performers believed that they could eliminate authority by challenging the sovereignty of a playwright's creativity along with all the forms of obligation that result from it. Consequently, they advocated artistic creativity in the play-production process beyond or without the playtext. Their rebellion was not necessarily deconstructive.

Nonetheless, the dissolution of the playwright's authority over the creativity of the other artists in a theatre company could be taken as a point of departure for deconstructive theory and practice in the twentieth century. From Filippo Marinetti's "theatre of variety" to Richard Schechner's "environmental theatre," the presumed forerunners of deconstructive thought undermined the playwright and his playtext. By attacking the seams which separate tradition from innovation, a malign concept of deconstruction emerged in French theatre in prewar years, and, like Artaud's plague, it spread quickly to the rest of the European and American theatres.

Deconstruction was indiscriminately allied with "contemporary" avant-garde, and hastily pitted against the "logocentric" theatrical tradition in which presumably the playwright is the supreme creator. In this tradition, his written words control the play-production process because he stands as the origin (*archē*) and end-goal (*telos*) of the creativity of the other theatre artists. The director and designers make the prompt-copy in the image of the playwright's intention; the director and the actors turn the rehearsals into a purposeful process whose meaning can be presented to an audience coherently during performance. The rehearsal-text presents the unified results of the interaction between the playwright's words and the other theatre artists. The various "texts" generated during a play production interrelate in such a way that they "mirror" each other: a change in the playtext automatically causes a change in the prompt-copy, the rehearsal-text, and the performance-text.

The logocentric theatre artists regard a playtext as a single, complete entity. The *logos* organizes the different parts of a playtext into a unified, coherent structure (Derrida 1976:18). The playtext and the playwright, therefore, become the origin from which "meanings" flow to the rest of the theatre artists who are involved in the production of the playtext. This privilege of origin gives the playwright the authority to exercise proprietary rights on the playtext and the subsequent performance-text. In other words, the playtext is protected by copyright, which seeks to limit the proliferation of significations during the play-production process (Foucault 1979:159). Copyright restrictions turn directors, designers, and performers into faithful interpreters, not co-authors, because the playwright controls the decomposition and recomposition of the playtext in rehearsal.

Western theatrical production condones a "theological" bias by allowing the *logos* of the "playwright-god" to govern the activities of the other theatre artists from a distance. The "absent" playwright-god is "present" during the production process through his playtext, which controls the meaning of representation in the prompt-copy, rehearsal, and performance. The directors, designers, and actors are permitted to represent the playwright's thoughts and intentions by rendering present the discourse of the playtext (Derrida 1978:235). They become the "mouthpieces" of their master's voice in the same way that the playwright's playtext "voices" the universal *Logos* which, allegedly, permeates society and nature.

Most logocentrists see theatrical production in representational (often "neo-Kantian") terms. The playwright "copies down" the *Logos*, and, in turn, the other theatre artists "represent" the *logos* of the playtext in their performance. The forerunners of deconstruction have fractured this chain of interdependence by redefining the playwright's contribution to theatrical production. Simply put, they challenge the notion of representation and reinterpret the concept of "author." First, they argue that the playwright's *logos*, manifested in the written words of a playtext, "rewrites" (does not "mirror") the universal *Logos*—if such a *Logos* exists. Rewriting involves creative interpretation (*poiesis*) not slavish imitation (*mimesis*). Therefore, if I may speak in the language of the pseudoclassical folklore in the field of theatre once more, playtexts have a presentational, not a re-presentational value.

If I have resumed abusing the intricate Western tradition of *logos*, I am doing so for the following reason: popular simplifications (and occasional misunderstandings) of controversial concepts have often affected the theory and practice of the theatre more powerfully than any informed scholarly interpretations. Western theatrical production was introduced to deconstruction when some theatre artists gradually realized that the "words" of playtexts had no representational value (Foucault 1970:304) and that the general *a priori* structures of cognition could not explain how things really are. Under the influence of Georg Hegel, some European theatre artists shifted their creativity from a representation of "the nature of things" to a presentation of "the artistic thought." Hegel had argued that Immanuel Kant's "thing-in-itself" does not designate an extra-mental reality but is, in fact, a cognitive construct which stands in critical tension with any form of knowledge. Consequently, authorship became creative, not imitative, for some playwrights. The separation between a playtext (characters) and its creator (playwright) caused playwrights such as Luigi Pirandello to send six characters in search of an author in 1921. His playtext, *Six Characters in Search of an Author*, challenged the relationship between the "dramatic" world (W_D) and the "real" world (W_o). Nonetheless, it was produced logocentrically because rehearsals and performances faithfully represented Pirandello's playtext.

Directors, designers, and actors cross the deconstructive threshold when they gradually endorse the following four premises: (1) playtexts do not point beyond themselves to the thoughts or intentions of playwrights; (2) playtexts do not embody the thoughts or intentions of playwrights; (3) playtexts are not composed of a finite number of signifieds; and (4) playtexts do not have a deep structure which lurks behind a surface structure. In other words, the "meanings" inscribed in a playtext can only be explained in terms of "transpersonal," conventional structures (semiotic systems or codes), not as the result of an individual consciousness which appropriates them. The deconstructors further dissolved the identity and integrity of the playwright and his playtext by dismissing the universal *Logos*, which allegedly was inscribed in the "deep" and "hidden" structures of playtexts. They broke free from the theological quest for the recovery of the *Logos*, which presumably stabilizes meaning.

Consequently, the deconstructors "transgressed" from every major school of thought (be it Aristotelian, Stanislavskian, Artaudian, Pirandellian, or Brechtian) not to mention the "masters" of the Japanese Noh, of the Indian Kathakali, and so on. Schools of thought of either Occidental or Oriental persuasion generally protect the purity of the tradition and guard the authority of the "master"— be he a playwright, a director, a designer, an actor, or a critic. By securing "paternity," theatre schools try to prevent "illegitimate" thoughts and practices in play production. Tradition and authority join forces to establish orthodoxy and to repress heterodoxy. The struggle against different opinion (heterodoxy) represents an effort to reduce difference and to promote unity in the quest for the origin—the master's thought or *logos*. The repression of difference regulates and regularizes play production. It establishes a normative canon of theories and practices for each school of thought that provides a standard against which "anomalies" can be judged and ruled out.

The deconstructors question the authority of the "great masters" of drama and theatre as well as the linear play-production process which ensures that authority is not dispersed but is properly channeled and delegated from the "master" to his "apostles." They submit that all Western theatrical production cannot be made to fit one single system. Theatre artists create collectively and their theories or practices form interdependent networks which sometimes co-exist in conflict. For example, the dissolution of the individual "playwright" through collective "playwriting" during rehearsals— frequently called "workshops" such as Jerzi Grotowski's Holidays— allows for anonymous subjectivity and collective creativity to materialize. Collective creativity replaces "productivity" with "festivity" and "mastery" with "process." In Happenings, experience can no longer be graphed along a line which had a definitive beginning and end. The production process becomes a wandering, a carnival, a "holiday" in which, reportedly, individual identities dissolve and social roles break down.

For a deconstructor, no single theory, or practice, or even school of thought is primary. Consequently, he proceeds to re-examine the network of interrelated functions in logocentric play production. This network, traditionally, includes at least five spheres of activity: the playtext, which is regarded as the domain of playwrights; the prompt-copy, which is viewed as the territory of directors and designers; the rehearsal-text, which is recognized as the beat of directors and actors; and the performance-text, which is considered as the ground of performers and spectators. This seemingly tight network has been disjointed and restructured in experimental deconstructive productions that explored how a "text" refers to other texts inside and outside the system of theatrical production.

Most deconstructive experiments suggest that "writing" is an endless process during which the "author" becomes a "reader" and the "reader" becomes an "author." The exchange of roles between "authors" and "readers" subverts any original or final authority. Therefore, it would seem that all "texts" (including the playtext) are derivative, never original. Each "text" repeats "texts" prior to it, and it does not express the intention of an individual author who poses as the origin of all meanings. Shakespeare's playtexts, for instance, rewrite other "texts." In sum, all writing involves rewriting.

The notion of "author" beyond the playwright has freed deconstructors from a fixed center, the playtext, and has allowed play production to wander in all directions. Several theatrical productions, which will be discussed in later chapters, have proved that the logocentric web of interrelations can be disrupted by turning the playtext into a prompt-copy, by transforming the rehearsals into workshops, and by eliminating closure in rehearsals or performances. Consequently, the deconstructors are promoting a new network of interrelations in theatrical production.

The power of origin, which a playtext enjoys in logocentric theatrical production, ensures that the playwright's word (*logos*) will control the play-production process. Like King Hamlet's ghost, the playtext forecasts a specific environment of experience for directors, designers, actors, and spectators. However, the influence that the playtext can exert depends on the responsive imagination of directors, designers, and actors, not on the playwright's intention. The playtext, therefore, is open-ended. Since meanings cannot be complete in open-ended playtexts, the logocentric directors, designers, and actors try to construct complete and "closed" performance-texts. Closure fixes meaning, ending the continuous "rewriting" that takes place during rehearsals.

Understandably, the deconstructors challenge the notion of representation and closure. If a playtext represents an image of the universal *Logos*, the prompt-copy, in turn, represents an image of the playtext. If the prompt-copy is an image of an image, what then is the rehearsal-text? An imitation of an imitation of an imitation? To move interpretation three Platonic steps away from its "object" is to demoralize the directors, designers, and actors—not to mention that the playtext which they imitate is already moved a Platonic step away from the *Logos*. Clearly, the logocentric game of "mirrors" favors duplication and duplicity, discourages creativity and innovation, and frustrates and alienates theatre artists.

The above effects are also promoted by the game of "closure." Closure turns a playtext into an organizing center of reference that helps the prompt-copy, the rehearsal-text, and the performance-text to achieve unity and coherence. In rehearsal, the logocentric directors ask the actors to recall, represent, and repeat the playtext and/or the prompt-copy. The actors who "write" the rehearsal-text are not permitted to replace or reject any meanings in the playtext or the prompt-copy. Consequently, logocentric directors and actors master space and time in rehearsal (1) by articulating sign-systems which re-present the playtext, (2) by rationalizing experience in the framework of the playtext, and (3) by remaining bound to the notion of a providential playwright.

Like the playwright who allegedly renders the universal *Logos* intelligible in a playtext, the director makes sure that the designers and actors render the playtext's *logos* intelligible in rehearsal and performance. The notion that this principle of structure and order transcends all "texts" ranks meanings to a primary, secondary, or tertiary status. The logocentrists believe that, by working backward and upward through the chain of "texts," they can arrive at the primary (original) meaning of the playwright (*logos*) or, of the divine universe (*Logos*), in an act of revelation. The logocentric director controls the creativity and expression of the designers and actors in the name of the playwright's *logos* or of the universal *Logos*. Logocentric theatre artists look backward, not forward.

In an effort to overcome alienation and to gain self-expression, several directors and actors rebelled against the playwright and attempted to master the "master." The conflict between playwright Anton Chekhov and director Konstantin Stanislavsky provides a clear example of the director's quest to dominate the playwright and the playtext. Chekhov called his *Cherry Orchard* (1904) a comedy, but Stanislavsky thought otherwise and produced it as a tragedy. "It is neither a comedy, nor a farce as you wrote," Stanislavsky told Chekhov, "It is a tragedy even if you do indicate a way into a better world in the last act" (Hingley 1950:180).

However, not all directors who overruled a playwright's interpretation of the world were deconstructors—especially if they claimed to have a more intimate understanding of the world than the playwright and his playtext. Playwrights, designers, directors, actors, and critics subscribe to logocentrism when they see "truth" as singular, simple, and permanent; not as plural, complex, or transient. Consequently, any discrepancies among the interpretations of logocentric directors, actors, and their critics are usually explained away as misunderstandings: either the playwright or the director or the actors must have confused the interplay between appearance (*phenomenon*) and essence (*ousia*) in the universe or in the playtext, respectively.

The logocentrists love to read two levels of meaning into playtexts. Stanislavsky, for example, founded his "realistic theatre" on a double reading of the "text" and its "subtext." The text was the sum total of the denotative, literal meanings, which were anchored on the words (signifiers) printed on the page. The "subtext," on the other hand, was the sum total of the connotative, figurative meanings "behind" and "beyond" the printed words on the page. In short, the text was "visible" while the subtext was "invisible."

Director Peter Brook founded his "holy theatre" on a similar visible/invisible binary opposition. "Can the invisible be made visible through the performer's presence?" he asked (1968:52), and he pressed his actors to make the invisible universal *Logos* visible through their performance. Even Bertolt Brecht based his "epic theatre" on the visible/invisible opposition, but he carefully inverted its direction. According to Brecht, ideology makes people's perceptions familiar, automatic, and therefore imperceptible. The defamiliarization techniques, however, can make the familiar (natural) look or sound unfamiliar (unnatural) and thus render the "invisible" visible to the spectator's consciousness.

In all three cases—Stanislavsky's familiar, invisible, deep structure; Brook's unfamiliar, invisible, deep structure; and Brecht's familiar, invisible, surface structure—decipherment is regarded as an act of revelation essential to logocentric understanding. Decipherment discloses and presents what otherwise would have remained "concealed" and, therefore, "absent" from human understanding. In sum, the logocentrists concur that playtexts possess determinate and determinable meanings which guarantee that interpretation is neither endless nor pointless.

But what if there is no universal *Logos*? What if the *logos* is man-made, an invention which helps theatre artists "humanize" the world and "read" nonexistent rationales and purposes "behind" the baffling disorder of life? As George Bernard Shaw prescribed,

> . . . the great dramatist has something better to do than to amuse either himself or his audience. He has to interpret life. This sounds a mere pious phrase of literary criticism; but a moment's consideration will discover its meaning and its exactitude. Life as it appears to us in our daily experience is an unintelligible chaos of happenings/ . . . / It is the business of Brieux to pick out the significant incidents from the chaos of daily happenings, and arrange them so that their relation to one another becomes significant, thus changing us from bewildered spectators of a monstrous confusion to men intelligently conscious of the world and its destinies. This is the highest function that man can perform—the greatest work he can set his hand to; and this is why the great dramatists of the world, from Euripides and Aristophanes to Shakespeare and Moliere, and from them to Ibsen and Brieux, take that majestic and pontifical rank which seems so strangely above all the reasonable pretensions of mere strolling actors and theatrical authors. (Shaw 1911:xxiv–xxv)

Clearly, Shaw argues that playtexts can only present dramatic worlds in which events and motives have discernible directions and form meaningful patterns even if the playwright believes that the world has no inherent order or meaning. Shaw's dictum also holds true with absurdist playtexts and playwrights: there is method in their madness! The playwright's *logos* weaves the playtext in a continuous, coherent (however absurd), complete (however fragmented) sequence which has a beginning, middle, and end.

Logocentric directors and actors treat rehearsals as a rite of passage. Despite the apparent fragmentation of the playtext or, rather of the prompt-copy, during rehearsals they present disparate scenes as interrelated episodes within a coherent pattern which emerges progressively. The logic of the narrative establishes a through-line which guides directors and actors to define every element in the dramatic world by its function and relation to the other elements. The narrative renders events and motives intelligible in such a way that the reader—whether or not he is director, actor, or spectator—grasps the point (theme) of the complete sequence. Meaning becomes a function of location of an element within the overall pattern. The rehearsals cannot extend the "end" of the playtext without altering its meanings. Consequently, directors and actors leave no loose ends as rehearsals approach the opening night. They overcome discontinuity by stitching everything together with the strong thread of narrative.

A director's desire for control emanates from the logocentric assumption that mastery is manifested through unity, coherence, and presence of meaning in rehearsal and performance. The director represses difference, chance, and absence by subordinating his understanding to the playwright's intention or vice versa. In either case, such a director fails to subvert the logic of repression and to break away from the theological frame of Western theatrical production.

Even self-conscious and conscientious directors could not escape from this pattern during (workshop) rehearsals. For example, Eugenio Barba who, among others, advocated an "alternative theatre," observed this theocratic structure of theatrical production in both Western and Oriental theatre.

> With great loyalty my companions tried to motivate their own work with my words, my explanations. But something was wrong, something didn't ring true, and in the end a sort of split became apparent between what they were doing and what they wanted to do or believed they were doing to satisfy me, to meet me. When I realized this, I gave up all explanation. After working

together many hours a day for many years, it is not my words
but perhaps only my presence that can say something. (Barba
1972:54)

In the absence of a playtext, the "director-guru" or the "myth
of technique" generally assumed control over the actor's behavior
during rehearsals. Although Barba himself questioned the "myth of
technique," he used it for one simple reason: the myth of technique
gave to his way of working a useful and logical justification and
subsequently made his way of working acceptable to others (Barba
1972:52–53). He believed that training offers the possibility of
bridging the gap between intention and realization (1972:47), but
he also argued that "virtuosity does not lead to situations of new
human relationships which are the decisive ferment for a re-
orientation" (1972:53). This quest for creativity made Barba arrive
at a deceptive juxtaposition between Oriental and Occidental theatre.

According to Barba, the actor in Oriental theatre must conform
to a tradition of techniques, which codify a performance style, by
"merely executing a role whose minutest detail has, as in a musical
score, been elaborated by some master in a more or less distant
past" (1972:48). Conversely, Barba thought that the actor in Western
theatre is—or should be—a creator, mainly because the Western
actor has no prescribed rules of action which should guide and
support his performance—except for the playtext and the director's
instructions. "His clash with the text," Barba explained, "through
his own sensitivity and his own historical experience, offers a unique
and personal universe to his spectators" (1972:48). This fallacious
binary opposition between Oriental and Occidental theatre—which
are seen as either static or dynamic—is founded on the
pseudostructuralist premises of Barba's "theatre anthropology."

Despite the research which has invalidated Western views of
the Orient as static (Inden 1986; Said 1978), Barba continued to
see Oriental theatre as the opposite of Western theatre for two
reasons: First, he came up with a dubious discipline which he
named "theatre anthropology." His theatre anthropologists, by
definition, study any recurrent principles which are common to the
performers of different cultures, places, and times; and they hope
that these principles, which cannot prove the existence of universal
and inviolatable laws, may be useful when applied to specific
theatrical performances (1982:5). Unfortunately, most of these cross-

cultural explorations indulge in qualitative analyses of oppositional tensions, reducing the history of world theatre into a binary molecular model. Barba, for instance, was quite convinced that theatre, in its long history around the globe, has always had a "visible, evident" dimension and an "invisible, subterranean" dimension (Barba 1986:1; Berberich 1984; Zarrilli 1988). Parenthetically, the binary opposition between Oriental and Occidental theatre or between visible and invisible dimensions in a theatrical experience is as fallacious as the binary opposition between logocentrism and deconstruction which I am pursuing here in the manner of my two good friends.

Second, Barba's essentially phenomenological "readings" of Oriental and Occidental theatre echoed the ever popular writings of Antonin Artaud and Bertolt Brecht, who, among others, introduced partial—if not misleading—views of the "Oriental other" to Western theatrical practice. Barba cherished the visible/invisible opposition, and he claimed that the "Oriental other" houses the invisible, intangible, and ineffable experience. "Once again," Barba insisted, "the exterior forms are of no importance" (1972:54). The actor's business is to describe the indescribable by creating the ineffable "presence." This presence is an invisible energy which transcends the visible aspects of an actor's technical training and physical performance. In the state of "presence," an actor is not interpreting or experiencing anything (Barba 1986:115).

Barba conceded that representational performance narratives are arbitrary inventions which make sense only in the specific, time-bound cultural contexts that generate them. But he was reluctant to accept that any presentational performance narratives are also arbitrary man-made cultural codes without recourse to the truth or reality. Barba's research, which stemmed out of the crisis of representation in the Western theatre, backfires because it tells us more about Barba's views than about the Oriental theatre (Clifford 1986). In a quest for universal essences and binary opposites, Barba overlooked the detailed description of the concrete sign systems and codes which are employed by performers and spectators, respectively, in a specific (social) space and (historical) time.

The logocentric directors and actors in Oriental and Occidental theatre alike, look backward to the "text"—which can be part of an oral or written tradition—through recollection, and they look forward in expectation to the performance-text during rehearsals.

Whether they practice a presentational or a representational theatre, they continue to operate within the framework of a theological metaphor. They regard play production as a straight line which organizes itself into a causal chain and controls everything from beginning to end in an inevitable sequence.

Allow me here to caricature—only for the sake of brevity—this "divine" metaphor. In the beginning, the "playwright-god" creates the playtext (Creation). Next, the "director-guru" and his "master-designers" produce a down-to-earth, imperfect image of the prototype in their prompt-copy (Fall). Then, the actors lend sight and sound to the playwright's words and the director's production concept through the presence of their bodies and voices in rehearsals (Incarnation). The performance that ensues from their joint efforts temporarily annuls "real" life (Death) and revives a "fictive" life (Resurrection). At the end, the theatre artists receive feedback (Damnation or Redemption) from their audiences and critics. It is in the phase of rehearsals that the theological metaphor of Western play production, along with its numerous variations, has cracked open.

Generally speaking, the logocentric directors and actors turn the rehearsals into a zone of discontent and restlessness because they feel suspended between a lost past (playtext) and an elusive future (performance-text). They try to preserve the past for the future—which are both absent during rehearsals—by suppressing the present that leaks in while the actors, in the manner of silkworms, are trying to create a cocoon of fictive time and/or space around them.

The deconstructors, on the other hand, do not endorse a central narrative; they prefer open-ended, unfinished playtexts which are extendible both backward and forward during rehearsals. Rehearsals are regarded as the work of creative imagination, and imagination is seen as being primarily productive, not reproductive. If that is not the case, why do directors, designers, actors, and audiences feel compelled to produce (not to reproduce) certain playtexts again and again? To whom are rehearsals presented? How are rehearsals different from performances? Isn't the performance on the opening night a rehearsal for the next night?

For example, Happenings and Holidays have no organizing center—whether that center is a playtext or a prompt-copy. The deconstructive theatre artist resists any tendencies—his own included—to achieve mastery. Interpretation has no end or beginning. There is no solid point in interpretation. Each interpretation results from a certain viewpoint which is produced in a figurational code. Consequently, no one code can be privileged over another. This unending play of signification/interpretation suggests that there is no exit from the vagaries of interpretation. Viewpoints do not have secure standpoints. They are relational, and, therefore, meaning becomes relative and liminal: that is, meaning appears and disappears at the seams of interrelated viewpoints. Meaning is equivocal rather than univocal.

A sign, however, can not have several or different meanings present simultaneously. A signifier does not possess multiple meanings. In fact, an isolated signifier means nothing. It generates meanings and equivocality only through interrelationships with other signifiers. Meaning therefore is unstable because it is inscribed in changing viewpoints and shifting contexts. The signifiers are caught in a semantic web. The synchronic network of signification is too extensive and complex to be mastered. The diachronic network seems to be boundless. The context, which informs the signs and the viewpoints to which signs are configured, remains unfinished. The open-ended diachronic web of signification leaves the semantic context indeterminable. The absence of an origin and of a finish makes the floating signifiers and signifieds yield only transient, migratory meanings. A deconstructor accepts the endless drift of meanings and does not attempt to fix meaning in rehearsal or in performance. As a result, he spells the end of the "author" and he inaugurates an open-ended rehearsal-text.

The deconstructors believe that texts depend on each other to produce meaning. This mutual interdependence turns every text into an intertext. Seen in this way, the rehearsal-text becomes a relational event which can not be self-contained because the signifiers that compose it are not self-contained. The rehearsal-text stands in a tangled relationship with other texts. The intertextuality in the play-production process has no end or beginning. Playtexts, prompt-copies, rehearsal-texts, performance-texts, and all other texts in and out of the theatrical world are entangled in an endless web, a "benevolent" circle which spirals but never closes. The loss of origin results from the elimination of an organizing center (e.g., a playtext) or principle (e.g., a myth of technique). Meaning always forms and re-forms but never stands or fully presents itself. For this reason, the deconstructors overturn the notion of producing a finished, closed, packaged product for their audiences.

Instead, the deconstructors invite the spectators to experience the activity of production. This is why their performances look or sound like rehearsals. They no longer consider interpretation a parasitic activity which feeds on an original source (the playtext). Unlike Barba, they see interpretation as a generative activity because there can be no "text" without interpretation. They contend that the "I" of each theatre artist is not the source of the sentences that he utters. Each personal voice is entangled in a web of linguistic and cultural references which precedes it and encompasses it.

A deconstructive theatre artist knows that he can never fully own his own voice. And so, he acknowledges his lack of authority over his "text." For example, Shakespeare's *King Lear* (playtext), Peter Brook's "King Lear" (prompt-copy), and Lawrence Olivier's "King Lear" (performance-text)—to mention only a few "King Lears" and fewer texts—are only masks which have attached a "voice," a "face," or an "identity" to the collective labor of many anonymous and eponymous contributors. These "texts" of King Lear resulted from the social activity and interaction of countless co-producers of meanings who were involved directly or indirectly with the "true chronicle history of King Leir" as early as the turn of the seventeenth century.

For the most part, the logocentrists have inscribed the history of Western theatrical production in binary oppositions on an evolutionist canvas—whether the issue is Gerhardt Hauptmann's naturalistic theatre or Brecht's epic theatre (Figure 3). The theatre artists and critics who draw such exclusive, hierarchical oppositions, share an undialectical attitude, and they cannot conceive that oppositions can co-exist as equivalents. Instead, they privilege one term (e.g., epic) and impoverish the other (e.g., realistic), or vice versa. In this way, they sustain a hierarchy within the axiological domain of a theatre company that allows one opposition to rule over the other.

It is against such hierarchies as the above that the deconstructors have rebelled, and they want to abolish the structures of domination/subordination which regulate Western theatrical production. Revolutionaries such as Adolphe Appia, Gordon Craig, or even Bertolt Brecht are not radical enough because they retain

The modern theatre is the epic theatre. The following table shows certain changes of emphasis as between the dramatic and the epic theatre.

DRAMATIC THEATRE		EPIC THEATRE
Plot	1.	Narrative
Implicates the spectator in a stage situation	2.	Turns the spectator into an observer, but
Wears down his capacity for action	3.	Arouses his capacity for action
Provides him with sensations	4.	Forces him to make decisions
Experience	5.	Picture of the world
The spectator is involved in something	6.	He is made to face something
Suggestion	7.	Argument
Instinctive feelings are preserved	8.	Brought to the point of recognition
The spectator is in the thick of it, shares the experience	9.	The spectator stands outside, studies
The human being is taken for granted	10.	The human being is the subject of the inquiry
He is unalterable	11.	He is alterable and able to alter
Eyes on the finish	12.	Eyes on the course
One scene makes another	13.	Each scene for itself
Growth	14.	Montage
Linear development	15.	In curves
Evolutionary determinism	16.	Jumps
Man as a fixed point	17.	Man as a process
Thought determines being	18.	Social being determines thought
Feeling	19.	Reason

FIGURE 3. Brecht's Model of Binary Oppositions Between Epic and Realistic Theatre. (Source: Bertolt Brecht, "The Modern Theatre is the Epic Theatre: Notes to the Opera *Aufstieg und Fall der Stadt Mahagonny*" (1931). In *Brecht on Theatre*, ed. & tr. by John Willett. London: Methuen, 178, p. 37.)

a hierarchical oppression. For example, Appia, in agreement with Gordon Craig, believed that the complete, composite performance-text required one creative mind, "one lordly dictator as designer-director," to bring all the elements into harmony by subordinating the actor and preventing him from making an independent display (Kernodle 1954:7).

The deconstructors argue that repression will not be eliminated from the play-production process unless theatre artists and critics avoid the trap of thinking solely in terms of domination and binary, conflicting opposites. Theatre artists and critics do not liberate themselves and their work from logocentrism by simply giving realistic theatre or epic theatre—to mention only two—a negative or a positive appraisal. A reversal of the dominant/subordinate relationship is not enough. Nothing fundamental will ever change unless the values of the binary oppositions dissolve through a dialectical inversion. Consequently, the deconstructors chisel out an analytical approach which will allow them to disorganize and, perhaps, reorganize the inherited order of Western play production presumably in a viable way.

At this point, deconstruction becomes an analytical tool which helps theatre artists and critics (1) to explore the structure of relationships of binary oppositions and (2) to reformulate these binary oppositions by dissolving and recasting—not just reversing—their former values. The deconstructive critics challenge the intelligence and integrity of such polarities in Western theatrical production, and they create a new future for theatrical practice away from the notions which have traditionally conditioned it. The deconstructors attack the logocentric theatrical network by turning its own tactics against it, "producing a force of dislocation that spreads itself throughout the entire system, fissuring it in every direction" (Derrida 1978:20). They expose the instability and contradictions of foundational notions and practices in theatrical production and search for viable alternatives.

PART ONE

The Domain of the Playwright

It must be definitely said that an actor's duty is to respect a play. Whichever way he delivers it, he must speak what the playwright has written, nothing more, nothing less.

Constant Coquelin, *The Art of the Actor* (1880)

A playwright doesn't want his play "improved" if the improvement leads to making a different play than his own. He wants *his* voice to be heard, unless he thinks of himself as a journeyman.

Harold Clurman, *On Directing* (1972)

CHAPTER ONE

Vocal Texts

My two friends, Jon and John, were not very kind to me after they heard my views about deconstruction, which I had expressed to them in the form of a "manifesto" (1989:31). Jon accused me of being a latent logocentrist, and John accused me of being a suppressed deconstructor. Does this mean that I am both?

John was upset because I quoted Derrida repeatedly in my "manifesto." He claimed that Derrida was a hypocrite. As a reader, Derrida preached that the limitless play of meaning in a text encourages multiple interpretations. But as a writer, Derrida discouraged the limitless play of meaning when he insisted that any reader of a text of his, such as John Searle, should yield an accurate, singular interpretation of it (Derrida 1977:162).

This alleged discrepancy does not prove that deep down Derrida believed that an author's intention controls the meaning of his texts, according to Jon. John failed to read the subtle irony in Derrida's rebuttal to John Searle's attack (Fischer 1985:40). But even if irony is deleted from Derrida's text, Derrida could only be accused of inconsistency, not hypocrisy, on this issue.

I dared to tell my friends that one could not invalidate deconstruction as an approach by simply undermining Derrida's credibility. Derrida is neither the origin nor the end of deconstruction—as my logocentric friend assumes. Deconstruction is not a mystique with a charismatic leader whose words can be interpreted only by a league of apostolic scholars and acolytes— as some of its enemies and advocates make it sound. Deconstruction is an analytical approach which helps researchers articulate problems, test hypotheses, process data, and arrive at conclusions. Every step of this approach is open to scrutiny on grounds of cogent argument and useful application. Like all analytical approaches, deconstruction can improve its art of inquiry—which is reinforced by a collection of the persuasive theories (i.e., particular answers) that the deconstructors have given to specific problems of the theatre. By generalizing from these answers, it becomes clear what the deconstructive approach can or cannot do for the theatre.

Jon protested and informed me that deconstruction is not an analytical approach. John laughed in my face and said that the deconstructive approach is useless because it cannot help researchers solve the problems of the theatre. For instance, Derrida's argument, that writing precedes speech, is illogical. All children learn to speak before they learn to write, and entire cultures (not only illiterate people) have speech without writing. On the other hand, no man or culture has writing without speech (except for handicapped people and primitive computers), and no writing can record all the complex features of speech such as intonation, stress, or pitch. Disregarding biological and historical evidence, Derrida argued that writing is not just a system invented to record speech, that writing has become more central to language than speech because writing is now encompassing speech.

Jon argued back that John missed Derrida's point and, at the same time, made Derrida's argument legitimate. By using biological and historical evidence in this inflexible logocentric way, John asserted (1) that human nature and culture, which he indicatively reduced to a monolithic model, have not changed since the days of Plato and (2) that writing should continue to be regarded as an inadequate, secondary activity which is preceded by speech. The theatre artists and critics who share this phonocentric perspective regard writing as a mere representation of speech. In other words, they think that speech is in touch with the origin of meaning (i.e., the speaker's consciousness), while writing stands one step away from it. Consequently, they view writing as being inferior to speech, and, by extension, they treat a playtext as a mere blueprint for the performance, which allegedly presents the "real thing" to an audience.

According to Jon, this phonocentric orientation prevents John from looking into how technology has affected the future of evolving cultural forms, such as theatre, which manifest "irregular" states of being and doing. Derrida's unorthodox thinking, for instance, is useful to discuss the problems of theatrical productions which start from a written playtext. The written playtext (which is viewed as either dead letters or an inscribed voice) precedes, encompasses, and controls the oral utterances of its readers (directors, designers, or actors) during readings, rehearsals and performances. Since nearly 90 percent of all professional theatrical productions around the world today are based on written playtexts, any investigation that endorses the seemingly "illogical" premise that writing precedes speech can yield far-reaching results.

John raised an eyebrow at Jon's argument and pointed out that speech precedes writing because this is a demand of human nature, not of a phonocentric orientation from Plato to Saussure. Derrida unjustly accused Saussure of relegating writing to a secondary, marginal position (Derrida 1976:8; Hawkes 1977:148). Saussure called attention to speech and the oral transmission of literature in all nations because he opposed the narrow ethnocentrism of earlier philologists-historians who, by privileging the study of writing and the written transmission of literature, favored only the discussion of Indo-European languages and literatures which had long written traditions. It is wrong to say that Saussure promoted an ethnocentric, pro-speech examination of language, literature, and culture.

The less time my friends take to explain the background of their rationals, the more confused I become about the issue that they discuss. Their evolutionary metaphysics reminds me of the old quandary: What came first, speech or writing? I think that they are both wrong because—regardless of their opposing views—they both use priority as an empowering lever which can dictate a hierarchical relationship of dominance and subordination between speech and writing. Take, for example, the structuralist quandary "Which came first, parole or langue?" in the context of theatre.

Saussure had described language as a network of structural relations which, like any other cultural system, can be studied from a sychronic perspective. He saw a structured economy in language which allowed a small number of distinctive features, as represented by the phonetic or written alphabets, to signify a great repertory of negotiable meanings. Meanings change when the position of consonants and vowels change within a specific linguistic system (e.g., opt, top, pot). Sets of signs (such as the English alphabet in the above example) and their acceptable combinations (such as opt, top, pot, but not tpo or, the word order verb-adjective-noun but not noun-adjective-verb) become institutionalized as a system of language (*langue*) which is employed by a community of speakers. By employing a synchronic perspective, the structuralists thought that they could distinguish the isolated oral and/or written linguistic behavior (*parole*) of an individual from the general system of accepted oral and/or written structures (*langue*) shared by the linguistic community.

It is easy to see that *langue* and *parole* can each exist in both oral and written forms on the sychronic axis. *Langue*, for example, can be stored in the individual (often called "collective") memory of the speakers of an illiterate linguistic community as well as in the grammar books and dictionaries of a literate linguistic community. *Parole*, too, can register as an oral or written utterance, depending on the level of technology—writing paper or magnetic tape—availabe to a playwright. Therefore, it would seem that neither speech nor writing can claim priority over each other because writing can exist the moment speech can exist and vice versa. The speech/ writing relationship, however, is easier to define on the synchronic than on the diachronic axis.

Diachronically, the *langue* of a linguistic community, say of the twentieth-century Bakas, vanished into thin air when its members, who only transmitted personal and collective experience or knowledge (literature) orally, perished. On the other hand, the *langue* of a linguistic community, say of the ancient Greeks, who also transmitted personal and collective experience or knowledge (literature) in writing, survived when its members died. In short, historically, the written utterances have "endured" longer than the oral utterances in the libraries of cosmopolitan centers, reclusive monasteries, enlightened monarchs, and educational institutions prior to the twentieth century.

Likewise, playtexts have been more effectively recorded and stored than performance-texts since the days of ancient Greek theatre—at least until the phonograph (record player), the magnetic audiotape (tape recorder, tape player), and the magnetic videotape (videotape recorder, videocassette) were invented respectively in the 1870s, 1940s, and 1950s. Technology corrected the imbalance in the twentieth century by making speech as "durable" as writing. Naturally, this imbalance between speech and writing, which existed prior to the twentieth century, affected theatrical production— especially when copyright laws were put into place. However, durability guaranteed survival, not dominance.

It would be misleading to assume that all theatre artists and critics promoted writing over speech, especially after modern printing was invented in the 1450s; or that all the theatre artists and critics who were involved in revival productions of classical texts from Aeschylus to Shelley gave writing priority over speech just because the playtext was usually the only surviving document; or, finally, that all the theatre artists who were involved in producing the plays of living playwrights in their day gave priority to speech over writing. The relationship between speech and writing in the context of theatrical production is more complex than it seems.

CHAPTER TWO

Same Difference

In his essay, "Exit Thirties, Enter Sixties," Richard Schechner wrote that the era of the Sixties had begun and the era of the Thirties had passed away while he was studying it.

> The men who made this era—Lee Strasberg, Elia Kazan, Robert Lewis, Paul Mann, Harold Clurman, and others—are still active in our theatre, and will be for some time. But they represent an aesthetic that is no longer representative. Their impress, so important and formative, is fading as another generation assumes leadership. Our theatre is undergoing basic revaluation. (Schechner 1966:13)

If, for the sake of the argument, I accept Schechner's premise that theatre generations cover thirty-year periods, can I also claim that the era of the 1960s has ended while I am studying it, and a new era is beginning in the 1990s? Can I argue persuasively that the theatre artists who "made" the 1960s (Schechner included) will be active for some time in the 1990s, but they represent an aesthetic which is no longer influential?

I do not think so because the "new" aesthetic, which Schechner and others introduced in the radical veneer of the Sixties, was founded on the age-old metaphysics of origin and presence. The quest for first causes and the nature of ultimate reality continues to dominate the aesthetics of theatrical productions. "In going back to the sources of language, we are returning to the source of meaning," Peter Brook said when he justified the production of *Orghast at Persepolis* (Smith 1972:80). The source of meaning was the consciousness of the speaker, not the memorized text of a playwright. "What you hear in a person's voice is what is going on at the centre of gravity in his consciousness at that moment"

(Smith 1972:46). The presence of the speaking consciousness in improvised performance was seen as offering an authentic experience of the "real thing."

Richard Schechner's insightful essay "Drama, Script, Theatre, Performance" (1973; revised 1988) inadvertently illustrates how this "new" aesthetic was clogged with structuralist residues. Schechner wrote his essay to propose a classificatory (taxonomic) model of theatrical production which would account for the points of contact among playtexts, prompt-copies, rehearsal-texts, and performance-texts.

The first version of his model (Figure 4a) has four concentric, overlapping circles. Each circle rests on the circle which is immediately larger than itself. Generally, the larger circle contains all the circles smaller than itself. The playtext (or drama) exists as a written text, a verbal code, that can be transmitted through time and space independent of any human transmitter, who simply acts as a carrier or messenger. The playtext, which allows for little improvisation, is the domain of the playwright (alias shaman).

The prompt-copy (or script), on the other hand, is the domain of the director, (*didaskalos, guru*) who "must *know* the script and be able to *teach* it to others" (1973:8). The prompt-copy exists as a verbal/visual code in the mind (like an interior map of a particular production) and can only be transmitted from person to person. It can be a traditional well-known plan, or it can be developed to suit certain new specifications of place and time.

In turn, the rehearsal-text (or theatre) is the domain of the performers. They have a concrete and immediate response to the playtext and/or the prompt-copy. The rehearsal-text is a specific visible/sonic set of well-known components or a score invented during rehearsals. It represents the visible aspect of the "invisible" prompt-copy to a certain degree. The prompt-copy may be the cause of the rehearsal-text, but the rehearsal-text can also influence the shape of the prompt-copy (Schechner 1973:24).

Finally, the performance-text (or performance) is the domain of the audience. It is the text shaped by both performers and spectators "from the time the first spectator enters the field of the performance . . . to the time the last spectator leaves" (1973:8). In many cases, a playwright can also function as a director and a performer. In other cases, a performer can function as a spectator.

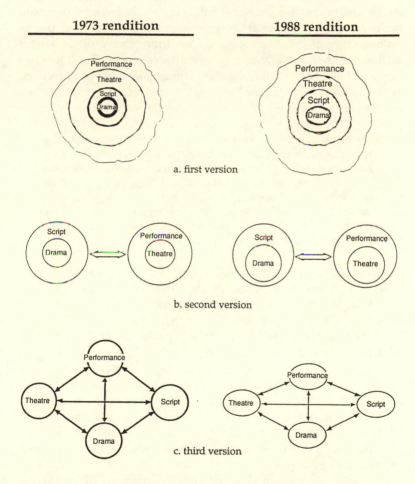

Drama = Playtext
Script = Prompt-copy
Theatre = Rehearsal-text
Performance = Performance-text

1973 rendition

1988 rendition

Performance
Theatre
Script
Drama

Performance
Theatre
Script
Drama

a. first version

Script
Drama

Performance
Theatre

Script
Drama

Performance
Theatre

b. second version

Performance
Theatre
Script
Drama

Performance
Theatre
Script
Drama

c. third version

FIGURE 4. Richard Schechner's Model of Play Production. (Source: Richard Schechner, "Drama, Script, Theatre, Performance" *Drama Review* (17:3 (1973), 8, 9, 13; also in *Performance Theory*, rev. & exp. edition, New York: Routledge, 1988, p. 72.)

Therefore, Schechner concluded, it is hard to define the performance-text because the boundaries separating it from the rehearsal-text and everyday life are arbitrary (1973:20).

Clearly, the first version of Schechner's model portrayed a logocentric view of the play-production system in phenomenological terms. The immutable playtext of the playwright-shaman occupied the center of the theatrical universe, immediately followed by the prompt-copy of the director-guru. The arrangement of the circles established the centrality of a consciousness whose vision reached the rest of the theatre artists through a transcendental rippling effect. Plato described this "divine" effect aptly by referring to the stone of Heraclea, a magnet. "This stone," Socrates told Ion,

> does not simply attract the iron rings, just by themselves. It also imparts to the rings a force enabling them to do the same thing as the stone itself, that is, to attract another ring, so that sometimes a chain is formed, quite a long one, of iron rings, suspended from one another. For all of them, however, their power depends upon that loadstone. Just so the Muse. She first makes men inspired, and then, through these inspired ones, others share in the enthusiasm, and a chain is formed. (Plato *Ion* 533d-e)

Schechner depicted the remaining circles of the play production process as a correlate of the playwright-shaman's consciousness (intention and extention) which stands as the source of meaning outside any specific sociohistorical conditions.

The second version of Schechner's model (Figure 4b) reformulated the above view in structuralist terms in order to account for conflicts in the theatrical process "regardless of geographical location." Schechner drew two oppositional pairs of circles because he believed that some cultures (especially Indo-European) emphasize playtext and prompt-copy over rehearsal-text and performance-text, while other cultures (especially African and Oceanic) emphasize rehearsal-text and performance-text over playtext and prompt-copy.

Schechner explained the universal application of the second version of his model by saying that "a strong Western influence is felt in non-Western nations, and an equally strong non-Western influence is felt within the Western avant-garde" (1973:9). Like a good structuralist, Schechner, first, depicted these conflicts in a model of two abstract sets of binary opposites which appear to him to be universally applicable, but then he could not explain why there was such an increasing attention among theatre artists to the points of contact (or seams) which "apparently weld" each circle to the others. "I don't know," he admitted, "why the seams, which traditionally have held the four elements together, are now being explored in ways that break them apart" (1973:9).

The third version of Schechner's model (Figure 4c) averted attention from a central playtext and bipolar tensions. Instead of each circle being a "link" in a straight causal line, all four circles become disparate, discrete units which may be in opposition to one or more of the others, exposing the points where theatrical production is "weak" and disjunctive. According to Schechner, TPG's production of Sam Shepard's *The Tooth of Crime*, which he directed, opened these seams of contact between playtext, prompt-copy, rehearsal-text, and performance-text—exposing their "weakness" to an audience of 120 spectators (full house). "It is this process of dissociation," wrote Schechner, "and its consequent tensions, ambivalencies, and novel combinations that characterize the contemporary avant-garde" (1973:13).

Schechner's contemporary avant-garde questioned, among other things, the voice of the playwright which has ordained the structure of the logocentric theatrical production since the day of the Classical Greek dramatists. The theatre artists and critics who challenged this structure in the era of 1960s argued that the production and perception of meaning in the theatre results from a series of interactive contacts among playwright, designers, directors, actors, and spectators—not in isolated reflection. "Differing circumstances of playing," Peter Brook postulated, "would alter the nature and meaning of the event both for the actor and the spectator" (Smith 1972:21).

If the production and perception of meaning in the theatre is a shared result of collective interaction among playwright(s), designer(s), director(s), actor(s), spectator(s), and critic(s) and if the production and perception of meaning in the theatre changes when the nature and structure of the interactive contact of the above agents changes, then why were the advocates of anti-logocentric practices in the 1960s unable to break away from a phonocentric bias, failing truly to introduce a new aesthetic as an alternative to logocentrism which still dominates Western theatrical production?

Schechner's problem was rephrased in semiotic terms by Keir Elam, who took the argument back to square one. Elam ended his account of *The Semiotics of Theatre and Drama* without answering a crucial question: "In what ways are the dramatic text and the performance-text related—what are the points of contact between them?" (1980:208). Elam's concept of "contact" is reflected in the way we still produce plays and in the manner subsidies are allocated to theatre professionals. For example, grant decisions of the National Endowment for the Arts to theatre applicants are based on a distinction between dramatic literature and theatrical performance (Marranca and Dasgupta 1983:4). At best, plays and performances are seen as independent, self-sufficient artifacts without being mutually exclusive (Veltrusky 1976:95).

Elam's concept of "contact," implies two things: (1) a separation—not necessarily an opposition—between the distinctive features of a playtext and its performance-text and (2) a hierarchy in which playtexts exert a logical and axiological control over performance-texts—the common perception being that playtexts are written prior to the realization of their performance-texts. This control, however, is not unidirectional because the writing of a playtext is reciprocally conditioned by the physical specifications of its future performance. "It is equally legitimate," argues Elam, "to claim that it is the performance, or at least a possible or 'model' performance, that constrains the dramatic text in its very articulation" (1980:208–209).

Elam's claim is not as widely applicable as it sounds even though most playtexts dictate how they should be staged—as in the case of elaborate stage directions or in the case of blocking an aside. Elam's claim conceals the assumption that a playtext can fully dictate or foresee the dissemination of its verbal and visual structures during production. John Styan had supported a similar assumption thirteen years earlier based on a study of Shakespeare's playtexts. "The language of the good dramatic poet," Styan wrote, "especially carries the submerged imagery of gesture and movement" (1967:56). This, however, may not be as universal a case as Elam and Styan suggested. For example, Sophocles and Shakespeare wrote playtexts which perhaps were "constrained" by the physical specifications of the Theatre of Dionysus and the Globe Theatre, respectively. But their playtexts could never have anticipated the thousands of revival productions in translation in languages, stages, and styles that they received in subsequent centuries. Playtexts and their performance-texts enter an intertextual relationship which is indeed problematic rather than automatic and symmetrical.

Unfortunately, Elam saw a partly co-extensive relationship between a playtext and its performance-text which left out all other "texts" generated during play production. "The written-text/ performance-text relationship is not one of simple priority," Elam wrote, "but a complex of reciprocal constraints continuing a powerful intertextuality" (1980:209). Like Anne Ubersfeld and other semioticians, Elam downplayed the role of prompt-copies and rehearsal-texts in the play-production process—what Schechner calls "script" and "theatre" (Ubersfeld 1977:16). So, Elam's question "What are the points of contact between a playtext and its performance-text?" becomes relevant to the investigations of Schechner's "new" aesthetic.

On the understanding of play production as a sequential system, both Schechner and Elam could identify borderlines and points of contact in their respective models of play production. However, Elam's question can generate a useful answer if it is broken down into two more specific questions: (1) Is there a contact between a playtext and its performance-text? (2) What is the nature of this so-called "contact"? In other words, can this "obvious" contact be the result of a misperception? The prevailing view, which was shared by Schechner, asserted that a playwright's thought is prior to and independent of the written language of the playtext. Likewise, the language of the playtext is prior to and independent of the audiovisual language of the performance-text.

Nonetheless, several poststructuralist directors, designers, actors, and critics have observed that any assumed lines of demarcation or priority between a playtext and its performance-text are, in fact, nonexistent because meaning skids in all directions, simultaneously, to and from extra-theatrical texts, playtexts, prompt-copies, rehearsal-texts, and performance-texts during play production. Within this understanding of the play-production system as a continuum, it is presumptuous to claim that one can identify any demarcation points between a playtext and its performance-text.

Post-Artaudian theory and practice revived the controversy over the playtext/performance-text dichotomy (Derrida 1978:235) and over hierarchy issues between the creativity of playwrights and

the creativity of the other theatre artists. Directors, designers, and
actors would alter the playtext. They would use nonverbal
communication "to reinforce text, to clarify subtext, or to negate
the text either unintentionally or through conscious artistic choice"
(Cobin 1983:159; Green 1983:166; Immoos 1983:303). As a result
of this activity during "rehearsals," playwriting stopped being the
domain of playwrights only, and it expanded from playtexts to
include prompt-copies and rehearsal-texts.

In sum, we need to re-examine the issue of how playtexts
connect with their performance-texts. Any time-honored
explanations about a dichotomous and/or hierarchical relationship
between playtexts and performance-texts have only affirmed the
sovereignty of playtexts and playwrights in terms of priority and
dominance. The motives of such established explanations were
rendered suspect by alternative modes of play production which
experimental theatre companies have introduced in the so-called
"era of the 1960s."

In the following chapters, I will show that Schechner's "new"
aesthetic did not shake off the age-old view that writing lures
language away from its authentic origins, which are founded in
speech and self-presence. In fact, the "avant-garde" aesthetic of the
1960s retained the binary opposition between speech and writing
by privileging speech over writing. Then, I will demonstrate that
the alleged "contact" (dichotomous or trichotomous) between
playtexts and performance-texts was discussed in the context of
animal play and encounter rituals in order to promote logocentric
values in a Darwinian guise.

Schechner acknowledged that his narrow definitions of the
widely used words "drama," "script," "theatre," and "performance"
could confuse his readers, but he chose not to coin new terms that
nobody would pay attention to (1973:7). In the 1988 version of his
essay, Schechner noted that "someone with a Derridean turn of
mind might say that what in 1973 I called a *script* a deconstructionist
would now call a *text*" (1988:104). Although his notion of "text"
is questionable, I took the liberty of replacing Schechner's four
terms with playtext, prompt-copy, rehearsal-text, and performance-
text, respectively, in the hope that I will not lose the attention of
my readers. I use the terms as equivalents for a while before I
depart from Schechner's limiting definitions.

I base my analysis on a careful reading of Schechner's published works. However, I draw my examples from his essay "Drama, Script, Theatre, Performance," and I confine my argument to it for a simple reason: the 1988 revision of the 1973 essay uses a "modernist" rhetoric to conceal the structuralist, logocentric residues that I undertake to expose. Although the 1988 revision of the 1973 essay is a mild one—confining itself to matters of clarification, paragraphing, terminology, and emphasis mainly—significant changes of content occur occasionally. For example, Schechner's touching (almost Socratean) acknowledgment of ignorance in the 1973 essay is erased by a dignified silence in the 1988 revision (1973:9; 1988:73).

I limited my screening of Schechner's sources to Johan Huizinga's influential *Homo Ludens* (1949). Of course, Schechner's postulate that young animals need play to improve behavioral patterns necessary for their survival goes back to Karl Groos' *The Play of Animals* (1896). Schechner's concept of fun during playful activity can be traced back to Karl Groos' *The Play of Man* (1901). His endorsement of the theory of evolution in nature and culture echoes Loomis Havemeyer's *The Drama of Savage Peoples* (1916) and so does his notion that body language, as an enactment of the prompt-copy, preceded articulate discourse. But finding out *who* (might have) influenced Schechner's work will not answer *why* or *how* Schechner and Ernest Kirby revived the theory of evolution in the era of the 1960s. Kirby's explanation that the origin of theatre has been neglected provided an excuse, not the reason, for his book *Ur-Drama: The Origins of Theatre* (1975). His project differed from Schechner's in the sense that Kirby gave the actor, not the playwright or the director, the role of the shaman. He saw in William Ridgeway's trance mediums (1915) the forefathers of later-day actors. So, he argued that the shamanistic trance performances, which depended on the audience's shared participation in a ritual, are the antecedent of subsequent more elaborate established theatre forms which lack the healing element.

I will follow two steps. First, I will examine how Schechner dealt with the finished playtexts and visions of living, independent playwrights. TPG's production of Sam Shepard's *Tooth of Crime* indicates that, like Shepard, Schechner as a director operated on two assumptions: (1) that a playwright's vision has an origin and a presence independent of the playtext and (2) that speech has priority over writing because the playtext emerged as a specialized form of the prompt-copy as soon as some Western theatre artists replaced ostention (a term derived from the Latin verb *ostendere*, meaning "to show") with description.

Second, I will investigate why and how the advocates of the "new" aesthetic attempted to efface the "written" text from the art of theatre. Schechner, in particular, associated the performances of participants in "theatre workshops" in the 1960s with the performances of cavemen in "temple-theatres" in the 2500s B.C. His ethological explorations indicate that Schechner, among others, deluded himself that he could somehow dispense with the text and could arrive at a pure, self-authenticating grasp of reality.

Finally, I should add that I will not argue against utilitarian aesthetics or against the introduction of methodologies from anthropology for the study of theatre. I will be critical only of the methodologies introduced by what I feel tempted to call the New York School of Anthropology by analogy to the so-called Cambridge School of Anthropology. Although I question Schechner's "modernist" rhetoric and "scientific" eclecticism, I hope that the validity of the theatrical experience (*ecstasis*) through ritual participation (*methexis*), which he and his colleagues advocated, will remain unscathed.

For Schechner, three kinds of directors have managed to assume a conflict-free control over playtexts: (1) directors who, like Richard Foreman and Robert Wilson, have written their own playtexts; (2) directors who, like Joseph Chaikin and Peter Brook, have controlled the visions of their guest playwrights, such as Jean-Claude van Itallie and Ted Hughes; (3) directors who, like Jerzi Grotowski, restructured existing public domain material to their needs. A fourth kind of directors who, like Richard Schechner, preferred the playtexts of living, independent playwrights, could not assume a conflict-free control over a playtext.

When Schechner directed Sam Shepard's *Tooth of Crime*, a mild conflict developed between Shepard and Schechner. The conflict created the misperception that playwright and director stood on opposite sides of the issue. Shepard wrote a letter to Schechner which rephrases a logocentric tenet that echoes Plato's *Ion.* "For me," Shepard wrote, the reason a play is written is because a writer receives a vision which can't be translated in any other way but a play. It's not a novel or a poem or a short story or a movie but a play. It seems to me that the reason someone wants to put that play together in a production is because they are pulled to its vision. If that's true then it seems they should respect the form that vision takes place in and not merely extrapolate its language and invent another form which isn't the play. It may be interesting theatre but it's not the play and it can never be the play. . . . I'm sure that if you attempt other plays by living writers you're going to run into the same situation. It's a question you should really look into rather than sweep it aside as being old-fashioned or even unimportant. (Schechner 1973:12)

Evidently, Shepard thought that a playwright is either the origin of the meanings in a playtext or the endowed agent of another source. On this authority, a playwright can check the accuracy and faithfulness of the interpretations of directors, designers, actors, and critics. Shepard suggested that their "respect" for the structure and vision of the playtext can minimize misinterpretations and can secure its accurate (re)production. He shunned the possibility that they could be attracted to a playtext because they wish, for example, to expose its latent ideology and contradictions. He also assumed that (mis)interpretation is less of an issue with the playtexts of dead playwrights that belong to the public domain, having lost their "voice" and "copyright."

In the context of Plato's metaphor, Shepard saw the playtext as a magnet which attracts the other theatre artists to the vision of the playwright. Shepard's claim to this "magnetic" vision raised the following question: To what degree must the vision of a playtext determine the vision of the other theatre artists who create the prompt-copy, the rehearsal-text, and the performance-text? (Schechner 1973: 13). How did Schechner deal with the controlling vision of living playwrights?

Schechner translated "vision" into "scening." He assumed that playtexts appear in the playwright's mind as "scenes" and that "this scening is coexistent with playwriting." For Schechner, playwright Samuel Beckett may have been a rare exception because he could "hear" rather than "see" his plays. Allegedly, Beckett had a keener ear for music and the sound of words than most playwrights.

> The act of playwriting is a translation of this internal scening into
> dialog + stage directions. The stage directions are vestiges and/
> or amplification of the internal scening. The whole scening process
> is, in my view, a scaffold that is best dismantled entirely once
> the play takes shape as dialog. (Schechner 1973:13)

This means that the playwright's vision ("scening") has a structure
that exists before the structure of the playtext. This vision has a
presence which can be *seen* or *heard* by playwrights. In sum,
Schechner endorsed Shepard's assumption that a vision has an origin
and a presence independent of the playtext. So, what initially
appeared to be a conflict between a logocentric playwright and a
differing director now looks like a coalition—with each party fighting
for independence (i.e., control) and validity in interpretation (i.e.,
supremacy).

In the 1988 version of his essay, Schechner comments that
what *attracted* him and the others to Shepard's playtext was its
wholeness and its *allusive language.* "We didn't want to deconstruct
his text," Schechner wrote. "But as we worked on the play, and
the seam between performance and theatre opened wider, definite
changes occurred in the script, if not in the actual words of the
drama" (1988:74). Although the contract with Shepard prohibited
Schechner from restructuring the words of the playtext, he altered
things "around" and "between" the lines.

Specifically, two characters (the chorus of the Keepers) spoke
the lines of four characters; the protagonist's opening song was
turned into a theme song that the protagonist (Hoss) never sang;
the antagonist (Crow) appeared at the end of the first act instead
of the beginning of the second act; and, instead of a rock band,
the performers, who were also musicians, composed and performed
the music of the play. Since musicians are performers, but not
actors, their performance was life-style role-playing, not
impersonation of characters in a play. Schechner as a director made
no attempt to harmonize the feelings of the performers with the
alleged feelings of the characters because the demands of the
playtext (drama) had low priority with him. It is about this that
Shepard warned Schechner in his letter (Schechner 1973:12).

Schechner gave speech priority over writing by differentiating
between the playtext and the prompt-copy and by relegating the
playtext to a secondary status. He argued that the playtext is encoded

in patterns of written words whereas the prompt-copy is encoded in patterns of enactments. In these enactments, speech is manifested as sound (breath-noise), not as a configuration of letters (words-as-written). Only at a later phase are the enactments associated with the written word in the form of dialogue and stage directions. In short, the prompt-copy, like a blueprint, pre-exists and affects any given enactment (1973:6-7).

Schechner justified the priority of speech over writing by arguing that, historically, the playtext emerged as a specialized form of the prompt-copy (scripting) long after writing was invented. Western theatre gradually replaced enactment (Schechner's term for ostention) with communication (Schechner's term for description). The expansion of literacy inverted the old relationship between ostention and description, and the playtext assumed priority over the prompt-copy. As a result of this, the enactments during play production became a code for faithfully representing the words of the playtext, instead of the words of the playtext representing the enactments of the prompt-copy. But the avant-garde theatre artists in the West, wrote Schechner, are refocusing attention on the enactments of the prompt-copy (1973:7).

Therefore, Schechner would not allow Shepard's playtext to govern the entire system of enactments during rehearsals or performances (Schechner 1973:12). Schechner's reluctance to serve Shepard's playtext faithfully, however, did not introduce a new aesthetic. Ironically, both playwright and director shared Plato's prejudice against the written word, and they replicated this old view which associated live speech and the speaker's presence with truth or authenticity.

Shepard regarded writing (description) as a recording tool which was preceeded and anticeded by enactment (ostention). A playwright, like a method-actor who practices emotional recall, retrieves, follows, relives, and records on paper audiovisual sensations of actual experiences stored in his "inner library" without intervening with "emplotment" techniques (Shepard 1977:51). "Words are tools of imagery in motion" wrote Shepard (1977:52). Their power lies in their capacity to evoke a partial glimpse of the world to an audience (1977:53). He believed that words were "living incantations," not signs, and he often spoke them out loud before he put them down on paper. Therefore, he avoided rewriting his playtexts to avoid interfering or changing his original vision. Rewriting required rescening.

Likewise, Schechner believed that directors, designers, and actors can rescene a playtext only in the context of their immediate circumstances. They cannot possibly "scene" it as the playwright envisioned it for several reasons: (1) the playwright's vision is generally unknown to them; (2) the playtext is generally produced in a culture outside the culture that it originated from; (3) the new theatrical and architectural conventions make it impossible to produce a play in the playwright's vision; and (4) the sociocultural matrix of a play as visioned soon changes, and the original vision, which is tied to the original matrix, decays with it (1973:13–14).

None of the above reasons, however, were applicable to the production of Shepard's *Tooth of Crime*. In addition, Shepard shared Schechner's phonocentric premise. He believed that the organization of "living, breathing words as they hit the air between the actor and the audience" actually possesses an affective power (1977:53). Shepard also believed that "the *living* outcome (the production) always demanded a different kind of attention than the written form that it sprang from. The spoken word, no matter how you cut it, is different than the written word. It happens in a different space, under different circumstances and demands a different set of laws" (1977:57). Clearly, Shepard agreed with Schechner that speech was separate from writing and preferable to writing. Once more, what initially seemed to be a dispute over living speech vs. dead letters, now looks like an agreement—with each man insisting on being treated as an affiliate, not as a subordinate, in the play-production process.

CHAPTER THREE

A Darwinian Performance Theory

Like Plato, both Schechner and Shepard suspected that writing undermined the authority of their visions because it sacrificed the intention of the live speaker to the vagaries of textual interpretation. Writing introduced indeterminacy in a communication system such as theatre, and it prevented listeners from experiencing the intimate link between sound and sense. For example, Shepard had an unusual sensation during which he could hear his characters speak. His sensation was similar to Socrates' "supernatural experience" during which "a sort of voice" would come to him and speak (Plato *Apology* 31d; Plato *Republic* 496c). "In my experience," Shepard wrote, "the character is visualized, he appears out of nowhere in three dimensions and speaks" (1977:50)—in a manner similar to that of the angels in the Old and New Testament.

The advocates of the Greco-Christian (i.e., Platonic) tradition have always regarded material texts as inferior writing and spiritual texts as superior writing. Material texts, such as playtexts, are used by people who, according to Plato, "rely on that which is written, calling things to remembrance no longer from within themselves, but by means of external signs" (*Phaedrus* 275a). Conversely, spiritual texts—such as Socrates' voice, the Pentecostal holy ghost, Shepard's living characters, or Schechner's internal scening—are all imprinted on the mind (or soul) directly through an act of revelation. This immediacy becomes the source of all authentic wisdom and truth.

Plato's distinction between live and written speech empowered live speech. Live speech, which is imprinted on the soul (or mind), knows how to defend itself, to explain itself, and to address the proper people. "There is not, nor ever shall be, a genuine art of speaking which is divorced from a grasp of the truth," Socrates told Phaedrus (260e). Conversely, a written text cannot explain or defend itself and "cannot distinguish between suitable and unsuitable readers. And if it is ill-treated or unfairly abused, it always needs its parent to come to its rescue" (Plato *Phaedrus* 275e; Plato *Letter VII* 341e).

By creating this double order of texts, which had sensible (visible, audible) aspects and intelligible (invisible, inaudible) aspects, the theatre artists and critics who worked within the Platonic tradition promoted the belief that the spiritual text should be protected from the material text. To rephrase this in the context of Schechner's concerns and metaphors, the prompt-copy (as a mental, interior map) should be rescued from the playtext (the physical, external vestige of internal scening). Why did the advocates of the "new" aesthetic take pains to "save" this "spiritual" prompt-copy? For four basic reasons:

First, the "dead" letters or "dead" voices in a playtext depend on the consciousness of the reader to come alive. This relationship of dependency empowers the reader (director, designer, actor, critic) at the expense of the playwright. It also subjects the voice(s) inscribed in the playtext to possible misinterpretations. In short, the dependency of the playtext on a reader's consciousness (type of personality and level of understanding) upsets and often alters the balance in Plato's "magnetic field." Likewise, a prompt-copy, if it is rendered in writing, can only jeopardize the director's position of power, which he usurped from the playwright.

Second, "internal scening" eliminates misinterpretations because it effaces textual interpretation. Internal scening goes beyond "reading" the dead letters or dead voices of a playtext recorded on paper or tape. It resurrects past experience "here and now" by recourse to universal behavioral patterns imprinted directly on the mind of a human being. A director recasts the lived experience—not the playtext of a playwright—through an interplay between genetically and culturally programmed codes of behavior shared by all who are involved in a theatrical production (Schechner 1988:218). These codes cannot be de-centered because they stem from a "living" consciousness, not a "dead" playtext.

Third, the living consciousness of a theatre artist conceals itself unless it speaks *in propria persona* by employing direct speech and by avoiding narratives (or manners of speech) that are affected by impersonation. Therefore, playwrights, directors, designers, actors, spectators, and critics can grasp and impart a sense of truth only if they stand and work outside dramatic texts. Dramatic texts always require impersonation regardless of disclaimers—such as in Peter Handke's *Offending the Audience* (1969). Plato frowned upon playwrights and actors because they spoke "in character," impersonating somebody else or something else. In "living out" the part through strong appeals to the emotions, an actor's blessed soul first lost its divine traits, forgetting what it once knew, and then it picked up impious, criminal traits from the roles that the actor performed (*Republic* 392d, 393a-398b). Not unlike Plato, Schechner deflated dramatization (i.e., impersonation) as a form of (en)acting in his "environmental theatre" (1988:74). In this, he joined Jerzi Grotowski and other advocates of the "new" aesthetic, who announced that the primary objective of their performers was not to impersonate characters or to imitate emotions (Grotowski 1968:246, 255–256).

Finally, dramatic writing becomes a deceptive, dangerous supplement because it fossilizes and conceals living thought while it simultaneously allows the indiscriminate dissemination of information to "worthy" and "unworthy" readers —i.e., directors, designers, actors, and critics. Being a relative new invention, according to Schechner, dramatic writing developed as a narrow form of the wider prompt-copy. For example, Aeschylus, as director-teacher (*didaskalos*) could personally speak and transmit the prompt-copy of *The Persians* (472 B.C.) to a group of chosen actor-disciples; they, in turn, could check their misinterpretations by listening to him because he was the source of all meaning in his playtext. In the subsequent centuries, however, *The Persians* encouraged an impersonal diffusion of Aeschylus' wisdom—often at the expense of his authority and original vision. The pirated, poorly edited, badly translated or ineptly adapted text of *The Persians* received "questionable" revival productions and interpretations. From this narrow perspective, Aeschylus seems to have empowered his interpreters to misconstrue his intention and vision because he committed his thoughts to writing and, therefore, submitted "his" text to the public domain.

In the above context of reasoning, many theatre directors-teachers more or less revived the mystique of origin and authority in performance groups, laboratory theatres, theatre ensembles, theatre workshops, experimental companies, or research institutes during the "era of the 1960s." They did not submit their vision to the lures of a playwright's fixed playtext because they wished to sustain their authority over interpretation and the dissemination of meaning. Instead, they generated (1) actor-centered, flexible rehearsal-texts through interaction with their "chosen" actors-disciples and (2) less flexible performance-texts through interaction with their select, often limited, spectators-participants. The potent theatrical experiences (attested or alleged) that they offered to themselves, their actors-disciples, and their select spectators-participants demonstrated the Socratic equation among truth, presence, and the primal authority of speech.

Although these theatre artists and their audiences challenged the primacy of the written text and modified the art of playwriting, several playwrights who shared Plato's reasoning about speech and writing collaborated with them. Even complainers, such as Sam Shepard, behaved like Plato expected a composing playwright to behave. Plato argued that playwrights are not in full control of their utterances when they compose (*Ion* 534; *Laws* 719c). Instead, they are under the spell of the Muse—i.e., the playwright's natural talent (*phusis*) and his Bacchic or Corybantic inspiration (*ecstasis*). Shepard, who started defending his right to guard his voice and vision in the playtext from the artistic creativity of directors and actors, realized that he had minimal control over anyone or anything, including his own voice. "I begin to get the haunting sense," Shepard wrote, "that something in me writes but it's not necessarily me. At least it's not the *me* that takes credit for it" (1977:54).

Shepard's fear illustrates how differently logocentrists and deconstructors view artistic creation. Generally speaking, a logocentric theatre artist sees his consciousness as a separate entity from its written and oral expression. However, he thinks that his "voice" is an authentic (re)presentation of his consciousness. He also believes that his consciousness can only appropriate and communicate meanings through *direct*, personal contact (dialectic) with another vocal consciousness. Writing confuses him and frightens him. Conversely, a deconstructive theatre artist believes that his "vocal" or "mute" consciousness can appropriate or communicate meanings to others and to himself only through "texts" which are based on visual, audible, tactile, olfactory, or gustatory conventional, transpersonal codes—i.e., a language. He thinks that his "voice," which can be expressed in speech, writing, or any other form, does not represent *his* consciousness. He believes that his so-called consciousness (his "I" or "Me") is not a separate entity (or reality) from the "texts" or "languages" that it uses to communicate.

In the logocentric habit of curving separate entities, Schechner presumed that playtext, prompt-copy, rehearsal-text, and performance-text are conceptually distinct realities, structures, or systems (Schechner 1973:20) and that "the center of each is very different from that of the others" (1973:20; 1988:86) even though their exact boundaries are somewhat arbitrary and overlap or blend into each other on a continuum (1973:26). Schechner soon realized that he could dissociate and segregate these "realities" only at the expense of the one over the other. In order to preserve a neat logocentric understanding of theatrical production, however, Schechner would not let the four circles merge into a "chaotic" continuum. Like a responsible structuralist, Schechner confessed the following: "I want to find ways of keeping three or all four in living tension. I believe that none has *a priori* precedence over the others" (1973:20; 1988:86).

In sum, Schechner preserved the perception that the various "texts" have opposing centers and overlapping boundaries during play production. So, he reduced "writing" to its inscriptional sense alone, and he did not realize that the "enactments" which make up part of his prompt-copy (script) are a system of signifiers— namely, a form of writing—that mediates between the sender's "intention" and the receiver's "understanding." Schechner could contain the effects of writing (i.e., of literary theatre) within the Platonic tradition by treating writing as a transcription of the elements of speech. In order to avoid any notions of "text," Schechner proceeded to locate the source of authentic thought in the moment of an awareness (enactment) which precedes articulate discourse. For Schechner, the genuine art of theatre depends on carefully *scripted* enactments, not on *written* texts (1973:6).

By giving enactment priority, Schechner relegated the playtext to an inferior place, while he raised and "restored" the prompt-copy to a superior position. To strengthen this perception, Schechner took a mental trip into the stone age, describing the hunting rituals (performances) of nonliterate cultures. Despite the lack of evidence, Schechner asserted that the prompt-copies contained and contributed to the efficacy of the enacted hunting or fertility rituals. "It is not until much later that power is associated with the written word,"

Schechner argued. "To conceive of these very ancient performances—some as far back as 25,000 years ago—one has to imagine absolutely non-literate cultures" (1973:7). As I will show, Schechner boldly and imaginatively taxed ethological and anthropological findings to usher into the theatre Plato's ideas in a Darwinian guise.

Schechner admitted that he knew nothing about the prompt-copies (scripts) used in paleolithic temple-theatres. "I don't say *texts*, which mean written documents," he wrote. "I say *scripts*, which mean something that pre-exists any given enactment, which acts as a blueprint for the enactment, and which persists from enactment to enactment" (1973:6; 1988:103). In this frame of mind, Schechner invited his readers to join him on a mental trip among archaic cultures and nowhere did he associate the drawings in the paleolithic caves to writing. Like a sixteenth-century cartographer, who drew maps of the New World without having actually seen it, Schechner charted a logocentric origin for the theatre with the excuse that all succeeding maps of the New World revised, but did not reject, the first sketches (1973:26).

Sadly, Schechner's trail-blazing metaphor is deceptive. The New World lay ahead of the seafarers and, thanks to improved technology which assisted observation in the following centuries, cartographers revised old errors. Conversely, the origin of theatre lies in the past, and technology cannot retrieve it for direct observation. If no critic can (in)validate Schechner's story about the logocentric origin of the theatre, then preference, not evidence, determines the issue of origin.

However, no critic or artist can overlook the motives and results of such preferences in observable, contemporary theatrical productions. What goals did Schechner's story serve? Take Schechner's claim that, besides human beings, other higher primates "perform" during playful activity and encounter rituals (Goodall 1972:66–67) or that human and animal performances in playful situations offer an aesthetic experience which has a vital, educational, "survival value" for them in serious situations because such performances provide species specific, vital know-how and exercise for sexual, combative, and status encounters. If animals, too, subscribe to utilitarian aesthetics, he thought he could invalidate any theory which advocated that the performing arts offer aesthetic experiences as a luxury or leisure.

"The only theory of aesthetics that I can tolerate," Schechner proclaimed, "is one in which aesthetics is considered a specific coordination of play and ritual" (1973:29). What motivated Schechner's aesthetic intolerance? Schechner wished to interrelate hunting, play, and ritual with the genesis of playtexts, prompt-copies, and rehearsal-texts, respectively (1973:33, 35). First, he linked animal play to human play because both humans and animals simulate motives and behavioral patterns in playful situations which seem qualitatively different from their equivalent motives and behavioral patterns in serious situations. In simulated situations, they are less involved, they experience their surplus kinesthetic energy as fun, and they fragment, reorder, exaggerate, and repeat their motor patterns because no immediate results are required (Loizos 1967:178).

Then, Schechner postulated that human play emerged from hunting practices and, in turn, play influenced hunting practices because it emphasized teamwork, animal disguises, strategic planning, beginning-middle-end sequence of events, crisis orientation, violent encounters, win-or-lose situations, prowess themes, and man-made ordeals (Goodall 1972:205). So, he concluded that hunting practices were inherently, not metaphorically, theatrical because a prompt-copy (script) was necessary for the hunters to develop strategies that culminated in a climactic attack-event (1973:32). In turn, human play gradually generated secondary symbolic activities—such as theatrical performances—which retained the above hunting elements in their storytelling through words, songs, dance, and music as dictated by local tradition (1973:36).

Here is the Darwinian foundation of Schechner's performance theory: Animals instinctively stage encounter rituals as an alternative to violent behavior (Lorenz 1966:57). Their fight-flight rituals (or performances) rather than direct combat (which could deplete the males of many species) decide territory claims, status challenges, and mating priorities. Their effective "performances" are selected and developed (in an evolutionary sense) because the members of a species which used them have survived. These selected and developed series of programmed behavioral patterns (or, performances) are based on instincts (i.e., genetically stored and transmitted information) which elude learning (i.e., information stored and transmitted through written texts and/or the "texts" of the oral tradition). Schechner transfered this line of thought into the context of theatre, and he made the "scripted" behavior of enactments the cornerstone of his prompt-copy, which, as a mental map, exists outside written texts.

Did the observations about the behavior of higher primates add any validity to Schechner's theory that the performances of human beings offer an aesthetic experience which has a vital, educational, "survival value" for them? I am afraid not. For example, Schechner could have (in)validated his theory quantitatively by distributing questionnaires among groups of theatregoers and by analyzing their responses to real-life situations prior to and after their exposure to a selected group of playtexts or performance-texts over a set period of time. Or, he could also have (in)validated his theory qualitatively by recording and analyzing, say, the nineteenth-century debate on whether art should be a model *of* life or a model *for* life. Instead, Schechner pursued a different, more colorful course to prove his case. One can only wonder why.

Schechner selected what suited his argument mainly from the work of ethologists, anthropologists, and historians. He thought he could "weld" together play, ritual, and theatre by pinning on the same skewer observations obtained by different methodological procedures in different disciplines with different objects of study—without screening their findings (1988:15). Schechner's skewer held together several different pieces of information—especially about encounter rituals among higher primates and about rituals among human beings in Western avant-garde workshops, in Oriental folkloric performances, in ancient Greek temple-theatres, and in prehistoric decorated caves. Ironically, Schechner's argument was held together not by the "scientific" evidence that he selected but by an etymological tale told by Johan Huizinga, a Dutch historian. Huizinga discussed play as a cultural phenomenon from a historical approach, not as a biological phenomenon from a scientific approach (1955:ix).

Schechner's approach was eclectic—in Cicero's fashion. He picked Huizinga's tenet that play was one of the cornerstones of culture (1955:5), but he rejected Huizinga's other tenet that play exists for its own sake. Schechner maintained that play is a rehearsal for *future* serious encounters, but he did not debate Loizos' comment that play only borrows, elaborates, and ritualizes behavioral patterns from past serious situations (Loizos 1967:179). Since the priorities of the "new" aesthetic took Schechner beyond written language to "scripted" enactments, he did not mention Huizinga's preoccupation with language. He overlooked the fact that Huizinga investigated the concepts of *play* and *agon* as they were expressed in written language—despite Huizinga's disclaimer in the title of his chapter "*Konzeption des Spielbegriff und die Ausdrucke für ihn in der Sprache*" (Huizinga 1955:28–45). Nor did he mention that Plato figured prominently in Huizinga's thought and examples.

Schechner pivoted a significant section of his argument around Huizinga's flimsy etymological connections among play, ritual, contest, and hunting, although his priorities were poles apart (1973:29–30). Huizinga's fundamental tenet (1955:28) that word and idea were born from creative language ran contrary to Schechner's tenet (1973:13) that ideas exist prior to their written expression. Huizinga's argument that play was anterior to, superior to, and separate from culture (1955:19) sounded like Schechner's argument that the prompt-copy was anterior to, superior to, and separate from playtext—but, with one crucial difference: Huizinga did not place his argument in a Darwinian context (1955:46); Schechner did. Huizinga tried to restore missing ideas (signifieds) by interpreting written words (signifiers) which he found in Greek and other texts. Huizinga stated his position so clearly that Schechner could not possibly have misread it. Then why did he? Five reasons seem plausible.

First, Huizinga's general concept of play suited Schechner's general goal to reintroduce ethology and anthropology to the study of theatre. "Thus defined," wrote Huizinga, "the concept seemed capable of embracing everything we call 'play' in animals, children, and grown-ups" (1955:28). This umbrella concept covered the playful activities of higher primates and human beings in both encounter rituals and theatrical events. "Huizinga's *Homo Ludens* made it possible to speak of play in a full variety of cultural contexts," wrote Schechner. "Huizinga connects playing to ritual, and stresses the idea of sacred time and place, and of contest, *agon*" (1973:30).

Schechner himself, in order to associate animal and human play in archaic communities, assumed that higher primates and human beings have homologous behaviors. Huizinga was convinced that the "primordial quality" or essence of play was to be found in the fascination and fun which is experienced by those who participate in it—either as players or spectators (1955:2-3). This experience "resists all analysis, all logical interpretation," claimed

Huizinga, because "play is irrational" (1955:4). Schechner agreed with the instinctive (irrational) nature of human play (1973:30, 33, 34). But Huizinga embarked on an etymological analysis of play because he believed that play had permeated such "archetypal" activities as language since their very inception.

Second, Huizinga shared Schechner's premise that languages or, better, cultures, segregate—while nature unifies—human experience and communication. "All peoples play, and play remarkably alike," wrote Huizinga, "but their languages differ widely in their conception of play" (1955:28). For Huizinga, language allowed human beings to name things and, by naming them, to raise them into the domain of the spirit. By expressing things linguistically, human beings created a cultural (mental) world alongside the natural (material) world (1955:4).

In an effort to account for behavioral patterns (performances) which are determined by both nature and culture in an evolutionary context, Schechner brought ethology and anthropology together (1988:248, 249). He thought that body language, for example, was partly learned behavior through culture-specific texts or contexts, and partly instinctive behavior. As instinctive behavior, body language was universal—neither culture-specific nor species-specific—because it was "fixed" genetically (1988:207). For Schechner, the alleged difficulty in distinguishing between genetically programmed patterns and culturally programmed patterns in body language, which expresses a large repertory of emotions from fear/anger to sadness/happiness, proved that culture affected human biology (1988:229, 228).

Third, Huisinga's concept of illusion (defined as "in-play") in ritual performances of archaic communities was explored by the "new" aesthetic of the 1960s. On the one hand, playing or performing a sacred ritual was not behaving in the ordinary sense because it entailed consciously simulating and (re)presenting unreal situations (1955:22). On the other hand, it went beyond illusion (as fake reality) because it (re)presented a mystical reality to the participants. "In it, something invisible and inactual takes beautiful, actual, holy form," Huizinga wrote, anticipating Peter Brook's holy theatre. "The participants in the rite are convinced that the action actualizes and effects a definite beautification, brings about an order of things higher than that in which they customarily live" (1955:14).

Although the participants do not completely lose consciousness of ordinary reality, they are transported beyond themselves (*ecstasis*). The ritual is a series of enactments (*dromena*) which actualize a spiritual world for the participants by representation, alias, re-doing. The represented action (*drama*) mystically repeats or (re)presents a cosmic event or happening. The representation results in identification because it actually (re)produces the event or happening instead of showing it figuratively. So, ritual performances cause "the worshipers to participate in the sacred happening itself" (Huizinga 1955:16). As the Greeks would have said, ritual performances are *methectic*, not *mimetic*, because "*methexis* gives way to *mimesis*, participation to imitation" (Harrison 1927:126). The advocates of the "new" aesthetic in the 1960s rejected imitation, and moved towards a *methectic* experience through participation.

However, Huizinga was unsure how ritual performances connected with an aesthetic perception of the cosmic order (1955:17). He felt that play and ritual both eluded precise aesthetic definition or analysis (1955:7). But Schechner did not feel that way, so he discussed play and ritual in an aesthetic frame. For Huizinga, the equation between play and frivolity was not a given (1955:6), nor was the contrast between play and seriousness (1955:5). Therefore, he interrelated play to ritual, and he examined their relationship outside the realm of aesthetics.

Huizinga defined play as a voluntary, repetitive, orderly activity which is similar to ritual and consciously different from ordinary life. He further described play as an activity that generates fun, absorbs the participants, is free from profit considerations or material interests, and proceeds within its own proper spatiotemporal boundaries in an orderly manner according to fixed rules, promoting the formation of social gatherings (1955:13). In short, Huizinga believed that play creates order, and the affinity between play and order can perhaps explain why play "seems to lie to such a large extent in the field of aesthetics" (1955:10).

Fourth, Schechner was lured by Huizinga's attempt to link play with ritual. Huizinga argued that ritual has all the formal and essential features of play—namely, order, tension, movement, change, solemnity, rhythm, and rapture which transports the participants to another world. Both play and ritual separate the participants from ordinary life in an artificial seclusion by

circumscribing a sacred space, a magic circle (1955:20)."Just as there
is no formal difference between play and ritual," wrote Huizinga,
"so the *consecrated spot* cannot be formally distinguished from the
play-ground" (1955:10). Huizinga summoned the Greco-Christian
tradition to support the connecting link—in particular, Romano
Guardini's *The Spirit of Liturgy* (1918) and Plato's *Laws* (345 B.C.).

In the chapter, "The Liturgy as Play," Guardini emphasized
the connection between play and Christian ritual by ascribing to
liturgy several features that, for Huizinga, characterized play.
Huizinga was particularly taken by the comment that liturgy is
"pointless and yet meaningful," but another question demanded his
attention in the context of religion: Can simulation (pretending) be
a feature of both play and ritual? Yes, answered Huizinga, because
make-believe is operative in all religions (1955:22). Here, Huizinga
paraphrased Jane Harrison, who saw the beginning of ritual and
theatre in a "thing re-done" as a mimetic act. "In all religion, as
in all art," wrote Harrison, "there is an element of make-believe,
not the attempt to deceive, but a desire to re-live, to re-present"
(1927:43). For Harrison, simulation was not beguiling; and neither
was it for Huizinga. "This identity of ritual and play was unreservedly
recognized by Plato as a given fact," Huizinga wrote. "He had no
hesitation in comprising the *sacra* in the category of play" (1955:18).

Plato did not exactly do or say that, however. Plato believed
that people take their lives too seriously although they should not.
Instead of doing their serious work (war) for the sake of their play
(peace), people should perform their role as God's toys and should
spend their life perfecting their *play* (peace) through certain games,
such as song and dance, which would keep them mentally and
physically fit (*Laws* vii 803b-e). From this, Huizinga hastily deduced
that "archaic ritual is sacred play" which, in turn, is indispensable
for the well-being of the community in Plato's sense (1955:25–26).

> If we accept the Platonic definition of play, there is nothing
> preposterous or irreverent in doing so. Play consecrated to the
> Deity, the highest goal of man's endeavour—such was Plato's
> conception of religion. In following him, we, in no way abandon
> the holy mystery, or cease to rate it as the highest attainable
> expression of that which escapes logical understanding. (Huizinga
> 1955:27)

The games that Huizinga—and to a certain extent Plato—had in mind were celebrated on a holiday in a festival mood as part of rituals which surrounded a central mystery (1955:21). Inside the enchanting circle of play or ritual, the rules of ordinary life relaxed, and the participants responded to simulated acts partly spontaneously and partly acting up to expected roles imposed by the traditional rules of the game (1955:12). In order to reveal how relative and fragile it is, a participant, who wished to be a spoil-sport, could shatter this play-world by walking out (1955:23). A participant, who wished to immerse himself in the play-world, could move toward the pole of ecstasis (1955:21) or illusion (1955:25) where the "one" *becomes* the "other" and vice versa.

Fifth, Schechner had a stake in Huizinga's effort to equate play with contest in a warlike, bloody context. Schechner used ethological interpretation to claim that higher primates modify their behavior when they shift from playing to hunting in the manner of human cadets who play "war games" before they are shipped to actual "theatres of war" where immediate results are required. Huizinga employed textual interpretation to argue that "play is battle and battle is play" especially in archaic cultures (1955:41). But he applied questionable evidence to support his conclusion. At this stage of my critique of Schechner's performance theory it may be useful to examine Huizinga's evidence that was endorsed so readily by Schechner.

CHAPTER FOUR

New Aesthetics for Old?

Huizinga postulated that each linguistic community has a concept (signified) of play which contains just what is expressed in the word (signifier) that describes it. He also believed that some languages, such as Hebrew and Latin, abstracted a general concept of play earlier and better than other languages, such as Greek and Chinese, by aggregating the various aspects of play under one general word (1955:28–29). According to Huizinga, Hebrew has one general word (*sahaq*) which "affords striking evidence of the identity between the agonistic and the play principle . . . in remarkable contrast to Greek with its changing and heterogeneous terms for the play-function" (1955:35). Likewise, Huizinga continued, Latin has really only one general word (*ludus*) to cover the whole field of activity from contest to play and from liturgical to theatrical representations (1955:35).

Huizinga would not let Greek and Chinese upset his "equation" between contest and play. So, he argued that the Greeks were not right in making a verbal distinction between contest (*agōn*) and play (*paidiá*). He turned his back to Hendrik Bolkestein who had argued that Huizinga could not legitimately subsume Greek contests under the concept of play because the Greek word for contest (*agōn*) did not clearly denote play (1937:26). Although Greek and Chinese are not the only languages which distinguish between contest and play, Huisinga was anxious to prove his theory at any cost. If the Greek linguistic community had two different words (signifiers) because it had two different concepts (signifieds)—one for contest and one for play—how could Huizinga outplay the Greeks without contradicting his earlier postulate?

He conceived of the signifier/signified relationship as a double structure. If he could not push two words (signifiers) into one on the surface structure, perhaps he could mold their meanings (signifieds) to merge on a "deeper" level. So, he argued that contest and play share an "underlying identity" in all cultures because the contest—which belongs to the sphere of the festival, which, in turn, belongs to the sphere of play—has all the formal features and most of the cultural functions of play (1955:48). Then, why did the Greek language distinguish between contest and play? Because, answered Huizinga, the contest (*agōn*) had become so intense a cultural function that the Greeks felt it existed in its own right. Therefore, Huizinga concluded, the Greeks failed to perceive the essential play-element in their contests, and they never united contest with play conceptually and linguistically in one general word (1955:31).

Interestingly, this explanation does not occur in the German edition of Huizinga's essay (Switzerland, 1944). It appears in rather obscure terms in his own English version of the same essay which he attempted before his death in 1945. Schechner read a version reconstructed by the translator of the 1955 American reprint of the 1949 English edition. Elsewhere in his essay, Huizinga claimed that the Greek linguistic community distinguished between contest (*agōn*) and play (*paidiá*) for the following reason: *paidiá* evoked vivid associations of child play whereas *agōn* had nothing to do with play proper originally because Greek contests were fought out in deadly earnest—sometimes ending in death. Here Huizinga contradicted himself. When he wished to link play with ritual earlier, he had acknowledged that *paidiá* also described serious, sacred play (1955:25–26; Plato *Laws* vii, 803b–e). Later, when he wished to disagree with Jane Harrison, who distinguished between bloodless contest (*agōn*) and gladiatorial combat, Huizinga ignored the hesitation of Plutarch who had only heard that, in the old days, the duels ended with the death of the defeated at Pisa during the festival at Olympia (Harrison 1927:221–222; Huizinga 1955:49; Plutarch *Symposiakōn Problēmatōn* 675c). Plutarch was afraid that he would become an object of ridicule if he insisted on the truth of his statement.

Oddly enough, Huizinga wished to equate play with contest because play can be bloody, not because contest can be bloodless. Despite the lack of solid evidence, Huizinga saw no reason for separating contest from play in archaic societies, and he handled etymological explanations in a self-serving way. Plato had conjectured that the origin of play lay in the need of young creatures, animal and human, to leap (*Laws* ii, 664e). From this, Huizinga concluded that "rapid movement must be regarded as the concrete starting point of many play words" (1955:37). Then, Huizinga attempted a skimpy etymological survey to find such words for play. He found two, one Gothic and one English.

The Gothic word *laikan* (play) occurs in the sense of "leaping" in all extant Gothic texts—except in the translation of Mark's gospel where Jesus, on the way to Jerusalem, tells his twelve followers that the people will mistreat him "and will mock him" among other even worse things (Mark x, 34). The Greek text reads "*kai empaixousin autō.*" The Gothic translation reads "*jah bilaikand ina.*" Unfortunately, Huizinga miscounted. The Gothic verb occurs in this "exceptional" sense two more times in Mark's gospel (xv, 20 and xv, 31), twice in Luke's gospel (xiv, 29 and xviii, 32) and once in The Epistle to the Galatians (vi, 7).

The English word *play* comes from the Anglo-Saxon *plegan*, which primarily meant "playful activity and rapid movement." Huizinga felt tempted to argue that the English *play*, the Anglo-Saxon *plegan*, the Old High German *pflegen* (vouch), the Old Frisian *plega* (warrant), the Medieval Latin *plegium* (pledge), the Old French *pleige* (surety) were identical formally and semantically (1955:40). Since all six words related concepts of taking risk, Huizinga concluded that they were very close to the sphere of play.

From this, he deduced that, unlike Greek and Chinese, all Germanic languages regularly use words of play to refer to armed strife or contest. Oddly enough, Huizinga did not refer to a Germanic text to prove "the identity of play and battle in archaic culture." Instead, he referred to a Semitic text, the Second Book of Samuel, where presumably a deadly conflict between two teams was called "play." A closer look, however, proves that Huizinga suppressed any evidence that suggested otherwise. The Bible reads:

> Abner the son of Ner, and the lads of *Ish-bosheth* the son of Saul, marched out from Mahanaim to Gibeon. And Joab the son of Zeruiah, and the lads of David, marched out from Hebron and met them at the cistern-well of Gibeon; and the two bands sat down on either side of the cistern-well. Then Abner said to Joab, "Let the lads stand up and *play* before us. And Joab said, "Let them stand up." And they stood up and took their place, twelve

lads for Benjamin and *Ish-bosheth*, the son of Saul, and twelve
lads for David. And each got hold of his neighbour's head with
his hand, and thrust his sword into his neighbor's side, and they
fell together: so, the place was named *Helkath-hazzurim*, which
is at Gibeon. And the ensuing *battle* was very tough that day;
and Abner and the men of Israel were beaten before the lads of
David. (Samuel, II 12–17)

Huizinga cared less if the biblical story was historically true
or was just a tale invented to explain a place-name in Gibeon.
Martin Luther's translation (1545) transliterated the Hebrew place-
name as "Helkath hazurim." The translator of the Geneva Bible
(1560) also transliterated it as "Helkath hazzurim" with a note on
the margin "Field of strong men." Huizinga's understanding that the
place-name "*erhalt einen Namen von heroischem Klang,*" was based
on the Vulgate translation "*Ager robustorum.*" So, Huizinga was
sure that the Septuagint translation *paizatōsan* and the Vulgate
translation *ludant* were faultless and that the Hebrew text presented
no question of poetic license in the use of the word *play*. "The
only point that matters," he wrote, "is that this action is called play
and that there is no mention of its not being play" (1955:41). At
this point, however, the text is somewhat enigmatic, and it does
not justify Huizinga's assertive tone.

First, the Hebrew text does not suggest that Abner equated
the deadly action with play according to Kyle McCarter, Yigael
Sukenik, Otto Thenius, August Klostermann, J.J. Glück, and Roland
de Vaux. They all read, more or less, "soldiers" (*hannĕ 'ārîm*) and
"gladiatorial duel" (*wîsahăqû*). Thus, contrary to Huizinga's claim,
they argued that Abner proposed a deadly combat by representatives
(*Vertretungskampf*) to settle the conflict between the two bands.
The battle ensued because, with all the "lads" having being killed,
the contest was indecisive (*Anchor Bible* 1984:95; Vaux 1971:131).
Combats between select men sometimes preceded the general battle
in Middle-Eastern warfare. "The fights between picked warriors were
not supposed to be a cruel entertainment *before* the battle, but
were meant to come *instead of* the battle," wrote Sukenik. "Their
object was not to increase, but to decrease casualties, and one of
the main rules, it seems, was that their result decided the course
of the whole battle, i.e., the army whose chosen warriors were
defeated was considered defeated as a whole" (1948:115).

Ironically, on the one hand, Sukenik's explanation contradicts Huizinga's theory of play on which Schechner built his own; on the other hand, it supports the Darwinian footing of Schechner's performance theory. In any case, J.J. Glück's analysis of the same incident at Gibeon discredits any Darwinian surmises. Glück argued that pre-battle duels were not fought instead of general battles. Pre-battle duels were "suicide combats" that served as preludes to all-out battles between recruited armies, which lacked professional training, discipline, and strategic mission. The death struggle of the duelists inflamed the passions of the troops who joined in the fighting sometimes before the suicide combat was over (Glück 1964:30).

Second, the text does not suggest that the "foul play" was battle, according to Herbert May, Bruce Metzger, Hans Hertzberg, Karl Budde, M. Segal, L. Batten, Julius Wellhausen, the Septuagint translators, and the Peshiṭta translators. They all read, more or less, "lads" (*hanĕ 'ārîm*) and "bloodless contest" (*wîśahăqû*) in the Hebrew text. So, they argued that Abner proposed a play which intentionally or unintentionally turned foul. In either case, and contrary to Huizinga's claim, the author(s) of the Second Book of Samuel did not associate the bloody contest with the battle which ensued according to these interpreters. For those who thought that Abner used *ṣaḥaq* denotatively, the play turned foul unintentionally. Something like a *tournament* or *mock duel* or *sport* was agreed upon, which at the heat of the game got out of hand and turned into an exchange of lethal stabbings, which, in turn, degenerated further into a real battle (Budde 1902:205; Hertzberg 1964:251–252; *Oxford Annotated Bible* 1965:376; Segal 1917–1918:95). For those who thought that Abner used *ṣaḥaq* figuratively, as a signal or cue, the play turned foul intentionally. The Septuagint translated the Hebrew placename *ḥelkat haṣṣūrîm* (field of the flints) as *meris tōn epiboulōn* (lot of the insidious). The Peshiṭta translated *haṣṣūrîm* as *sdn* (opposing sides or plotters) pointing to either *ṣdm* = *ṣodim* (plotters) (Wellhausen 1871) or to *ṣrm* = *ṣārîm* (treacherous fellows) (Batten 1906:92). It would seem that either the team of Abner and Ish-bosheth (meaning "Man of Shame") or both teams concealed their intentions, if not their swords, and used the (wrestling) match or (sword) dance as a deadly surprise attack.

The relief no. 182B discovered by Max von Oppenheim in Tell Halaf probably belongs to the same period as the battle of Gibeon (Figure 5). The deadly duel between the two men looks like the deadly contest between the two twelve-lad teams in the Second Book of Samuel. They stab each other as they are holding each other's head. But, does the relief represent a real duel or a mock duel? Does it depict a pre-battle "suicide combat" or an isolated incident in a general battle? Does it portray a conventional "method of gladiatorial fighting" or a conventional "method of artistic representation" fashionable in Palestine and Mesopotamia? The relief no. 182B is as enigmatic as the Second Book of Samuel, and it does not explicate Abner's use of the verb *ṣaḥaq*. Contrary to Huizinga's assumption, words, like pictures, have context-dependent, not inherent, meanings.

The verb *śiḥēq* (Huizinga's *sahaq*), as an isolated dictionary entry, can denote both carefree play (cf. roots *śhq* and *ṣhq*) and gladiatorial play (cf. Samson's "play" as *sahaq* and *ṣahaq* in Judges 16:25–27). But in the above excerpt, its meaning is text-bound, and the text is vague as to how Abner or, rather, the author(s) of the Second Book of Samuel meant the word "play." Nonetheless, two things are clear:

First, if the verb *ṣahaq* is associated with "battle" here, perhaps figuratively, it does so nowhere else in the Hebrew Bible. If the root *śhq* is not a homonym which has nothing to do with the root *śhq* (to play), but *śhq* acquired a connotation (subcode) which, as Huizinga thought, could refer to the combat described in the above passage, it still remains unclear whether Abner used it denotatively or connotatively. This is certainly a truly exceptional use of the word in the vague context of a corrupt text and, as a controversial exception, it provides no solid foundation for Huizinga's generalizations and theory.

Second, if Huizinga had included one more sentence to his partial quote of the excerpt cited above, he would have had to admit that the Hebrew text (and its Greek and Latin translations) used two different words—one for play in the beginning and one for battle at the end of the story. The incident begins with the Hebrew *wîśăḥăqû* (let them play). The Septuagint translates *paixatōsan* (let them play), and the Vulgate *ludant* (let them play) as in a match. The slaughter that ensued is described in Hebrew as *milḥāmāh* (war, battle), in Greek as *polemos* (war, battle) and in Latin as *bellum* (war, battle).

FIGURE 5. Relief No. 182B from Tell Halaf (Gozan) in Syria ca. Tenth Century B.C. (Source: Max von Oppenheim, *Der Tell Halaf.* Leipzig: Brockhaus, 1931, Plate 36 [182B].)

Evidently, Huizinga's conclusion "that play may be deadly yet still remain play" (1955:41) is questionable. The Second Book of Samuel does not support his proposal that the concepts of play and deadly contest should remain united in Hebrew, German, or any other language. So, when he concluded that "for all the above reasons it would not seem overbold to consider the terminological disparity between contest and play in Greek as the more or less accidental failure to abstract a general concept that would have embraced both," I part company with him. Moreover, the "lads" who were killed in the Second Book of Samuel in their effort to help David ascend the throne falsify Huizinga's claim that "the contest is largely devoid of purpose" or that its "outcome does not contribute to the necessary life-processes of the group" (1955:49).

Huizinga's etymological hunt for the signified proved to be a wild-goose chase. He inadvertently showed that a text is not a sum total of words that, as discrete linguistic units, convey a single meaning inscribed by an Author-God. The excerpt from the Second Book of Samuel proved to be a multidimensional space in which a variety of writings from many cultures, none of them original, merged or differed. Although I intended to be brief, my argument turned into a kaleidoscope of quotations as I drew information from the Second Book of Samuel in Hebrew, in Syriac, in Greek, in Latin, in German, in English, and in the multilingual commentary of nineteenth- and twentieth-century interpreters.

Huizinga's attempt to attach a final signified to the Greek or the Hebrew words for "play" or "contest" imposed a limit on the text and its translations. He "closed" the text in the sense that he "explained" it. And he "explained" it because he "deciphered" it by giving it a conclusive meaning. My intervention suggested that the text cannot be explained authoritatively; it can only be disentangled. "A text is made of a multitude of writings," wrote Roland Barthes, "drawn from many cultures and entering into mutual relations of dialogue, parody, contestation, but there is one place where this multiplicity is focused and that place is the reader, not as was hitherto said, the author" (1977:148).

The reader is someone who holds together in a single field some, if not all, the traces by which a written text is constituted. Because the reader walks on the axis of sychrony, he may seem to be "without history" as Barthes preached and Huizinga practiced. However, the reader's field is historically (diachronically) determined—whether the field registers on a human memory or a computer memory. In fact, the human brain and its products (hardware and software) are delimited historically, influencing the range and quality of the reader's "field" or "text." The field of traces by which the Second Book of Samuel was constituted, say, by King David in Jerusalem in the tenth century B.C. was historically different from the field of its alleged seventy readers (translators) in Alexandria in the second and third centuries B.C., or from the field of St. Jerome in Bethlehem in the fourth and fifth centuries A.D., or from the field of Martin Luther in Wittenberg in the sixteenth century A.D., and so forth.

Finally, on the authority of his exegesis, Huizinga drew "a further conclusion" which was music to Schechner's ears. "Given the indivisibility of play and battle in the archaic mind," he wrote, "the assimilation of hunting to play naturally follows" (1955:41). Schechner readily adopted such *non sequiturs* in his essay because it suited him (1973:32). Huizinga's goal was to prove (1) that play is anterior, superior, and separate from culture and (2) that hunting, play, ritual, and contest are, if not indivisible, at least similar. If, indeed, Huizinga misconstrued his methods and conclusions to prove his pet theory as shown above, how will this change our perception of the third version of Schechner's model and of the "new" theatre aesthetics in the era of the 1960s? By pulling the plug on Huizinga's methods and conclusions, will Schechner's project sink?

Schechner's goal was to prove (1) that the prompt-copy is anterior, superior, and separate from the playtext and (2) that hunting, play, and ritual are related to the genesis of playtexts, prompt-copies, and rehearsal-texts, respectively. Schechner drew support and credibility for his argument partly from Huizinga's essay. Infected to some degree by Huizinga's authority, Schechner even suffered a bout of aesthetic intolerance for theatre performances which did not combine play and ritual.

Huizinga argued that play "is not matter" (1955:3). Play, like a singular Platonic idea, exists prior to the various cultures which appropriate it, materialize it, and, thus, segment it in ostensible manifestations which, on the surface, differ from culture to culture. Likewise, Schechner argued that the prompt-copy is a mental interior map or "script." Genetically, the prompt-copy (like Schechner's body language earlier) is allegedly as universal and, therefore, singular as a Platonic idea. But, as soon as the various cultures appropriate it, they materialize it and segment it, say, in the specific visible enactments of body languages, which differ from culture to culture. Therefore, body languages—as plural—are always culture-specific and limited.

So, Schechner complained that culture affects human biology (1988:228, 229), and he concluded that a playtext, as a written manifestation of "internal scening," is limited by the language and the culture in which it is expressed (1973:6; 1988;103). Therefore, the playtext is not universal (1) even though it developed as a specialized kind of prompt-copy (1973:7) and (2) even though it periodically achieved dominance over the prompt-copy when "maintaining the words grew in importance" in theatrical productions of such cultures as Greek and Chinese (Schechner 1973:36).

Ironically, Huizinga unwittingly implied that the Hebrews, who presumably unified all playful activities in one word (*ṣaḥaq*), were closer to Plato than the Greeks who kept play and contest apart! Although Schechner set aside Huizinga's philological-historical perspective for an ethological-anthropological perspective, he retained the Platonic view. Therefore, Schechner contended that any difference between human play and animal play is one of degree, not of kind—although elsewhere fifteen years later he admitted that evolution helps "differences in degree become differences in kind" (1988:14).

For Schechner, therefore, human performances result from more conscious, deliberate and flexible responses to stimulation than animal "performances." Animal performances, as alternatives to violent behavior, are more *instinctive* whereas human performances are less *automatic*. Nonetheless, both animal and human performances are "scripted," thanks to genetically transmitted information, not to written texts (1973:28). "Scripted" performances are orderly. Their orderliness constitutes the metaphysical cornerstone of Schechner's performance theory (1973:34-35). This principle of order, like a skewer, holds together and rotates the above disparate approaches and remarks into an appetizing aesthetic theory.

Schechner's orderliness (or *Logos*) is not a man-made law. "One of the qualities of play in higher primates in the wild is its improvisational manner, and yet its orderliness" wrote Schechner. "In fact, play is improvisational imposition of order, the making of order out of disorder" (1973:32). Even the most unconventional human play always generates rules—no matter how swiftly they change—for one simple reason: it imposes an order which sustains communication and keeps misunderstandings at bay—especially when performances (encounter rituals) test the boundaries between simulation and reality for the participants (1973:33).

This principle of order unmasks Schechner's project and, in part, defines the "new" aesthetic in the era of the 1960s. Why "unmasks"? Because, on the one hand, Schechner announced that "origin theories are irrelevant to understanding theatre"; therefore, he did not intend to replace the origin theory of the Cambridge School of Anthropology with a theory of his own (1988:6). On the other hand, he offered yet another theory about the logocentric origin of the theatre despite his disclaimer. Schechner took his argument into the 2500s B.C. because he wanted to prove that enactment, speech, and writing—in this "natural" order—constitute the evolutionary links in the development of the art of theatre. If enactment, followed by speech, stands as the origin of the art of theatre, he could reclaim the priority and privileges of presence and speech over writing in theatre theory and practice.

In other words, Schechner could assert that a director's speech and presence during play production is superior, if not anterior, to the playtext of a playwright, who, as in Shepard's case, may also write admonitory letters to the director. Several directors of the "new" aesthetic, such as Peter Brook and Robert Wilson, achieved both priority and superiority when they controled the visions of their guest-playwrights, actors-disciples, and spectators-participants. In this context, Schechner could claim that the individual fantasies of theatre artists and audiences—such as those of Robert Wilson and Christopher Knowles in *The Life and Times of Joseph Stalin* (1973)—created "on stage the interplay between genetically fixed (universal) patterns and culturally invented (learned) ones" (1988:218).

In short, Schechner called upon the "authority" of ethology and anthropology to defend and expand his directorial turf and the tradition of theatre workshops which had mushroomed in the 1960s. Schechner believed that these theatre workshops emerged in a world of many distinct cultures which were fast becoming global. For Schechner, these theatre workshops temporarily replicated the secure environment and circumstances of small, autonomous, cultural groups. In this protected time and space, the workshop participants experienced rational, prerational, and irrational impulses which led to playful, ritualized, symbolic, *scripted* behavior.

Whenever the theatre artists of the "new" aesthetic and their audiences rejected impersonation, they created an environment of adventure—sometimes similar to that of therapy workshops—which allowed the participants to "come out" showing idiosyncratic aspects of their own personalities as the director led them on. Like in group therapy, the participants played around with reality by fragmenting, reordering, repeating, and exaggerating their behavior. The playtext and the playwright were often absent. "I associate the workshop environment," wrote Schechner, "with those ancient, decorated caves that still give evidence of singing and dancing, people celebrating fertility in risky, sexy, violent, collective, playful ways" (1973:36).

In sum, Schechner intended one thing and did another. However, he could be held responsible for inconsistency, not hypocrisy. His theory of origin connected animal and human performances even though animal simulation (e.g., camouflage) is genetically programmed whereas human simulation (e.g., impersonation) is willful both on stage and in life. Misguided by Huizinga, he blended play, ritual, contest, and hunting. He took for granted that these "performances" overlap in some higher primates, but he failed to prove that they merge in human activity in both archaic and modern communities. Huizinga, who stayed out of theatre aesthetics, and Schechner, who "left" theatre to establish an ethosemiotics of performance, did not mention that, perhaps, the above four activities merged in Old Attic Comedies. This task was accomplished for them by Francis Cornford, a member of the Cambridge School of Anthropology.

Cornford, who attempted to explain the ritual origin of Old Attic Comedies, endorsed the idea that the contest (*agōn*) was a symbolic battle between the gods of summer and winter (1914:67). He noted that, in these theatrical presentations, the contest (*agōn*) followed the entrance of the chorus (*parodos*), whose members were costumed as animals (1914:2, 70–82, 105). During the *agōn*— a dramatized debate that involved choral matches in abusive language (*aischrologiai*) and mock ritual combats of fertility—the comic protagonist(s) had to overcome all obstacles by any means (1914:73–74; 110–111). Although Schechner, in attempting to provide a phonocentric origin for the theatre in the era of the 1960s, conducted his research outside extant playtexts, he replicated two basic flaws from the methodology of the Cambridge School of Anthropology.

First, Schechner took for granted that the development of cultural phenomena—such as theatre—follow profound universal patterns of development even though surface details may vary from place to place and time to time. So, he reconstructed a phonocentric origin for the theatre by eclectically selecting and citing secondhand observations as "evidence" from different areas, cultures, and even species from much later, often contemporary, historical periods.

Second, Schechner used analogy to compensate for lack of evidence. What the record shows that happened at one place and time could have happened at another place and time about which the record shows nothing. So, he straddled over continents, centuries, and species, forcing disparate anthropological, historical, and ethological observations together in order to make up for the lack of assumed intermediate developmental steps which would allow him to link hunting, play, ritual, contest, and theatre. Since he was working within the frame of a Platonic-Darwinian model, he could not entertain the possibility that theatre has not evolved from a singular source or in the same way in all cultures at all times.

The Platonic-Darwinian model led Schechner, like Johan Huizinga and James Frazer prior to him, to mix "scientific" inquiry with "imaginative" explanations (1973:4). Frazer's reductive tenets that human communities evolved in three stages from hunting to agriculture figured in Schechner's polarizing tenets that hunting rites emphasize playtext and prompt-copy while agricultural ceremonies emphasize rehearsal-text and performance-text (1973:35). For the same reasons, Huizinga's assumption, that the culture of *homo ludens* originated from play, sounds like an extension of Gilbert Murray's assumption that Classical Greek tragedy originated from a *sacer ludus*—even though Huizinga conducted his research outside the realm of (Greek) theatre and he disagreed with Jane Harrison on the issue of contest.

The closest point at which Huizinga was able to pull real-life conflict and simulated conflict together in the context of theatre was when he observed that playful, self-contained activities—such as theatrical performances—may sometimes become the occasion of real-life competition for prizes—as in the case of the competitive Classical Greek theatre festivals (1955:47). In such cases, play functions as either a contest *for* something or a representation *of* something. These two functions can unite in such a way that play "represents" a contest or else becomes a contest for the best representation of something to an audience. But, instead of analyzing these two functions in an ancient or contemporary social context, Huizinga analyzed etymologically the armed ritual sports and dances of the Cretans and Spartans. He argued that Plato's phrase *enoplia paignia*—plural for *enoplion paignion*, meaning "armed play" (*Laws* vii, 796b)—indicated that contest and play were interrelated.

My argument in the preceding pages suggested that the alleged originality of the theatrical avant-garde since 1960 may be just another modernist myth and that its contributions to the art of theatre should be reassessed and be revised as a necessary first step before anything new or different can be achieved in the era of the 1990s. I demonstrated that a major advocate of the deemed "new" theatre aesthetic in the 1960s traveled from phenomenology to structuralism before he knocked at the door of deconstruction. His admittance was delayed because he carried in his mental luggage the age-old phonocentric bias that writing lures language away from its authentic origins, which are supposedly founded on speech and self-presence. He used a "modernist" rhetoric in the 1988 revision of his 1973 essay, but he failed to conceal the logocentric residues that clogged his argument. His "avant-garde" aesthetic tried to contain the effects of writing (i.e., of literary theatre) within the Platonic tradition by treating writing as a transcription of the elements of speech.

Specifically, Schechner retained the binary opposition between speech and writing by privileging speech over writing. He associated the performances in several theatre workshops of the 1960s A.D. to those in cave theatres of the 2500s B.C. He undermined the playwright as the origin of meanings in theatrical production—a deconstructive move—but he agreed that a playwright's vision is separate and anterior to his playtext. He differentiated between playtext (writing) and prompt-copy (enactment) to claim that the prompt-copy, like the playwright's vision, pre-exists and affects any given enactment. He argued that, historically, the playtext emerged as a specialized form of the prompt-copy but literacy helped the playtext gain priority over the prompt-copy. Therefore, he restored the prompt-copy to a position of power by creating a double order of texts, which promoted the belief that the spiritual text (prompt-copy) should be rescued from the material text (the playtext).

The "new" aesthetic attempted to "save" the "spiritual" prompt-copy for four reasons: A written prompt-copy depends on a reader's consciousness to come alive and, therefore, ends up like a playtext because it deprives the director of the position of power that he usurped from the playwright. The director's "internal rescening" eliminates (mis)interpretation because it emanates from a central consciousness which "relives" the playtext according to shared genetic and cultural dictates. Theatre artists—playwrights, designers, directors, actors—can grasp and impart a sense of truth only if they stand and work outside dramatic texts, which always require impersonation. Dramatic writing is a deceptive, dangerous supplement because it conceals living thought and often disseminates information to "unworthy" readers. In short, the new aesthetic tried to reverse the process from imitation to participation by modifying the art of playwriting and the nature of the theatrical experience.

I also showed how phenomenological, formalist, and structuralist models have created a presumed notion of contact among texts because they fostered separate centers, overlapping peripheries, and priority sequences among the various texts in theatrical production. In the logocentric habit of curving separate entities, Schechner sliced theatrical production into several conceptually distinct "structures" and used, in part, the misconstrued theories of Huizinga about hunting, play, ritual, and contest to prove that the prompt-copy is anterior, superior, and separate from the playtext. Like Huizinga's play and Plato's idea, Schechner's prompt-copy is singular and universal before it is appropriated and materialized by specific languages and cultures. Since a playtext is dependent on a language (learned behavior), it cannot be universal even though it developed as a specialized kind of the prompt-copy (instinctive behavior) and occasionally overruled it.

The orderliness of the prompt-copy as manifested in enactments became the metaphysical cornerstone of Schechner's performance theory. If enactment, speech, and writing (in this "natural" order) constitute the evolutionary links in the development of the art of theatre, then Schechner could reclaim the priority and privileges of the director's presence and speech over the playwright's absence and writing during play production. Eventually, Schechner realized that he could separate these "realities" only at the expense of the one over the other—a deconstructive thought—but like a good structuralist, he wished to keep them all in a living tension.

So far, I have discussed four of the "laws" that govern the old and "new" logocentric esthetics of Western theatrical production. The logocentrists have always attempted four things: to establish the signifier (playtext) as a window with a view of an autonomous signified (e.g., Shepard's vision); to establish the signifier (playtext) as a provisional sign which functions in the absence of a presence that must be reappropriated at a future point in time (e.g., Schechner's rescening); to establish the priority of enactment and voice (the live, spiritual prompt-copy) over writing (e.g., the dead, material playtext); and to establish a residence (e.g., the chamber of human consciousness, Plato's cave, or Darwin's genes) which will protect this intangible prompt-copy from external contamination.

PART TWO

The Domain of the Designer-Director

We know very little about the *Chironomia* of the ancients, i.e., the nature of the rules prescribed by the ancients in the use of the hands. We know this, that they carried gestures to a perfection which we can hardly imagine from seeing what our orators can accomplish in this respect. Of this whole language we seem to have retained nothing but an inarticulate cry, nothing but the power to make movements without knowing how to give these movements an accurately determined meaning and how to connect them together so that they may be capable of conveying not only one idea, but one connected meaning.

Gotthold Lessing, *Hamburg Dramaturgy* (1767)

The day I first saw a demonstration of Kathakali, I heard a word completely new to me—the *Mahabharata*. A dancer was presenting a scene from this work and his sudden first appearance from behind a curtain was an unforgettable shock. His costume was red and gold, his face was red and green, his nose was like a white billiard ball, his fingernails were like knives; . . . and his fingers spelled out strange coded messages. Through the magnificent ferocity of the movements, I could see that a story was unfolding. But what story? I could only guess at something mythical and remote, from another culture, nothing to do with my life.

Peter Brook, *The Shifting Point* (1987)

CHAPTER ONE

Under Plain Cover

My two good friends were outraged with my "defense" of deconstruction last night—each one for different reasons. Jon opened the discussion by saying that all deconstructors (whether they are black, gay, feminist, or whatever) question every aspect of the theatre, undermining any authority or consensus which enforces interpretations and dictates tastes and policies at any level. They question the priorities and standards which serve the interests of dominant groups. In doing so, the deconstructors loosen up the pockets of conservatism in the professional and the academic theatre.

John sneered at the wishful thinking of Jon and said that the deconstructors promote rather than erode established theories and practices because their radical attacks give their opponents the excuse to justify their dominance as a legitimate alternative to deconstructive chaos (Cain 1979:368). The deconstructors overrate the degree of inventions that they introduce to theatre theory and practice. Any early retirement plans for senile faculty and any technological inventions for theatre companies clear the air faster than 1001 obscure deconstructive research papers.

Jon argued back that retiring or firing and hiring faculty can bring no significant change for one simple reason: it empowers the university managers, who are already a dominant group. Their managerial planning cannot produce the artistic and technological inventions needed by theatre companies. For this reason, the deconstructors attack any authority which attempts to "guide," "stimulate," or inhibit their productivity and independent thinking. They do not accept traditional, dominant views unquestioningly.

John smiled and said that the traditionalists do not accept new, subversive views unquestioningly either. They follow a model of inquiry that makes sense. They question any established theory. If they find it inadequate, they modify the theory by reassembling its parts into new relationships. If this does not work, they replace it with a new more defensible theory. Then, they question the new theory, and the cycle of inquiry repeats its grinding course. Do the deconstructors do the same? No, the deconstructors follow an unorthodox cycle of inquiry. They question an established theory. If they find it inadequate, they neither modify it nor replace it with a new more defensible theory. They just keep the old theory. So, the deconstructors cannot offer any truly progressive ideas because their approach does not really help them abandon established opinions (Ellis 1989:81–83).

Jon protested that John swept under the carpet of deconstruction errors committed by the structuralists. It was the structuralists who retained irreducible bipolar tensions and articulated answers (i.e., theories) which privileged one side of a fundamentally unresolved binary opposition. The deconstructors question the hierarchical oppression of binary oppositions in the axiological domain of a theatre company or a university, trying to reverse, dissolve, and recast its values into new relationships.

To John, this sounded like a goal of the formalists whose interpretations presumably resolved bilevel tensions by enforcing an overall coherence and unity. For example, the Anglo-American formalists known as "New Critics" showed how discrepancies, tensions, and paradoxes result when elements in the "deep" structure (e.g., images) undercut and complicate elements in the "surface" structure of a playtext (e.g., plots). And they resolved these discrepancies by pushing for unity and coherence through more inclusive theories.

Jon informed John that the above description was partly true for the formalists but completely false for the deconstructors. Many formalists sanctioned their interpretations on the authority of their "objective" readings of playtexts. And many structuralists achieved their interpretations by repressing one side of a binary opposition. The deconstructors avoid either approach, and they formulate new answers (theories) which ask for fundamental changes in established habits of thought and practice in the field of theatre—whether these habits are phenomenological, formalist, structuralist, or even deconstructive. Deconstruction has become popular with all those who are dissatisfied with the current state of theatre research and development.

I interrupted them to make sure that I followed the argument. As a first step, the deconstructors reverse structuralist binary oppositions, such as central/marginal, essential/unessential, because they wish to subvert the axiological (hierarchical) distinctions of what should be judged as essential or unessential, central or marginal. Fair enough! But what researcher can function intellectually unless he discerns what is central or marginal to his project? Exclusion is a function of the human brain, not a ploy of the logocentrists to preserve their power and authority against the deconstructors. The deconstructors, too, use exclusion when they expel central, canonized playtexts and theories to the margins. Jon looked at me annoyed and enunciated "as-a-first-step"!

John laughed again and said that Jon and I could take as many steps as we wished. Eventually, all deconstructors drive themselves into an undesirable situation when they empower the margins. Will the deconstructors stop supporting, say, the feminists and the Marxists, when the feminists and the Marxists come to dominate the discourse in the theatre world and the real world as much as in the academic world? Will the deconstructors begin supporting the male chauvinists and fascists when they become marginal? Should feminism be defended because it is suppressed or because it has an inherent value that should not be cast aside? A structuralist binary opposition—say, between dramatic theatre and epic theatre—entailed that epic theatre had an inherent value for Bertolt Brecht and some of his Marxists followers—and so did dramatic theatre for their opponents. In a reversed deconstructive binary opposition, feminism has no inherent value; it only acquired value when and because it was pushed to the margin.

Jon pointed the finger at John with resentment. Does feminism and do all the other isms have any inherent values? No, they do not! Adolf Hitler had argued that racism (Aryanism) had an inherent value. When feminism becomes female chauvinism or another fascism, the deconstructors will attack it at any phase of its development before it becomes a dominant ideology.

John was pleased to hear Jon speak against some ideologies, but was displeased to hear that all ideologies had no inherent value. So, John took things from the beginning to set the record straight. A playwright's activity created a playtext. A phenomenological reader would read the playwright's mind subjectively through the playtext, which allegedly functions as a transparency. In turn, a formalist reader would read stable meanings objectively because they are inscribed on the playtext, which presumably functions as an autonomous object. Next, a structuralist reader would read unstable meanings contextually because they are inscribed on a playtext, which supposedly functions as a binary opposite to the reader's competent (i.e., stable) interpretation.

I got confused, so I asked John to come to the point faster. John came to the point immediately. For the deconstructors, a reader (such as a designer, a director, or an actor) displaces the playwright in the making of a playtext, but his or her interpretive texts (such as prompt-copies, rehearsal-texts, performance-texts) are as unstable as the playtext. Neither the intentions of the various "authors" nor the rules of theatrical language can stop the signs from playing indefinitely against each other during play production. If the meanings of a playtext are inexhaustible, then its interpretations are endless. If texts refer only to other texts indefinitely, it follows that interpretation can never accomplish itself because there is nothing to interpret. Then what on earth do the deconstructors (designers, directors, actors) interpret as mediators of the meanings which they invite the spectators to watch?

Jon smiled and said that the readers (actors, directors, designers) take the role of the playwright because, as the structuralists demonstrated, the playwright cannot control the unstable meanings of a playtext. The readers explore the range of meanings of a playtext and, then, produce any meanings that crop up during play production. The readers' work is as creative as the work of the playwright. Their interpretations do not humbly serve a playtext or a playwright. Nor do their interpretative texts have any higher authority than the playtext. The deconstructive readers know that they are not in control of the unstable meanings of their interpretations whereas the structuralist "competent readers" thought they were in control. During the play production process, reading and writing trade places and become two names for the same activity.

John did not dignify this last remark with an answer. So, I took this opportunity to rethink the issue quickly. A set of signs can signify to me when I can distinguish this set from another set of signs by form or function. If a set of theatrical signs, say the twenty-six letters of the English alphabet, played against each other indefinitely, they would not be able to communicate any meanings because they would produce unrecognizable combinations and, therefore, they could not signify at all. But is this a logical error as my logocentrist friend argues or an age-old way of coining new words over the years as my deconstructor friend argues back? The more I listen to their quarrel, the more uncertain I become about my "apology" for deconstruction.

If a playtext must be liberated from any unobservable mental vibrations between playwrights and readers (i.e., from the phenomenological approach), from any isolated objective readings (i.e., from the formalist approach) and any conventions of its theatrical language (i.e., from the structuralist approach) to mean whatever the reader thinks it means, then can the playtext mean anything at all? Can a playtext communicate meanings without any conventions that are shared by the speakers of a linguistic community of theatregoers and theatre artists? Peter Brook raised similar questions at the International Center of Theatre Research in Paris in the 1970s (Brook 1987:129).

However, Brook's answers caused a controversy. My two friends, for example, held opposing views about both *Orghast* (1972) and *Conference of the Birds* (1973), not because each "text" had, say, two meanings that co-existed in conflict, but because the interpretation of my one friend is the very error denounced by my other friend. I cannot return to these "texts" to resolve the controversy for several reasons. The "texts" themselves are the loci of the dispute, and, except for publicity interviews and random recollections, there exists no *consistent* record (audiotape or videotape) of their improvised variations as they changed over time and space. I will not solve anything by adding my view to those expressed already. My view can create either further dissention or further consensus. In either case, singular opinion or total unanimity does not establish truth. My friends would remind me of Henrik Ibsen's *An Enemy of the People* (1883) or Bertolt Brecht's *Galileo* (1943), which illustrated how politics motivate the consensus of public opinion and of secular or clerical institutions.

Then, how can I resolve this or any other controversy? If every personal or collective opinion is equally (in)valid, a "text" in the theatre or in life means whatever any "reader" or "observer" seriously believes it to mean since the mind finds in a "text" whatever it is looking for. If a "text" can have more than one interpretation, how many interpretations are equally correct or acceptable? If the range of meanings that a "text" like *Macbeth* can acquire is indefinite, then will *Macbeth* eventually come to mean what *Hamlet* means or vice versa? This may not be permissible, but if it is possible, then the various producers of meanings (i.e., the "authors" of playtexts, prompt-copies, rehearsal-texts, performance-texts, reviews, interviews, research papers, books, and films) arbitrarily segment and copyright in separate bottles with different labels an ocean of theatrical and extra-theatrical "texts" for their own purposes.

The possibility of undermining the theory and practice of such "authors" threatens the economic and ideological foundation on which play production and theatre research have rested in the theatre industry and the academic world to date. I always thought (1) that my knowledge of the theatre developed through conflicting opinions, such as those of my friends, as a communal process during "table" talks and (2) that my friends and I changed our mind and endorsed a theory (alias, answer) to a problem because it was based on compelling evidence and, when applied, yielded useful results. Useful to whom? My friends shot down my theories and each other's theories because their application would be useful to the interests of the one and harmful to the interests of the other. In fact, the "answers" that worked for John were a "problem" to Jon. They do not think that this is mere posturing on their part.

Power struggle surrounds the implementation of each theory, and the established forces in the theatre market and the academic market try to "kill" new, subversive theories before they take root. This ideological and economic Darwinism of the "market forces" minimizes the alternatives offered to the development of theatre— especially when some of the "killed" artistic and technological innovations, like mutations, took place well before the arrival of the environmental circumstances which would make them beneficial to all. Unlike the structuralist binary oppositions, the deconstructive reversals nourish rather than suppress new and old possibilities. Of course, the structuralists accuse the deconstructors that they will damage play production and theatre research because they allow "creativity" to move beyond the restraints of compelling evidence and specific application.

Consider the question of power, which preoccupied Peter Brook. "How a single actor can impose his will on the rest of the company" (Smith 1972:25). The question implies that a playwright already knows what the actor ignores. For example, some formalists maintained that a playtext exerts a generative power which joins and keeps the other theatre artists within a shared task—the production of the play for an audience. This view nourishes the misperception that a "powerful" playtext is the cause for a playwright's control over the creativity of the other theatre artists. The structuralists, on the other hand, demonstrated that a playtext not only affects but is also affected during production by the other theatre artists and by the theatregoers. However, this mutual influence was neither as symmetrical nor as horizontal as several structuralist models made it look.

The structuralists did not emphasize sufficiently that relationships of power require reciprocity in order to function. One cannot be a "director-teacher" unless someone temporarily agrees to be his "actor-student." It was the interests of logocentric designers, directors, actors, theatregoers, and critics which caused the rise to power of certain playwrights. For example, logocentric directors allowed a playwright (even a dead one or an absent one) to control their creativity because the position of the playwright, as *archē* and *telos* of the play-production process, sanctioned all the other vertical relationships in theatrical production to their advantage.

In formalist productions, the director co-ordinated all the aspects of the production (set, costume, lighting, sound, and acting) into a unified whole. The designers harmonized their work with the playwrights' text as interpreted by the director's production concept. For many decades, theatre artists and critics believed that this formalist unity of blending colors and shapes gave a production its coherence. A poor design was one that disrupted the harmony and continuous flow of the produced stage picture. The structuralists challenged this assumption, but not the logocentric foundation that supported it.

Usually, a logocentric director derived his or her power and authority from a playtext. Whenever the actors argued that they had a greater understanding of their parts, the director claimed that he had a greater comprehension of the overall playtext. Whenever the set-costume-light designers complained that they had a greater knowledge of their individual tasks, the director claimed that he had a greater understanding of the overall production concept. In short, those directors who claimed that they had a unifying (formalist) vision of the whole process and of the final product often implied that they were the only persons to whom such revelations could have occurred. These director-gurus (*didaskaloi*) posed as the only competent interpreters of a playtext—sometimes by deifying the playwright and sometimes by mystifying the job of directing.

When the logocentrists allowed a playwright to control their creativity, they also made themselves accountable for errors and responsible for differences in opinion. Whenever a "subordinate" designer or actor challenged a director's "superior" interpetation of a playtext or a playwright's "superior" interpretation of the world, he asserted his equal rights as a creative artist. To reinforce conformity to order, the logocentists used the fear of anarchy. They described deconstructive theatrical production as a disordered state, prey to the innovation and inefficiency of the deconstructive theatre artists.

Every time logocentric opinions and practices go uncriticized, they influence how things are seen and done in the theatre. These perceptions and practices soon solidify into structures which bear the air of reality—the way things are. So, the continuous criticism of all established structures, practices, and perceptions becomes imperative for two reasons: First, the theatre artists and critics who appropriate and preserve a sense of order (read "hierarchy") or community (read "conformity") are not known to have instigated changes in the art of theatre or in the society of the theatregoers. Novelty and change require deviations from the norm. Second, the deconstructors cannot acquire any power and eventually change the established order of things in theatrical production, unless, ironically, their approach and practices take an institutional form. This contradiction needs the vigilant attention of deconstructors and their opponents.

Logocentric theatrical production provided playwrights, designers, directors, actors, spectators, and critics with an accepted repertory of artistic behavior that consists of perceptual patterns in interacting roles. These patterns and roles enable them to relate to each other in an orderly way founded on standards, expectations, and norms by means of which theatrical production proceeds. However, patterns and roles can change over time as the means of theatrical production change, thanks to artistic and technological innovations. Any audience member who is a house-husband, a homosexual governor, a woman doctor, or a black millionaire knows that social and professional roles can be changed.

The deconstructors are changing conventions and expectations as to what it means to be director, designer, actor, spectator, critic, or playwright. Theatre folks slip easily out of one role into another because formal education and hands-on-the job training require them to familiarize themselves with several professional roles within the theatre. As theatre artists and technicians develop their artistic consciousness, they can reconsider their artistic behavior, can recombine learned experience, or can question and modify standard practices. The deconstructors explore the potential for change in theatrical production and training. They do not attribute errors unilaterally because artistic and professional relationships do not result from one-sided activity, but rather they depend on dynamic interactions which change from time to time and from place to place.

The relationship among designers, playwrights, and directors has not remained static, but it has not improved the status and role of designers in logocentric play productions either. Theatre artists, often afraid of taking chances or permitting changes, have deceived themselves that artistic conformity stands for financial security. Despite the compromise, however, the precarious world of theatre continues to threaten their sense of order and security which is fostered by the social and artistic patterns that they are familiar with. As social and aesthetic conditioning foreclose any alternative patterns or responses, these theatre artists are losing their capacity to change the art of theatre over time.

The theatre artists, who suffocate artistically and financially under this established inertia, have a right to oppose it and try to change the course of things. If designers, technicians, directors, and actors are responsible for the process and the final product in a logocentric production, they deserve to have equal say and equal pay in the creative process. The deconstructive theatre artists assert their artistic independence against the playwright and his playtext. They declare their right to initiate, create, and produce their own thoughts in their own way. The playwright has not ordered the process of theatrical production. The playwright has only given it possibilities.

The deconstructors not only clear the path by exposing and sweeping aside some of the shortcomings of logocentric play production, but they also develop alternatives. In this part of the book, I will explore some of the suppressed alternatives available today in play production and theatre research. Technological inventions—from the writing paper to the magnetic tape—have empowered some theatre artists at the expense of others in the theatre and the academic world. Will the advent and application of computer graphics shift the power balance in favor of those who work in the area of theatre design and technology?

The number of students and faculty working in graduate and undergraduate programs of theatre design and technology has shrunk in the 1980s reportedly for six reasons: heavy workloads, slashed budgets, short deadlines, uninteresting tasks, long hours, and low pay (Nowell et al. 1987:6). Computer technology helped them do things faster, but time saved was time spent on learning how to operate new software packages and how to use the computer as a research tool. But the use of computers as labor-saving and cost-reducing devices, has not changed, so far, the artistic or professional function and status of designers and technicians in the theatre or the academic world.

Training programs in theatre design and technology continue to perform an auxiliary function, serving the priorities and goals of the acting-directing training programs. Of course, training opportunities—and professional opportunities—for designers and technicians exist when they have a right to experiment and grow along with the directors and actors as part of a production team. The logocentrists kept the contribution of designers and technicians under control, and they reduced it in Schechner-like "environmental" productions and Grotowski-like "poor" productions by focusing on the actor's speech and presence.

Although the trend toward a poor theatre gradually lost its appeal to the nonprofit sector of the U.S. theatre industry, it still holds sway in acting-directing training programs, whose aesthetic priorities and funding privileges, among other serious factors, caused the absence of designers and technicians in academic programs, in the 1980s. Several directors, such as Richard Schechner, acknowledged the *presence* of the technicians on stage during several of their productions, but many designers and technicians could do without this kind of theatrical credit.

The work of many Western theatre designers and technicians, such as El Lissitzky and Frederick Kiesler, has run against the logocentric aesthetics of acting and directing since the industrial revolution of the 1760s. If current technological inventions and the economics of the theatre industry give theatre designers and technicians the upper hand by the end of the twentieth century, they may modify the nature of the theatrical experience for theatregoers and theatre artists alike. The deconstructive approach uncovers and articulates any "weak" trends in theatre design and technology which, if implemented, may change the face and the course of academic and professional theatre in the early decades of the twenty-first century.

While the artist-scholars and artist-scientists borrowed their approaches (concepts and tools) from the Humanities and the Social Sciences respectively, the artists who work in the area of theatre design and technology borrowed their approaches (concepts and tools) from the so-called "hard" or "applied" Sciences—such as Mathematics, Physics, Statistics, Engineering, and Architecture. So, their photos and credentials in academic yearbooks or theatre company programs look as respectable and reliable as those of their colleagues. Their "scientific" projects often sound less embarrassing than the artistic "dabbling" of their colleagues in acting-directing training programs or in international centers for theatre research.

> Brought up in a scientific family, Peter Brook has believed for a long time that the theatre, like science, cannot go forward without research. In the arts, the word "research" customarily means a scholarly sifting of what has been done and written in the past; although he is exceptionally well informed about the history of theatre, as his book *The Empty Space* testifies, Brook, however, means a form of research much closer to that of scientists in an experimental laboratory: the search for processes, combinations, causes and effects hitherto unknown. (A. Smith 1972:15)

Anthony Smith presented director Peter Brook as an artist-scientist after the fashion of the structuralist approach which dominated theatre in the era of the 1960s. And so did John Heilpern, who reported that Brook spent "all his working life in search of opposites, believing it's the only way he can find a reality" (1978:15). "We've a lot to thank" Brook's scientific parents for, wrote John

Heilpern, because, next to giving birth to Peter, "they invented Brooklax, the laxative" (1978:10). However, Brook's "scientific" or "laboratory" experiments in Iran and in Niger, among other places, did not meet the standards of his colleagues in the area of theatre design and technology. Brook had interesting questions, but his "scientific" method, which allegedly provided some (if any) answers, remains questionable.

Brook dreamed of a universal theatrical language which would make sense to all audiences regardless of their language, culture, or class. To carry out his project, Brook founded the International Centre of Theatre Research in Paris in 1970 on a $1 million subsidy from the Ford Foundation for a three-year program. Brook brought together actors who had "no shared signs" of common language, common ideology, and common culture. He did so in opposition to the common practice of other companies which brought together actors who shared the same culture, the same ideology, the same language, and sometimes the same class (Brook 1987:129).

During the experiments in Iran and in Niger, the actors of the International Centre of Theatre Research were exposed to unfamiliar languages, to unfamiliar myths, and to unfamiliar environments—human and natural. In Iran, Brook investigated the conditions which allow simple aesthetic forms to communicate meaning to multinational audiences directly without the help of familiar references to shared sociocultural forms (Trilling 1972:35). In Niger, on a $60,000 expedition, Brook repeated himself. "We set out to explore what the conditions were through which the theatre could speak directly," Brook explained. "In what conditions is it possible for what happens in a theatre experience to originate from a group of actors and be received and shared by spectators without the help and hindrance of the shared cultural signs and tokens?" (Gibson 1973:47).

Brook's experiments in Iran and Niger were interrelated and so were his conclusions. According to Brook, they discovered three things: (1) the "sound fabric" of language is an "emotional code" that reflects the passions that forged it; (2) a myth of the past exists in the present when it reflects a living reality; and (3) audience research complements formal education as a theatre company learns to question, respect, trust, and satisfy the expectations of specific, diverse audiences (1987:130, 132). In both experiments, Brook's phonocentric orientation determined how the questions were phrased, the observations were recorded, the data were interpreted, and the results were reported.

To put things in perspective, this orientation of some theatre artists, such as Peter Brook, has been less about the priority of speech over writing and more about three related issues: (1) How do words (seen as phonetic writing) vocalize meanings? (2) How do words relate to their referents? (3) How is a playwright's voice recovered from a playtext? In this context of inquiry, these theatre artists endorsed four phonocentric premises, and have treated writing as a representation of speech since the "genesis" of Classical Greek drama.

First, they subscribed to the essentialist theory of language. They postulated that meanings exist independently from any language that is employed to express them. Meanings are autonomous, real essences in the mind of a speaker, and speech is a direct and natural reflection of these essences. In short, spoken words reveal, do not produce, the categories of meaning that are present in a speaker's consciousness—also known as mind, thought, vision, or reason. For Brook, in particular, speech is in direct touch with the source of meaning, and sound is in closer touch with meaning in some languages than in some others. "In Avesta, there is never any distance at all between sound and content," Brook wrote. "In listening to Avesta, it never happens that one wants to know *what it means*" (1987:130).

Second, they subscribed to the referential theory of language. They postulated—partly thanks to an etymological hunt for origins— that most words had or have a one-to-one, natural, direct relation to real-life categories. So, they assumed that a language reflects, not produces, these categories. In short, they presumed—partly on the score of cases of onomatopoeia—that spoken words mirror or mirrored the categories they denote in the real world. In the case of Brook, the sound patterns of speech express and crystallize the emotions of a linguistic community. "It is because the ancient Greeks had the capacity to experience certain emotions intensely that their language grew into the vehicle it was," Brook wrote. "If they had had other feelings, they would have evolved other syllables" (1987:130).

Third, they subscribed to the intentional theory of consciousness. They postulated that real-life categories could be grasped only as a correlate of the human consciousness. This consciousness looked like Siamese twins because it resulted from the inseparable blend of meaning (subject) and being (object). Thanks to this blend, human consciousness was the origin (i.e., the order of meaning or *logos*) of any definition about real-life categories because these categories expressed its intention. In short, spoken words about real-life categories function as transparencies which present a privileged consciousness as the origin of truth. For Brook, speech, as the expression of a live, present consciousness, can resuscitate the anemic meanings of a printed text. "Zoroaster's poems, which on the printed page in English seem vague and pious platitudes," Brook wrote, "turn into tremendous statements when certain movements of larynx and breath become an inseparable part of their sense" (Brook 1987:130).

Fourth, they subscribed to a neo-Platonic dualism which separated material (inferior) texts from spiritual (superior) texts. For Brook, translations, as inferior written texts, cannot express the true meaning of superior texts, such as spoken Avesta. "Translations at once lead one into the colorless and flavorless world of religious cliches," Brook wrote. "But as spoken, Avesta is meaningful directly in relation to the quality made by the act of speaking" (1987:110). The experiment in Iran, known as *Orghast* (1972) evolved from the study of Greek, Avesta, Latin, and "Orghast"—a language of sound invented by Brook's guest playwright, Ted Hughes. The experiment in Niger, known as *Conference of the Birds* (1973), was based on the Persian story about a symbolic journey undertaken by birds. Without the journey, the birds would have never understood that what they were searching for could be found at home. Ironically, the lesson of the birds did not teach Brook to stay home to search for the answers to his questions instead of launching his costly experiments abroad.

On the one hand, some logocentric theatre artists and critics assumed that the actual phonic shape of speech is not as arbitrary and conventional as is its graphic shape. On the other hand, they regarded the written words in a playtext as phonetic-alphabetic writing (Derrida 1981:24-25). For them, speech and writing expressed the same consciousness in different degrees of accuracy or proximity, but their phonetic-alphabetic writing differed from speech only quantitatively. This view is especially apparent in the way they wrote down the utterances of those characters who spoke in dialect. In sum, by endorsing the above three tenets, some logocentrists repressed the medial transformations of writing because they believed that the presence of the actor's speech acts revived the playwright's thoughts, not his playtext (Hawkes 1977:146; Jameson 1972:173).

Other theatre artists and critics who, thanks to Saussure, swerved away from the essentialist and the referential theories of language bumped into a similar metaphysics of presence. Saussure argued that words or, to put it more accurately, linguistic signs are arbitrary because they have no inherent meaning or ability to reflect every single real-life category. Meanings or, to phrase it more properly, concepts are the creation of language and do not necessarily exist outside language—as, for example, the concept of "unicorns" today and the concept of "airplanes" prior to the 1890s. So, Saussure argued for three things:

First, the combination of phonetic sounds in the making of a word (e.g., "top" but not "tpo") and the combination of words in the making of a grammatical sentence (e.g., Greek vs. Hebrew syntactical rules) are arbitrary. However, once usage establishes these combinations among the speakers of a linguistic community, they become forbidding "combinatory rules." A speaker must respect them if he or she wishes to communicate quickly and effectively with others. Nobody can prevent an innovative playwright from calling a pot "tpo." However, no theatregoer will understand that "tpo" means "pot," and the wider linguistic community will not immediately or necessarily endorse the playwright's usage once the equivalence between "tpo" and "pot" is explained to them.

Second, an individual speaker or writer is not capable of fixing a single value alone because, usually, the choice of linguistic signs does not rest with the individual. For Saussure, "the individual does not have the power to change a sign in any way once it has been established in the linguistic community" (1959:69). The community is necessary if arbitrary values, which exist solely thanks to usage and general acceptance, are to be set up. The concrete and conceptual system of a language—i.e., both signifiers and signifieds—is the common property of its speakers. However, although the speakers support the arbitrariness of such a system in order to communicate effectively, meanings are not indeterminate.

Third, meanings are established through a system of differences in a language, not through positive terms—i.e., terms with inherent meanings to be found outside a linguistic system. These differences "mean" by their place in a system of concepts and by their function in a system of features (Eco 1976:48-49). The basis for the differentiation and, therefore, for meaning is when a specific system of concepts introduces a particular set of features or vice versa. The system of concepts is as arbitrary as the system of features because they both result from a process of organization and simplification. Unless a letter has a place in a system of letters (i.e., an alphabet), or a word has a place in a system of words (i.e., a lexicon), or a phrase pattern has a place in a system of phrase patterns (i.e., a syntax), there is no language, no meaning, and, therefore, no communication.

Saussure's postulates became the mainstay of the structuralist approach in theatre studies. Saussure proposed that, even though languages represent only one particular semiological system, linguistics could serve as a model for all branches of semiology because its signs, which are entirely arbitrary, realize better than other signs the ideal semiological process (1959:68). When structuralist theatre artists and critics began to explore the related levels of signifying activity at the various steps of play production in the early 1930s, they observed that language is only one of many audiovisual codes employed in theatrical production and that the other codes did not follow the master pattern of language. Consequently, they questioned the role of linguistics in dictating the methodological priorities of the structuralist approach to the theatre. For many structuralists—from Petr Bogatyrev to Cesare Segre—linguistics gradually lost its pre-eminence to semiotics.

Nonetheless, most of the early Czech, French, and Italian advocates of theatre semiotics—from Tadeuz Kowzan to Patrice Pavis—inherited Saussure's linguistic quandary. On the one hand, the individual oral or written utterances (*parole*) of a theatre artist precede language (*langue*) because, historically, it was the utterances of individual theatre artists which made it possible for the "languages of the stage" to evolve. On the other hand, a theatre artist cannot speak or write "theatrically," so-to-speak, unless he draws on a theatrical language (*langue*) which exists prior to his oral or written utterances; he cannot produce readily acceptable meanings (structures) unless he follows the arbitrary ground rules shared and supported by the community of theatre artists and theatregoers. How did the structuralists—regardless of linguistic or semiotic inclinations—resolve this discrepancy?

Most of them handled the paradox by accepting a dialectical relationship between a theatrical *langue* and a theatrical *parole* which could not be reduced to any clear-cut hierarchy based on priority. Roland Barthes confused the issue for the theatre structuralists of semiotic inclinations when he proposed to reinstate linguistics over semiotics because "we are, much more than in former times, and despite the spread of pictorial illustration, a civilization of the written word" (1968:10). Derrida, however, argued that this reinstatement, which ostensibly favored writing over speech, would not help semiotics overcome its structuralist "blindness" which privileged speech and the speaker's (implied) presence (1976:29). The early work of Schechner, which I discussed in the previous chapters, provided an examplary case.

New analytical tools and new technological inventions are gradually changing the way we do research in theatre today and the way we will produce or market plays in the 1990s. How semiotics and high technology will modify—evolutionize rather than revolutionize—our traditional perceptions on theatre theory and theatre practice remains a controversial issue. But the way we sever our ties with past methods and means of production will certainly define our ability to improve performance quality, to increase company productivity, to enhance artistic opportunity, or to tap latent audience demand in the twenty-first century.

The changes which could make a significant difference tomorrow emerge in the artistic and technical efforts which go into making prompt-copies (not prompt-books). To date, the prompt-copy has been viewed as a "subsystem" in the overall logocentric process of theatrical production. So, in the following chapters, I will raise two questions as a means of exploring and realizing the potential for change in theatrical production and training: (1) What cybernetic capabilities did computer graphics introduce to play production in the 1990s? (2) Can the work of deconstructive designers be coopted by the logocentrists, and then twisted back into "shape," becoming part of the logocentric theatre without altering the fundamental framework of mainstream Western theatrical production?

CHAPTER TWO

The Original Dittos

Can theatre artists and critics find their way out of Darwinian performance theories? Yes, but no change in the 1990s can guarantee that theatre theory and practice will arrive at any viable alternatives by the twenty-first century. "Change" has served as a catchword that attracted public attention to the work of many theatre artists and critics over the years. The popularity of a "change" depends on who defines it, who introduces each one of its definitions, and who implements it. Historically, it has been easier to talk about change than to implement change in the professional and academic world of theatre. It has also been easier to talk about some kinds of change (caused by evolution) than about some other kinds of change (caused by revolution—technological or otherwise).

In this and the following two chapters, I will try to show how and why Anne Ubersfeld and Keir Elam, among other theorists of the theatre, underestimated the significance of the prompt-copy in theatrical production. The prompt-copy is becoming a focal point for artistic, scholarly, and scientific-technological research in the 1990s. The prompt-copy allows designers and directors to estimate space and movement on stage in terms of frequency, rhythm, duration, complexity, dominance, and coordination. It interrelates speech with movement within a "found" or designed space, and it allows the study of the differential involvement of the various parts of the human body (e.g., head, hands, legs) in a performer's total activity within a specific situation and environment. For the deconstructors, the actor's "animate" body and the designer's "inanimate" sets, costumes, lighting, and sounds have equal semiotic status. The sonic and graphic notational systems on a computer screen, which represent acoustic and visual impressions, make no claims to reality or to realism.

I will argue that Peter Brook's call for a scientific re-examination of the theatrical phenomena—especially of the underlying "codes" of such a signifying system as theatre—remained a noble intention that yielded valuable insights but poor results. Brook's disclaimer that in the theatre there is no place for the "*author as god*" (A. Smith 1972:56) paid only lip service to deconstruction. Brook undermined "the dictatorship of the playtext" (Artaud's term), but he replaced it with the authority of the director-guru. In addition, Brook's "experiments" retained the phenomenological assumptions of Artaud about the languages of the stage and the structuralist assumptions of Claude Levi-Strauss about "nature versus culture." However, Brook failed to prove (1) that under the surface of linguistic and cultural diversity, there exist regularities (patterns) which cut across all distinctions of culture and national language and (2) that by going back to the sources of language (sonic elements), he was returning to "the source of meaning" (a universal tonal consciousness), which could be communicated outside the various linguistic and cultural frames (A. Smith 1972:79-80, 181, 248).

In all fairness, Brook never advocated that words have to be banished forever from the theatre "in favour of gesture and primitive sound" (1979:249). Nor did Antonin Artaud. However, Brook was unable to discover a formula of geometric power and simplicity—such as his idealized circle—which would express the logic underlying the dispersed corpus of the improvisations of the CIRT group. He simply retained the phonocentric bias of Saussure and the obsession for origins and presence of Jean Jacques Rousseau. Phonocentrism and logocentrism converged in a dialectic between "nature" and "culture" and expressed a desire for some lost primordial sequence of speech-before-writing along the lines of Schechner's environmental theatre. Nature was identified with unmediated speech (*Orghast*) and with the dawn of tribal awareness (*Conference of the Birds*).

Brook's "experiments" in the 1960s and the 1970s, which revived a misguiding notion for "scientific" research in Theatre Studies, produced flimsy results because they were based on poorly stated and inadequately tested observations. Semiotics stepped into the picture when the debate over the loosening of logocentric bonds emphasized a need for more comprehensive tools that could deal with both the verbal and nonverbal aspects of theatre. The development of notational systems which could record stage movement and display it on a computer screen for semiotic analysis and/or for the compositional purposes of designers and directors opened new avenues in the methods and means by which we will produce plays and do our research in the twenty-first century.

Although some phenomenologists talked about timeless themes (archetypes), some formalists about desirable skills (techniques), and some structuralists about interpretative competency (processes), for all of them "colaboration" meant that (1) a designer should serve the playwright or his playtext, the director or his production concept (model production), the actor or his inspiration and (2) a designer should not question any of their preset notions on what is historical or ahistorical, desirable or undesirable, competent or incompetent. So, they underrated the designer's "decorative" art, or "unregarded art" (Gombrich's term). When "auteurs" such as Bertolt Brecht realized that theatrical production is a series of functions without a fixed center, they empowered the playtext as an ideological core which, as a printed book and a model prompt-copy, stood both inside and outside the structure of (capitalist) theatrical production trying to control it.

In doing so, Brecht and many other anti-Aristotelians ignored the notion of the "supplement," which was introduced by Aristotle, regarding the art of the designers and the art of the playwrights. Aristotle's notion of the "supplement" was less strict than Brecht's notion of the "model production." Brecht treated playtexts and model productions as handy mouthpieces for his own superior grasp of their meaning and style (mode) of production, impinging on the work of the other theatre artists. I will demonstrate that the mere substitution of terms—such as epic for naturalistic, public for private, Marxist for capitalist, and so on—do not place the discussion of theatrical production outside the realm of metaphysics.

Whereas the phenomenological, formalist, and structuralist approaches theoretically "close" and "control" the various "texts" in theatrical production, I will show how deconstruction "reopens" them (1) by re-examining how the frames and codes of the various theatrical texts are constructed, (2) by analyzing the rhetorics of earlier analytical approaches which generate and sustain a set of theories and practices, and (3) by reinscribing the "author" who is entrapped within a restricted economy. For most formalists, the idea that the meaning of the playtext could be translated (paraphrased) into any kind of equivalent "text" during theatrical production was unbearable. Theatrical production threatened the autonomy and purity of the sacrosanct playtext even when designers, directors, and actors tried to serve it faithfully.

It almost became a doctrinal commitment among some formalists to retain the "substance of God" (St. Augustine's term) in every playtext, and this ought to be respected by designers, directors, actors, and critics. Their readings of a playtext for the public turned them into mediums who communicated "deep-laid intuitive responses" (Leavis' term). Leavis treated language itself as a medium of "lived" or "felt" experience. The perfect medium for exposing the Unconscious in terms of the theatre was "the talking picture" (Jones' term). From Edmond Jones' "talking picture" (1941:17) to William Wimsatt's "verbal icon" (1954:217), designers, directors, actors, and critics of playtexts enacted their intuitive responses. It will become evident that the formalist notion of playtexts as "verbal icons" and of sets as "talking pictures"—i.e., as timeless, self-possessed structures of meaning—were undermined by the very (dialectical) tensions (*oxymorons*) which these artists sought out in order to praise and contain them. Organic form turned out to be a product of the formalist and structuralist desire for order rather than anything vested in the playtext itself.

Since, all texts (forms of writing) in theatrical production raised questions of meaning and intent, playtexts could no longer sustain their privileged status and primal authority by effacing the importance of the texts "written" by designers, directors, actors, and critics. This view contributed to the weakening of the logocentric system of priorities which defined the relation between "creative" (primary) and "derivative" (secondary) texts. The distinction rested on the view that playtexts embodied full, authentic meaning which, through an inward self-surveillance, insured a perfect intuitive fit between intention and utterance. This mystique of origins and presence was challenged by annulling the various territorial imperatives which—like the Berlin wall—marked off playtexts from prompt-copies, rehearsal-texts, performance-texts, and extra-theatrical texts. The "autonomous" playtexts were invaded by the "insubordinate" texts of designers, directors, actors, and critics. All in all, instead of discrediting materialism, some theatre artists revealed that their idealism was an attenuated naturalism. Edmond Jones illustrated my last point when he said, "Do not think for a moment that I am advising the designer to do away with actual objects on the stage. There is no such thing as a symbolic chair. A chair is a chair" (1941:26-27).

Of course, one may argue that the changes which technology introduces to theatrical production may not necessarily modify the structure of its functions. This argument implies that the structure of functions in theatrical production rests on forces other than technological and economic development—such as artistic and educational goals. I will explore the validity of this argument by briefly examining two such goals which resist technological and economic change. I will argue that the forces of "traditional" art and "scholarly" rationalizations support each other, but they cannot control entropy and experience. I will also argue that dissemination occurs when the "text" does not return to its author and that theatre theory and practice has abandoned hope of returning to the playwright's word (*logos*) or the Word (*Logos*) that was in the beginning by way of imitation.

Computer-animated design has opened new possibilities for restructuring hierarchical roles in play production. Although computer-animated design does not ban improvisation and artistic innovation from the stage, many designers and directors who abhor detailed stage composition before rehearsals and detest lectures on productivity or the jargon of marketing and engineering felt threatened. They claimed that the mind of a good designer or director is cheaper, if not faster, than a cost-reducing computer; that the work of improvisational directors may be more time-consuming and costly than when it is assisted by a computer, but it is often more creative and it is worth it.

Consequently, they are reluctant to abandon the pencil and the paper, and they resist the dissemination of computer-animated design by refusing to train themselves and their students in this high-tech drawing tool. They forget that the Europeans imported paper as advanced technology item from Baghdad (Iraq) before they built their own paper mills at the turn of the fourteenth century or that, likewise, the pencil was considered high technology in the 1560s when the naturalist Conrad Gesner described a new writing tool in which graphite was inserted into a wooden holder. The mass dissemination of paper and pencil (as well as the printing of plays) divided the world of theatre into literate and illiterate theatre artists by the end of the sixteenth century. One could not be a playwright unless he or she knew how to write plays, and one could not design, direct, and act in a play unless he or she knew how to read plays.

Professional opportunity decreased for the illiterate theatre artists who felt that the proliferation and dissemination of written playtexts and prompt-books threatened the oral tradition in the theatre which privileged the playwright as a director-guru (*didaskalos*). Understandably, any theatre artists who were worried about their professional survival resisted the new technology in the 1580s. In a similar manner the introduction of computer-aided design in the 1980s called for computer literacy, and it divided theatre artists into computer literates and computer illiterates. The old guard who lacks computer training complains that the computer-aided or animated design enables (empowers) mediocre designers—who otherwise were incapable of drawing with pencil on paper—to produce better results, especially in drafting.

The mass dissemination of this new technology—which upsets established patterns of expression and power in the art of theatre— has a "democratic" or "equalizing" function because it enables the less capable to perform at more acceptable levels. On the other hand, this very same technology sets new standards which are both "authoritative" and "discriminating." These standards redefine "artistic ability" and "professional skill" and, therefore, concentrate professional power only in those who possess the ability, can afford the training, and can acquire the skills of computer literacy. The other theatre artists who simply have the abilities and skills required by improved fourteenth-century tools, must make the extra effort to train themselves in computer-animated design—if they wish to maintain their professional and artistic influence in the future.

Clearly, the conflict has not developed between human brains and electronic brains as some designers and directors made it sound. The conflict has developed between logocentric scripts and deconstructive texts because computer-animated design is subverting the traditional means of production, expression, and accreditation. During historical periods of sweeping transitions, which are caused by new lines of technological inventions—writing paper or magnetic tape—the deconstructors seem to regain power over the logocentrists. In a sloppy effort to confuse the issue, director Richard

Schechner tried to "gloss over" the difference between logocentric "scripts" and deconstructive "texts" while he hastily put all notational systems in one bag.

> From a 1986 perspective, I might differently gloss the distinction between "text and script." Someone with a Derridean turn of mind might say that what in 1973 I called a "script" a deconstructionist would now call a "text." There are many different kinds of text—performance texts, dramatic texts, musical texts, movement texts, painterly texts, etc. A text is a way of inscribing—encoding—information. Such inscriptions may be on stone, vellum, or paper—or they may be charges of a silicon chip, memory traces in a dancer's body, or what have you. Various notation systems exist: alphabetical, digital, analogical, graphic, etc. New languages can be constructed. Information can easily be translated from one of these inscriptive-storage systems (languages) into another. That's why I can so easily write this text on my computer: The machine almost instantaneously inscribes and translates the several languages it uses—while what comes up on my screen is the one language I know fairly well, English. This translatability promotes discourse across disciplines. (Schechner 1988:104)

The deconstructors dissolve dichotomies, not differences as Schechner seems to think in his attempt to equate "text" with "script." The designers, who break the rules of logocentric production, go beyond structuralist dichotomies such as Steen Jansen's "plan textuel vs. plan scenique" (1968), Marcello Pagnini's "complesso scritturale vs. complesso operativo" (1970), and Schechner's "drama vs. script" (1973)—or earlier phenomenological dichotomies such as Roman Ingardern's "Haupt-text und Nebentext" (1958). For the deconstructors, the various "texts" in theatrical production function as each other's trace—neither as parts nor entities with overlapping boundaries and conflicting centers. Each text leaves no point at which completion or closure can be attained in the next text. In other words, the playtext, the prompt-copy, the rehearsal-text, and the performance-text are neither parts of a formalist organic whole nor conflicting entities in a structuralist binary system of oppositions.

Dissemination and difference result from denying the existence of a final (transcendental) signified. Meaning becomes indefinite when there is no final authority present—such as a playwright-god, a director-guru, a master-designer, an actor-star, a leading critic, or a theological, scholarly, and scientific consensus on the meanings of man-made, natural, or divine "texts" and "contexts." Meaning is dispersed and cannot be gathered back because there is no fixed matrix or ultimate authority. In the absence of an "initial" author, one or more of the other leading experts tries to fill the gap by speaking in the name of the author-god. In this way, they posit determinancy where none existed otherwise, and their determinate meanings become performative acts.

Their performative acts entail a willful, egocentric imposition of closure which suppresses or eliminates any other differing opinions and meanings, retaining a hierarchical (metaphysical) structure. They also entertain the misperception that each side of the opposition can have meaning "autonomously" without the other. The presence of a playwright (as artist-in-residence) reaffirms this hierarchy, but the other theatre artists do not get any closer to the truth by obeying the directions of the playwright than by disobeying them.

If theatrical signification is not determined by the presence of a signified (embodied by a playwright) standing inside or outside of theatrical production, but, instead, it is determined by a system of differences in which each signifier is inscribed, then theatrical production and the various languages of its "texts" have no central source. This means that the playtext or the mind of a playwright are no longer the "womb" of meaning which sustains the rest of the "reproductive" chain in play production. Signifiers and signifieds do not merge along this chain of pairs; they only approach each other by interpretive approximation. Only the victims of illusion think that signifiers and signifieds (structural bipolarities) merge into a whole (formalist unity).

From Plato to the present, theatrical production has rested on widespread dualisms, such as subject/object, spirit/matter, self/ world, signified/signifier. In turn, these pairs have rested on fixed, polarized frames of reference which formed global wholes. It was assumed that a gifted theatre artist had the ability to grasp and reveal the (Platonic) ideas reflected in the objective world through playwriting, designing, directing, and acting for the benefit of his colleagues and their audiences. A spectator who borrowed the ears or eyes (so to speak) of a gifted theatre artist could see through the "text" what the theatre artist beheld directly. In other words, the playtext, the prompt-copy, the rehearsal-text, the performance-text, or the critical essay functioned only as the means (metaphysical windows) which helped the "viewers" grasp a supreme or deep reality intuitively.

Each "window-text" (i.e., system of signifiers) made no cognitive contribution of its own. The more "invisible" these systems of signifiers were, the better because, supposedly, the viewers responded not to the signifiers of a playtext or a performance-text, but to what these systems of signifiers disclosed. This Greco-Christian perspective allowed actors and spectators alike to relate themselves to a higher Reality or Being through incarnation, not interpretation, and through participation, not discourse. Popular formalisms and structuralisms reduced the various histories of Western theatre to monisms and dualisms. They also guaranteed the full presence of meaning in performance thanks to the presence of the actors and their "direct" speech.

Jerzi Grotowski's poor theatre (kabbalistic *via negativa*), Peter Brook's holy theatre (voodoo rites), and Richard Schechner's environmental theatre (dionysiac orgies), among many others, proposed a subversive revision of Western theatrical production. However, these revisionists, instead of breaking from tradition, re-established its fundamental tropes and functions. Their theory and practice resulted in a nonconformity that was deeply traditional, and neo-Platonism returned by way of heresy into their alternative theatres.

The phenomenological project of disembodying the "texts" in theatrical production by overlooking the signifiers that comprised them rested on the Platonic theory of imitation and the concept of medium. The medium—say, Brook's actor—sacrificed his own identity so that something else ("the Other") could be made present ("visible" and "audible") through the actor's body and voice. "You must act as a medium for the words," Brook guided John Kane. "If you consciously color them, you're wasting your time. The words must be able to color you" (A. Smith 1972:27).

In scenography, sets, props, lighting, and costumes were external forms of something else. This something else was seen as a fixed, intrinsic meaning or essence, and it eventually produced a fixed perspective in the work of many scenographers by the seventeenth century. The fixed perspective supposedly imitated ("represented") an (historical) external reality as a glittering gate to an internal reality. In other words, verbal, pictorial, or body language were transparent, neutral media which transmitted a deeper reality or essence.

These languages became physical, "visible," nonneutral media only to the theatre artists and critics who realized that the signifiers were not just vehicles for communicating thoughts, but also governed the organization of their verbal, pictorial, or corporeal "texts" as well as their readings of those texts. Instead of receiving intrinsic meanings neutrally or passively, each reader actively participated, through interpretation, in the co-production of meaning based on the specific configurations of words, colors, shapes, movements, gestures, and what-have-you that comprised the playtext, the scenography, and the acting. In brief, each designer-director "rewrote" a playtext in different ways, each actor "rewrote" the prompt-copy in different ways, and each spectator viewed the performance-text in different ways. Consequently, the meanings of these "texts" were thought to be reader-related or spectator-related, and they were stabilized by the parameters set by theatrical and extra-theatrical conventions.

When formalist designers, directors, and actors abandoned the fixed perspective by rejecting representational scenography and imitative acting, they assigned (so to speak) to themselves (as readers) the responsibility for giving order ("harmony") and meaning ("unity") to a playtext and to its performance-text. However, although they established their own frames of reference, they still believed that they delivered—did not invent—the meaning of a playtext on stage. Their stagecraft became self-referential (conceptual), and, in a way, ahistorical. But if point of view determines the appearance of physical reality—as Luigi Pirandello argued in his plays—then meaning and value inhere in their relationship with each other, and they change as their relationship changes.

This last point was taken up by the early structuralists, who, unlike the formalists, maintained (but did not always practice) that artistic intention was historical—i.e., artistic intention was governed by socioeconomic and psycholinguistic systems operating in a culture when a playwright, designer, director, or actor produced their own work. Although the revival of a playtext from a different historical period or from a different culture raised serious questions about shifting contexts and dominant components along the synchronic axis and the diachronic axis, a structuralist "competent" reader never doubted the validity of his interpretations. Meaning and value were relative, but not the knowledge that a competent reader could yield about the meanings and values that the playtexts possessed in their historically or culturally different production conditions.

In this way, the structuralists separated the issue of stable interpretations from the issue of unstable meanings and values during theatrical production. In their view, any conflicting propositions on stage could co-exist in binary oppositions because the nature of reality itself was self-contradictory, manifesting itself in such pairs as old/new, good/evil, capitalism/communism, body/soul, history/ fiction, and so on. In fact, the work of the theatre artists was truthful when it presented the contradictory nature of reality. Under this premise, a playtext which was set apart by the cultural codes of a society at a certain historical period for presenting unreal events in a fictive environment about imaginary creatures could still possess meaning and value although it did not contain one speck of truth. In short, the meaning and value of the various "texts" depended on how a theatre company "produced" or "framed" these texts as objects of interpretation at a given place and time.

With their left hand, the structuralists erased the dividing line that the formalists had drawn between poetic language and ordinary language; but with their right hand, the structuralists drew circles and frames around the various languages of the stage in order to define the nature of theatrical experience. A language qualified as stage language if theatre artists and theatregoers had agreed to draw a frame around it which indicated their decision to see with "special" self-awareness the resources that verbal, pictorial, or corporeal languages usually possessed outside the theatre (Fish 1980:108–109; Pavis 1982). But how could they discuss the linguistic, pictorial, kinesic, or musical signifying functions that these "theatrical" languages acquired and yet avoid the mystical trappings of dualism? They thought that they could do so by replacing the symbol with the sign and by emphasizing that the conjunction between the signifier and the signified was arbitrary.

The structuralist replacement turned theatrical signification into a man-made, conventionalized system which, at a surface level, was historically determined but, at a deeper level, retained the belief in the presence of universal structures. In other words, at one level, the languages of the stage—as sign systems—signified only as coded by theatre artists and theatregoers in the process of their production, and varied from culture to culture over time. At another level, they introduced the rather ahistorical concept of "the latency of structures" (Riffaterre 1983:10). Stanislavsky, among other designers and directors, assumed that playtexts had a surface structure and a deep structure (or subtext). Then it became easy to claim an opposition between surface structure and deep structure, based on the archetypal contrast between appearance and reality.

The tendency to think about theatre in double terms—often presented in captivating works such as Artaud's *Theatre and Its Double*—and to seek out hidden meanings has been an age-old trend in the analysis of theatrical texts. Most phenomenologists, formalists, and structuralists agreed that theatrical texts (playtexts, prompt-copies, rehearsal-texts, performance-texts) did not signify in the same way as extra-theatrical texts (drama reviews, actor interviews, scholarly lectures, and so on). Their agreement ended when it came to explaining the semantic mechanisms of a theatrical text. Were the semantic mechanisms located inside the text, outside the text, or both inside and outside the text? If they were outside the text, were they located inside a reader, outside a reader, or both inside and outside a reader? For example, Roland Barthes located the semantic mechanisms outside Jean Racine's playtexts and outside the reader of these playtexts. "The Racinian theatre finds its coherence only on the level of ancient fable, situated far beyond history or the human psyche" (1977:9). This meant that a theatre artist, such as Brecht, could gain no advantage by comparing a playtext or a production style to reality.

All three approaches, with different degrees of commitment, shared one criterion: words as signs (signifier/signified) were judged in relation to the "things" (referents) that they represented. It follows that they evaluated a theatrical text in comparison to reality— regardless of whether they wished to approach reality or to distance themselves from it. If, for example, the meaning of a set design was based on verisimilitude, a director would stress how apt the colors and shapes were and would praise the designer for his ability to make others "see." If, on the other hand, the meaning of a set went against verisimilitude, a director would respond in one of two ways: he would interpret it as a distortion (again in terms of reality) and would attempt to justify it by theorizing on the intentions of the designer. Or, depending on his aesthetic priorities, the director would either admire or reject the design. In either case, "reality" was used to measure the discrepancy between the theatrical "text" and the "text" of reality.

Unfortunately, the measuring of discrepancies between reality and the various theatrical texts does not explain why a viewer accepts the shift from the usual arbitrariness of the linguistic, pictorial, corporeal, or musical signs to a different kind of arbitrariness specific to the theatrical experience. I will try to answer this question in the third and fourth chapters of Part Three in this book. Here, I would like to point out that the recourse to "reality" isolated meanings from one another because each meaning was conceived as the relation between one textual component and something outside the text. Meaning was not considered in its intertextual combinations with other meanings during play production.

Deconstructive analysis, such as the one that I undertake in this book, exposes how others and myself give in to our own processes of making order through persuassive rationalizations (Derrida 1970:249, 262). Thanks to René Descartes' division between subject and object, the organizing "I" of a logocentric theatre artist, critic, or historian assumes a convenient position from which to observe "internal" and "external" realities in the world of theatre. If, however, external reality is a cultural construct or "fiction" (Nietzsche's term), its definition and origin depend on the desire of the consciousness of a theatre artist, critic or historian. If, on the other hand, their consciousness is also "derivative" (Derrida's term), then internal reality has no original foundation as well.

Consequently, the sharp division of the logocentrists between fiction and reality becomes blurred because fiction cannot exist without reality anymore than presence can exist without absence. They are accomplices inside as well as outside the theatre. The deconstructive approach turns theatrical production into an activity without an organizing center and without a stabilizing frame. The theatre artist, who stands "inside" theatrical productions, and a theatre critic or historian, who stands "outside" theatrical productions, cannot be separated from the tools (verbal, pictorial, corporeal, or musical languages) that they use to understand and express reality and fiction. Therefore, fixed perspectives, impartial observations, original thoughts, and objective descriptions are popular self-deceptions.

Whereas Saussure based his notions of reality on the binary opposition between signifier and signified (1959:67), Derrida based his on the differing and deferring function of signifiers and signifieds (1981:27). The possibility of a (theatrical)sign, which substitutes for something else in a system of differences, depends on deferring (putting off) into the future any grasping of the "thing itself." This means that interpretation has no closure or end that could import a final meaning into theatrical and extra-theatrical texts—except for a play of differences. It also demonstrates how precarious is the grasp on meaning. Under this premise, the various theatrical "texts" do not put the "real thing" on stage.

The temporal interval between two "texts" in theatrical production defers into the next step the full presence of the "thing" or "reality" or "meaning"—from the playtext to the prompt-copy, from the prompt-copy to the rehearsal-text, from the rehearsal-text to the performance-text, from the performance-text to the critical essay, and so on. Nothing escapes textuality just because artistic production moves from the "lifeless" page to the "live" stage. In other words, deconstruction asks theatre artists, theatregoers and theatre critics to change certain habits of thinking about the production of theatrical "texts." The conflict between deconstruction and other approaches has been fierce because the habits of thought, which are called into question, have supported the theory and practice of Western theatre since the ancient Greek festivals.

Deconstruction shows how theatrical texts fail to achieve perfect closure, absolute truth, and final meaning. It does not imply that these texts are worthless for a group of theatregoers and theatre artists just because the texts are the product of an arbitrary union between signifiers and signifieds. It only shows that these texts are man-made products, not the products of a genius in direct contact with the laws of nature or with a divine author of the world. If there was no gap between nature (being) and culture (meaning), then sign production would hardly be necessary to human beings. Any logocentric "texts" which upheld their unassailable status of truth in the name of their proximity to primate ethology (Schechner), to primal consciousness (Brook), and to historical reality (Brecht) fell victims to their own rationalizations. In their effort to turn their anticipated failure into success, they made themselves vulnerable to deconstruction.

The arbitrary union between signifiers and signifieds manifests the capacity of human beings to endow old and new material forms with (new) meanings which these forms do not possess naturally. A material form, however, may not have a meaning only when it is turned into a man-made, "unnatural" sign. The art of the theatre uses, explores, and revises this process of sign production. If all texts are man-made, they lack intrinsic value and their significance is relative to time (historical period) and place (social or geographical space). When meaning becomes contextual and continuous, the "real" world seems theatrical and the world of theatre seems real. The activity of interpretation—i.e., the disclosing of the meaning "within" a material form—becomes gratuitous. If a "text" cannot exist without interpretation, then interpretation itself constitutes a "text."

The interpretative ability of a "reader" to create "meaningful" texts from natural or man-made "sign systems" points the way to understanding how the (human) mind can bewitch itself by its own powers of signification. The power of self-bewitchment (illusion) has been strong enough among human beings as to separate consciousness from its referents. The whole process of signification has been reduced to an endless "chain" of displacements and inversions of signifiers. These signifiers constantly turn back on themselves, but without ever getting any closer to the world they signify. In other words, the art of theatre travels on the surface of signifiers which present themselves from rewriting (detour) to rewriting (detour). In this way, they reveal that the origin of meaning has lost its central source and, therefore, no "text" can return to its author[s].

If we exclude mime, many nonverbal communication experiments in avant-garde theatrical productions have been conducted with the view that the performance-text is not a representation of people, events, or things but rather a process of direct sign production. In other words, these experiments have rejected the mirror theory which, since the day of Plato, defined imitation (*mimesis*) as a technique reflecting reality in its "rhetorical isomorphism" (Berke 1978:46). The mirror theory could not explain the production of dramatic worlds which have few, if any, perceivable structural parallels in the real world as, for example,

Peter Handke's *Kaspar*. The theatre artists of such nonverbal communication experiments have viewed the performance-text as the production of artistic thought in theatrical signs.

Logocentric directors, designers, and actors enhance upon the "nonliterary" dimension of a playtext by designing a prompt-copy and rehearsing it. During this process, several "nonliterary" elements take the form of nonverbal communication. Most structuralist theatrical experiments posited that people share an innate faculty for producing and understanding information according to some regular, universal patterns. People exhibit this innate faculty by manipulating learned codes—such as spoken or written language—based on a repertory of signs and a set of combinatory rules. While the innate faculty seems to be universal, the learned codes succumb to change mainly due to spacial (geographical) and temporal (historical) factors.

The "behavioral margins" that exist between a playtext and its performance-text allow for variations in language, paralanguage, and kinesics. It is through "cultural fluency" (Poyatos 1980:235) that directors, designers, and performers of the logocentric tradition think that they (can) preserve—as closely as possible—the cultural attitudes embodied in the playtext. In the case of Shakespeare's *King Lear*, for example, the codes of the playtext, prompt-copy, rehearsal-text, and performance-text presumably corresponded most closely to each other during its first production "before the kinges majestie at Whitehall vpon Sainct Stephens night" on December 26, 1606. The implication is that, in all subsequent productions of *King Lear*, the margins between the linguistic code printed in the 1608 quarto and the language of the theatre artists and their audiences in the following centuries grew increasingly wider.

Consequently, the question whether a performance-text should preserve the linguistic, paralinguistic, and kinetic codes of its contemporary audience or of the Elizabethan society printed and suggested in the quarto became a matter of choice as well as of skill for designers, directors, and actors. In short, as Peter Brook pointed out, the transitory nature of codes which are employed in theatre segment the theatrical experience both diachronically and synchronically (Gibson 1973:46). Can there be, therefore, a universal, stable "language" for play production? "In Paris, in 1972," Brook wrote, "we worked with deaf children, touched by the vividness, eloquence and speed of their body languages. The American

National Theatre of the Deaf spent a very rich period with us, experimenting both in movement and in sound, and extending the possibilities of both companies" (1987:133). The deaf actors gave Brook's actors words to translate into body movements (Heilpern 1978:21).

However, the popular belief that sign language, such as the one used by the American National Theatre of the Deaf, is a universal language based on an iconic gestural system was disproved by the mid-1970s (Jordan and Battison 1976:70). James Woodward and Suzan De Santis compared the Parisian version of the French Sign Language (FSL) and the modern version of the American Sign Language (ASL). Although the two sign languages share a common ancestor, 42.7 percent of the compared iconic and indexical signs "were found to be noncognates, i.e., signs with neither formational nor semantic relationships to American signs" (Woodward and De Santis 1975:330). Similar experiments in the 1970s proved that sign language is not "gestural speech" but that it has its own syntax, grammar, vocabulary, and idioms (Stokoe 1960; 1972:119).

Intelligibility among "speakers" does not depend solely on the amount of shared vocabulary of signs (cognates) between two sign languages. It also depends on a set of combinatory rules that make shared signs in French and American sign languages unintelligible to the signers of each in discourse. Deaf foreigners, for example, stop using their own sign language and start using gesture and artless mime in order to communicate. Such communication decreases accuracy, of course, and is slow paced and very repetitive, involving a back-and-forth checking of possible meanings as the signers establish a crude, tentative code of shared signs and meanings. In sum, sign languages do not differ from spoken languages as far as being limited to culture-specific communication.

Director Peter Brook attempted to use a universal "code" for play production at the International Institute for Theatre Research in Paris. He observed that languages frame and segment human experience in (historical) time and (social) space. So, he attempted to devise a "new theatrical language" which (1) would "enable his 25 actors of ten nationalities and as many divergent cultures to find a common phonetic, aesthetic, and sensual mode of expression" and (2) would help them communicate meaningfully with a multinational audience (Trilling 1972:33). Despite evidence to the contrary, Brook assumed that body language could serve as a universal "code" for communication without reference to the sign systems of any particular (sub)culture. "Therefore, one can work without roots," Brook believed, "because the human body, as such, becomes a working source" (Gibson 1973:50).

Brook unwittingly discovered that Antonin Artaud's theories of *glossopoeia* do not test out. *Glossopoeia* is the creation of a language which "takes us back to the borderline of the moment when . . . the signified and the signifier are not united yet" (Derrida 1978:248). Artaud opposed the premise that a concept does not exist unless it is formulated in words. Artaud argued that speech cannot express all human experiences accurately. Polar emotions such as joy/fear, anger/bliss belong to the nonverbal aspect of consciousness which is expressed in bodily sensations like quick/slow pulse, tense/relaxed muscles, etc. The inability of words to communicate such tense feelings or unconscious images cannot negate the existence of such feelings or images. So, Artaud sought a theatrical language made of natural signs which would communicate ineffable messages. "Speech will cease to govern the stage, but will be present upon it" (Artaud 1958:124).

Unfortunately, Peter Brook's experiments in Niger and Iran did not yield reliable data because he had a general investigating question but no specific hypotheses to test; he had a focused set but no control of the variables involved; he had a theatrical jargon but no unambiguous language through which to carry out and record his observations systematically; and he had potential experimental subjects (actors and spectators) but no method for selecting audience response data for analysis. Brook neither adopted the methodological devices of other disciplines from the Social Sciences nor developed his own at the International Institute of Theatre Research in Paris. Brook's experiments played with the idea of finding a universal theatrical language but offered no solutions.

Let me briefly illustrate the above points one by one. Peter Brook had two general questions. Can meaning be communicated outside coded speech or gesture? What happens when gesture substitutes for speech (A. Smith 1972:41, 42)? The first question could only provide a reliable YES/NO answer if Brook had tackled two more specific hypotheses earlier: (1) comprehension is (or is not) context-bound regardless of the codes employed; (2) repetition of uncoded verbal or gestural signifiers does (or does not) establish a correlation between the sound or gesture and an idea in the addressee's mind (signified)—namely, a crude, tentative code. The second question that Brook asked indicates more clearly than the first question that he and his group only went on a "fishing trip" to Iran and to Niger. The question was not stated as a hypothesis that could be proved or disproved.

Brook had hardly any control over the variables involved in his experiment. Improvisation and accident generated the decided effect, leading to speculation and conclusions. "We and the African group sang," Brook reported from Agades in Niger, "and suddenly we found that we were hitting exactly the same language of sound. Well, we understood theirs and they understood ours, and something quite electrifying happened because, out of all sorts of different songs, one suddenly came upon a common area" (Gibson 1973:45). This happy accident did not show which variables made it happen because Brook had established no control over them. The "electrifying" effect remains one of the numerous unreproducible broad observations of his trip.

Brook's experiments are reported in a diffuse language. His disciples, who followed him across the fields, reported that their fieldwork investigated two things: (1) "the simple relationships of movement and sound that pass directly" and (2) "the single element which has the ambiguity and density that permits it to be read off simultaneously on a multitude of levels" (A. Smith 1972:250). I guess (it is only a guess) the above questions could be rephrased as follows in semiotic parlance: How does an unspecified number of uncoded paralinguistic and kinesic signs communicate meaning to an audience, thus facilitating polysemy? The discoveries reported are equally confusing:

> Perhaps, the most important discovery of the work done through the Avesta and Greek is the difference between a small number of words which, all their overtones being present, carry simultaneously a rich band of meaning, and the opposite, which is the diffuse use of words, obligatorily diffuse, because each single unit in the contemporary vocabulary is not atom-charged, energy-charged, in the same way. (A. Smith 1972: 250)

Brook and his reporters had no clear and specific language (even a jargon) in which to carry out their research and to record their observations systematically. Unambiguous language facilitates communication and consensus among researchers because it allows them to replicate experiments and offer fruitful criticism.

Despite his alleged intentions to be scientific, Brook prepared no preliminary work to select actor responses and spectator responses for analysis. Brook rather imposed his interpretations on his subjects. For example, Brook gathered the performers after the first performance of *Orghast* and told them: "The audience's concentration made it possible tonight to be closer to each other and to the place than ever before. The closer the silence, the larger the opening to each other" (A. Smith 1972:205). The quadrolingual performance-text of *Orghast*, according to playwright Ted Hughes, "communicated" a story of crime and revenge between matter (she/animal) and mind (he/human). At the animal level, crime and revenge created a self-perpetuating situation. At the human level, the vicious circle of crime and revenge broke "by creating a being which, like Prometheus, includes the elemental opposites" (A. Smith 1972:132-133).

The audience had mixed feelings about the performance and clearly could not follow the abstract story line. Random remarks by spectators include: "Will there be a dictionary of *Orghast*?"; or "The audience should have been helped by a guide to the key symbols in the language, without which the work was elitist"; or "To the unaided observer, it does offer some striking moments of theatre, but these moments seem not at all united by any intelligible plan"; or "Most spectators were bewildered and overwhelmed" (A. Smith 1972:209; Henry Hopkin, *The Guardian* 7-9-1971; Richard Findlater, *The Observer* 12-9-1971). In short, the results of these otherwise interesting experiments remain inconclusive.

Finally, Brook did not adopt the methodological devices of other disciplines nor did he develop his own at the International Institute for Theatre Research. A significant number of papers were published in the area of communication accuracy or intelligibility, introducing new techniques in the 1960s which could have helped Brook conduct his experiments more quickly, cheaply, and with greater reliability at home (Mehrabian and Reed 1968). Simply stated, intelligibility is a measure of how well the addressee (spectator) can understand the addresser (actor).

In order to measure intelligibility precisely, communication researchers extensively use what is known as a Referential Communication Design (RCD) (Osgood and Sebeok 1965:200). An RCD is a situation in which the addresser (actor) describes a specified referent to the addressee (spectator). Because the referent is known to the experimenter (say, director Peter Brook) in advance, he can measure intelligibility. The communication is considered intelligible when the addressee observes the addresser's communication and identifies the correct referent from among others.

RCDs were used in the study of sign-language communication of deaf people of similar or different sign languages. The results of such experiments raise provocative research questions in the context of theatre—especially for theatre companies that perform for deaf audiences or for multinational audiences at international festivals. Konstantin Stanislavsky was perhaps the first director to conduct an RCD experiment. He asked an auditioning actor to make forty different messages by repeating the phrase *segodnja večerom* (this evening). The audience had to understand these forty different messages only through the actor's paralinguistic variations because the actor was asked to hold the linguistic and kinetic aspects of the utterance constant (Jakobson 1960:354).

Apart from the above methodological errors, Brook mistook iconic and indexical theatrical signs for "natural" and "nonintentional" signs (Eco 1979:16, 17; A. Smith 1972:43). So, he designed the nonverbal communication experiments in such a way as to "break down" the arbitrariness of the symbolic signs. Symbolic signs require the spectator's prior knowledge of the code in order to decode a message (A. Smith 1972:43-44). Brook seemed oblivious to the findings in semiotics, kinetics, and communication research in the late 1960s. In kinetics, for example, it had been observed that each culture selects a limited number of kinetic units (kinemes) from a stock of potential material—an observation similar to that in linguistics about phonemes (Birdwhistell 1971:54). Iconic signs and indexical signs are not natural or nonintentional signs just because they are thought of as similar or causally connected with the objects to which they refer.

Indexical signs, for instance, always convey a content, even when there is no observable referent—as in the case of Macbeth who asks "Is this a dagger which I see before me?" (*Macbeth* 2.1.33). Either as speech or as a gesture, "this" acquires meaning not because something is close to it but because it signifies that there *must* be something close to it (Eco 1979:116). Macbeth's pointed-finger gesture toward the invisible dagger and the articulation of the demonstrative pronoun in English are, in a sense, arbitrary choices. The Guna and Navaho Indians prefer the "pointing-lip gesture" and the Macedonian Greeks, occasionally, the "pointing-chin gesture." Theatrical signs, whether verbal or visual, depend on arbitrary, culturally determined codes.

In sum, the syntactic and indexical functions of theatrical gesture are founded on cultural sign systems whereby they become recognizable, intentional, and thus expressive. Theatre communicates within a system of reference among signs because it works within a broader cultural and social system. Naturally, such broader systems of reference which help a community of theatregoers share a common experience are not universal. Consequently, the possibilities of a common theatrical language are limited in time and space by "using the local slang and local references" (Gibson 1973:49). So, although nonverbal communication allows a performance to enhance a playtext, the enhancement is as culturally specific as any verbal communication. Today

> . . . we need a study of exactly what goes on when the playtext
> is turned into a performance-text and of what is their theatrical
> (not natural) interaction made of exactly. (Poyatos 1982:92)

Experiments and developments largely concerned with forms of nonverbal communication allow, to some degree, such an understanding for the makers of the prompt-copy.

In the following pages, I will show that the "cybernetic" capabilities, which are introduced to play production by computer graphics, can change the way in which directors plan, designers stage, actors perform, playwrights compose, and audiences watch plays. I will also show that high technology, which empowers the work of deconstructive designers, could be manipulated to appropriate their work in such a way that would preserve—instead of changing—the framework of logocentric theatrical production.

To date, those drama scholars who have confined themselves to the analysis of playtexts have regarded "stagecraftness" as an area that lies beyond their methodological capability and research domain. They have narrowly defined "poetics" as a process of writing and reading playtexts—not of rewriting, rereading, and reproducing playtexts for an audience (Culler 1975:128). They have ignored "nonliterary" elements such as stage, sets, props, blocking, movement, business, lighting, sound, and costumes. Designer-director Gordon Craig remarked sardonically in 1921 that "professors explain the dramatic art by talking much about the dramatic characterization, logic of construction, three unities, and so forth, and quote from Brunetière, Edmund Burke, and other wise men who study the moon by looking at it in deep wells" (1983:20). In a similar, skeptically humorous manner, I will discuss the art of theatrical communication by talking about the logic of formalism and structuralism and by quoting Gordon Craig and Peter Brook, among others, who studied the languages of the stage by looking at them in the "deep well" of metaphysics.

The analysis of the poetics of theatrical production was eventually facilitated by the advent of semiotics in the 1930s. The concepts of "writing" and "reading" expanded from the printed page to the various "texts" of the stage—i.e., the prompt-copy, the rehearsal-text, and the performance-text. Theatre artists and critics began to regard the poetics of play production as an organized system of multimedial, recurring, identifiable, symbolic operations. Those who subscribed to the structuralist approach, however, stressed the importance of performance-text analysis over playtext analysis. In this way, they reversed the traditional emphasis, but they also created an axiological binary system which slighted the role of intermediate "texts" such as prompt-copies and rehearsal-texts.

For example, Anne Ubersfeld proposed a model (Figure 6) which emphasized a partly co-extensive relationship between a playtext and its performance-text (1977:16). Consequently, her model did not account for sign-system transformations brought about by the work of designers and directors. For this reason, I will proceed to my task by abandoning Ubersfeld's binary model. In fact, I will show that the prompt-copy and the rehearsal-text are pivotal in the play-production process, and they require a different diagrammatic representation.

I will base part of my analysis on a meticulous reading of the published works, interviews and travelogues of Peter Brook and his colaborators. I will quote Brook from secondary, "impartial" accounts when he did not dispute them publicly to my knowledge.

Since the "experiments" were reported in ways that do not encourage independent replication, I will interpret what has been written about them. I will question the "scientific" value, not the artistic value, of Brook's phonocentric work at the International Center of Theatre Research in Paris or elsewhere.

A few improvisations that were filmed offer a poor semiotic record of how each improvisation changed when the CIRT group performed in the African bush, in the suburbs of Paris, among the Chicanos in California, and the Indians in Minnesota. Reportedly, each improvisation changed forms and meanings even within the same day because the communication frame changed. When the CIRT group performed an improvisation as "rough theatre" at 8 p.m., as "holy theatre" at 12 midnight, and as "chorale theatre" at 5 a.m. on street corners in Brooklyn in 1973, Brook claimed that they discovered "that its contents were truly universal, that it transcended all cultural and social barriers with ease" (Brook 1987:154).

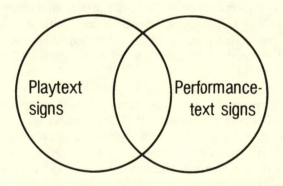

FIGURE 6. Anne Ubersfeld's Model of Play/Performance Relationships. (Source: Anne Ubersfeld, *Lire le théâtre*. Paris: Messidor/Editions sociales, 1977, p. 16.)

Why can't I believe Peter Brook, and how can I stop believing the worst? In discussing my skepticism, I will follow two steps. First, I will examine how the prompt-copy enhances the paraverbal, kinesic, and visual dimensions of a playtext and how nonverbal communication allows the "nonliterary" elements—which are developed in the prompt-copy—to escape from the logocentric dictates of playtexts. History indicates that these nonliterary elements frequently fell prey to the subtle logocentrism of idealist designers such as Appia and Craig, or pseudonaturalist directors such as Stanislavsky and Brook.

I will look further into Brook's "scientific" inquiries which explored the relationship between verbal and nonverbal theatre, the transformation of gesture into word, and the exact place of words in theatrical expression (Brook 1987:110; A. Smith 1972:42). Brook endorsed Schechner's notion of a universal consciousness of enactment, but Brook—like Craig—privileged a universal consciousness of tone which allegedly ran deeper than the languages or cultures that segregated people into separate groups.

Second, I will explore how the prompt-copy delivers the intentions (*logos*) of playwrights, designers, and directors to dominate the work of the actors and their interaction with the audiences in rehearsals and performances, respectively. I will take up the case of Brecht, who, like other theatre artists before and after him, linked the process of renovating theatre with new scientific developments and new production styles.

While production styles—naturalist, symbolist, expressionist, or epic—have been neatly defined and kept apart in theory, they converged "dangerously" into one and the same thing in practice (Gorelik 1962:234, 309, 310, 334). Their advocates shared an introspective attitude which addressed a limited circle of spectators (read "initiates") until they reached a point where they were talking only among themselves. "The style of the symbolist wing of the new stagecraft had turned out to be only a thin naturalism," Gorelik wrote. "It was the theatricalist section which caught style in bushel baskets. Did this achievement of the theatricalists do away with the contradictions which we noted in the symbolist theatre? It did not" (1962:309). Gorelik's formalist rhetoric, however, confused rather than clarified the issue.

Brook's program to re-establish the spirit of scientific inquiry in the field of theatre at the International Center of Theatre Research in Paris in 1973 echoed Emile Zola's earlier project to introduce the experimental and scientific spirit of the nineteenth century to the field of theatre in Paris in 1873. "Outside of a certain stage-related know-how," wrote Zola, "what today one would call the science of the theatre is no more than a mass of little tricks of the craftsmen, a kind of narrow tradition which stifles the stage, a stereotyped code of language and situations written long ago, which every original mind will strongly refuse to use" (1873:9). A century later, Brook shared Zola's dissatisfaction about the stale state of knowledge and practice in twentieth-century stage production, which he labeled "deadly theatre" (1968:10).

André Antoine, a designer, director, and actor who was inspired by Zola's manifestos, challenged the "deadly" baroque conventions of the 1880s. He replaced representational, pictorial design (i.e., two-dimensional, "unreal" sets and props) with presentational, sculptural design (i.e., three-dimensional, "real" sets and props). A setting no longer "represented" a wall; it "was" a wall as real as the actor. Antoine also replaced representational acting (i.e., "unrealistic" gestures and diction) with presentational acting (i.e., "realistic" gestures and diction). The actor no longer "played" a part; the actor "lived" the part. "I experienced a phenomenon hitherto unknown, the almost complete loss of my personality," Antoine wrote in his diary on 30 May 1890. "From the start of the second act, I do not remember anything, neither the audience, nor the effect of the performance, and when the curtain closed, I recovered myself but I was shivering, enervated, and uncapable to regain my self-control for a while" (1921:183). Brook, who likewise abandoned "the debased ideals of the Deadly Theatre" in search of a living theatre in the 1960s, called this kind of intense experience "holy theatre" (1968:64).

Stanislavsky was among the first to analyze in detail how an actor should begin to "live the part" and recreate this experience consistently from performance to performance. He developed a technique (alias "system" or "method") which supposedly has helped most actors in Western theatres to replace external imitation with internal impersonation for their stage(d) behavior. It was no longer enough for an actor or actress just to imitate the behavior of a character in love in *Romeo and Juliet*. The actor or actress now reproduced within himself or herself a sensation which approximated the state of mind of Romeo or Juliet by resorting to personal experiences of similar or lesser intensity.

So, "naturalist" theatre artists—from Antoine to Brook—pushed for authentic emotions, authentic sets, authentic costumes, authentic speech, authentic gestures. They measured "authenticity" and "accuracy" by recourse to direct observation (personal experience) and indirect observation (historical testimony). Whenever direct and indirect observations conflicted, they relied on personal experience rather than on historical testimony.

In search of truth and authenticity, Konstantin Stanislavsky and the MAT group left the libraries of Moscow and traveled to ancient Russian towns (*Tsar Fyodor*, 1898) or the Khitrov Market (*Lower Depths*, 1902) (1963:230, 305). In a similar quest for truth and authenticity, Peter Brook and his CIRT group left the libraries of Paris and traveled to the ruins of Persepolis (*Orghast*, 1972) and as far as Daru Lapidu's open-air theatre in Oshogbo, Nigeria (*Conference of the Birds*, 1973). Of course, the MAT group brought back "unfamiliar" experiences and performed them to "familiar" audiences at home, whereas the CIRT group took "familiar" experiences and performed them to "unfamiliar" audiences on site.

The presence or absense of technology in the (re)creation of an enviromental experience or a theatrical experience has always been at issue between naturalist designers and idealist designers. Should a designer achieve the desired effect by using the latest technology, by using historically authentic technology, or by avoiding technology as far as possible?

Antoine, for instance, used only lanterns on the table for the war council in the third act of Leon Hennique's *The Death of Duke D'Enghien* in 1888. The so-called "photographic realism" of the early naturalists encouraged the use of the latest technology—such as photography and film—and stimulated involvement in technological innovations—as in the case of painter-designer Louis Daguerre, who co-invented photography (heliography) with Nicephore Niepce in the 1820s.

However, photographic realism was quickly discredited as an "external" skin-deep explanation of the social and psychological "realities" of the common people for two basic reasons: First, the theatre naturalists fell prey to a neo-Platonic dualism, paying only lip service to scientific materialism. For example, Antoine and

Stanislavsky never fully endorsed Zola's spirit of science for the theatre. When Henry Bauer labeled Antoine a naturalist, Antoine was embarrassed and protested on 6 May 1889 (1921:143-144), preferring a more diversified and "ecclectic" approach to theatrical production.

Stanislavsky, too, recanted naturalism. "Those who think that we sought for naturalism on the stage are mistaken," wrote Stanislavsky. "We never leaned towards such a principle. Always, then as well as now, we sought for inner truth, for the truth of feeling and experience, but as spiritual technique was only in its embryo stage among the actors of our company, we, because of necessity and helplessness, and against our desires, fell now and then into an outward and coarse naturalism" (1948:330-331).

Second, the idealist theatre artists opposed the "false and futile" practice of the naturalists who used authentic or historically accurate language, gestures, sets, costumes, or lighting. They could not bear the uncomfortable, external, material "coarseness" of the signifieds of referents in naturalist theatrical performances. They questioned the use of authentic costumes or facsimile streets since the staged environment was never actually real. They argued that nothing was fully authentic, solidly real, or genuinely historical in naturalist performances. Nikolaevich Evreinov, mockingly, advised the naturalists to build up a real fourth wall between the actors and their audience, if they desired authenticity, and to avoid acting plays in Russian translation when the characters were supposed to be Germans in Germany. Instead, the idealists sought to depict "inner" or "poetic" truth, not external "reality" (Moussinac 1922:8, 14).

The idealist theatre artists looked for the essence (alias "soul") of things in their environment. Their designs and acting supposedly expressed the spiritual (read "disembodied") side of their material reality on stage, establishing an emotional rapport with their spectators. The material aspects of their art and technology were ignored. The physical side of scenography—which marked naturalist productions—almost "evaporated."

Their performances ranged from symbolist to expressionist styles, communicating meaning and emotion to the audiences with "ahistorical" or "unnatural" language, gestures, sets, costumes, or lighting presumably just as effectively as the performances of the naturalists. To a great extent, their introverted art replaced history and social analysis with metaphysics and psychoanalysis. It reduced a concrete environment into a nebulous atmosphere, specific motives into abstact moods, and often wrapped up disparate elements in life and on stage into a "harmonious" aesthetic unity.

The controversy between idealist and materialist theatre designers and directors unfolded through several "waves" over the decades, and it took several "new" shapes which, in fact, disguised and repeated old patterns. In the 1960s, for example, "when most experimental theatre artists were emphasizing the actor and were emulating Grotowski's *poor theatre*, Robert Wilson began creating a brand of formalistic theatre based on dreamlike images that, through the use of minimalist music and incredibly slow pace, intended to take the viewer into a dream like state to allow the subconscious to emerge" (A. Aronson 1986:12).

Wilson called these "new" shows operas, but, in fact, they were an extension of Appia's old operatic tradition of design and technology. Equally old was the "new" variation of scenographic theory known as "action design" practiced by such designers as Jaroslav Malina in the 1980s. "The basic premise of Action Design is the emptying out of the theatre," wrote Delbert Unruh. "The typical trappings of *scene design* or even *scenography* are left out in the alley along with atmospheric lighting and museum piece costumes" (1987:8–9).

The working methods of designers changed according to the idealist or the materialist premises to which they subscribed. For the idealists, truth in the theatre stood above and beyond mere accuracy to fact. Real life died in the theatre unless it was recast on stage and it was transformed into art. "*The artist should omit the details, the prose of nature,*" Edmond Jones wrote epigrammatically and emphatically, "*and give us only the spirit and splendor*" (1941:82). Following the steps of his idealist predecessors, Jones retained a phonocentric understanding of theatrical production, and he belittled the material side of scenography.

For example, he believed that in Elizabethan England, "the written and the spoken word held a peculiar magic" which helped playwrights and their mouthpieces, the actors, to transport the audience from place to place, from time to time, and from mood to mood by a spoken stage direction that "all the elaborate mechanism of our modern stage cannot match" (1941:136, 139). Obviously, for Jones, technology could affect only the spectators' senses of sight and hearing and could not "rise from the domain of the senses to a superior region"—if I may quote Plotinus here (*Enneads* 1.6.1).

In a manner that predated the explorations of Grotowski and Brook, Jones believed that the Theatre, like the Church, had a consecrating, purifying function on its members (1941:153). Jones was persuaded that actors experienced a sense of dual personality, of otherness, of being possessed, of another's voice speaking through them. This voice uplifted human beings into a spiritual realm above their base animal nature (1941:155). So, any actors who casually said that they gave a good performance, "what they meant was that a spirit was present in them for a time, making them say things that they themselves did not know they knew" (1941:157).

This widespread metaphysical idealism among designers and directors cast a shadow on scenography for two reasons: it made them turn their back to the material conditions of theatrical production, and it encouraged them to assume that the consciousness of a "possessed" theatre artist is ahistorical—i.e., emanating from a primordial Voice or Idea, not from historically developing social relations. "I think of the words of Plotinus," Edmond Jones wrote,"*For the soul, a divine thing, a fragment as it were of the primal Being, makes beautiful, according to their capacity, all things whatsoever that it grasps and moulds*" (1941:157).

Jones, among other designers and directors, struggled to grasp and mold universal, immutable truths on the stage by following (read "partaking into") the discriminating taste of Plotinus' eternal soul. As soon as the soul saw or heard something ugly, the soul "rejected it as something foreign" to her nature. A design (sets, costumes, lights, sounds) was partially or completely ugly when it partially or completely remained "foreign" to the divine design or reason (*Logos*). This reason proceeded from the universal soul and, through the soul of a theatre artist, changed matter (actuality) into form (reality)—by turning, for example, two meaningless sticks into a meaningful cross.

It follows that a (set, costume, lighting, sound) design could be beautiful only if it had acquired form by eliminating matter. "Something is ugly," wrote Plotinus, "if it is still matter and has not been entirely molded by informing reason into perfect form"

(*Enneads* 1.6.2). Plotinus' aesthetic position explains to a certain degree why the idealist theatre artists turned their back to the material aspects of scenography.

In the context of this neo-Platonic tradition, the idealist theatre artists campaigned for the comfortable, internal, spiritual "refinement" of the signifieds of signifiers. "Stage designing should be addressed to the eye of the mind," wrote Edmond Jones. "There is an outer eye that observes, and there is an inner eye that sees" (1941:26). With a firm belief in this assumption, Jones preached that "a good scene, I repeat, is not a picture. It is something seen, but it is something conveyed as well; a feeling, an evocation. Plato says somewhere: It is beauty I seek, not beautiful things. That is what I mean" (1941:26).

Economically, this scenographic neo-Platonism was more viable than scenographic naturalism. It no longer required the purchase or rental of an original chair or costume because, thanks to Plato, the "original" was actually a copy of an Idea. A stage prop or a stage costume, which was a copy of a historical chair or costume, may have been an imitation of an imitation, but it was cheaper and most spectators could not tell the difference.

Since economic and ideological considerations go hand-in-hand, Zola was charged for ignoring the internal, spiritual, invisible side of man and things. Alexandre Dumas *fils* argued that Zola misunderstood theatrical conventions because Zola wished to "stage" reality; that the naturalists, despite their quixotic desire to create an exact replica of nature, produced only inferior copies of the original. The sensible idealists, instead, tried (1) "to discover and reveal to us that which we do not see in what we daily observe" and (2) "to idealize the real that is seen and make real the ideal that is felt" (1898:178).

Dumas' Platonic understanding of theatre, however, misconstrued the case of the naturalists. The issue was whether theatrical experience should be founded on the signifieds of referents or on the singifieds of signifiers. Ferdinand Brunetier tripped over this moot point when he accused the naturalists of dealing with the "actual" rather than the "real."

Of course, Brunetière regained his step and, following the rhetorical track already set before him, went on to argue that true artists—including "true" naturalists—depict both the physical and spiritual aspects of "all of nature, interior as well as exterior, invisible as well as visible" (1888:335). For Brunetière, this dualism created a "balanced" and "complete" artistic depiction of the world which "rescued" the art of theatre from the material, external focus of naturalism.

This dualism, which was phrased in the context and rhetoric of neo-Platonism, corroded the scientific materialism of the "new masters" from André Antoine and Konstantin Stanislavsky to Peter Brook and Richard Schechner; it encouraged scenographic suggestive simplicity (read "material reduction") of means and effects; and it influenced the way designers and directors have used technology over the years.

The Repressive Liberators

Most idealist theatre artists, from Richard Wagner to Stéphane Mallarmé and from Adolphe Appia to Edmond Jones, felt that the "spirituality" of a playtext was threatened by the material nature of stages, actors, sets, props, costumes, and lighting. Wagner used the "integrative" power of music to "spiritualize" (read "control") the stage and breathe inner life into inert matter. Mallarme would rather give poetry the unifying, uplifting function that Wagner gave to music. For Malarme, the material presence of actors, props, and sets reduced the expressive potential of a playtext. So, Malarme reserved a mental space, a "holy of holies," where a reader could recreate the imaginary world, instead of realizing it on a three-dimensional stage structure (1885:199).

Likewise, Appia puzzled over how the audiovisual stage realization of Wagner's texts could preserve their spirituality. So, Appia emphasized two of the less "material" and more "animated" elements in scenography—namely, stage lighting and actor movement. Wagner was concerned about the playwright's lack of control over the stage presentation of his text, and Appia tried to solve this problem. Appia envisioned a stage-design apparatus which would enable the opera composer to control all aspects of stage production, including space, setting, and movement.

Appia thought that music, which created and controlled both time and emotion, could unify all the other acoustic and visual elements into an organic whole only if it extended to the physical setting. Appia also assumed that the mediating presence of lighting could help music integrate the living actor with the inanimate settings. Music and lighting together could unify the various elements most effectively if actors, costumes, props, and sets expressed only

133

the spirit of the text adding no new information. Any scenographic inspiration should arise from the text itself—not from theatrical conventions or from extra-theatrical reality.

Appia's idealist project gave music priority over speech. However, it retained a logocentric orientation because it subordinated the work of actors and designers to the authority of the playwright-composer. Appia made them serve the master's score, and he wished to control the elements of their work by music and lighting. Unlike spoken theatre (i.e., naturalist theatre), which could only *signify* the internal aspects of a life indirectly through representation, musical theatre (i.e., Wagnerian opera) could *express* the internal aspects of life directly through the medium of music according to Appia.

In fact, Appia thought that musical theatre was superior to "spoken theatre" because it could simultaneously express internal feeling and signify external action, convincing an audience about the real life which animated the stage presentation. Music was the animating spirit or soul in musical theatre, and it fixed an actor's verbal behavior, leaving no freedom of initiative. In Appia's musical theatre, actors abdicated their personality and renounced every interpretative right of their roles. "The more complete this renouncement is, the better the actor will fulfill his mission" (Appia 1983:270). However, music could not determine the relationship of the actor with his inanimate setting. But again Appia, who admitted that it was impossible to "avoid the care of interpretation," thought of a way to confine the interpretive liberties of actors and designers.

Appia claimed that the actor served as an intermediary between the playtext and the decorative form and that the union between the inanimate setting and the actor existed latently in the playtext score prior to its staged presentation. Consequently, the actor determined the setting, but the music predetermined the proportions of the setting, which assumed a musical texture. In sum, music (read "the playwright-composer's intention") prescribed the exact measure of expression required by all elements in theatrical production (including actors and designers) and depended on their collaboration.

The ideal stage space, for Appia, was a cube with totally flexible sides (floor, ceiling, walls), thus permitting each playtext to develop its own unique performance space where emotional and dramatic possibilities could occur thanks to a continuous "play" of electric, not natural, light. Appia conceived the setting as a three-dimensional static, inanimate frame or structure that complemented the dynamic figure of the actor.

Computer-animated design in the 1990s offers the stage design-apparatus and the dramatic possibilities that Appia dreamed about in the 1890s. Computer-animated design also addresses some of the priorities of both pseudoidealist and pseudonaturalist designers because, despite their alleged differences, both parties were concerned with achieving an organic unity in their staged productions.

The idealist directors usually strove to synthesize the various elements (such as language, gestures, sets, props, costumes, and lighting) into a rhythmic fusion and artistic unity (Macgowan 1921:23). Likewise, many naturalist directors and designers visualized their productions as if each element played its part like an instrument in an orchestra, contributing to the total impression. As early as 1875, Duke Georg of Saxe-Meiningen went into production of Schiller's *Fiesko* in Berlin only after making detailed drawings of entire scenes showing the actors in the proposed settings.

These designers-directors did not regard setting as separate from acting or secondary to acting. "I know the objection: i.e., that the stage setting is secondary," wrote Antoine to Françisque Sarcey on 24 November 1890. "Yes, perhaps, in the repertory" (1921:199). Antoine, however, insisted that stage setting was "the indispensable complement" of naturalist plays "in which the theory of environments and the influence of external things have taken so large a part" (1921:200). In Antoine's Darwinian universe, setting and actors formed an interactive system. Computer-animated design gave the above theories and practices a new twist.

In logocentric production, the prompt-copy evolves from the interaction among directors, set-costume-lighting designers, actors, and crews who respond to the playtext and to one another's interpretations of the playtext. The prompt-copy synthesizes both literary and nonliterary elements in order to prescribe verbal and nonverbal communication on stage. The prompt-copy, therefore, is an audiovisual structure which results from an interpretation (analysis or decoding) and reconstruction (composition or encoding) of playtext information to suit the concrete specifications of a production.

"The scene designer must work in a hundred ways," wrote Edmond Jones, "but in his mind's eye he must see the high original intention of the dramatist and follow it" (1925:16). Since playtexts are structured sign systems that impart a meaning—even the meaning of nonsense—on the readers, accordingly, the prompt-copies replicate, the rehearsals stabilize, and the performance-texts present a programed aesthetic and ideological experience to the audiences.

In deconstructive productions, the prompt-copy emphasizes the compositional and interpretative priorities of directors and designers—regardless of the playwright's intentions and the structure of the playtext. If I may retain for a moment the idealist lingo evident in Stanislavsky's logocentric terms, the prompt-copy emphasizes the priorities that will appear in the performance-text as both "inner action" (content) and audiovisual orchestration (form) (Stanislavsky 1963:383–384).

In fact, the deconstructors often show how intentions and structure work against themselves. They inscribe a systematic "other message" through what has been said in the playtext. They make the playtext differ from itself as they transform it into a prompt-copy in ways that the playwright had not anticipated. They continue this division and difference in rehearsal and performance. So, difference results not from error, but from the intervention of deconstructive directors, designers, actors, and critics to undermine—not necessarily through parody—the dominant statements in a playtext. Consequently, they see themselves as producers, not interpreters, of the playtext because the "other" message requires their creative work to be realized.

The logocentric concept of the prompt-copy as a subsystem in play production includes all four steps of stage composition (i.e., production design, ground plans, blocking, business) in both their visual dimension (e.g., sets, movement, lighting, costumes) and their acoustic dimension (e.g., verbal/nonverbal, rhythmic/arhythmic flow of sounds). These dimensions of the prompt-copy are interdependent and are the product of collective work and interaction. Teamwork and specific artistic and economic priorities, of course, seem essential to a successful outcome.

Generally, however, the director is the only person fully aware of all steps of stage composition as he coordinates the overall process. The director briefs the designers on his concept of the production, and each designer—and subsequent crew—proceeds to fulfill his own task independently. As the prompt-copy moves toward rehearsals, the director functions as the key link and reference point for the produced designs.

The deconstructors agree that the above designs require careful and detailed planning, but they decline to give the director a central role—if any at all. Let me sketch these complex operations in three brief paragraphs. The *production design* comprises the playhouse (site, size, stage type, seats, spectators, style of architecture) and the set system (single realistic or abstract set, multiple realistic or abstract sets, and "no" set). The *ground plan*, in turn, illustrates the stage and sets as seen from above. It determines the visual pattern of the play's action—especially the actor's blocking. For example, the shape and arrangement of doors, walls, windows, and furniture are tested to look proper and functional. The ground plan, then, accomodates and emphasizes the action of the play by establishing focus and encouraging blocking.

Blocking prescribes the placement and movement pattern of all characters so that they instantly and clearly reveal the action in meaningful ways. Placement and movement create perceptual effects and give focus to the expressions and the beats (i.e., the moment-to-moment actions) of the characters, guiding audience attention through binary opposites such as motion/stillness, balance/imbalance, one/many, speech/silence, light/darkness, attack/retreat, rhythm/randomness. Blocking reveals dominant/subordinate relationships and the characters unstated thoughts and emotional shifts by segmenting and presenting precise, often contradictory, beats. "If we consider that in a three-hour Shakespearean play with an average of six actors on stage at a time, the director stages over 1000 man-minutes of stage time, we realize that a lot of blocking goes on in the theatre" (Cohen and Harrop 1974:137).

Business defines the detailed, limited, physical movements of a character in a position, such as smoking, eating, and the like, adding significant information about the personality and frame of mind of the character. *Costume design* tacitly informs on the fictional or historical, social, and personal circumstances of the characters. *Incidental music* and *lighting*, on the other hand, create focus, mood, and rhythm that can complement or contradict the previous compositional tools. For example, a lighting plan, which creates focus, may destroy a sense of time. In sum, lighting, costume design,

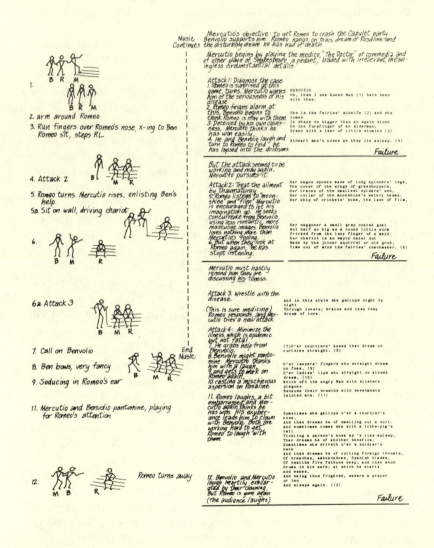

FIGURE 7. A Sample Page of a Prompt-Copy: Mercutio's Speech (1.4.53–91) in Shakespeare's Romeo and Juliet. (Source: M. Gallaway, *The Director in the Theatre*. New York: Macmillan, 1963, pp. 202–204.)

blocking, business, ground plan, and production design are all complementary, yet interacting, compositions which guide and control audience attention.

Directors gained power and control over designers because someone was needed to check on all these interactions during the designing process to make them functional. The rehearsal and the director have always made up for the inability of the designers to calculate in simulated, three-dimentional space the interacting details of the prompt-copy's compositional tools and to check errors in their designs.

"Lovely sketches and renderings don't mean a thing, however impressive they may be," wrote Josef Svoboda. "You can draw anything you like on a piece of paper, but what's important is the actualization" (Burian 1971:15). Experience taught Svoboda that Gordon Craig's optimism seventy years earlier was unfounded. "When I make the same scene on the stage," Craig told the theatre manager, "it is sure to be quite different in form and colour, but it will create the same impression on you as this design in front of you now" (1983:33-34).

For centuries, speech and movement were transcribed into two different time scales on paper—the pages of prompt-books (Figure 7). Detailed and complete planning in the prompt-copy before rehearsals began saved time and money because it diminished error and the uncertainty of the producers about target-audience response. The prompt-copy recorded—in detail and carefully drawn to scale—sets, props, ground plans, blocking, costumes, lighting, sound, speech, and the movement of set, props, and actors on stage. The ground plan drawings were placed on the left page facing the playtext on the right page—including every position and movement which would be tested during rehearsals. The foresight, which a prompt-copy made possible, saved rehearsal time and helped crews meet production deadlines.

The above compositional tools are interrelated systems of signs which offer a nexus of interacting functions. Despite their rigorous imagination, artistic skill, and careful work, the designers could not anticipate these functions in every detail. However, technology gradually offered them viable alternatives which often were perceived by entire generations of theatre artists and critics as irrelevant or inimical to theatrical concerns.

The invention of talking movies in the 1930s and videotapes in the 1960s, for instance, registered speech and movement in two different channels anchored in a common time scale. This made possible to time-match speech and movement. It also helped those who filmed and studied the semiotics of (theatrical)performances in the 1970s to achieve a more accurate, more integrated, and more detailed description of the behavioral organization on stage and in the auditorium—whereas in the past they had to resort to drawings, pictures, and tape recordings. Research in computer graphics in the 1980s improved the analytical control that a researcher (and, subsequently, a designer) could have over setting, speech, and movement in the theatre. It also improved the creative transcription and matching of verbal and nonverbal data.

Gordon Craig envisioned a future for the designer-director that computer-animated design and computer graphics made possible in the 1980s. "If you cannot make an idea pay," Craig told the theatre managers at the beginning of the twentieth century, "that but reveals your ignorance of how to handle it, and you fail at your own game—but, observe, the idea has not failed. It waits for someone better fitted to develop it" (1983:35). The visual subtleties, which were beyond the comprehension and imagination of the theatre managers when Craig was first talking about "painting in light," acquired new possibilities thanks to computer-animated design and computer graphics (Figure 8).

Next to fulfilling artistic dreams, computer-animated design will also have an economic impact because it helps designers visualize multiple factors and so minimize production error which would require last minute redesigning. In this way, computer graphics and semiotic research are slowly reducing the need for long rehearsal periods and for autocratic directors, promising significant savings in time and cost.

Thanks to computer-animated design and figures, the designers can now see how their proposed designs and patterns will function and how they will look from various angles. Rather than build a replica of the set in order to view it in three dimensions, they can generate a graphic display which helps them view a drawing in seconds and decide quickly on how to improve the result of their production concept (Figure 9a). They can delete, magnify, reduce, rotate parts of the drawing, specify scale, and automatically calculate and display distances between points. They

FIGURE 8. Gordon Craig's "Painting in Light": Suzanna (1908), Yorick (1913), and Hamlet's Speech (3.3.73) in Shakespeare's *Hamlet* (1914). (Source: Gordon Craig, *On the Art of Theatre*. London: Heinemann, 1911, plates 4, 5, 6.)

can use the computer as a labor-saving device while they bring into the prompt-copy their artistry, experience, imagination, and aesthetic values.

The performing arts industry in the U.S.A. uses computer graphics in film and dance. Rapid and inexpensive cartoons have been produced since 1968 when the mathematical techniques for creating smooth-flowing figures among a set of positions became available to filmmakers. "Computer animations are 20 times cheaper than movies produced in the conventional way" (Anderson 1971:721). The movie *Tron* (Walt Disney Productions 1982) was an unprecedented demonstration of this new technology in computer animation. "Some 53 minutes of the film consist of animation done purely by electronic means, without resorting to pen, pencil, or brush" (Schickel 1982:63). The ambition to construct simulated worlds and to create human figures that would move and interact in simulated environments has been a long-standing challenge for artist-engineers in computer graphics.

Their efforts to create computer-animated human figures whose motions appear natural, self-generated, and coordinated have resulted in three types of figures: stick figures, ellipsoid figures, and spheroid figures (Figure 9b). Stick figures are the simplest and therefore the easiest display representations. They lack aesthetic appeal, however, and give ambiguous spatial limb interpretations (Herbison-Evans 1982:27). Still, they are most efficient for the designer's blocking purposes. The movements of all independent body segments can be observed and the minor disadvantage of ambiguous spatial interpretation—i.e., whether a limb is behind or in front of the body—is eliminated when a perspective is generated.

Ellipsoid figures, on the other hand, are "fleshed-out" stick figures; they require more complex data and programs and more computation between frames. Nonetheless, a figure of twenty ellipsoids solves any aesthetic and ambiguity problems. Finally, spheroid figures provide a three-dimentional, solid view of the human body. Their limbs change size according to their distance from an operator-defined point of view, and they project shadows from a light source defined by the designer (Dooley 1982:24).

Two forms of graphic display draw these three types of figures: the vector and the raster displays. The vector display draws stick and ellipsoid figures. The raster display draws spheroid figures. While vector-display figures lack the "realism" that raster-display

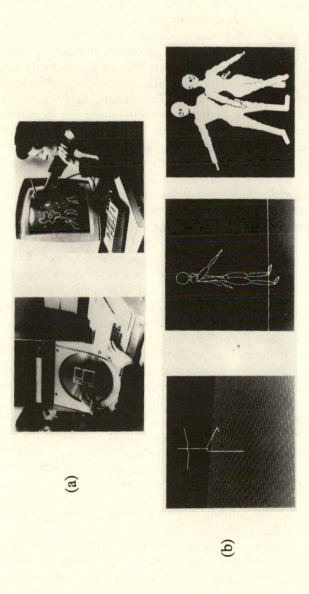

FIGURE 9. Computer Graphics. (a) Computer-animated Design. (b) Computer-animated Figures: Stick, Ellipsoid, Spheroid. (Sources: R. Parslow and R. Green, eds. *Advanced Computer Graphics.* New York: Plenum, 1971, p. 447; R. Parslow, et al., eds. *Computer Graphics.* New York: Plenum, 1969, p. 64; T. Calvert et al., "Aspects of Kinematic Stimulation of Human Movement" *IEEECG&A* 2:9 (1982), 48.)

figures can obtain, vector display is faster because it requires fewer calculations (Herbison-Evans 1980:355). In considering display speed, if a frame rate of twelve frames per second cannot be maintained, the display misses significant segments of movement patterns or its speed appears slower than real time (Calvert et al. 1982:45). Real-time display allows designers to explore various blocking compositions without engaging performers in rehearsals.

Such programs in computer graphics are useful to theatre designers because they can create and display various physical and functional interfaces between human figures and their setting. By manipulating both human figures and their setting, the designers can (1) check and modify layouts of sets and blocking quickly, (2) remove or insert various props rapidly, and (3) study with greater speed a larger variety of acceptable alternative environments. Of course, all this is at an experimental stage, but if ever applied widely, it could affect the current structure of theatrical production.

For the time being, one focus of semiotic research is on how an actor's movement patterns on stage are broken down into a notation (e.g., Labanotation), which is then fed into the computer to generate the same movement patterns executed by a stick figure on the screen. Labanotation has been used to describe (notate) movement and gesture in ballet since 1928. The actual symbols of Labanotation or their alphanumeric equivalent have been entered as input into a computer-based system to generate dancing stick figures on the screen since 1980.

When a notational system—such as Labanotation today and the English language tomorrow—can be transformed into sets, props, and figures which interact with one another on the computer screen as soon as a designer, or a playwright, types in his "text," this technological breakthrough may change the way plays will be written and produced in the future. In the meantime, researchers create libraries of macros—i.e., preprogrammed sequences of support changes such as those that arise in walking, running, or jumping— by using the alphanumeric representation of Labanotation as the standard input. The first substantial segment of notation produced was completed in 1982. It involved an improvisation sequence from the *Nutcracker* ballet (Calvert et al. 1982:48).

Of course, the visual side of a prompt-copy contributes only one part to the total aesthetic experience presented by its performance-text. Historically, the tactile, olfactory, and gustatory sides of a prompt-copy have contributed very small parts to the total aesthetic experience even in experimental theatres, dinner theatres, and cabaret theatres of an Aristophanic or Epicurian proclivity. So, the acoustic side—both verbal and nonverbal sounds—contributes the remaining significant part.

Since the semiotic construction of a prompt-copy involves both digital and analog notational systems—which produce speech, writing, music, dance, and other visual or acoustic images—the problem is how to synthesize sign systems of different semiotic status in meaningful ways. The seemingly single-leveled, homogeneous series of signs in the playtext—which Schechner described as dialogue and stage directions—eventually become a weave of multichanneled, multisystemic codes in the prompt-copy. How should designers and directors organize the analog and digital sign systems in the prompt-copy so that these sign systems express their artistic (aesthetic and ideological) goals?

As early as 1727, Franciscus Lang called attention to an integrative analysis of both verbal language and body language in relation to the cultural sign systems that support them (1968:85). However, the selection and combination of the semiotic units of these sign systems depends on how each designer defines "unit." This definition, in turn, determines how the prompt-copy, as a multimedial text, will be segmented and organized.

Gotthold Lessing, who set for himself the task of bringing together dramatic literature and theatrical performance into a productive relationship, regarded the art of stage production as a "reproductive" process which conjoined heterogeneous media in order to produce meaningful units of sign systems. In other words, designers and directors selected linguistic, paralinguistic, and extralinguistic signs from medial repertoires and combined them meaningfully into a chain of multimedial scores. Signs were selected and combined because of their visible or acoustic properties. For example, an actor's "feeling is something internal of which we can only judge by its external signs," observed Lessing (1962:12).

Lessing thought that the art of stage production unified poetic speech and painting (scenography). He assumed that playwrights, designers, and directors created an illusion in order to affect an audience. Both painting and poetic speech produced similar effects—i.e., pleasing illusions—on an audience by representing absent things as if they were present and by making fiction look like reality. Both pleasures proceeded from the same source, Beauty, which had external and internal applications—from thoughts to forms (1984:3).

However, the art of playwrights, designers, directors, and actors could reveal the truth (Beauty) with a lie (i.e., illusion) only if it had the stamp of authenticity about it according to Lessing. Authenticity depended on how well their artistic work corresponded with the "natural order" of the Highest Genius (*Logos*). So, Lessing thought that truth had a double nature—as immanent structure and desirable form. This belief that a stage production resulted from a series of acoustic and visual imitations which replicated either an ideal reality or an empirical reality was popular before and after Lessing.

Lessing's dualism nourished two popular misperceptions even though his initial materialist premise—i.e., that the medium and the sensory organs determine the limits of representation—was correct. First, he argued that a playtext was limited by its material reproduction on stage because dramatic poets, unlike designers and actors, could maintain a high level of illusion on the page even when the represented objects were invisible.

On the other hand, painters ("designers") and actors faced the impossible task of representing invisible objects on canvas or on stage (Lessing 1984:76). Lessing would allow them to think for themselves while they were translating the playwright's model-text from one art into another and to prove that they were as great in their art as the dramatic poet was in his (1984:40). Nonetheless, Lessing reserved a spiritual dimension for playtexts and a material dimension for scenography thanks to a problematical syllogism.

Lessing's syllogism went as follows: "If it is true that, in its imitations, painting uses completely different means or signs than does poetry, namely, figures and colors in space rather than articulated sounds in time, and if these signs must indisputably bear a suitable relation to the thing signified, then signs existing in space can express only objects whose wholes or parts coexist, while signs that follow one another can express only objects whose wholes or parts are consecutive" (1984:78).

In other words, painting represented the visible properties of bodies in juxtaposition, whereas (dramatic) poetry represented the actions of bodies in succession. So, Lessing drew the tautological conclusion that (1) "painting alone can imitate material beauty" because beautiful things, whose parts lie in juxtaposition, are represented by painting and (2) the (dramatic) poet "abstains entirely from the description of physical beauty as such" because beautiful things, whose parts are shown in succession, are represented by (dramatic) poetry (1984:104).

Second, Lessing adopted the distinction between arbitrary signs and natural signs as they are used "to render the visible invisible and the invisible visible" (1984:70). He maintained that dramatic poetry was the highest genre of poetry because it could fully transform conventional (i.e., arbitrary) signs to natural signs. On the page, dramatic poetry, like other poetic genres, relied on devices such as words, tone, meter, and figures of speech. On the stage, however, Lessing believed that the words ceased to be conventional signs and they became natural signs for conventional objects thanks to the actor's acting, which approached nature or reality (1904:291).

In other words, staged playtexts communicated vivid thoughts and feelings in such a way that the spectators felt that they had real impressions. During "this moment of illusion" the affected spectators "ceased to be conscious of the means which the poet used for this purpose, that is, his words" (Lessing 1984:85). By endorsing the popular assumption that playtexts were "designed for living presentation by the actor," Lessing drew one more fallacious conclusion: "we do not merely believe that we see and hear a screaming Philoctetes," wrote Lessing, "we do actually see and hear him" (1984:24).

Lessing's misconception in the 1760s that words become natural signs in the theatre was repeated by Peter Brook in the 1960s, leading to the conclusion that a stage production offers an experience of the *real thing* either through a naturalist ostention or through an idealist revelation. In more recent years, Judith Milhous and Robert Hume repeated the worn-out belief that "performance analysis enjoys the distinct advantage of dealing with actuality, with a production complete in all its details, with the experience of the real thing" (1985:33).

However, a theatrical performance neither ostentates a material object (say, the historical Hamlet and the castle that still stands at Elsinore) nor does it reveal an original Platonic Idea (say, an Ur-Hamlet or an archetypal castle). The performance is just another interpretive text, the performance-text, which is inscribed in different semiotic systems and medium (stage) from the semiotic systems and medium (page) of the playtext.

The props, sets, lights, sounds, costumes, actors—bodies and voices—are never fully "real" or "present" as objects on the stage because they serve as signifiers, standing for something else. So, their material presence during a performance is never fully disclosed to an audience even when, for example, the paint is removed from the sets or the costumes from the actors. Likewise, the concepts (signifieds) that each spectator forms during a performance result from his or her interpretation of man-made, man-controlled signifiers, not from an original Idea, Spirit, Logos, Voice, or the Muse, which supposedly manifests itself on stage through the words of the playwright, the lines and colors of the designers, or the voice and body of the actors.

A performance-text, for instance, could never fully reveal the Holy Ghost to an audience even if ghosts existed. A performance-text can only present a material signifier (an actor or a broomstick) "standing for" the immaterial ghost of Hamlet's father. In this sense, when Sarah Bernhardt played Ophelia in 1886 or Hamlet in 1899, she simultaneously *was* and *was not* Ophelia or Hamlet, the sets *were* and *were not* Elsinore, the stage light *was* and *was not* sunlight or starlight, and so on.

In sum, presence of full meaning and closure in interpretation during performance are misperceptions facilitated by the shifting semiotic modalities of the performance-text. The critics who protested about Bernhardt playing Hamlet, but not Ophelia, displayed once again the widespread prejudicial attitude that the trained body and voice of an actress are not conventional vehicles (signifiers) but have some inherent connection with the (masculine or femine) part that she plays.

The above misperception encouraged discourse analysts, such as Deidre Burton, to argue that (1) playwrights could be regarded by sociologists as fellow researchers of the structures of verbal interaction and (2) the dialogues of plays could be read as condensed forms of ethnographic observations of naturally occurring talk. The similarity of "play talk" with "real talk" could be explored at the level of discourse analysis (Burton 1980:8).

Burton maintained that dramatic dialogue often sounds like natural conversation. Therefore, discourse analysts could use staged talk as if it were a transcript of real conversation (1980:96). Dramatic dialogue, next to courtesy books, conversation manuals, oratory handbooks, conduct prescriptions, and notations of actual conversations, could help conversation analysts understand discourse patterns in past and present times.

Ironically, the similarity between natural and staged behavior was unwittingly disproved in three steps by Konstantin Stanislavsky when the Moscow Art Theatre Company produced Leo Tolstoy's *The Power of Darkness*. First, Stanislavsky confessed that the actors could not reconcile themselves "to a theatrical stencil of the Russian muzhik" because they perceived a difference between real muzhik behavior and its run-of-the-mill theatrical representations. Second, Stanislavsky admitted that the closer the MAT actors copied the external (verbal)behavior of the muzhiks, "the more ethnographical it was," stifling their performance because "real talk" served a different function from "play talk" (1963:309). Third, Stanislavsky revealed that the "discourse" of a real muzhik on stage made the "discourse" of the actors look and sound unnatural. When the MAT actors returned to Moscow from Tula Gubernia—where they observed "the real muzhiks" in their natural environment—they brought back with them not only costumes, dishes, and furniture, but also "two living specimens of village life"—an old man and an old woman (1963:309–310).

During rehearsals, Stanislavsky replaced the ill actress who played Matryona with the old woman, and he discovered to his dismay how authentic and natural she was. If "she interpreted the inner and outer contents of Toltoy's tragedy so fully and truthfully," if "she justified each of our naturalist details of production to such an extent," then why didn't Stanislavsky allow her to perform with the rest of the actors?

Stanislavsky gave two reasons: (1) the old woman occasionally threw aside Tolstoy's text to use her own words "which no censorship would ever allow on the stage"; (2) her behavior on stage had "such veracity that it was impossible for any one of us to appear on the stage after her exit" (1963:310). So, Stanislavsky further reduced her performance from just crossing the stage to singing in the wings. "But even this proved dangerous for the actors,"

Stanislavsky recalled. "Then we made a phonograph record of her song and used it as a background for action without breaking up the ensemble scene" (1963:310–311).

The deconstructors reveal the contradictions committed by discourse analysts who endorsed both formalist and structuralist tenets. For example, some discourse analysts, on the one hand, assumed that staged talk differs from real-life talk because staged talk is presumably more condensed, more emphatic, more focused, and more typical than real-life talk (Schlieben-Lange 1980:239; Spillner 1980:279). On the other hand, they analyzed staged talk with the linguistic methods used for real-life talk. If there exists a modal difference between staged talk and real-life talk which prohibits quoting evidence from staged talk as evidence for real-life talk, how could they claim a structural identity between staged talk and real-life talk in order to regard staged talk as a model for hypotheses about real-life talk? For this reason, the deconstructive designers and directors call for a reconsideration of the issue of staged/real talk. Even if a playwright (say, Shakespeare) could competently reproduce the structures of real-life talk in his playtexts, the staged talk in a revival production of his playtexts (say, *Macbeth*) would be significantly different from the real-life talk of the audiences in subsequent years. The ahistorical or synchronic perspective of many formalists and structuralists made muddy water even muddier for the designers of prompt-copies. Intentionally or unintentionally, most designers and directors face the inevitable task of transforming—either by "updating" or by "translating"—the verbal and visual codes of a playtext, which may belong to their own or to a different culture.

Research about how ordinary people in some kind of verbal interaction organize their behavior in relation to one another in order to make their "encounter" or "communication" possible in real life emerged in the early 1950s (Ruesch and Bateson 1951). These researchers postulated that interactional events among people have an organization specific to their nature and frame. On the assumption that staged interaction has an organization specific to the theatre of a historical period and to the scene enacted on stage, semiotic research analyzed observable, communicative behavior in order to discover the "rules" of staged interaction (Elam 1980:135). Some studied body language and considered posture, spacing, orientation, and gesture. Others examined interactive speech, looking for hesitations, rhythms, tunes, and tones of voice as conscious or unconscious signifiers of meaning. Despite the poor results, Peter Brook's experiments at the International Center for Theatre Research acquire significance in the context of this type of research.

Brook's experiments may have failed to give clear, specific answers, but, upon re-examination, they circumscribed intriguing problem areas for future research. Reportedly, under the influence of Noam Chomsky's linguistic theory, Peter Brook and his CIRT group investigated whether human beings—regardless of their racial diversity, national identity, and cultural conditioning—could share an underlying, universal theatrical language. In search of this universal language, the CIRT group in Africa improvised performances without words or dialogue. Brook's theatrical adventures and Heilpern's humorous description of them covered a large, serious field of inquiry.

The CIRT group performed at seventeen different places: at the marketplace of In Salah, at the marketplace of Tamanrasset, at the outskirts of Tamanrasset, at the marketplace of Agades, at a Tuareg village, at the Peulh's hut at Agades, at a Hausa village, at the village of Gangara, at the Emir's mud palace in Kano, in a village in the fields outside Kano, under a dead baobab tree, in a small town, at the village of Wuseli, at the village of Dungung, in the town of Gboko, in the bush a day's drive from Ife, at the village of Itagunmodi, in Ife, and in Daru Lapidu's open-air theatre in Oshogbo. These open-air performances showed how (1) the cultural frame and (2) the spatial organization of the people (actors and spectators) who enter a focused or unfocused encounter affects the nature of the transaction.

For example, some spectators from among the unreceptive audience at the marketplace of Tamanrasset thanked the actors for their "dancing." "This was doubly embarrassing," wrote Heilpern, "because there hadn't been any dancing" (1977:89). It soon became clear that they had never before seen a theatrical performance and that they referred to the CIRT performance as "dancing" because, according to Heilpern, their local language had no word for "theatrical performance." The absence of the appropriate cultural and linguistic frame for the CIRT performance resulted in misframing it as "dance," a word or concept that raised the wrong expectations in the audience and perhaps can explain why the audience was not receptive, did not applaud, and "drifted away."

Interestingly, the smaller audience at the spacious, peaceful marketplace of In Salah was more receptive than the larger audience at the narrow, bustling marketplace of Tamanrasset—even though both audiences were "theatrically naive" (Heilpern 1978:74). It would seem that the shifting spatial arrangments of actors and spectators expressed how their attitudes changed during the performance— as they also did at the village of Gangara. "There was such a powerful sense of occasion," wrote Heilpern, "that I couldn't help wishing Brook had something prepared to offer, a *real* show" (1978:148). When actors and spectators progressively frustrated each others expectations, their orientation on and around the carpet changed. The spectators fidgeted with noisy indifference, perhaps thinking of the local storyteller and four singers on horseback, who were waiting for their turn to perform. Reciprocally, the performing CIRT actors retreated behind a "fourth wall" until several women and children, pushed by a horse, spilled screaming onto the carpet, breaking the performance (1978:151).

In John Heilpern's text, *Conference of the Birds*, Peter Brook did not raise any questions about the spatial organization of actors and spectators during a theatrical encounter. However, Brook's trial-and-error improvisations offer valuable insights as to how a designer-director can use space in order to increase the spectator's involvement through risk-taking strategies without breaking the actors' performance.

For example, does a spatial organization derive its properties from the requirements of the interactional event or from the separate needs of each participant? During the improvised performance of the *Shoe Show* at the Tuareg village, the CIRT actor Yoshi Oida "presented the shoes" to the village schoolmaster, who was sitting on the edge of the carpet in the audience (Heilpern 1978:119). The schoolmaster thought that the shoes were a genuine gift and refused to give them back—making it impossible for the show to continue. Three actors in character—i.e., the sorceress and the thieves—tried and failed to get the shoes back. The schoomaster returned the shoes only when he was begged by the shoe collector in a manner that he thought to be satisfactory.

If sustained spatial arrangements define an encounter as a coherent, distinct event, designers and directors can use them to define phases of postural configurations within an interactional event, serving as frames. The concept of "frame" has been used in theories of person-to-person interaction and small-group interaction. In making a prompt-copy, designers and directors need to know how such frames are created, sustained, changed, and disbanded.

For example, Heilpern noticed that the CIRT actors, even though they performed on a carpet in open spaces under the desert sun, often retained the acting frames required by indoor proscenium stages—i.e., they paced nervously around in their new costumes as if they were waiting for the five-minute bell, and they waited in a space behind a tree to make their entrance on the carpet— as if the tree were the wings of a theatre (Heilpern 1978:72, 75). And they did so despite Brook's reminders that their journey was an exercise in heightening their awareness at all levels—meaning that they should beware of the frames that they carried in their mental luggage on their trip to Africa.

Brook assumed that the actors needed (1) to cast off the "sophisticated" linguistic, theatrical, and cultural frames of Europe and Asia like dead snake skins and (2) to attain a simplicity of expression that could touch all spectators—regardless of their level of understanding. Only then could the CIRT actors offer a rich (read "dense") experience to the African spectators, who were theatrically illiterate, naive, or innocent. The circle symbolized this kind of theatrical experience for Brook. "A cat, a child, and a sage can all play with a circle in their own way," wrote Heilpern, "finding in it whatever they want" (1978:174). Unfortunately, Brook failed to see that one can easily frame the circle and that the circle is not an open frame itself. Brook himself framed the interactive system (or circuit) between his actors and their spectators when he decided the sequence of their improvisational routines or when he set several rules about the location and size of their performing areas and the number and manner of people who could attend the performances (1978:181). Brook became aware of these initially "invisible" frames whenever his actors failed to please good, kind, open, welcoming audiences. The audiences felt disappointed, and the actors felt rejected.

Heilpern claimed that the Africans did not understand the content of the improvised, nonverbal performances. "The harsh truth to be swallowed," wrote Heilpern, "was the simple undeniable fact that the audience couldn't understand what the hell we were supposed to be doing" (1978:185). Heilpern's appraisal of the situation was inaccurate, underestimating the audiences' native intelligence. When Brook asked some villagers after an unsuccessful performance of the *Shoe Show* to tell him what they had seen, the village chief, in consultation with several others, answered that they had seen something about a pair of shoes which changed people in some way (Heilpern 1978:184). Evidently, they understood what the actors were doing, but they saw no value in it. Nor did the Westerners in the audience, who either walked out (missionaries) or voiced their disappointment (Professor Beier). Despite their awareness program, the CIRT group did not realize that the involvement of their audience required more than understanding.

Neither Brook nor Heilpern asked how the silly *Shoe Show* and a pair of "magic shoes" related to the problems of the villagers, who were suffering from drought, hunger, unemployment, and poverty. Instead of performing a story about the shoeless feet of the starving children who were begging them for money, the CIRT group obstinately focused on the "magic" boots of a well-fed, Greek-American actor who was complaining about the heat and the mosquitoes. The plight of the African children was "beyond words." The *Shoe Show* was merely "without words" and beyond the immediate concerns and frames of reference of the villagers. Heilpern thought that the supposedly "universal" language of the *Shoe Show* failed to communicate its message because the *Shoe Show* was built around a Western theatrical convention—i.e., that shoes can magically transform people, bringing luck or disaster. Therefore, Heilpern concluded, the African audience could not follow the story because it could not share this cultural frame of reference. "We were still trapped in restricted art forms that made sense only to ourselves, which is why the rehearsal of the show was a success and the performance a failure" (1978:186).

However, the feedback that Brook and his actors received, when they cared or dared to ask the villagers, proved that the Africans followed the enacted story as well as the Europeans. Their lack of involvement may have resulted from their frustrated expectations. Nowhere did the CIRT group conduct preperformance or postperformance audience surveys for comparison and analysis. The CIRT group was on the road giving "hit-and-run" performances, taking no time to know their audience or understand their frames of reference—even when the villagers said things that falsified their preconceptions (Heilpern 1978:218–219). For example, the teacher of the village of Wusely did not know who Adolf Hitler was

(1978:213). When Heilpern told Chief Godunyilwada that life in the village of Dungung was simple, the chief disagreed with him (1978:224–225).

In spite of such clues, the CIRT members retained their own frames of understanding: They thought that Europeans and Asians see a division between a visible and an invisible reality; that the Africans see no division between the tangible and the intangible reality (1978:60-61); that power in expressive sound or movement always comes by a process of elimination—not by addition—of outward forms (1978:129); that an actor, like a cat, should be trained to think visibly with his body, becoming one sensitive responding, animated organic whole (1977:131); and that, ironically, one can discover something new only when one takes absolutely nothing for granted (1978:84).

In view of the above, Brook's experiments broached the question once again: How are framing agreements established in the opening of an encounter in the theatre? Frames, based on cultural conditioning, seem to be a primary factor. For example, when the CIRT group started performing *Orghast* at Kano, their Nigerian audience was not present. Reportedly, the Nigerians in 1973 went to a show only when they sensed action. "If you want an audience," Brook was told, "you must begin a show without one" (1978:169).

Frames, based on theatrical conditioning, seem to be a secondary factor. When the Hausa audience heard the bird cries and monkey shrieks of *Orghast* for the first time, they convulsed with laughter—mistaking the performance for a satirical comedy— perhaps a parody of Aristophanes' *The Birds* and Edgar Burroughs's *Tarzan of the Apes*.

Frames, based on linguistic conditioning, seem to be a tertiary factor. When the CIRT actor Malik Bagayogo, who played the God of Darkness, pronounced the deliberately contrived nonsense words "BULLORGA TORGA," the audience burst into snorts of laugher. When the actor repeated the phrase, the audience echoed back "BULLORGA TORGA?" When the actor shouted again the nonsense syllables rising above the tumult, the audience went hysterical. "BULLORGA TORGA, a word invented by Ted Hughes," explained Heilpern, "happens to be very similar to the Hausa slang for cunt. In the gravity of the moment, Bagayogo was wailing on about cunts" (Heilpern 1978:171).

Framing agreements are not negotiated and established only between actors and spectators during performance. They are also negotiated and established among the theatre artists—from the playwright (Ted Hughes) to the director and from the director (Peter Brook) to the actor (Malik Bagayogo). "When I asked Malik why in God's name he didn't get on to another word," wrote Heilpern, "he looked most indignant. *Mais c'est dans le texte!* The actor trained for so long in the arts of improvisation had stuck to the script. I think Ted Hughes would have been proud of him in a way" (1978:172).

This example illustrates how the frames, which are established by the logocentric tradition, exert a powerful influence over the creativity and decision-making of individual theatre artists. Although the playwright may be absent (as Ted Hughes was), the actor risked ridicule by going against his better judgment and the frames of understanding of his "untrained" audience. "We must learn to *train* the audience," said Brook. "We must learn to build a real relationship" (1978:95). However, Brook's urgency to "train" an audience casts a shadow on the relationship.

Establishing a communicative relationship requires definitions of role, purpose, and attitude. In transcultural situations—such as the above that involved African audiences and European, American, and Asian performers—it was necessary to formulate these definitions in ways that made sense to all the participants in the improvisational performance. But Brook experimented more with his performers than with the audiences in order to find circumstances conducive to fruitful exchange. In the rare case of the Peulh performers during which Brook abdicated his role as director-teacher, neither party explored the areas of their common interests nor did they clarify their mutual viewpoints and attitudes (Heilpern 1978:124–129).

More importantly, Brook failed to pay serious attention to the responses of his African spectators, and therefore he risked turning transnational communication in theatre into another form of cultural imperialism. For instance, the manipulation of "ethnic" and "national" groups in the U.S.A. and the European Economic Community, respectively, has become common practice in the semiotics of advertising. The advertisements which promote products or politicians to ethnic or national minorities illustrate the differences between dominant and subordinate cultural images by framing the affect as an interplay between iconic (analog) and symbolic (digital) expressions in the specific (sub)cultural context of a target audience.

Back in the African bush whenever Brook and his actors failed to engage the attention of their audiences, they explained away their failure by either blaming the audience or themselves. For instance, the audience was "tough" or "rough"; the actors failed to "sense out" or to "get in step with" the mood of an audience and the like (Heilpern 1978:111). Their haphazard pondering, however, leads to a serious question. How is an interactional routine changed within the context of an ongoing encounter when one of the participating individuals or groups nonverbally indicates readiness for a new kind of interactive relationship which is not included in the range of possibilities of a current frame?

At the Tamanrasset performance, Brook advised his actors to "change direction, switch with the different moods of the audience" (Heilpern 1978:77). Brook repeated himself at the Agades performance by advising his actors to "change and develop with the audience, or they are lost" (1978:111). This is easier said than done. How can an actor tell one or more of the changing moods of one or more spectators while he is busy acting and interacting with the other actors on a carpet or on stage? How should an actor interpret the behavior (say, silence or laughter) of one or more spectators? How can a terrified actor "win over" an audience, particularly when some spectators are booing and hissing at the time? (1978:111–112). For directors such as Peter Brook, who advised his actors to "avoid the mini-world of indulgence and interpretation" and to kindle a "true creative flame," these questions become very perplexing (Heilpern 1978:228, 243).

How is frame attunement established in order to end an encounter? In life, each participant gets the other to agree that a move to terminate their encounter is a move of this sort—through nonverbal pre-enactments of departure such as partial withdrawals, looking away, and incomplete vocal signs, indicating a "closing section." In theatre, the problem is for the actors to get the spectator to agree that such a move on their part is, indeed, a move of this sort. Semiotic research pays as much attention to the above paralinguistic and kinetic features as to the observable organization of actual conversations.

Several paralinguistic and kinetic signals are regularly associated with changes in a speaker's role, and with juncture points in the utterance exchange. In real-life talk, the participants can predict the juncture points in each other's speech because utterances are highly patterned both in word order and in rhythm, disclosing from the very beginning how they will end—as it frequently happens in staged talk among actors who have rehearsed their interaction. Some conversation analysts reaffirmed what designers and directors intuitively knew all along: all behavior is structured in time, and rhythmic convergence is fundamental for the development of any focused encounter.

All this pertains to developing techniques that would help designers and directors create a prompt-copy which would be able to sustain audience attention for about 120 minutes under one or more chosen performance styles. If audience attention depends on the modulation of the rhythm of action planned and controlled by the designer and directors, then a well-designed, flexible prompt-copy can engage, maintain, and excite the attention and feelings of both actors and audience during rehearsals or (improvised) performances.

The rhythm construction by the monitors of a prompt-copy and the rhythm sharing by the viewers of a performance-text operate at many organizational levels—from beats to scenes and from scenes to acts. The ability of the participants in a theatrical event to sustain their relationships satisfactorily for an extended period of time depends on how well the "creators" of the prompt-copy provisioned to help actors and spectators share a spatiotemporal patterning of action.

In sum, Brook's program to re-establish the spirit of science in the field of theatre fell victim of his haphazard inquiries, his muffled neo-Platonic dualism, and his pseudo-Oriental phenomenology. Any theatre designer schooled in the scientific method would doubt Heilpern's testimony that "there have been times in the work of the group when all cultural associations, all barriers of language and class have been swept away. In their place a new power and freedom: a spirit" (1978:130). The almost biblical mysticism that shrouded the "holy" or "unholy" experiences of the CIRT believers drained Brook's rationalizations from any explanatory power.

"Such moments can't really be explained," admitted Brook after the Peulh actors joined the song of the CIRT actors. "Yet they're not accidental anymore" (Heilpern 1978:130). For Brook, such ineffable experiences do not result from the artists' painstaking interpretations, which, in turn, can be inscribed in the carefully executed design of a prompt-copy for further interpretations by actors and spectators. Instead, these brief experiences are unique, spontaneous, momentary revelations, which erupt at random intervals. Brook's revelatory "science" rendered the role of the designers obsolete.

In Brook's nonverbal theatre, director and actors found "other means of expression beyond traditional language" which freed them from serving the playtext of an "absolute ruler," the playwright (Heilpern 1978:165–166). However, Brook's initial deconstructive move was paralyzed under a heap of phenomenological assumptions. In Brook's nonverbal theatre, the actor-author and the director-editor replaced the playwright and reversed the hierachical relationship. Like a privileged medium working under the guidance and approval of a director-priest, the actor had, occasionally and momentarily, direct access to the vital source or essence of life. The essence of life was to be found in and through the actor's consciousness.

Perhaps, like the *pythia* at the Oracle of Delphi in Greece or the *babalowo* at the Oracle of Ife in Nigeria, the actor, who attuned his consciousness with the cosmic vortex, could become the center or the navel of the theatrical universe. "Truth, a truthful life and vitality, bursts from the center," said Brook according to Heilpern. "It is never the other way around. But to arrive at the center, the actors must undertake the most intense life of self-exploration" (1978:141). In Brook's scheme of things, playtexts, sets, props, costumes, lighting were physical layers which occasionally stimulated but generally prevented the actors from reaching the underlying essence of things. Brook thought that "without the help of costume or scenery, dialogue or script, an actor, who enters the carpet, cannot lie" (1978:196).

Brook reiterated several truisms of the logocentric theatrical tradition. If Heilpern's account is accurate, Brook lectured him on organic communities (1978:42); he believed that "theatre imitates and animates life" (1978:230); he deemed that an actor finds the essence of life through a transformative repetition which helps him penetrate and remove, like snake skin, the external frames of social conditioning and personal habits—including his language and personality (1978:110, 141); he thought that his exercises helped his actors arrive at a higher level of awareness by ascending from a physical level to a spiritual level (1978:141, 163); he maintained that there exists a universal body language or movement language which can fully express a state of being; and he expected that "beneath the structures of all languages can be found the lost primal speech of the universe, God's speech" (1978:161).

At the International Theatre Congress in Rome, Italy, in 1934 the fascist theorist Silvio D'Amico repeated the idealist claim that theatre could be saved only by those dramatic poets who shall recapture and speak the Word (1931). His neo-Platonism left no role for designers, directors, and actors other than to serve the playwright's word (*logos*), which supposedly reflected the divine Word (*Logos*). A similar claim was launched in 1932 by the American designer Lee Simonson. "The development of scene-designing as an art," wrote Simonson, "must wait upon the arrival, in sufficient numbers, of dramatic poets capable of interpreting life profoundly" (1932:458). Until these playwrights arrive, the theatre designers, no matter how talented, "can do little more than mark time." The creative force is the playwright. "In the modern theatre, as in every other, the beginning is in the word" (Simonson 1932:464).

The belief that playwrights alone can initiate change, progress, and revelatory experience rested on the assumption that the job of designers, directors, and actors was largely interpretive—if not a threat to the integrity—of the playwright's intended meaning (Gorelik 1962:158). Anita Block, for instance, sought a "permanent life" for a playtext after its "ephemeral existence as *theatre*" was over. "The play must be regarded as an independent art-form which stands or falls on its own intrinsic merits," Block argued. "It is shocking to listen to groups of educated and informed persons invariably discussing plays in terms of their productions" (1939:5).

For Block, even the most effectively executed stage design was "surely entirely extraneous to the values of the play as such." Good directing, good designing, good acting could add "certain theatrical values," but they could never "add a hair's weight of value to the play itself." Mordecai Gorelik was among the first to detect that this form of neo-Platonic dualism, which fathered a desire to devaluate—if not to eliminate—the artistic contribution of designers, directors, and actors, stemmed "from the notion that theatre consists of a priceless soul—the script—and a mere body—the production" (1962:23). The playtext, which passed through the ordeal of theatrical production unscathed, could deliver the playwright's message to the audience "with almost virginal purity" (1962:23).

Unfortunately, Gorelik blurred his sharp focus by adopting the same rhetoric of origins which defaced Schechner's "deconstructive" project. Namely, he resorted to flimsy scientific, historical, and etymological explanations to secure priority and power over the playwright. Gorelik claimed that "science has established that gesture came before language"; that, historically, "the playwright was a late comer" to a dramatic ritual which already included dance, gesture, music, costume, and setting; and that the words "drama" and "theatre" originally denoted action (*dromenon*) and spectacle (*theatron* < *theatēs* < *theaomai*). So, gesture came before the word, performance preceded playwriting, and the spectator's eye predated the audience's ear. Inadvertently, his argument supported rather than undermined the priority sequence, value system, and power structure of logocentric theatrical production.

Gorelik remained a formalist in the tradition of Gordon Craig, Bertolt Brecht, Harold Clurman, Elia Kazan, and Robert Lewis, among others, who, despite their artistic differences, were "united in their poetic insight into the meaning of stage technique" (1962:xiii). He regarded theatrical production as a unified, co-ordinated, organic whole whose members worked along a production line (Figure 1). Each member depended on all the others, and true progress could only be achieved by all and for all. Otherwise, the progressive, rich work of a playwright would be frustrated by the backwardness of poor design, poor directing, and poor acting. Gorelik contended "that *all* the forces of stage production are creative, that each of these factors can and should make progress, that the fight for a better theatre has to be waged all along the line of production" (Gorelik 1962:41, 18). However, his attractive egalitarian posture on creativity dissipated quickly.

Gorelik never questioned the privileged, leading role of the playtext—either as written or spoken words—in theatrical production. "The script has a leading function, moreover, above that of the other elements of production, because it is a *chart* of production, it rallies the forces of production," wrote Gorelik. ". . . This leading function is an important privilege of the script; but it is a quality which must not be confused with creativeness" (1962:29). In fact, Gorelik believed that institutionalized directors, designers, and actors subordinated and limited the work of a playwright in times of "weakened" theatre. For instance, the established, old-style romantic productions destroyed early naturalist playtexts according to Gorelik.

Second, Gorelik never questioned the notion of originality. He argued that designing, directing, and acting were as original as playwriting. Consequently, designers, directors, and actors did not have to "draw their breath of life" and their interpretations from the playtext. Like the playwright, they creatively used the resources of their cultural heritage. "Shakespeare borrowed practically every one of the plots of his plays," wrote Gorelik. "Does that make him only an *interpreter?*" (1962:28). Gorelik answered his question in the negative for two reasons. First, he thought that playwrights of Shakespeare's caliber possess a creative genious which breaths originality into their playtexts. Second, he believed that, thanks to this creative breath, "every script is a living organism capable of development or adaptation" to the demands of production through rewriting by the playwright far into rehearsals (1962:34).

Finally, Gorelik complained that drama scholars presented the history of the theatre as a succession of "immortal playscripts"— as if theatrical production existed only to illustrate a playtext in various kinds of performances without ever altering it (1962:17). So, these scholars neglected the "theatrical truths" disclosed in production (1962:3). Like the truths yielded by any other humanistic, scientific, or artistic field, Gorelik believed that theatrical truths are accurate, revealing comments on some phase of existence. Theatrical truths are manifested with the help of all theatre artists and production personnel through the stage apparatus (Gorelik 1962:4). Depending on the historical period, the stage apparatus was dominated by playwrights, directors, designers, or actor-stars. Regardless of their struggle for power, all these theatre artists set out to present a truthful image of Nature and Man—especially in modern times. Their dramatic technique was a means to an end, and the end was "*to influence life by theatrical means*" (1962:5).

Gorelik was concerned about the implications that this power struggle had over the artistic process and product presented to an audience. So, he astutely articulated the problem—which periodically preoccupied formalists, structuralists, and deconstructors. What comes first, the dramatist's script or the forces of theatre in general? Can it be said that the script alone is truly creative while the other elements of production are "interpretive"? What is the value of such a distinction? Or is it of no more pressing importance than the question of which came first, the chicken or the egg? It happens to be a question of great theoretical and practical importance whether the script alone is creative while the other factors of production are interpretive. (Gorelik 1962:17)

Gorelik asked the right question but gave the wrong answer because he was determined to prove that the work of designers, directors, and actors was as original as the work of a playwright— instead of proving that their work was as interpretive as the work of a playwright (1962:22). Gorelik blamed the production methods of Broadway and Hollywood—the proverbial scapegoat of formalists and structuralists alike—for attaching to the playtext an overwhelming importance at the expense of the other "texts." Gorelik argued that the playtext stands at the center of the economic set-up of Broadway theatre because Broadway productions are assembled by the "casting-office" method. "The productive forces are assembled temporarily for a specific play after which they are disbanded" (1962:18).

Gorelik failed to note that the playtexts of the ancient and modern "masters" of drama—whom he revered—also stood at the center of theatrical production in the darling theatres of the formalists—namely, resident repertory theatre and college or university theatre—despite their different economic setup from Broadway or Hollywood. Although the artistic (i.e., both ideological and aesthetic) orientation and production policy of these companies—as Gorelik justly noted—caused certain types of plays to be composed which would not otherwise be written, such play-production policies did not alter their logocentric orientation, their hierarchical structure, and their general mode of production significantly.

Artistic activities in most theatre companies on and off Broadway continued to be organized after the model of the industrial production line, emphasizing the need for discipline, leadership, and productivity. The energy of the various theatre artists converged into a singular concentrated "aesthetic line." Any detection of individual artistic expression, which disrupted this line, was suppressed for the following reason: regardless of whether the emphasis was on the process or the product, any undisciplined disruption of the aesthetic unity supposedly distracted the other artists and the audience, weakening the impact of the overall effect. So, the crews and the actors turned the prompt-copy into a performance-text, and stabilized its aesthetic unity through technical and dress rehearsals. But who controlled this aesthetic unity, in whose name, and on what criteria?

Gordon Craig assigned to the designer-director the task of bringing all these elements into a harmonious, integrated, aesthetic system for each stage production. Craig's first Platonist dialogue (written in 1905) was a plea for the designer-director as overlord. The designer-director's dictatorial mastermind planned and fashioned everything—from the playtext to the performance-text—skillfully welding together many separate artistic talents and their work (1911:137–181). Craig was determined to found a "new theatre" and to influence "many thousands of younger artists—and older ones too" by offering spectators an experience that would take them "beyond reality" (1983:11, 21).

Craig's new theatre was not a literary theatre such as that founded by the "unnatural" efforts of Goethe, who "marshalled his army of words" (1983:15). Craig's project was intended to free the theatre artists of the "new theatre" from the wordy dominion of literary theatre and from the domination of the playwright. In this sense, Craig proposed to deconstruct the foundation of logocentric theatrical tradition. However, Craig's "new" theatre proved as restrictive and authoritarian as the "old" theatre. Why did Craig's reformation backfire? What corroded his innovative program and preserved, instead of changing, the framework of logocentric theatrical production in his work?

Craig's new theatre preached an elitist directorial gospel which recognized as kindred spirits only those who interpreted playtexts with superior understanding and staged performance-texts with a self-reliant closure. In the vein of the neo-Platonic tradition, Craig joined the vampire dance of the other idealist theatre artists and critics who supposedly revived theatre from its "deadly" slumber by feeding on the blood of the living as they embraced their young victims—and older ones too—into eternal society. Originality would help them transcend time by breaking the confining mold of history and materialism because, by definition, *originality (prototypia)* projected the prototypes of the past as "novelties" in the future. However, their idea of originality also exposed their bias by showing that the history or the materialism of the art of theatre had first to be conceived as a restricting mold.

In search for universal truths, both formalists and structuralists raised material reality to an abstract, ahistorical level—from concrete buildings to human relations. Formalists, such as Boris Aronson, for instance, wanted "to remake reality in the form of abstract visual metaphors" (1989:5). "I strongly believe that for each play you first and foremost create a space which, inherent in its design, already holds the mystique of the entire event," Arronson reportedly said. "My main approach to theatre design is to recognize the individuality of each production in terms of theme and concept of the script" (1989:5). So, Aronson compared hell with the labor conditions in a sweatshop factory on Essex Street on a hot summer day. However, instead of describing specific labor conditions and relations, he represented "hell" as a state of mind and he designed the "factory" in the shape of a huge human profile—a fiery red crucible with steep ladders—in which twenty actors were sliding down the fire pole and returning up the staicase, and sliding down again. Supposedly this design conveyed to the spectator "the flame of work and passion, labor and drudgery" (Figure 10).

Structuralists, such as Ted Hughes, who subscribed to the ideas of T.S. Eliot and Claude Levi-Strauss, believed that myths and poetic speech affect the mind of an audience before they are conceptually understood (Levi-Strauss 1969:12). On the assumption that all languages originated in the physiology of man, Hughes imagined that the mythology of *Orghast* was being enacted within Prometheus' body (Figure 11).

Hughes' sketch of the "physiology" of *Orghast* showed the parts of Prometheus' body in which the myths took place and the sounds they gave rise to. "The figure of Krogon, a great bird of prey, squatted on the shoulders of Prometheus," Anthony Smith described Hughes' sketch, "blotting out the light—Orghast— which, however, was repeated inside him, in the womb, surrounded by fertile, female darkness" (1972:91). In short, Hughes deprived myth of its social and historical dimensions.

The reductive symbols of the theatre formalists (e.g., Boris Aronson's design of Hell in Figure 10) and the oxymoronic myths of the theatre structuralists (e.g., Ted Hughes' drawing of Orghast in Figure 11) attempted to tap the resources proper to the art of theatre and to reformulate the role of this art in the "modern age" (read "scientific age"). If the "laws" of (social) science were timeless (read "ahistorical") and could be harnessed to change the current state of affairs in the world, then these theatre artists and critics wished to repeat the "success" of the (social) scientists in escaping and reshaping history. Their subsequent claims to scientific objectivity and ideological freedom which legitimated the practices of institutionalized power structures—from companies to schools— are being unmasked by the deconstructors. Deconstructive analysis exposes the hierarchies of binary oppositions, inverts and dismantles these oppositions, and resists the emergence of a synthesizing theory or practice which would produce a new organic unity or hierarchical structure.

I will try to show that Craig's reforms backfired because, under the influence of formalism and dualism, he proposed a synthesizing theory which combined (1) several artistic functions in one theatre person and (2) several artistic elements in one aesthetic whole. The trend of combining several functions in one theatre artist can be observed in the work of many theatre artists from Victor Simov and Konstantin Stanislavsky to Mordecai Gorelik and Bertolt Brecht. "To a certain extent the designer was required to be a stage director too," recalled Stanislavsky. "One of the first, and one of the few, well-known painter-directors in those days was Victor Simov" (1963:382).

The trend of combining several artistic elements in one aesthetic whole can be observed in Craig's theory of the five elements. For Craig, the art of theatre was composed of five equally important elements or factors—action, words, lines, colors, and rhythm. Action was "the very spirit of acting"; words were "the body of a play"; lines and colors were "the very heart of scenography"; and rhythm was "the very essence of dance." However, Craig gave action and rhythm, the less tangible of these elements, the privilege of origin by pronouncing action and rhythm the parents of theatre (1911:138). According to Craig, "the (ur)dramatist made his first piece by using action, words, line, color, and rhythm, and making his appeal to our eyes and ears by a dexterous use of these five factors" (1911:140).

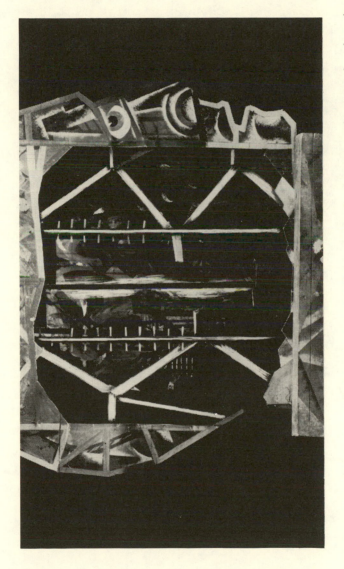

FIGURE 10. Boris Aronson's Design of Hell in Abraham Goldfadden's *The Tenth Commandment* produced at the Yiddish Art Theatre of Maurice Schwartz in 1926. (Source: Boris Aronson, *Stage Design As Visual Metaphor*. Ed. by Frank Rich. Katonah, N.Y.: Katonah Gallery, 1989, p. 6.)

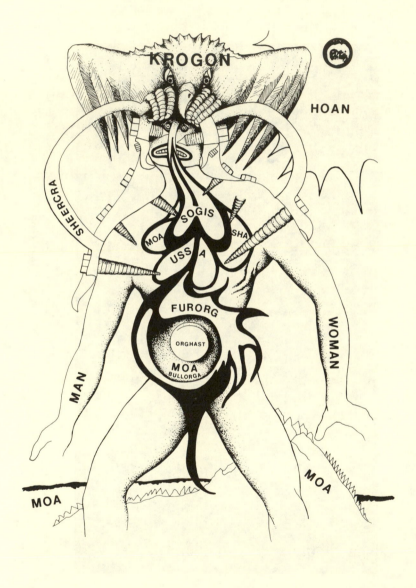

FIGURE 11. Ted Hughes' Physiology of *Orghast*. (Source: Anthony Smith, *Orghast at Persepolis*. New York: Viking Press, 1972, p. 92.)

Therefore, all subsequent playwrights who overlooked action in order to please an audience's ears wrote poetic plays (closet dramas). Poetic plays were readable, not performable, because words were all-important and "the addition of gesture" produced inharmonious results. For example, Shakespeare's *Hamlet* had "so complete a form when read" that it lost heavily whenever it was presented to an audience "after having undergone stage treatment." *Hamlet* was a finished, complete aesthetic object when Shakespeare wrote the last word, and "for us to add to it by gesture, scene, costume, or dance, is to hint that it is incomplete and needs these additions" (Craig 1911:143). Craig proposed such an airtight closure to stop the playtext on the page from leaking onto the stage that makes me wonder why. Lending an ear to Craig could prove as deadly as lending an ear to King Claudius, whose rhetoric of balanced antitheses infected his audience (*Hamlet* 1.2.1–39) as effectively as the poison that he poured into King Hamlet's ear.

If I may switch metaphors here, Craig reminded us that, unlike readers, spectators have been invariably "more eager to *see* what the playwright would *do* than to *hear* what the playwright might *say*" (1911:141). Therefore, all good playwrights who wrote producible playtexts, whether they were using poetry or prose, always spoke "in action"—either poetic action (i.e., dance) or prose action (i.e., gesture). Only these "good" playwrights had "any birth-claim to the theatre —and that a very slight one" (1911:142). Craig allowed even good playwrights a very narrow margin because he wished to reserve the stage and the birthrights for a special kind of designer-director. "*Hamlet* will go on being performed for some time yet, and the duty of the interpreters is to put their best work at its service," Craig wrote. "But, as I have said, the theatre must not forever rely upon having a play to perform, but must in time perform pieces of its own art" (1911:144).

What were those "pieces" that should have replaced the playtexts of playwrights? They were any performances—from pageants to masques—which were entirely intended for the stage and which looked or sounded incomplete when they were written down or were just recited. Clearly, Craig used closure to segregate playtexts from performance-texts, to reverse their hierarchical position, and to displace the playtext from the stage. Craig knew that by shifting around priorities he would create a need for a new kind of theatre artist, the director. Only a technically trained director could interpret the playtexts of dramatists, could recover the ground lost to the theatre, and could restore the art of the theatre "by means of his own creative genius" (1911:147). However, a director could not rise above the status of a master craftsman as long as he interpreted a playtext by means of his designers and actors.

In order to rise to the status of an artist, a director had to know how to control effectively the use of actions, words, line, color, and rhythm. When a director was in control of these five factors, his art was self-reliant and he no longer needed the assistance of a playwright (1911:148). In other words, the designer-director became a capable dramaturge, too. By uniting three functions into one person, Craig turned artistic consciousness into a meat grinder which mashed everything and everyone into a unified aesthetic pulp regurgitated on the stage for the aesthetic pleasure of an audience. The consciousness of Craig's designer-director-dramaturge could always appropriate to itself (read "devour") what was alien or external to it.

This view turned artistic consciousness into a watchdog with three heads, who—like Cerberus at the gates of Hades—controlled everything that went into theatrical production. In the narrow margin that was left for the remaining artists, very few daring deconstructive designers and actors could introduce something else ("other") which Craig's monstrous theatre artist and theatregoers could not bite into ("penetrate" in Grotowski's sense) and appropriate. These supressed designers and actors hoped to make the formalist monster (1) listen to the many barks that constituted its own "singular" voice, (2) realize that its own "internal" voices were as entropic as their "external" voices, and (3) accept that pluralism in interpretation may undermine formalist interests in the theatre but not theatre at large. So, they questioned the margins by which designer-directors, such as Craig, insulated and defined their "new" theatre.

Of course, the various logocentric approaches have been a fundamental resource of making sense of the activities and discourses that constitute what has been generally called "Western theatre." These approaches and the deconstructive approach have been compatible so long as each became a setup for the other to take place. However, some logocentric theatre artists and critics (including Craig) ignored those setups whose rhetoric framed (read "undermined") their innovative endeavors. It is hard to tell to what extent Craig or history controlled the rhetoric of his texts beyond

such changes in terminology as "stage manager" for "stage director."
For example, Craig could not (fore)see the liaisons between "painting
in light" and "computer graphics" nor could Delbert Unruh as late
as 1974 in his essay "Composition in Light" (Unruh 1974:18, 20).
And yet these links go on working of themselves. In spite of Craig?
Thanks to Craig? In Craig's texts? Outside Craig's texts?

If the "discourse" of change cannot be located in one text
or a limited series of texts, then those theatre artists and critics, who
habitually tie their theories and practices to a canon of authoritative
texts, have unjustly excluded all the other texts. Craig, for instance,
created an opposition between playtext (the past) and performance-
text (the future). He presented either text as an autonomous,
indepedent, self-reliant aesthetic object. Then, he oscillated between
page and stage in order to define "modernity" as a timeless value,
not as part of a historical process. His dictatorial designer-director
set up his own house in order to sustain his quest for self-justification.
But he was unable to turn out, turn down, and turn over the inviting
distinction between writing and reading, drawing and speaking.

Craig's director "promised faithfully to interpret the playtext,"
but he read only portions of the text, disregarding the playwright's
stage directions as voices that were "alien" either to the designer-
director's art or to the playwright's text. The case of Shakespeare's
playtexts allowed him to argue that "all the stage directions, from
first to last, were the tame inventions of sundry editors" (1911:154).
Instead, Craig's designer-director focused on the "pictures" painted
by the unraveling speech acts of the characters, and he envisioned
the main properties of the five elements—i.e., movement, tone,
hue, shape, and rhythm—which the playtext must assume on stage
(1911:149). In other words, Craig's designer-director gave priority
and power to speech in determining the properties of the
compositional elements. For this reason, an actor could offend a
playwright by omitting words from the playtext. "It is an offence
to poach on what is the sole property of the playwright" (1911:151).

Likewise, a playwright who "dictated his stage directions,"
could be equally offensive because he "tampered with the art of
the stage director" (1911:151). Since Craig agreed that the stage
directions were of value to the reader, he implied that his director
was not an ordinary reader. He was not an ordinary director either
because he also assumed the function of the set designer, costume
designer, and lighting designer.

> *A* has written a play which *B* promises to interpret faithfully. In
> so delicate a matter as the interpretation of so elusive a thing as
> the spirit of a play, which do you think, will be the surest way
> to preserve the unity of that spirit? Will it be best if *B* does all
> the work by himself? Or, will it do to give the work into the hands
> of *C, D,* and *E,* each of whom sees or thinks differently from *B*
> or *A*? (Craig 1911:156)

Craig argued that it is best that *B* does all the work himself because
"that is the only way the work can be done, if unity, the one thing
vital to a work of art, is to be obtained" (1911:157).

His designer-director did not draw historically accurate
designs. First, he chose certain hues "which seemed to him to be
in harmony with the spirit of the play," rejecting other colors as
out of tune. Then, he wove certain objects into a pattern, using
them as the center of his design. Next, he added the necessary
props, each character in the play, each movement of each character,
and each costume of each character. "Slowly, harmoniously, must
the whole design develop, so that the eye of the beholder shall
be satisfied," concluded Craig. "While this pattern for the eye is
being devised, the designer is being guided as much by the sound
of the verse or prose as by the sense or spirit" (1911:157–158).

Finally, he supervised and guided the building of the sets,
the painting of the props, the tailoring of the costumes, the
memorized lines of the actors, and their interactive movement on
stage. Then, guided by the specific sets, costumes, words, and stage
movement, he took care of the lighting design. "If the word *harmony*
held no significance for him," insisted Craig, "he would of course
leave it to the first comer" (1911:160). His lighting design suggested,
did not reproduce (imitate), natural light. His goal was to bring all
these elements into harmony with one another. The director alone
knew how to preserve the harmony which he started to create.

Consequently, the rest of the theatre artists and crews should
comply with the superior dictates of the director because "the right
and just interpretation of the play, is the all-important thing in the
modern theatre" (1911:166). In the name of unity, harmony, and
"just" interpretation of the play, Craig's "modernism" made theatrical
production regress into a feudal system under an enlightened despot.
Like the captain who controlled every man on a ship, the director
controlled every man on stage and guided the show, like a ship,
to its destination. The slightest disobedience ("mutiny") on the part

of the other theatre artists would be disastrous to the unity and harmony imposed by the director. Therefore, it should be punishable with dismissal (read "exclusion") from the production team—if not the theatre company (1911:171).

The external, rough force by which the idealists established obedience and unity (i.e., power and authority) could not be swallowed (i.e., internalized) by the other theatre artists unless it was sugarcoated. Otherwise, authoritarian designer-directors would risk running one-man companies. So, Craig turned "external" obedience into "internal" discipline. He asked theatre artists to obey willingly the director's authority and vision. He articulated false truisms (1) in attractive slogans, such as "the finer the actor, the finer his intelligence and taste, and therefore the more easily controlled" by the director (1911:168), and (2) in scary aphorisms, such as "until discipline is understood in a theatre to be willing and reliant obedience to the manager or captain, no supreme achievement can be accomplished" (1911:172).

Craig deplored the fact that in the theatres of his day discipline was not held to be of such vital importance as in the military and the navy. Craig assumed that the theatre artists and crews were "enthusiastically willing" to obey the director. They became unruly and disobedient only when, occasionally, their judgement was at fault (1911:172). Craig assumed that his designer-director was infallible and uncorruptible because he was shielded by a "new" orthodoxy (a "new" church) which exorcised evil influence by upholding the "high standards" of the Greco-Christian theatrical tradition. Difference of opinion (*heterodoxy*) was a sinful transgression which debased and prostituted their art—the wages of disobedience. The "bad" officers of the "theatrical navy," who catered to "vulgar" audience demand, took advantage of those fallen theatre artists. "What the theatre people have not yet quite comprehended," declared Craig, "*is the value of a high standard and the value of a director who abides by it*" (1911:172).

Craig would allow a playwright to become a designer-director in his "modern theatre" only when the playwright had studied and practiced set design, costume design, lighting design, acting, and dance (1911:175). However, Craig would not allow an actor to become a designer-director even though, historically, many actors had become leading directors. Craig explained his reasons for this discrimination in formalist terms: if an exceptional actor becomes a director to the play in which he has a part, he will lose perspective. As a director, he should have a complete view of the performance, but as an actor, he will only have a partial view of it. He cannot do both, and he will gradually cease to look upon the work as a whole. "And this is not good for the work," concluded Craig. "This is not the way a work of art is to be produced in the theatre" (1911:173).

Craig's modern theatre would come to be when a technique was invented that would turn it into a "masterpiece of mechanism" and would allow it to "develop a *creative art* of its own" (1911:176). Since the entire art of theatre was divided into many parts of tightly interrelated crafts—set design, costume design, lighting design, acting, dancing, singing, and so on—significant change could take place only if all the crafts of the theatre—not just one or two— were reformed in the same theatre company simultaneously, evenly, in a systematic progression. "*The whole renaissance of the Art of Theatre depends upon the extent that this is realised*" (1911:177). In short, Craig entrusted the reform of the art of theatre only to the hands of those "watchdogs" who had studied and had practiced all the crafts of the theatre and, therefore, had at least three heads in one body (1911:177). The global, not fragmented perspective, of a playwright-designer-director would help theatre "stand self-reliant as a creative art, and no longer as an interpretative craft" (1911:178).

Craig, therefore, advised the theatre artists to use or invent different material from the material of the dramatic poet in order to give form to an idea. They should create their masterpieces from the materials of action (both gesture and dancing), scene (lighting, costume, scenery), and voice (1911:180). "When I say *voice*, I mean the spoken word or the word which is sung," Craig explained, "in contradiction to the word which is read, for the word written to be spoken and the word written to be read are two entirely different things" (1911:181). Bertolt Brecht pursued Craig's agenda.

In sum, Craig took the long detour above because he followed two misplaced arrows: How could a theatre artist avoid interpretation which was branded as a secondary activity? How could a theatre artist secure creativity which was esteemed as a primary activity? Craig proposed two solutions to this problem. (1) He could avoid interpretation and secure creativity by condensing the functions of three separate artists into one master-brain. (2) He should no longer (re)present a playtext written by a playwright to an audience—which implied that theatre artists should stop taking it for granted that what "is presented to an audience must be made of words" (1911:179). In either case, Craig's project reaffirmed the values of phonocentrism and idealism.

Like the weird sisters in Shakespeare's *Macbeth*, the three functions of playwriting, designing, and directing met again in the master-brain of Bertolt Brecht, who realized Craig's dream before the advent of computer technology in the field of theatre. Peter Brook was among the first to notice this connection. "There is an interesting relationship between Brecht and Craig," wrote Brook. "Craig wanted a token shadow to take the place of a complete painted forest and he only did so because he recognized that useless information absorbed our attention *at the expense of something more important.* Brecht took this rigour and applied it not only to scenery but to the work of the actor and to the attitude of the audience" (1968:75).

The first duty of the designer-director, according to Craig, was "to create a simplified stage" by reviewing and discarding theatrical material from past epochs and retaining only what was capable of renewed expression (1983:51). For Craig, theatre was a composite art with its own laws which, by foregrounding a few parts from the whole, permitted the "soul" to be separated from the "body" of the environment. To a certain extent, Brecht forged ahead on the trail that earlier was blazed by Appia and Craig in his quest for "gestic music" (1964:104) and for simple gests (Craig's "images") which could replace "one thousand words" because they could distill and expose the deceptive rhetoric of everyday life and, in this way, transcend and enhance its meaning. Brook, as a structuralist, was concerned about Brecht's formalist virus.

> Brecht himself always insisted on directing his own plays. He would take many months to direct the first production, and for him, that first production then became the blueprint for every successive production, and he would have every detail noted, and then would send these elaborate prompt books and photographs around Germany for other people, assistants, to use. But that is terrifyingly dangerous. It seems one is on a knife edge, where there is a balance between two opposites. (Brook 1988:58)

Brecht's desire to control both the first production that he directed and all subsequent productions of his plays infringed upon the artistic freedom of designers and directors who staged his playtexts or rather his prompt-books. "Your representative Frau Berlau gave full information about your wishes to myself, the producer, the scene designer, and the actors," director E. Winds told Brecht in 1949. "This was backed up by a large number of stage photographs together with explanatory texts and also by your written stage directions. As it's hardly usual in the theatre for an author to influence a production in such a detailed way, and we in Wuppental are trying the experiment for the first time in this clear-cut form, it would be interesting to know your reasons for evolving a model production and setting it up as a definitive example for others to work on" (Brecht 1964:222).

Recent technological innovations make Brecht's dream and Brook's nightmare come true in the twenty-first century because they will enable a Brecht-like or a Craig-like playwright-designer-director to "write" a computer-animated prompt-copy of his play and design it for two standard stage types—square (box) and rectangular (procenium). In the 1980s, computer graphics gave a playwright-designer-director the capability to design human figures (characters) in various settings (locales), and then light ("shade") and color this animated prompt-copy with numerical spotlights. The 1980s technology also allowed him to record the animated scenes of his prompt-copy on an Abicus which was a still-frame storer that could record 750 frames—i.e., about 35 seconds of animation—at a time. Then, the images which made up a scene could be shown on a monitor and edited onto a one-inch videotape. The playwright-designer could add music, "fades," and "dissolves" in the final editing process.

In Craig's theatre of the future, the playwright-designer-director will be able to store a complete prompt-copy on a disk and mail it to all perspective theatre companies at a reasonable price. The control that both Craig and Brecht desired over the dissemination of their work was achieved for lighting design in the 1980s. From the productions of *A Chorus Line* to *Les Miserables*, the idea of computer memory control of lighting was introduced into the theatre in a big way. However, I should note here that the producers of such shows were not after the idea of repetition of the original production in subsequent productions in the manner of Craig or

Brecht. For example, the designers involved in *Les Miserables* computerized the lighting so that they could save money and so that all subsequent performances of the original production would be lighted the same—wherever and whenever they happened—in Chigaco, New York, London, or Vienna.

Nonetheless, the inventions used in productions such as the above can also be used to advance plans—similar to those of Craig and Brecht—to exert control over different productions, produced by different people at different places at different times. In short, lighting design was the first "craft" (Craig's term) to benefit from computer technology. The audiences of such performances enjoyed flawless, smooth transitions, cross-fades, and turntable movements controlled by the microprocessor. To the dismay of the humanists, the audiences did not lament the loss of "the human touch" in lighting changes during the show.

CHAPTER FOUR

Visual Presentation

Theatre has been perceived as an institution—i.e., an objectified social activity with established, predictable roles and functions—since the days of Plato and Aristotle. These "established" roles and functions among playwrights, designers, directors, actors, spectators, and critics were often stretched or altered over the years by "unpredictable" technological inventions and artistic innovations. Among other things, inventions and innovations affected (1) the way in which designers and directors expressed their production concept(s) in a series of (computer-animated) sketches, shaping the signifying capability of their work, and (2) the degree to which designers served their own artistic goals or the objectives of playwrights, directors, or actors.

At the beginning of the twentieth century, for example, Stanislavsky complained about the "painter-designers" who were attracted by the popularity of the theatre and used theatrical productions to exhibit their paintings. "Indeed, art exhibitions are visited only by hundreds of people and that for the brief period that they are open," Stanislavsky remarked. "The theatre, on the other hand, is visited by thousands, day after day, month after month. It was only natural that the painters saw this advantage" (1963:382). Not withstanding the publicity tricks of the "painters," which Stanislavsky readily exposed, his dissatisfaction with them had three more serious motives.

Stanislavsky supported an actor-oriented performance-text; he searched for "inner realism" rather than for "external naturalism"; and he advocated a formalist organic unity founded on military discipline (1963:312, 334, 382). "I was becoming more and more disappointed in the work of artists," he explained, "in canvas, in paint, in cardboard, in the outward means of production, and in the stage direction hokum" (1963:336–337). Stanislavsky became acquainted with Craig and his ideas in 1908. "Like myself," wrote Stanislavsky, "he had come to hate theatrical scenery. What he needed was a simple background for the actor, out of which one would be able, however, to draw an endless number of moods with the help of lines and light spots" (1963:388). Since Stanislavsky, many directors—from Antonin Artaud to Jerzi Grotowski—have challenged the status and significance of the designers by reducing scenography in their productions or by drafting their own designs.

Except for the "unruly" painters about whom directors sometimes complained, the collaboration between designers and directors generally implied that the designer served the priorities of directors and actors—not the other way around. "The best designer evolves step by step with the director," Peter Brook argued, "going back, changing, scrapping, as a conception of the whole takes form" (1968:92). In short, the "best" designers effaced their artistic priorities in order to serve those set before them by playwrights, directors, or actors who patronized their artistic and professional "evolution."

In this artistic and professional climate, the designers were transformed into shortsighted servants who, unless assisted, could not see beyond the surface into the inner, deeper truths of art and life explored by their masters. According to Edmond Jones, the designer should serve the actors because the actors were "seers" who, thanks to their inspiration, excited by that of the playwright, expressed timeless themes, and they intimated immortality (1925:14). According to Gordon Craig, the designer should serve the playwright's thoughts otherwise disharmony would erupt. "The question here is not how to create some distracting scenery," wrote Craig, "but rather how to create a place which harmonizes with the thoughts of the poet" (1911:22).

Despite his anti-formalist, anti-naturalist, anti-Aristotelian, and anti-Stanislavskian posture, Brecht cherished similar views roughly from 1930 to 1950 when he described the work of his designer Caspar Neher—revealing an alarming level of formalism in his theory and practice of the art of theatre. For Brecht, the "best" designers first gave the playtext a masterful reading, but they then avoided pedantically copying external, inessential (background) decorative details which would distract the spectator's attention from the intellectual and artistic statement of reality made by the playwright and the actors. Instead, the "best" designers showed only "the essential" details which were graced with beauty and which were carefully selected and placed in three-dimensional sets that expressed the atmosphere of the playtext, making significant statements about reality (1964:230). Specifically, many props were museum pieces and the hand-props were "always authentic".

However, Brecht's designer represented interior and exterior spaces by indication, which supposedly stimulated the spectator's imagination. According to Brecht, imitation numbed imagination. So, the basic impression was of "very lightly constructed, easily transformed, and beautiful pieces of scaffolding, which furthered the acting and helped to tell the evening's story fluently" (1964:232). Overall, the sets and props reminded the audience of the artificial nature of the environment on stage, and they displayed "a lovely mixture" of the handwritings ("signatures") of the designer and of the playwright (1964:231).

Brecht's designer sometimes helped the director with blocking, gestures, and idiolects, but he always started his designs from the characters' situation and thoughts as revealed in the playtext by the playwright. "He is a great painter," Brecht said in praise of the designer of many of his productions. "But above all he is an ingenious storyteller. He knows better than anyone that whatever does not further the narrative harms it" (1964:232). With this last statement, Brecht raised narrative on page and on stage to a privileged, all-important position. Unless the designers placed their art in the service of the playwright's narrative, they could only create a damaging dissonance. This restriction illustrated Brecht's desire to control the visual representation of his playtext on stage, but it also touched upon a more serious problem that I will discuss here.

Brecht proposed the epic production style as an alternative to the production styles established by what he called the Aristotelian and the Stanislavskian traditions. He believed that the epic style would help theatre artists to change the patterns set by capitalist theatrical production, and, in turn, it would enlighten theatregoers gradually to alter their restrictive social structures. Unlike the socialist-realist production style which was employed under Eastern-Block communism and emphasized reconstruction, the epic production style was employed under Western capitalism and emphasized the deconstruction of the "shaky foundations" of the German socioeconomic structure.

The collapse of the Berlin Wall and of the communist regime in East Germany in 1989 as well as the revitalization of communist economy by West German capitalism created an embarassing paradox for the advocates of the Brechtian tradition, who had high hopes for the mission of their theatre as an ideological platform. The decreasing influence of theatre in postwar societies can explain, in part, why Brecht and his followers failed to have as massive an appeal to the public as their rivals who controlled more technologically advanced media, such as radio, film, and television. But it cannot explain why Brecht retained in his epic production style several logocentric tenets of the Western theatrical tradition which he would have rejected based on his alternative approach.

Brecht was aware that new technology enhanced the narrative capabilities of theatre artists and that it was new technology which made the epic production style possible—as an alternative to what he called the Aristotelian production style. He also realized that the narrative technique of the epic production style was far from perfect, and it could be further improved with new technological and artistic innovations. However, Brecht did not suppress or reject the Aristotelian production style, even though he insisted that it should not be allowed to monopolize the stage and further its social goals. "I myself," Brecht admitted, "can use both Aristotelian and non-Aristotelian theatre in certain productions" (1964:135). And so he did in *Galileo* (1938), *Mother Courage* (1939), and *The Good Person of Szechwan* (1940).

Does this mean that he occasionally compromised his anti-Aristotelian posture or that he nourished a latent formalism which, at least in theory, helped him reconcile "irreconcilable" production styles and ideologies? Brecht's formalism can be detected in his desire to create a production style that was both instructive (socialist realism) and entertaining (bourgeois realism) while, at the same time, it would turn the playhouse from a "home of illusions to a home of experiences." His desire for theatrical experiences that would both instruct and entertain goes back to Horace. "I have here Horace's *Ars Poetica* in Gottsched's translation," Brecht wrote. "He really expresses a theory that often concerns us, one that Aristotle proposed for the theatre" (1964:270). Brecht cited both Horace and Johann Gottsched, but not Aristotle.

Horace advised Roman playwrights and actors in Rome in 13 B.C. in a manner similar to that of Stanislavsky in Moscow in A.D. 1913: if they wished to make their readers or their spectators weep, they must first express suffering themselves; only then would readers or spectators feel the blow of the characters' misfortunes (*Ars Poetica* 101–104). Brecht also mentioned that in this passage Gottsched cited Cicero's description of how Polus, a Roman (sic) actor who played Electra, receiving an urn supposed to contain her brother's ashes in Sophocles' *Electra* used an urn containing the ashes of his recently deceased son. Polus' personal loss made him weep real tears and move the audience. Brecht regarded this "Aristotelian" acting style as "barbaric," but obviously he read Aristotle's text through the eyes of Horace, Cicero, and Gottsched.

Gottsched, a critic and professor of logic and metaphysics at the University of Leipzig in 1734, introduced the standards of eighteenth-century French critics such as Nicolas Boileau to the German theatre. In collaboration with actress Caroline Neuber, he established the Leipzig school of acting and criticism. They followed neo-Classical models in their attempt to raise German theatre from a "base" medium for "crude" sensual entertainment to a "respected" medium for serious literary drama. Ironically, Brecht's anti-Aristotelian, Marxist project rested on Gottsched's idealist interpretations of Greek and Roman theatre—exposing Brecht's weak knowledge of Classical theatre. For example, Polus was not a Roman actor as Brecht thought, but a Greek actor of tragedies who probably lived in Aegina and was son of Charicles from Sounion (*Noctes Atticae* VI.v; *Menippus ē Nekyomanteia* 16, *Zeus Tragōidos* 3, 41; *Dēmosthenēs* xxvii.3). Indicatively, Brecht, who opposed Aristotelian poetics, never quoted Aristotle's *On Poetics* directly or in translation.

Instead, Brecht based his anti-Aristotelian posture on four premises. First, the epic and the dramatic were no longer two separate, rigidly opposed ways of telling a story to the public through the medium of the written word and the medium of the living actors, respectively. Instead of being a contradiction in terms, the "epic theatre" pointed to the fact (1) that epic works and dramatic works had both dramatic and epic elements in their narratives and (2) that some epic works (e.g., Homer's *The Iliad*) were performed whereas some dramatic works (e.g., Goethe's *Faust*) were more effective as books. "This is no place to explain how the opposition of epic and dramatic lost its rigidity after having long been held to be irreconcilable," Brecht wrote. "Let us just point out that the technical advances alone (mechanized stage and film projection) were enough to permit the stage to incorporate an element of the narrative in its dramatic productions" (1964:70).

Second, pleasure and instruction were no longer two separate, rigidly opposed goals for telling a story to the public. Thanks to the "gestic principle," epic theatre showed (1) that the "inexorable fate" of human affairs was of "human contrivance," not of invisible metaphysical powers outside man or of personified, primal "motive forces" inside man and (2) that the pleasurable spiritual cleansing (*catharsis*) of the spectators did not need to take place through empathy or identification with the protagonist's archetypal, spiritual, or psychological conflicts brought about by carefully contrived plots which made the connection of the events appear believable (1964:181, 183). In this sense, an "Aristotelian play" was static because it showed the world as it was by appealing to the emotions of the spectators as a mob, whereas a "learning-play" was dynamic because it explained how the world was changing or could be changed by appealing to the reasoning and judgment of the spectators as individuals (1964:80). Brecht's theatre became a place for philosophers—not necessarily of the Gottsched type.

Third, the natural and the stylized were no longer two separate, arbitrarily disconected modes of presenting a story to the public. Instead, stylization turned nature (real world) into art (dramatic world) because—by Brecht's definition—stylization produced a "general elaboration" of what was natural in order to show the spectators what was important in the story for their society. The activities of playwrights, designers, directors, and actors became art only though a stylization which heightened, but did not destroy, "naturalness" in the process. For instance, the text of a playwright was "sacred" when it was "true" to the real world (society) rather than to the implausible whims of his imagination. So, regarding the style of presentation, Brecht agreed with Aristotle that a probable story (narrative) is the kernel (soul) of a social drama (tragedy). Brecht also endorsed an Aristotelian closure, even though Brecht insisted that the story should never confine itself only to spiritual or psychological conflicts. For Brecht, the story "ought to contain everything and be the object of all of our attentions, so that once it has been told the whole thing is concluded" (1964:183, 213).

Fourth, the designer's work was no longer a separate entity under the epic production style, which theoretically had rejected symbolism and had turned Stanislavsky's naturalism into realism. In fact, Brecht, whose enthusiasm made him disregard history at this point, thought that a "complete revolution" took place in stage design just because Neher designed pleasing (beautiful) and instructive (didactic) sets that were based on the actors' needs as established during rehearsals. According to Brecht, this setup encouraged collaboration and mutual influence among playwright, designer, and actor (1964:134). Brecht, who sounded like a distant echo of Lessing, claimed that the designer regained his independence and was able to express his view of the theme of the playtext through his own artistic means. "The integrated work of art (or *Gesamtkunstwerk*) appeared before the spectator as a bundle of separate elements" (1964:134).

Interestingly, Brecht's anti-Aristotelian premises, which emphasized unity and integration, did not deviate significantly from the course set by Aristotle's text. In his third premise, for instance, Brecht openly endorsed Aristotle's fundamental tenet that the story is the soul of a play. However, Brecht was "hooked" on Aristotle more deeply than he cared to admit or suspected. For example, Brecht argued in his first anti-Aristotelian premise that epics and plays had both dramatic elements (impersonation) and epic elements (description) in their narratives. Aristotle could not have said it any better when he praised Homer for being aware that the epic poet should speak in his own person as little as possible, otherwise the poet is not being an imitator (*On Poetics* 1460a 6–15).

In the following chapters, I will try to explain how and why Brecht's "deconstructive" project, which was based on an anti-Aristotelian posture, nourished a formalism and a neo-Kantian idealism which were more logocentric and authoritarian than Aristotle's views about the written playtext and its visual presentation in the theatre.

First, I will challenge the allegation that Aristotle underrated the art of the designers. In order to prove that Aristotle gave the designer's art an equal, complementary status to the playwright's art, I will examine the misinterpretations of several popular formalist and structuralist translations of Aristotle's *On Poetics*. Second, I will explore how idealist concepts and dominant production conditions undermined Brecht's project by guiding him into preserving (instead of rejecting) several patterns of the logocentric theatrical production.

Brecht, of course, consulted Gottsched's translation. However, the popular English translations of Aristotle's *On Poetics* that I selected for discussion, have been important in establishing pro-Aristotelian as well as anti-Aristotelian perceptions in the English-speaking world of theatre. Next to translations such as John Willett's *Brecht on Theatre*, these texts account, to a certain extent, for the Brechtian and anti-Aristotelian tradition in the English-speaking sector of the academic and professional theatre. My focus is on the legacy of (mis)perceptions which condition current Brechtian practice in this sector, not on the "original" sins and errors committed by Brecht and other anti-Aristotelians.

The formalist "virus" that Peter Brook detected in Brecht's aesthetic theory has been traced back to the Russian formalists (Bennett 1979:31; Brook 1987:58; Hoover 1973:39; Mitchell 1974: 76, 78, 81; Willett, in Brecht 1964:99) although its alleged source of origin was occasionally doubted (Brooker 1988:62). However, in Brecht's case, the dissemination of concepts may have taken more intricate paths than any direct borrowing can explain. For example, Roman Jakobson's "the dominant" (*dominanta*), Viktor Shklovsky's "defamiliarization" (*ostranenie*), and Jan Mukařovský's "semantic gesture" were concepts directly affected by Broder Christiansen's ideas of "the dominant" (*dominante*) and "quality of divergence" (*differenzqualitaten*). Whether Brecht developed the concepts of "gest" (*Gestus*) and "alienation effect" (*Verfremdungseffekt*) working independently within the mindset of the 1930s or borrowed them from texts such as Shklovksy's "Art as Technique" (1917), Jakobson's "The Dominant" (1935), or Christiansen's neo-Kantian *Philosophy of Art* (1909), the fact remains that idealist notions found their way into Brecht's Marxist project and were readily absorbed by the English-speaking sector of the Brechtian tradition in academic and professional theatre (Brooker 1988:17; Esslin 1971:126; Gray 1976:182).

In his treatise *On Poetics*, Aristotle identified six necessary ingredients that Athenian playwrights used in writing tragedies: *muthos, ta ēthē, dianoia, lexis, melopoiia, and opsis*. These were widely and repeatedly mistranslated as "plot," "character," "thought," "diction," "song," and "spectacle," respectively. The translation of *opsis* as "spectacle," "scenery," or "visual adornment" encouraged the following assumption among formalist theatre artists and scholars who often called themselves (neo-)Aristotelians: Aristotle ranked the six ingredients according to their importance—with *muthos* at the top and *opsis* at the bottom—and he dismissed *opsis* as the least artistic of all ingredients (Tr. Halliwell 1987:93). Since Aristotle wrote that one could be affected by reading a tragedy without seeing it performed by actors, they also assumed that Aristotle considered the designers' art as secondary or extraneous to the compositional art and emotional affect of tragedy.

Many reputable and popular translations supported the above misperception. For example, Samuel Butcher translated Aristotle's text (lines 1450b 17-21) as follows: "The *scenery* has, indeed an emotional attraction of its own, but of all the parts, it is the least artistic, and connected least with the art of poetry. For the power of Tragedy, we may be sure, is felt even apart from representation and actors. Besides, the production of *spectacular effects* depends more on the art of the *stage machinist* than on that of the poet" (1898:29). In the 1951 edition of Butcher's translation, which was prefaced by John Gassner, the word "scenery" was replaced with the word "spectacle."

The students of English who consulted Lane Cooper's "amplified" translation read a similar view: "The *element of Spectacle* though it arouses the interest of the audience, is last in importance, since it demands the lowest order of artistic skill, and is least connected with the art of poetry as such. A tragedy can produce its effect independently of a stage performance and actors—that is, when it is read; and besides the business of *preparing the stage and the actors* is the affair of the *costumer* rather than of poets" (1913:27–28). Cooper's interpretation, in turn, influenced Ingram Bywater's translation: "The *Spectacle*, though an attraction, is the least artistic of all the parts, and has least to do with *the art of poetry*. The tragic effect is quite possible without a public performance and actors; and besides, *the getting-up of the Spectacle* is more a matter of the *costumer* than the poet" (1920:39). To put it mildly, the above translations underplayed the importance of the designer's art.

The tide changed in the 1960s when the structuralist approach encouraged the English-speaking theatre artists and scholars to observe the art of theatrical production "scientifically" and to describe the structure of its functions in "binary oppositions." Kenneth Telford, for instance, translated the above lines afresh: "*Spectacle*, though it attracts the soul, is the most unartistic and least appropriate to *poetic science*. For the power of tragedy is possible even without a contest and performers, and moreover, *the execution of spectacles more authoritatively belongs to the art of the costume-maker than to that of the poet*" (1961:14). Likewise, Gerald Else proposed a slight variation: "The *visual adornment* of the dramatic persons can have a strong emotional effect, but is the least artistic element, the least connected with the *poetic art*, in fact, the force of tragedy can be felt even without benefit of public performance and actors, while for *the production of the visual effect the property man's art is even more decisive than that of the poets*" (1967:29). To put it mildly again, the translations after 1960 overplayed the importance of the designer's art.

Evidently, the translations of Aristotle's text changed as the dominant mind-set of theatre artists and scholars changed over the decades—illustrating the deconstructors' notorious thesis that "all" interpretations rest on misinterpretation. Then, how would Jon or I translate the above text before we would begin deconstructing our own interpretations? I do not know about Jon, but I would point out that, speaking of the *opsis* (i.e., the *visual presentation*, which included what today is the combined result of directing, acting, set design, costume design, and lighting design), Aristotle observed that:

> *hē de opsis psuchagōgikon men, atechnotaton de kai hēkista oikeion tēs poiētikēs; isōs gar tēs tragōidias dunamis kai aneu agonos kai hupokriton estin, eti de kuriōtera peri tēn apergasian tōn opseōn hē tou skeuopoiou technē tēs tōn poiētōn estin. (peri poiētikēs* 1450b 17–21)

and the *visual presentation* is indeed persuasive, but it is most unartistic (on the page) and the least related to playwriting; perhaps because the strength of tragedy exists even without stage-contest and actors, and because the art of the designer is more important for the completion of *visual presentations* than the art of the playwrights.

Apparently, Aristotle did not talk about the "art" or about the "science" of poetry in the above excerpt. He did not decide "authoritatively" on behalf of either the playwright or the "designer" (alias "property man," "costumer," "stage machinist," or what-have-you). He did not create a hierarchy with the specific purpose to rank the *opsis* (visual presentation) at the bottom. In fact, in two separate instances, where he enumerated the six necessary ingredients of tragedy (1450a 13–15 and 1450a 7–10), he placed the *opsis* (visual presentation) first and fifth, respectively. If indeed "*opsis*" meant "visual presentation," then it appeared last—not at the bottom—in Aristotle's discussion on the composition of Greek tragedy because, from the playwright's standpoint, the "visual (re)presentation" of a playtext was the last step in the linear progression of logocentric theatrical production, and it was often beyond the playwright's immediate control and expertise—as Aristotle suggested.

The different interpretations of the term *opsis* in Aristotle's *On Poetics* exemplify the main concern of this book—not only because the term is the first recorded instance of what later came to be regarded as a dichotomy between playtexts and performance-texts, but also because "interpretation" has been used by successive generations to establish a preferable hierarchical order in the functions and working relationships among the theatre artists during logocentric theatrical productions. Indeed, Aristotle talked about two media in the above excerpt: the page and the stage. A reader could feel the force of tragedy by *reading* it without *seeing* it performed on stage. In this case, the designer's art was the least artistic element to the goals of the playwright because the costumes, props, sets, etc., played no role in affecting the reader or in the composition (i.e., the actual "writing") of the tragedy. Conversely, a spectator could feel the force of tragedy by *seeing* it without *reading* it. In this case, the designer's art was more important than the art of the playwright in "completing" the performance-text for the spectator. In short, Aristotle gave the designers and the playwrights an equal, complementary status in their respective areas, the page and the stage. The playwright's art assumed a primary position in the reader's experience, whereas the designer's art assumed a primary position in the spectator's experience.

If indeed Aristotle discussed the composition of tragedies from the standpoint of playwriting in the above excerpt, then any formalist philologist would demand that Jon or I present solid textual proof that the word "*opsis*" (signifier) among Greek speakers in the fourth century B.C. generated a concept (signified) similar (equivalent) to the concept (signified) elicited by the term "visual presentation" (signifier) among the English speakers in the twentieth century A.D. My friend would simply refuse to be dragged into a "wild goose chase" for a transcendental signified. If pressed harder, I would point out instances of interpretive impass (*aporia*) that I found in formalist and structuralist translations of Aristotle's text. For example, the following sentence provides a clue—not solid evidence—that the ancient Greek "*opsis*" may be equated with the Anglo-American "visual presentation" as "performance": "*kai gar opseis echei pan,*" wrote Aristotle, "*kai ēthos kai muthon kai lexin kai melos kai dianoian ōsautōs*" (1450a 13–15).

Butcher translated this sentence as follows: "in fact, every play contains Spectacular elements as well as Character, Plot, Diction, Song, and Thought" (1898:27). Bywater, too, translated this sentence as shiftily as Butcher: "as every play, one may say, admits to Spectacle, Character, Fable, Diction, Melody, and Thought" (1920:36). Gerald Else avoided translating the sentence altogether, and explained his reasons in a note at the end of his book:

> I omit an interpolated (as I consider it) subject of the verb: "not a few of them, more or less" (the expression is crude, perhaps corrupted), and, following "use," another list of the six "parts." Its purpose, even its connection with the preceding passage, is unclear, and the order appears to be even more random than before: "for in fact the whole (?) contains visual appearance(?) and character and plot and verbal expression and song and thought in the same way (?!). (Else 1967:90-91)

Else could not make heads or tails of Aristotle's sentence. Nor could his formalist predecessors who glossed over the moot point with their smooth (i.e., "pulverizing") harmonious translations. Aristotle's sentence expressed a parenthetic opinion which was dissonant to their readings of Aristotle's "familiar" voice. This "other" opinion or "different" voice of Aristotle embarrassed their interpretations because it reversed the seasoned hierarchy of the ingredients (alias, "elements" or "parts") that Aristotle discussed in detail shortly thereafter. Butcher and Bywater "hushed" this "deviant" opinion in the text of their translations whereas Else "deleted" this "interpolation" from the text of his translation. Else considered it a "crude" and "corrupt" sentence that no longer merited inclusion because it suggested a "different" or "random" order of things.

I would translate Aristotle's sentence as follows: "and likewise, of course, visual presentations ("performances"?) have them all, and *ēthos* and *muthos* and *lexin* and *melos* and *dianoia*"—without translating the terms which are not at issue here. I would also avoid glossing over the "different" opinion or exclude it from the text of my translation. Aristotle's sentence reads like a parenthetic statement in which Aristotle shifted his attention from playtexts to mention that, likewise, the visual presentation of a playtext has the same ingredients. This momentary shift in Aristotle's text threw many generations of interpreters off balance. They regained their step and confused the issue by bringing Aristotle's statement (1) "in line" with his earlier train of thought about playtexts and (2) "in focus" with their mind-set—not the other way around.

Thus, they interpreted *opsis* as spectacle, scenery, *mise en scene*, visual adornment, and so on, making it difficult for themselves to see why Aristotle felt free to upset his "hierarchy" by placing the *opsis* first. They assumed that this was a contradiction, failing to realize that, according to Aristotle, *opsis* (as visual presentation) can exist as a separate system in which the traces—i.e., the other five ingredients regulating the composition of playtexts—could reappear in a different order. All this confusion manifests the slipery relationship among signifiers, signifieds, and their referents. It shows that dominant mind-sets make people blindly or deliberately suppress or exclude different opinions and voices from (their) texts. And it calls for a reinterpretation and re-evaluation of two major traditions in the field of theatre: the Aristotelian tradition—with its philological, humanistic, and artistic gear—and the anti-Aristotelian tradition, whose advocates, such as Brecht, based their polemics on (mis)interpretations of the above kind.

It is significant that the advocates of anti-Aristotelian aesthetics did not elevate the art of theatre design from the secondary, supplementary status which supposedly Aristotle had assigned to it. I will argue that their negligence was motivated by three reasons: (1) a dose of dualism which retained a hierarchy both between two artistic functions and between two theatrical "texts"; (2) an adverse economic-ideological environment which lured them to retain a repressive, logocentric orientation in their alternative theatres or production styles; (3) a subtle formalism which, under the cover of Marxist rhetoric, privileged the study of playtexts apart from their "visual presentations" (*opsets*). Brecht's epic theatre presented such a case of anti-Aristotelian aesthetics.

Brecht inadvertently showed the authoritarian side of his epic project in 1949 when he gave two reasons why designers, directors, and actors ought to follow his "model productions" (i.e., "model prompt-copies") as a definitive example. To begin with, Brecht distinguished between "imitation" (i.e., the way in which a naturalist production style "copied" reality) and "model building" (i.e., the way in which an epic production style "explained" reality). Thanks to its explanatory power, the epic production style could reverse the order of things and become a model *for* reality. So, the *best* way designers, directors, and actors could approach epic theatre was first by copying Brecht's model production and then by explaining the reasons why Brecht designed groupings, movements, gestures, and settings the way he did. "Probably one needs to have made a copy before one can make one's own model" (Brecht 1964:222). Copying preceded model-building and was differentiated from model-building, which was regarded as a superior activity.

Model-building required higher skills than copying. A theatre artist could "evolve" from the low art of copying into the high art of model-building through training. However, regardless of skill and training, there was always "slavish imitation" and "masterful imitation" according to Brecht. The turning point where a theatre artist's "copying" was transformed into "art" occurred when "routine" and "rigidity" were eliminated from his work. Brecht wanted his "model production" (i.e., "prompt-copy") to be taken as the starting point for the rehearsals—especially by those theatre artists who were unfamiliar with blockings that could "tell stories," or with playtexts whose stories required an epic production style.

Although Brecht did not consider the copying of his production models a disgraceful activity for designers, directors, and actors, he did not think very highly of them. Brecht claimed that the directors, designers, and actors who copied his "model productions" did not restrict or lose their artistic freedom because they lived in a period when theatrical production was in a state of anarchy; they were already enslaved to old prejudices, conventions, and complexes; and they already obeyed audience demand—writing and producing plays to satisfy their patrons' tastes. So, "how can they have much freedom to lose?" Brecht wondered (1964:223). Instead of catering to audience demand, Brecht proposed that designers, directors, and actors should cater to the demands of an "enlightened" playwright. Obviously, Brecht wished to replace the "anarchy" of the capitalist theatre market with the "new order" of an inegalitarian communism where now the Marxist playwright-seer reigned supreme over the other theatre artists and their audiences.

Brecht ranked Marxist playtexts higher than their "tainted" performance-texts which went through a capitalist theatrical production. He advocated "an increasingly precise description of reality" through the development of "a genuinely realistic" production style—i.e., the epic production style, which could theoretically make the new socialist reality visible to the public (1964:224). So, Brecht designed his "model productions" exclusively to make the process of representing and influencing reality more precise, differentiated, imaginative, and charming (1964:225). Brecht expropriated realism—as an inherited bourgeois concept—before he used it to describe the "realism" of sets and words in his epic production style. For example, the sets, whose materials ought to be visible, should give the spectators truthful representations of life. There should be no faking by making a canvas backdrop look like a brick wall (1964:107, 233). Like the words in a playtext which tell a verbal story, the sets should tell their own visual story and have their own climax.

Both verbal and visual representations needed a "thorough cleanup" before they could be thrown together to be "smelted" and used by the epic production style. In short, words and sets needed to be cleansed of their impure, historical, bourgeois past and to be recharged by their (historical) socialist present (1964:107). Brechtian realist writing on paper and on stage was conditioned to the last detail by the question of how, when, and by which class it was used (1964:109). Brecht felt that the sanitized dramatic worlds of his playtexts and model prompt-copies risked contamination when they were disseminated by decadent capitalist theatrical productions.

Brecht mistrusted the capitalist theatre market, which resisted any change of its functions (MacGabe 1974:21). So, it seemed desirable to him—and by implication to all Brechtian Marxists—to read the plays which were written with the specific purpose of changing the established capitalist theatre industry instead of watching them performed by one or more of its theatre companies. Why would such a policy seem desirable to Brecht? He felt that the capitalist theatrical production neutralized the social message (i.e., the playwright's intention) which was embedded in a playtext:

> Today we see the theatre being given absolute priority over the actual plays. The theatre apparatus' priority is a priority of means of production. This apparatus resists all conversion to other purposes, by taking any play which it encounters and immediately changing it so that it no longer represents an alien body within the apparatus—except at those points where it neutralizes itself. The necessity to stage the new drama correctly—which matters more for the theatre's sake than for the drama's—is modified by the fact that the theatre can stage anything: "it theatres it all down." Of course this priority has economic reasons. (Brecht 1964:43)

Brecht's statement goes beyond Joahann Gottsched's call for a literary drama and his reproaches of "cheap" theatrical entertainment. In order to prevent the capitalist mode of production from bleaching the ideological color of his playtexts before it served them to the public, Brecht preached his own brand of formalism and logocentrism. He valued the (Marxist) playtext over its (capitalist) theatrical production, so he proposed the "literalization" of the art of theatre in the 1930s. He argued that "this literization of the theatre needs to be developed to the utmost degree" because the playwright should "speak" (communicate his intention) to the audience directly through titles and footnotes projected on screens (formulation) during a performance, not through the action (representation) only (1964:44).

My allegation about Brecht's formalism sounds preposterous in the context of Brecht's anti-formalist statements. However, Brecht spoke against formalist production styles, not against the formalist approach to theatrical production. Significantly, Brecht did not attack the doctrine of socialist realism drafted at the Soviet Writer's Congress in 1934 when, because of his defamiliarization effect (*Verfremdungseffekt*), he was branded as an advocate of the formalist approach in the U.S.S.R.. Brecht likened a formalist production style to a husk (artistic form) without a kernel (social content). He branded a design or acting as formalist when it was a superficial, mechanical, abstract, ahistorical representation that failed to show specific (contemporary)problems of average human beings in typical social-historical environments. "We shall get empty, superficial, formalistic, mechanical acting," Brecht warned, "if in our technical training we forget for a moment that it is the actor's duty to portray living people" (1964:234).

So, Brecht supported the Marxist "campaign against formalism" in the 1930s because he believed that artistic form should grow out of a social content, not the other way around. The Marxist campaign demonstrated that the development of social content is "an absolutely essential precondition" for "the productive development of artistic form" (1964:119). In the 1950s, Brecht continued to approve of the Marxist campaign against formalist production styles because he deplored the fact that "the question of form became a question of style," that "the unity of form and content" was rapidly breaking up, that artistic form became an end in itself, and "what used to be an organic whole became an effect of montage" (1964:249). Formalist production styles functioned like "corsets" or "paddings" which, by cramming the content, blurred the playwright's cohesive social statements.

Brecht's desire for an organic unity between form and content fathered his tenet that the development of new social contents required the development of new artistic forms. So, as a playwright for the working class, he regarded the campaign against the senseless games of "purely formalist" production styles as a political task with a political content. Formalist production styles were associated with decaying bourgeois art, and the campaign against them turned into a metaphysical quest for authentic, organic forms as opposed to arbitrary, artificial forms (1964:270). The campaign against formalist production styles "is part of the working class' struggle for authentic solutions to social problems," Brecht wrote, "so that phoney solutions in the arts must be combated as phoney social solutions, not as aesthetic errors" (1964:267). For Brecht, formalist production styles forcibly (i.e., "arbitrarily") imposed themselves on a playtext, its content, and its message.

Traditional production styles tamed the content and message of a playtext whereas modern formalist production styles distorted the content and message of a playtext in both original and revival productions according to Brecht. "Formalist *revival* of the classics is the answer to stuffy tradition, and it is the wrong one," Brecht declared in the 1950s. "It is as if a piece of meat had turned bad

and was only made palatable by saucing and spicing it up"
(1964:272). In other words, the distorted taste "of a declining and
degenerate bourgeoisie" could no longer sense the authentic nature
of things, thoughts, or feelings. Having lost its center, it drifted
"further and further away from human greatness." Formalist
production styles "have only made things worse" (1964:273).

> The true pathos of the great bourgeois humanists gave way to
> the false pathos of the Hohenzollerns, the ideal to idealization,
> winged sublimity to hamming, ceremony to unctuousness, and
> so forth. The result was a false greatness that was merely flat.
> (Brecht 1964:273)

What production style could preserve or restore the ideal
and the sublime in theatrical experience? Which production style
could end the drift and could bring theatregoers back in touch with
the kernel of things, with reality? Brecht's desire for an organic
unity between form and content laid the metaphysical cornerstone
on which he built a (social) realistic (alias, "epic") production style.
Unlike the average spectator who went to the theatre to escape
reality, Brecht's philosophic spectator went to the theatre to find
reality (1964:171). Consequently, "the theatre has to become geared
to reality," argued Brecht, "if it is to be in a position to turn out
effective representations of reality and to be allowed to do so"
(1964:186).

Brecht imagined a Valhalla for theatrical production styles in
the golden age of Johann von Goethe, where "theatre itself was
still a reality" and inventive imagination could "turn nature into art."
According to Brecht, during that period, the "primitive" state of the
"mechanics of illusion" (i.e., stage machinery) helped designers
provide some—but not enough—elements of deception. Hence,
they could represent reality on stage without making the spectators
forget that they were in the theatre (1964:218). Even when Duke
Georg of Saxe-Meiningen later introduced authentic costumes, this
authenticity (read "deception") was "compensated" with unauthentic
modes of speech that shattered the makings of an illusion. What
distinguished the epic production style from other naturalist or
formalist production styles was the quality of its divergence from
reality.

Brecht admitted very few production styles into his deceptively historical hall of immortality. Any production styles—from extreme naturalism to extreme formalism—whose divergence from reality "numbed" a spectator's critical judgment were never transported to his theatrical Valhalla. Naturalist production styles were too factual and trivialized reality. Formalist production styles—especially expressionism—were too abstract and distorted reality (1964:233). Brecht's desire for a seminal production style gave birth to the realistic "epic" production style. "Restoring the theatre's reality as theatre," Brecht wrote, "is now a precondition for any possibility of arriving at realistic images of human social life" (1964:218–219). The restoration of theatrical reality no longer required the faithful representation (e.g., copying) of social reality on stage.

Nonetheless, Brecht's rejection of naturalist and formalist production styles had idealist, not materialist, underpinnings. For Brecht, as for many theorists from Broder Christiansen to Jan Mukařovský, the "dominant" was the main principle which dictated the integration, perception, interpretation, and evaluation of the various "qualities of divergence" in a work of art, affecting both its mental form and its physical structure. In other words, they believed that a playtext consisted of external, material, sensory manifestations (Christiansen's "outer work," Brecht's "exterior husk," Mukařovský's "signifiers") and of internal, immaterial, spiritual manifestations (Christiansen's "aesthetic object," Brecht's "model production," Mukařovský's "signifieds"). The immaterial manifestations were shared by the members of a given group as an intersubjective, phenomenological, aesthetic object.

Consequently, a playtext had a double ontological status because it rested on both objective (external) and subjective (internal) realities (manifestations). The internal realities afforded mental impressions—such as associations of similarities or dissimilarities with the dominant aesthetic and cultural norms—which shaped the consciousness of a given group of theatre artists and theatregoers (1909:41, 82). According to Christiansen, the dominant dissimilarities formed the "qualities of divergence," and the sum total of all the dominant associations established the phenomenological aesthetic "object" (1909:118, 241). Brecht subscribed to this line of reasoning because he thought that the material manifestations (signifiers) of his playtexts could not guarantee the identity of his immaterial, phenomenological aesthetic "object" (Marxist signifieds) in capitalist theatrical productions. In order to safeguard the identity of his playtexts, Brecht tried to achieve a "phenomenological closure" by extending his influence further into theatrical production, through his "model prompt-copies."

Christiansen defined the phenomenological aesthetic object as a "teleologic structure" which resulted from the dynamic interaction of the various "qualities of divergence" in the perceivers' minds. "The dominant is the same as the structure of bones in an organic body," wrote Christiansen. "It contains the theme of the whole, supports this whole, enters into a relationship with it" (1909:242). Brecht built his epic production style on this interplay between dominant and subordinate qualities of divergence in order to expose automatized perceptions through "gest" and "defamiliarization" techniques. Like Jan Mukařovský, Brecht realized that the component(s), which occupied a dominant position, depended on the specific role of their aesthetic function against other functions.

> The hierarchy—the mutual subordination and superordination of components (which is only the expression of the internal unity of a work)—is in a state of constant regrouping. In this process those components which temporarily come to the fore have a decisive significance for the total meaning of the artistic structure, which constantly changes as a result of their regrouping. (Mukařovský 1946:4)

Any deliberate or accidental reordering of the dominant components in a Brechtian playtext during a capitalist theatrical production would change its meaning.

Brecht thought of a performance-text as a flexible bundle of aesthetic functions (values) which dissolved into other extra-aesthetic functions (values). The signifying aesthetic functions had a practical orientation or end-goal (*telos*) which lay outside the material side of the playtext because the material side served only as their vehicle. Therefore, Brecht valued only those playtexts which could alter and regroup the existing hierarchy of (bourgeois) aesthetic functions (values) and set a new (epic) aesthetic norm. Evidently, his epic production style would collapse if the interplay between the components were only a mental exercise and the dual ontological status of his dramatic representations a convenient fabrication. Consequently, Brecht felt the pressing need to anchor his theory safely on (historical) reality.

For Brecht, as well as for the Russian formalists earlier, the quality of divergence, on the level of representation, stood for the "divergence" from the actual—from reality (Erlich 1980:252). For Christiansen, the various "qualities of divergence" in a work of art determined the degree that the work deviated from customary aesthetic norms that were established by other works (1909:118). In an attempt to pin down the phenomenological aesthetic "object," Brecht established his criteria for a definition of a realistic (epic) production style by comparing the "picture" on the stage with the actual life that it claimed to portray. And he refused for two reasons to compare the picture on the stage with any surviving playtexts, designs, and acting methods from past historical periods—which were thought to be realistic in their day.

He believed that realism did not only inhabit external artistic forms. As a means of representation, external artistic forms (signifiers) were susceptible to change because the historical reality (signifieds) that they portrayed changed (1964:110). So, Brecht resisted the idea of comparing external artistic forms only, because he deemed that he would be compelled to decide on the definition of "realistic" production style for his "epic" theatre with only formalist (i.e., external) mechanical criteria (1964:112).

In this sense, Brecht expressed a neoformalist approach to the theatre which stood closer to that of Viktor Zhirmunsky, Yury Tynyanov, and Jan Mukařovský than to earlier mechanistic notions of formalists such as Viktor Shklovsky. Brecht's historical (diachronic) view helped him overcome the initial formalist view which considered playtexts as autonomous entities and "literariness" as an immutable, inherent essence of dramatic texts. Having lost their autonomy and their immutable, inherent essence, playtexts were regarded as relational phenomena which were susceptible to change during their theatrical productions—a change which Brecht did not welcome. His epic production style, like all production styles, was not founded on a harmonious blending of interacting factors. It presupposed a hierarchical organization which promoted the supremacy of certain components, and it functionally subordinated any conflicting components which opposed Brecht's priorities.

Theoretically, Brecht distinguished his epic production style both from the formalist production styles—which he found to be "restrictive" models—and from the so-called naturalistic production styles, which copied "reality" from a canon of "naturalistic" playtexts or designs (i.e., "conventions") rather than real life. Brecht replaced "literariness" with "naturalness," which he located in the reality of the theatregoers as members of society, and he borrowed materials from art as well as from life in order to put "living reality in the hands of living people in such a way that it can be mastered" (1964:109). According to Brecht, his epic theatre could help theatregoers master living reality (1) because it removed the many masks of rhetoric from both art and life, uncovering society's causal network, its dominant ideology and (2) because it defended a class which offered solutions for the most pressing problems of the broadest section of society, explaining the dynamics of progress in concrete terms that encouraged abstraction (1964:109).

Brecht believed that, within the hierarchy of a playtext, the strife of the components for domination caused major (interpretative) shifts from historical period to historical period. These shifts reflected the changes within the aesthetic "object" (signified) which took shape whenever new "qualities of divergence" surfaced in the minds of a society of theatregoers and theatre artists. The epic production style helped them not only to recognize the represented reality but also to understand it without being misled (1964:279).

However, this clear Marxist understanding that Brecht envisioned through an epic production style was rather misleading. Brecht identified and measured formalist production styles and stylized realist production styles by their degree of abstraction (i.e., "their degree of absurdity") from "natural" (i.e., "common sense" or "logical") reality. But, unless Brecht defined this reality as a communal property in a society of theatregoers, he could not measure any degree of abstraction that would identify and distinguish his epic production style from other formalist or naturalist production styles.

Brecht resorted to a normative, comparative definition to describe this "natural" reality in the theatre. "The theatre must acquire *qua* theatre," Brecht prescribed, "the same fascinating reality as a sporting arena during a boxing match" (1964:233). Obviously, Brecht did not distinguish between pure and mixed performances as the structuralists did later. Unlike pure performances (e.g., theatrical performances), mixed performances (e.g., boxing matches) require that the contestants act as if something were at stake beyond the entertainment of their audiences (Goffman 1974:126). Brecht would rather define his epic performances as mixed performances because his theatre fought for social reforms and acted as if humanity, justice, and other worthy causes were at stake. So, Brecht proposed two ways of achieving "authenticity" in theatrical performances.

He insisted that "a genuine story" could not emerge unless the scenes (*tableaux* or episodes) unraveled in linear procession *as if* the actors did not know what followed from moment to moment or what was "the play's overall sense" (1964:278–279). Only then could the sum total of the scenes—which did not necessarily complement each other—"unfold authentically without any cheap all-pervading idealization" (1964:279). In short, as Roland Barthes noted, each of the successive, contiguous "tableau" was absolutely meaningful and aesthetically perfect, and it expressed an ideal meaning directly (1974:35). Like Lessing's painter who tried to capture a "pregnant moment" on the canvas, Brecht's epic theatre artist told a meaningful story through a series of carefully selected and "immobilized" pregnant moments ("social gests").

Brecht also promoted the notion that only the present was real. "If the set represents a town, it must look like a town that has been built to last precisely two hours," Brecht advised the designers. "One must conjure up the reality of time" (1964:233). In other words, the dramatization of the (historical) past was unreal (dead) on stage, whereas the dramatization of the (historical) present was real (alive) in the auditorium. The present was real in the sense that the course of the theatrical events—and, by implication, of historical events—was underdetermined and full of possibility (suspense) during a theatrical performance.

However, despite Brecht's prescriptions, Brechtian theatrical performances remained as "pure" as Aristotelian theatrical performances for two reasons: (1) they were based on playtexts that had already predetermined the course of the fictive action on stage; (2) they were based on overdetermined prompt-copies (Brecht's "model productions") that had already limited the artistic freedom of the other theatre artists in making changes as they deemed fit or necessary during their interaction with their audiences.

In short, the fullness of the "resurrected" presence remained as elusive under Brecht's epic (Marxist) production style as it was under both naturalist and formalist (bourgeois) production styles.

In sum, Brecht practiced what he wished to avoid despite his anti-Aristotelian posture and his desire to introduce "scientific" consistency to his theory and practice of the theatre. In part, this discrepancy resulted from Brecht's normative definitions, which failed to prove that the epic production style was different—in degree or in kind—from the other naturalist and formalist production styles. His diachronic perspective helped him realize that, at different times and places, different components acquire the role of the dominant in a performance-text. This being the case, however, no production style (including his epic production style) could claim to have a permanent, stable hierarchy of dominant and subordinate components. This meant that Brecht had no "stable" criterion to differentiate his epic production style from other production styles. The actual "hierarchy" of the various components in playtexts, prompt-copies, rehearsal texts, performance-texts, and extra-theatrical texts became relational and relative—much to his chagrin.

PART THREE

The Domain of the Actor

Reflect a little as to what is *being true* in the language of the theatre. Is it showing things as they are in nature? Certainly not. If it were so, truth would be the commonplace. What, then, is truth for stage purposes? It is the conforming of action, diction, face, voice, movement, and gesture, to an ideal type invented by the playwright, and often enhanced by the actor. That is the strange part of it. This ideal type not only influences the tone, it also alters the actor's very walk and bearing.

Denis Diderot, The Paradox of Acting (1778)

The tragedy of the present-day theatrical revolution, which is greater in scope and more complicated, is that its dramatist is as yet unborn. And this when our collective creation begins with the dramatist. Without him the actors and the stage director can do nothing. This, it seems, is something our revolutionary innovators do not want to reckon with. And this, naturally, leads to many mistakes and misunderstandings that push art on to a false outer path.

Konstantin Stanislavsky, My Life in Art (1925)

CHAPTER ONE

Is There a Text in This Rehearsal?

*M*y two friends were displeased with my "apology" for deconstruction, but they joined me at the dinner table tonight for our "last supper," as John put it. Jon smiled amused, leaned to my side, and asked me if I was cast to play the role of Judas. I replied that I had no desire to play any role at all because role-playing always contains an element of dishonesty. I intended to be honest and true to both of my friends—especially if this, indeed, was to be our last dinner.

John and Jon exchanged glances and hid their smiles by raising their wine glasses to their lips. I guess that what I had just said pleased them although they did not believe me. According to Jon, honesty and truth could get me in trouble just as well as dishonesty and lies. I was reminded of the case of St. Genesius, the patron saint of Christian actors. Genesius, who was a pagan Roman actor, tried to play the role of a Christian as honestly and truthfully as he could. He spoke and acted like a Christian with such a genuine feeling that he convinced not only his Roman audience, but also himself that he was a Christian. Emperor Diocletian had Genesius executed after the performance.

John chuckled, and told me that Lope de Vega's play Acting is Believing *(1608) investigated the case of St. Genesius and the effects of role-playing in the theatre and in society. "I want to see how you play a Christian," Diocletian told Genesius. And the actor promised that the emperor would see him at his best in the role of the baptized Christian who remains steadfast in his faith as the Roman soldiers are dragging him to jail (1986:84). Indeed, Genesius played the role of the Christian so well that his audience could not tell the difference between his impersonation and the real thing. Nor could Genesius himself as it appears.*

As I was refilling his wine glass, I asked, "What do you mean? They were attending a theatrical performance, weren't they? Their awareness of this simple fact should have prevented them from thinking that Genesius was truly a Christian. The theatrical conventions of their time should have helped them realize that Genesius was only presenting an imitation of what his community of theatregoers recognized as a 'Christian'."

Jon brought to my attention that John had said "impersonation," while I had said "imitation." To John, my remark revealed that I had not read Lope de Vega's play. John informed me that Genesius deprived his audience, his fellow actors, and himself of their conventional theatrical frame. During the performance and without warning, Genesius started improvising to the great confusion of the other actors who had memorized the playtext in rehearsals. Genesius assured them that he had not forgotten his lines nor was he in need of a prompter to remind him of his lines. His Prompter, who put the new lines in his mouth, was the Christian God, and the playwright was Jesus Christ (1986:98). So, the other actors in the midst of the performance, which they had rehearsed earlier, no longer knew how the play would end.

"What about Diocletian and the other audience members?" I asked. Jon explained to me that Diocletian was displeased, and he rebuked the actors for performing what he assumed to be a poorly rehearsed play and for arguing among themselves in front of the audience. Diocletian was rather uncertain whether Genesius was playing a dramatic role or a social role when he denied Jupiter and declared himself a Christian. So, Diocletian told Genesius "Since you've lived in a play, you will die in a play" (1986:98), and he sentenced him to death. Genesius, who admitted that he played the role of a Christian so well that it seemed real, also said that, as a Christian actor, he performed the "divine comedy" instead of the meaningless "human comedy," earning for himself the title of the "supreme actor."

To John, the case of Genesius exemplified how social role-playing can influence dramatic role-playing and vice versa. Genesius tried to "get inside" the character, to see how it felt to be a Christian. So, he began saying, doing, and feeling things, which he would not under normal circumstances, until the identity of the Roman actor assumed the identity of the Christian character completely. This total "honesty," which precluded a distance between one's private identity and one's theatrical or social identity (role), was unacceptable to Diocletian and the other Romans. Diocletian and the actors in Genesius's theatre company kept their private identities separate from their social and theatrical identities. They were never converted or transformed by the social roles and the theatrical roles that they assumed.

John's explanation left Jon unsatisfied because it suggested that a person —spectator or actor—can stand "outside" before he decides to get "inside" a social or theatrical role. Jon argued that one cannot "slip" into a role as one puts on a costume—such as a monk's robe, a surgeon's glove, a lawyer's wig, a housewife's apron, and a knight's armor. Roles do not have "hollow" spaces "inside" them which shape and are shaped by the identities of the persons that occupy them. If John was looking for an irreducible center (essence), he would wind up like Henrik Ibsen's Peer Gynt. Gynt was peeling an onion, layer by layer, searching for the core, which he never found.

According to Jon, Lope de Vega knew that a social or theatrical role does not depend on an autonomous central consciousness "inside" it. So, Lope rendered all social and theatrical roles in his play quite unpredictable and unstable. His Diocletian must have thought that dramatic roles are more predictable than social roles because he stepped into the dramatic world in order to sentence Genesius to death. What the Roman emperor and John did not realize is that Genesius sought a metaphysical experience, a passion play, which would turn a theatrical fiction into the ultimate reality. The actors who had eagerly followed the earlier version of Genesius' playtext during rehearsals refused to follow his new version during the performance because Genesius was crossing the borderline of safe acting.

John had no quarrel with this interpretation as long as Jon would agree that Genesius adhered to the Greco-Christian tradition. Whether it was Dionysus or Christ that Genesius accepted as the Author of the signs that he "deciphered," Genesius apprehended a continuity or correspondence between two levels of being (realms of reality), and he read a hidden significance at the deeper level where nothing was meaningless or fortuitous (Schneidau 1976: 223). Genesius, the convert, felt that he had discovered a lost treasure box of fascinating symbols which helped him resemanticize the ancient world. Genesius was one among many theatre artists who felt tantalized by the possibility of being able to comprehend a deeper level of reality. From Euripides' The Bacchae to Peter Brook's "holy" theatre, all these theatre artists assumed that the world was a text written in a cryptic language and that they could learn how to read it when they were properly enlightened.

Jon questioned this explanation because the supernatural agent who "properly enlightened" privileged folks, such as John, was missing from Lope de Vega's play and the experience of Genesius. Vega and Genesius did not invite us to contemplate the powers of (super)natural forces in the comfortable way of the Greco-Christian tradition. The signs in the play—even the miraculous ones such as the Voice and the Angel—pointed beyond the (super)natural order to a realm of existence that escaped incarnation. In Lope's play, the pagan (Greco-Roman) tradition and the Christian tradition entailed different mind-sets because Diocletian and Genesius saw the same signs but they read them differently. Their readings (interpretations) were equally contrived and arbitrary regardless of the Roman code or the Christian code of understanding that they applied to the world. Lope's play broke the presumed unity of the Greco-Christian consciousness, and Genesius' experience did not "glue" it back together. Instead, his experience offered a critique of itself by reopening the issue of role-taking and role-giving in society and in the theatre.

John disagreed with the way Jon read the play, so he reopened the issue of role-playing. An actor playing a role has to go beyond the dramatic character (i.e., beyond language) in order to find truth for a simple reason: as a linguistic text, a character is a series of marks on a page, and, like an empty costume, a character has no ontological status. It is the actor's presence—body and voice—that gives life to the dramatic character and reopens the contact with reality. When an actor-playwright, such as Genesius, writes or says "I" in Latin, in Spanish, or in any other language, that "I" is nothing more than an instance of "writing" or "speaking." A language knows only an abstract "subject," which is indicated by the personal pronoun "I," not the specific person who writes or says "I" (Barthes 1977:145). A dramatic character, like a linguistic subject, is hollow. What holds a dramatic character together is the actor who steps "inside" the linguistic "subject." The character is empty outside of the actor's very enunciation which defines it.

Jon looked at the three bowls with the French onion soup that I had just served and added one more comment before we began eating. As a rule, a good logocentric actor—and all sides agreed that Genesius was a superb actor—notices all the marks of the unaccountable (anacoloutha *or* non sequiturs*) in the rehearsal-text and tries to make them accountable. So, he reduces the inexplicable to the explicable trying to help the performance-text sustain the illusion of unity, coherence, meaning, and truth. Despite Genesius' disclaimers, his "improvisation" turned the intelligible and familiar into an unfamiliar territory for all concerned. Like all performance-texts, the one presented to Diocletian and his court was prone to disunity, incoherence, meaninglessness, and error—conditions which are prevalent in rehearsals—to such a degree that Diocletian was displeased and Genesius was executed. In a way, St. Genesius became a forerunner of modern-day "prompters" who advise actors to* "always try to show the unknown side of things to the spectator" *(Grotowski 1968:237).*

For John, not all actors and spectators are eager to experiment with the unknown and the unexpected in their lives. But those who do experiment are responsible for the decline of standards and attendance in the theatre in recent years. They produced incoherent, meaningless performance-texts at the expense of the theatregoers and the taxpayers. They produced playtexts without any respect for the playwright's intentions or the spectator's expectations (Riess 1990:66). Even a classic such as King Oedipus—*which survived time and space because it dealt with eternal problems and universal values—was butchered time and again for the purposes of an "experiment." These "experimental" companies blocked access to the eternal problems and universal values of the play by updating its dialogue, by giving local color through dialects, accents, and movements, by dressing the characters in modern clothes, and by designing sets that the play did not need.*

I kept quiet. Perhaps I could understand why the destiny of Oedipus seemed credible to an audience when it was placed in ancient Thebes. If Oedipus were to marry Jocasta in contemporary Thebes, the records at the City Hall would have told him that his intended bride was his mother. In the era of computers, the case of Oedipus becomes less probable. But there were three things that

I could not understand. First, did the hyphen (-) between Greek and Christian suggest a continuity or an opposition? According to Jon, the "new" readings of Genesius opposed and undermined the "old" readings of Diocletian. Genesius' two identities (pagan and Christian) appeared to be mutually exclusive, and the one suppressed the other. This structuralist polarity dictated a rigid separation, an absolute difference, and a distinct identity which precluded any relation between pagan and Christian. Why then did John insist on the continuity of the Greco-Christian tradition?

Second, did the presence of the playwright in rehearsals complicate or simplify communication among the actors who constructed a unified rehearsal-text or performance-text? According to Jon, Genesius' presence confused matters even though he had the unique advantage of being the actor and the playwright of what he was rehearsing and performing. When all the actors were interrogated, they revealed that their "unified" performance-text was in fact a "mosaic" of texts which resulted from the different methods of acting that each one of them practiced—from complete identification with a character (Genesius) to complete detachment from a character (Salustius). If the presence of an actor behind the "texts" that he rehearses or performs is as necessary as John assumes, then a playtext is broken into a kaleidoscope of rehearsal-texts by the different methods of acting that each actor brings to rehearsal or performance. Why then did Jon insist that a method of acting (the "I" of the actor) is as arbitrary as a rehearsal-text (the "I" of the character)?

Third, did the various texts in theatrical production (playtexts, prompt-copies, rehearsal-texts, performance-texts) become expressions of transcendence as they moved from one medium to another, from one identity to another, from one reality to another, from one historical period to another? If I deny them any transcendental value, then these texts cease to refer to one another. For Jon, when a text cannot refer to an earlier text, it cannot secure its truth and validity; it no longer has access to the origin of meaning, and it is deprived of its "theological" foundation. When severed from its theological origin, the text of Genesius becomes an "object" for scientific study. It loses all pretentions to depth, to Christ as a playwright, or to a playwright as god, to transcendence, to interiority, and to all the other terms which denote an authoritative, conclusive "presence" of meaning in theatrical production. This anti-theological motive would challenge the status both of an actor's interpretative knowledge of all these texts and his values and convictions (Krieger 1979:172). Then, why did John insist on telling me that whoever tried to turn the study of theatre into a science would soon discover that the spiritual experience worked against their "scientific" projects?

In the following chapters, I will try to continue the process of secularization of the theatre which theatre artists, such as Peter Brook, Jerzi Grotowski, and Joseph Chaikin, tried to arrest in the era of the 1960s. In doing so, am I chosing to understand theatrical phenomena at the expense of theatrical experience? But how else can I rearticulate the "absent something" that reportedly actors and spectators continue to experience in the theatre if I do not put a historical or a scientific frame around the theological aspirations of theatrical consciousness? I keep reminding myself that all historical projects and scientific theories are cannon-specific, however universal they may seem. They belong to the past of the theatre. But I cannot forget that theatre can have no future without privileging (temporarily) some theories or projects over some others. Nonetheless, this widely endorsed idea of "progress" in the world of theatre may be misleading.

For example, theatre rehearsals stimulated, circulated, and established several orders of assumptions. Over the years, the formalist assumption that a rehearsal-text was an organic whole gave way before the structuralist assumption that, thanks to the conflicting interpretations of directors and actors, a rehearsal-text could disintegrate into two or more "rehearsal-texts" which often entered an intertextual relationship. When intention and wholeness disintegrated, rehearsal-texts no longer adhered to the hierarchical constraints dictated by a playtext. Instead, rehearsal-texts were monitored by the coherent interpretations of the competent readers—directors and actors—who often asserted their views very definitively while they were arguing for the indeterminacy of a playtext. But intertextuality and hegemonic readings gradually eroded the distinctions among the various texts in rehearsal. When differences dissolved or were suppressed, the various texts merged again into a "whole" which contained bipolar tensions. Under this idea of "progress," theatre research moved in circles—always returning to what was conceived to be a point of departure.

Collective playwriting through improvisation during workshop rehearsals freed the actors from submitting to the meanings of a playtext. A great number of rehearsal sessions were broken up so that the actors could construct their own rehearsal-texts. A supervising director (such as Peter Brook or Joseph Chaikin) unified these different rehearsal-texts into one patchwork quilt (performance-text) as the opening-night deadline got closer. However, this type of "writing" of performance-texts (1) delayed, but did not eliminate, the totalizing tendencies in theatrical production and (2) covered, but did not solve, the issue of the indeterminacy of meaning. Why should the meaning (intention) of a playwright's playtext be less determinate than the meaning (intention) of an actor's rehearsal-text? Why should the written "I" of a playwright be absent behind the playtext while the spoken "I" of the actor be present behind the rehearsal-text? The assumption was that acting—especially improvisational acting—was "fixed" in the present. Acting was not a homage to the truth of the past or to the truth of "others." The pleasure of acting was in making one's own rehearsal-text at the expense of a playwright's text or a designer-director's prompt-copy.

Reportedly, an improvisational actor was not obliged to (re)present a fixed text in rehearsal or in performance. His rehearsal-text was always provisional, and his relationship to his rehearsal-text could constantly change. Without a playtext, an actor's rehearsal-text looked immediate, dominant, and transient. Presumably an actor could faithfully follow his own impulses. The rehearsal-text became largely an opportunity for instant, direct interpretations by a community of theatre artists (workshops) who were bound together by shared assumptions. However, most of the performance-texts, which were developed from improvisations of the above kind, proved to be as restrictive as conventional performance-texts. Actress Glenda Jackson, for instance, removed all her clothes when she thought that an improvised situation required it in one of the performances of *US.* Her action made some spectators feel tense because they feared that the "unexpected" may have no limits during that performance (Brook 1968:30). But Brook quickly realized that the "shocking" value of all improvisations wears off soon because the unexpected becomes expected in the next performance and repetition—a trait of "deadly" theatre—embraces all "open-ended" performance-texts (1968:54).

Similar observations introduced the haunting suspicion that an actor had limited power to "break" his old text in order to make his new intention (meaning) present. The "deadly" touch of repetition suggested that perhaps an actor was never fully present behind the texts that he (re)presented. Many theatre artists exorcized this deadly thought by inviting the active participation of spectators during a performance—hoping that direct interaction would keep texts open. Like Genesius, they did not realize that the interpretative community of theatregoers, like Diocletian and his court, becomes another source of authority which imposes a definitive closure to the meanings presented to them. The formalist constraints that were imposed on the actors by a playwright's intention or a director's extension were replaced by the structuralist constraints that were imposed on the actors by a community of theatregoers. Most actors sustained these bonds because either they were afraid of risking any socioeconomic retributions or they had internalized these bonds, experiencing an insurmountable psychological barrier.

Of course, a workshop, a laboratory, or a theatre company was an interpretive community, too. It required agreement among its members even though it did not preclude disagreements caused by individual differences in intelligence, temperament, function, or purpose. However, the definition as to what counted as a performance-text or a rehearsal-text proceeded from a collective decision, and it remained in force as long as the majority of the members continued to abide by their perceptions and definitions. But the theatre artists of these workshops and companies never explained why a collective decision or definition was less arbitrary than a singular decision. Consensus made decisions seem less arbitrary and interpretations less heterogeneous. The motives which established a consensus among the members of a theatre laboratory, workshop, or company were not purely scientific, purely artistic, or even purely economic. An understanding of these motives could perhaps explain how the freedoms or constraints of interpretation were established in such groups.

The actors' interpretations in rehearsals generally exhibit their skill to turn a playtext or a prompt-copy into a rehearsal-text. Each actor's interpretation displaces portions of a playtext (dramatic characters) from the page into his consciousness. It would appear that a dramatic character could not occupy the same "space" with a live actor because the "I" of a character cannot know itself and the actor who impersonates "it." If this is true, then it would seem that an actor experiences nothing during the act of acting except for the activity of his own mind. But it is only by stretching the meaning of experience that we can speak of acting. We assume that an actor can know himself and the "I" of the character—even though the actor may never possess the entire range of implications about himself and the "I" of the character. The actor determines the interpretation and defines the character. But which is more important: to know about the "I" of the character or about the "I" of the actor? And how can we know what constitutes the experiencing "I" of an actor or the "I" of a character—not to mention the "I" of a playwright? Thus, acting became a reflection of the conditions of acting with the structuralists.

The stakes are so high in the present quarrel between my two friends that I must be circumspect and tiptoe slowly, testing the ground carefully and taking nothing for granted. I will try to re-examine some of the "founding" texts and "founding" conditions of Western theatrical production with patience—applying a "slow reading" (Nietzsche's term). I will gradually introduce and tentatively use some of the "scientific" jargon of the structuralists in order to build an alternative theory to the Darwinian performance theory. I will try to do it as persuassively as I can, but I hope that I will not fall prey to the same conditions which sealed the fate of Genesius, "the supreme actor."

Konstantin Stanislavsky often described his system or method of acting by repeating terms and concepts which were used by Ivan Pavlov when he explained primary respondent conditioning.

> I grasped the well-known truth that in our profession everything must be turned into a *habit*, which makes the new (art forms) one's own, organic, *a second nature.* Only after that can one use the new (art form) *without thinking of its mechanism.* This applied to the case in point: the *creative mood* could save an actor only when it was a normal and natural phenomenon with him. Without that he would unconsciously copy the outer form of the Leftist trend without inwardly justifying it. From that moment, I reduced my demands and decided to restrict myself to simpler problems in order to apply to them the discoveries I had made in my *laboratory work.* (Stanislavsky 1963:361)

Like Pavlov, Stanislavsky recognized that the relationship between form and content (or between signifier and signified) was as arbitrary as the relationship between a conditioned stimulus and a conditioned response. "I realized more and more that the inner content which I put into a role in creating it," Stanislavsky wrote, "and the outer form the role eventually assumed were as wide apart as heaven from earth" (1963:346). However, unlike Pavlov or the Leftist formalists and the poststructuralists, Stanislavsky considered this disjointed state of affairs to be a decadent order of things and wished to conceal the "mechanism" of innovation under a genuine spontaneity of habit, so-to-speak. "How was I to save my roles from degradation, from spiritual petrification, from stodgy habits and customs?" Stanislavsky asked himself (1963:348).

His response was simple. He tried to reverse this "entropic" order and to restore "a genuine art" in the theatre by finding a "staged-behavior" (alias, system or technique or method of acting) which would reunite the "empty shell" with the "inner truth" and both with life (referent or unconditioned stimulus). Ideally, a Stanislavskian actor would recreate for himself, in himself, the conditions of an unconditioned stimulus ("living material") which would trigger a psychological experience ("inner truth") that, in turn, would inform his staged behavior ("theatrical habit"). This creative task needed to be repeated for every single performance. Otherwise, an actor would deplorably wind up in repeating, habitually and mechanically, the fixed, external, "physical signs"— without feeling any emotion or any real need for action from performance to performance (1963:348).

For Stanislavsky, an actor was in a "natural" state of mind when he behaved as he did in everyday life. An actor was in an "unnatural" state of mind when he expressed what he did not feel, trying to "live" his part spiritually and physically by recreating the conditions of life and their reciprocal emotions. "It is this spiritual and physical dislocation between the body and the soul that actors experience and live through the better part of their lives in our theatre," Stanislavsky wrote, "from 12 noon to 4:30 p.m. when they rehearse, and from 8 p.m. to midnight, when they perform" (1963:349). Daily, the actors felt exposed to the intimidating presence of an audience, and they resorted to methods of artificial acting which were less taxing because they did not require the expression of genuine emotions.

Only the "creative mood" could save an actor from the rut of artificial and superficial acting according to Stanislavsky. The technique which would help an actor induce the "creative mood" in himself by promoting "favorable conditions for the creation of inspiration at will" required two physical states of being: (1) an actor could express the emotions of his soul with his body only if his entire body (physical apparatus) was relaxed and subordinated to his will (1963:351); and (2) an actor could stop being afraid of the audience only if he concentrated his attention on all his physical and spiritual sensations while he impersonated a character, forgetting that he was on the stage (1963:352). This impersonation was seen as a process of "incarnation" during which the character's soul assumed the body of the actor.

"We do not hold dear the inner image of the role which naturally assumes scenic outer forms in the process of incarnation," Stanislavsky complained about external, mechanical acting. "We fix these forms in our mechanical theatrical habits the moment we grasp them, forgetting the soul—the main content of the role" (1963:354). When actors fall into the "grip of senseless acting habits," they lose all sense of center and direction, degrading their art for the sake of their trade. Stanislavsky advised the actors to keep in touch with the truth of their emotions as they seek self expression. Only if their emotions were true (authentic) could the actors believe that what they and their colleagues were doing on stage was also true (authentic).

Richard Boleslavsky, who introduced his version of Stanislavsky's system in the United States, was a teacher of many well-known American directors and actors. Formalist director Harold Clurman was a student of Boleslavsky. Clurman pursued "authenticity of feeling" (or "humanity") in performance. Clurman believed that Stanislavsky's system of acting enabled performers to use their bodies and minds more consciously as instruments for the attainment of "truth" and for "true interpretation" on the stage (1975:43). It helped them experience the "direct roots" of life and rid themselves of the familiar cliches of "stage deportment" which made theatrical experience the antithesis of human experience. Without direct human experience, a playtext, which was transformed into a performance-text during theatrical production, lacked a creative justification.

The question was, How did this transformation take place, and what, if anything, was lost in the process? For example, playwrights, such as Lynn Riggs, were afraid that the above rhetoric and emphasis on the creative contribution of actors and directors "boiled down" to a contempt for the work of the playwright (Clurman 1975:36). In order to bridge the formalist gap between playtexts and performance-texts and to place them on an equal footing, Harold Clurman concocted his own brand of logocentrism with a soft deconstructive hue.

First, he assigned theatre a dual origin in order to argue that playtexts and performance-texts offered equally significant experiences ("quality of life") to readers and spectators, respectively. The essence of this experience could be defined when it was placed "in some personal or traditional scale of values" (Clurman 1958:2). Standing on this personal-traditional scale, Clurman looked at the "origins of the theatre," and he saw that live theatre was "an outgrowth of two forces which at a certain point mingled and became unified." The one force was the raw impulses and spontaneous expressions of the "primitive folk," and it produced dramatic festivals. The other force was the reasoned thought of educated "priestly interpreters" and "university chaps," and it produced dramatic literature.

> Almost every stage "show" betrays the duality of these origins. It is historically true that action precedes the word, and that the theatre's "body" was present before it learned to speak. It is still true that without the "body" —the physical dimension, the presence of the actor—there is no theatre. (Clurman 1958:4)

Likewise, almost every written playtext betrayed the duality of these origins because it was a structure of action with set words which organized human experience while, at the same time, it emphasized a sense of free play to "the masses."

Second, Clurman endorsed an enlarged concept of organic unity in order to guarantee a "natural" continuity between playtexts and performance-texts. The art of theatre consisted of interdependent parts ("organs") which formed "a single organism" instead of being "arithmetically cumulative." All interacting organs—the playwright, the director, the designers, the actors, and so on—were important, but no organ was more important than the others because none could stand alone and, besides, the "*heart* of the theatre" was not situated in one of its organs (1972:5). Clurman made a point to distinguish and acknowledge the artistic contributions of the different "organs," even though he actually perceived and evaluated their work as a whole (1958:5). "The theatre cannot live through any single organ of its being," Clurman rephrased the formalist premise. "The theatre as an art is indivisible" (1972:4).

This indivisibility defined, and occasionally strained, the relationships of the various "texts" in theatrical production. For example, despite his earlier claim, Clurman thought that generally a playtext was the beginning and the heart of a theatrical production. "Under ordinary circumstances, the playwright's script is the core and basis of the theatrical event," Clurman wrote. "To begin with, the playwright is the director's closest collaborator" (1972:42). Indicatively, the rhetoric of Clurman's statement suggested that no longer was the director the playwright's collaborator even though traditionally the playwright initiated or confirmed the choice of director and entrusted him with his playtext. It was the playwright, the designers, the actors, and the audience who became the collaborators of the director.

Ideally, they all merited the director's respect for their co-operation. In reality, however, neither respect nor admiration eliminated an element of uncertainty among them, and their teamwork was disrupted by individual interests (1958:281). Often the work of a "great actor, a great director, or a great ensemble," equaled or excelled, according to Clurman, the significance of a fine playwright—even though these members of a producing unit rarely matched the creative capacity of a gifted playwright. However, a "bad" director, who thought he could "fix" a play with cuts and alterations, would only destroy "the play's unity on the stage" because the form of a play rose out of its "own organic nature" (1972:49). Only a "good" director, who showed respect for the organic unity of the playtext could preserve its unity on the stage. So, under the rhetoric and the pretext of "saving" the text, Clurman dropped his egalitarian organic mask.

Clurman showed his true feelings when he made his kind of formalist director the "heart" (i.e., a vital, unifying, co-ordinating center) of the creativity of the other theatre artists. He warned that "the finest text is often seriously damaged or destroyed by an inadequate cast or improper direction, occasionally by inept physical (scenic) treatment or even by the wrong playhouse" (1972:4). The messiah who would save the playtext from damage or destruction was not the playwright. It was the actor under the guidance of Clurman's director. Like a music conductor, Clurman's "contemporary" director brought ("conducted") all the elements of theatrical production into one work—a performance-text (1972:10). His director, however, was not as contemporary as Clurman thought because Gordon Craig had invented this type in 1905. "The relation of the stage-director to the actor," wrote Craig, "is precisely the same as that of the conductor to his orchestra" (1911:147).

Clurman added to Craig's authoritarian director a twisted Darwinian sense drawn from Boris Aronson's pet opinion that the theatre was a collective art in which the strongest man ruled. Contractually, organized theatrical production may be pivoting around a playwright, but, pragmatically, playwrights rarely exercised their legal rights because, according to Clurman, either they were timid or they realized their inexperience with "the means which most suitably served to embody their playtexts" (1972:10). "Many playwrights hardly understand" the process whereby a "written play" is absorbed into the whole context of a theatre production because they think in a different medium from that of the director (Clurman 1975:73).

For Clurman, the director's medium is "the behavior of living men and women, physical shapes, lights, color, movement" (1972:38). The director "rewrites" every element on a "staged play," and "the others" (i.e., the actors) play the director's "score." "One might say," Clurman wrote, "that the director is the author of the theatrical production, except for the fact that in the collective art of theatre no one can be more than a crucial collaborator" (1958:244). Despite the seemingly humbling posture, Clurman endowed this "collaborator" with power to veto the artistic contribution of the other theatre artists. Clurman's formalist director could "controvert" a playwright in order to arrive at a "more congruous" result with what the playwright *had conceived* rather than with what the playwright "believed" he *had written* (1972:38).

This implies that Clurman's director had a better grasp of the signifieds of the playtext than the playwright—unless the playwright was "truly a man of the theatre" and could "see" his play on the stage as he was writing it. Of course, every playtext—through dialogue and stage directions—implied how it ought to be physically presented on stage (1972:6). However, "the director—if permitted—has the right to do what he pleases with a script," Clurman wrote, "provided what results is persuasive, enriching, and consistently intelligible in itself" (1972:40). In short, the director translated his understanding of a playtext into a self-consistent, coherent "stage-language" (alias performance-text) that was all one piece, revealing no discrepancy between the "text" that the spectators heard and what they saw (1972:38).

The director also had "the right and duty to veto what he considered inappropriate or misleading" in the performance of the actor who "willy-nilly contributed to the direction of a play through his natural temperament, intuition, imagination, and skill" (Clurman 1972:6, 7). According to Clurman, a director should be forgiven when he took credit for some of the actor's improvisations and accepted compliments for them. Playtexts owed their revival and subsequent survival to the directors and actors who resurrected them in the theatre. During play production, a transformation took place which "materially altered or enhanced the quality of the original script" (1972:4). The actor's art was not just to "recite lines" (Samuel Johnson's phrase). The words were incarnated into the person of the actor who was "the body of the art of the theatre" (Stark Young's phrase) in the specific environment of a performance. The playtext no longer existed in the theatre as a written text. Instead it was absorbed in the process of production.

For this reason, "the theatre never dies," Clurman declared, "because it is an act of *actual presence*" which brings in immediate contact people, not their images, who wish to celebrate and express themselves (1975:315). Did Clurman mean to say that the theatrical occasion was more important than the "texts" that it (re)presented? Perhaps so, but Clurman remained a theatre formalist. His art of the theatre was an ordered, unified, self-contained, meaningful entity which did not spill outside of the theatre into extra-theatrical texts (1972:14). Clurman tried to reverse the hierarchy between drama and theatre by following the same path of reasoning that Richard Schechner and others took in the early 1970s.

Clurman had noticed that many performance-texts in the 1960s came into being without an initial playtext. Instead, they were based on the audiovisual improvisations on a theme by the actors under the guidance of a director. The director, in collaboration with a playwright, often shaped the verbal (i.e., literary) aspect of a performance-text in "its final form"—as in the case of Joseph Chaikin and Jean-Claude van Itallie's *The Serpent* (1972:21).

> This tendency, much in vogue today, is often dubbed "new theatre." Actually, it marks a return to the theatre's origins. Words did not constitute the core of the rituals and tribal celebrations of primitive communities. Even in the classic Japanese theatre the dramatist or "playwright" was considered a minor figure. The acting or performance was the crucial factor. Theatre precedes drama. This historical fact has immense aesthetic importance. But in our traditional modern theatre we reverse the process: we convert or "translate" drama into theatre. This creates a confusion from which theatre criticism and theatre practice have both suffered. (Clurman 1972:xi)

Clurman's "new" order of things would restore the drama/theatre relationship to its "natural" place in order to establish a "director's theatre."

Joseph Chaikin, among others, advocated a "new theatre" in the era of the 1960s by focusing on the theatrical occasion (event) and by exploring the immediate contact among actors and spectators. Chaikin observed the fictive world on the stage and the real world in the auditorium, and he concluded that the living situation of "actually being in the theatre" was "more present" than the situation enacted on the stage (1972:1). His preference for the "real" over the "fictive" world encouraged a redefinition of Stanislavsky's method of acting. "Acting is a demonstration of the self with or without disguise" (1972:2). In other words, acting entailed a demonstration of the fictive self of a character and the real self of the actor or spectator. When their images of fictive or real selves became fixed, they prevented themselves from further discoveries. Such self-limiting actors and spectators could only see what they were "*conditioned*" to see—failing to serve the "real" art of theatre (1972:3).

The concept of "conditioning," which recurred in many theories of acting from Stanislavsky to Chaikin, was seen as an impediment by those who wished to arrive at a genuine art of the theatre. Most theorists assumed that their method (system or technique) of acting could help actors (1) free themselves from "old habits," (2) achieve authentic, communicable experiences from performance to performance, and (3) avoid reconditioning themselves to "new habits." Technique was conceived as a means to free the theatre artists and, subsequently, the spectators from established (mis)perceptions and values (1972:5). They also assumed that the director—as *didaskalos* or *guru*—could play a vital, leading role in guiding a team of designers and actors through encouragement or intimidation to achieve artistic freedom and authenticity.

If the director's medium of artistic expression was live people, then the "collective" activity for the creation of a "performance-text" during rehearsals was directly affected by a director's leadership style and by the conditions of dominance or subordination that he or she imposed on the other theatre artists. The creation of the rehearsal-texts—and eventually of the performance-text—was also influenced by "naturally" or "unnaturally" induced states of consciousness which prompted, in the participants, a dissociation—i.e., a spiritual and physical dislocation—among signifiers, signifieds, and referents. Under such induced states of consciousness, the transformation of a playtext into rehearsal-texts or into a performance-text was viewed by logocentric directors, actors, spectators, and critics as an act of incarnation and presence.

Theoretically speaking, the variety of theatrical experiences that a community of theatregoers can enjoy depends on the variety of production styles available to its theatre artists—say, from naturalism to expressionism. Historically, the different production styles led to different methods of acting and vice versa. Each novel method of acting affected the structure of traditional theatrical production by creating yet another type of theatre—say, from Brecht's "epic theatre" to Brook's "holy theatre." Dissimilar methods of acting resulted from dissimilar strategies which determined how a role was acquired and how the members of a production unit interacted. The popular polarities—say, between "external" and "internal" naturalism or between "bourgeois" and "socialist" realism—chose not to see that the interacting singular "souls" of the characters and actors were sociocultural constructs or that their social and theatrical realities were products of individual conditioning.

Polarities of the above kind failed to explain (1) what caused a "cycle of renewal" among methods of acting, production styles, and types of theatre and (2) how the "authentic experience," which all parties claimed for themselves, could be attained by mutually exclusive methods of acting. In order to propose a verifiable explanation to these questions in the following chapters, I need to ask three related questions which old and new methods of acting, despite their differences, answered either explicitly or implicitly: (1) To what degree of proximity or distance should an actor's staged behavior be to (his or her) real-life behavior? (2) To what degree of involvement or detachment should an actor's emotions and thoughts be to those of a character? (3) To what degree should an actor renew his or a character's thoughts, feelings, and actions in order to avoid "lifeless" repetition and to achieve more effective portrayals?

Peter Brook compared a Stanislavskian actor to a Pavlovian dog in order to expose how limited the margins of artistic freedom were that Stanislavsky's method of acting offered. Unlike "baroque" acting, which was rejected in later years because it was based on "frozen" systems of expressions and attitudes, "method" acting had not yet been rejected because, according to Brook, it offered a deceptive sense of artistic freedom. Instead of drawing on "any deep creativity," Stanislavsky's actor adjusted his observations about external behavior to his internal spontaneity.

> He is reaching inside himself for an alphabet that is also fossilized, for the language of signs from life that he knows is the language not of invention but of his conditioning. His observations of behavior are often observations of projections of himself. What he thinks to be spontaneous is filtered and monitored many times over. Were Pavlov's dog improvising, he would still salivate when the bell rang, but he would feel sure it was all his own doing: "I'm dribbling," he would say, proud of his daring. (Brook 1968:112)

Brook thought that improvisation—under Stanislavsky's method of acting and its Anglo-American variations—reached the limits of its freedom very rapidly. And so thought many "avant-garde" theatre artists in the era of the 1960s who abandoned Stanislavsky's method of acting in search of a new method that would tap "deep creativity."

These theatre artists rejected naturalist acting methods because they usually associated such methods with mirror representations of behavioral patterns fostered by the dominant ideology of a society. "Naturalism corresponds to the programmed responses of our daily life—to a life style which is in accord with the political gestalt of the time," Joseph Chaikin told Schechner. "To accept naturalism is to collaborate, to accept society's limits" (Schechner 1969:144). As an antidote that would transgress the limits of both society and Stanislavsky's technique, Chaikin used the technique of "transformations." This technique retained "naturalistic" acting, but it introduced rapid changes of situations and roles for the actor. These changes required that an actor should give up his conventional, fixed identification with only one role (character) throughout a play and to (re)act in discontinuous, often unrelated and self-contained roles and situations without establishing logical or motivational connections.

Unlike Stanislavsky's actor, who played by the rules of his shifting "inner" reality, Chaikin's actor played by the rules of rapidly changing "outer" realities. "Transformations do not change acting but the rules governing the use of acting," Schechner observed. "In changing these rules, however, new situations are possible for performance and through that for playwrights" (1966:10–11). If Stanislavsky's method of acting made actors and audiences perceive their motives and actions as natural and logical, "transformations" called into question any dependence on established perceptions of nature and logic—along a pattern set by Brecht. Brecht's epic theatre had challenged actors and spectators to consider the possibility that their motivation and behavior was arbitrary to a large extent. It only seemed real (i.e., "natural" and "logical" in their historical time and social space) because the daily repetition (conditioning) of their social routines reinforced this impression.

A character was no longer seen as a case study with a fixed psychological profile (*historia*). Instead, a character was known by his universal external situation and his potentially flexible social action (*praxis*). By emphasizing action in terms of potential universals over fixed particulars, these theatre artists paid tribute to Aristotle (*On Poetics* 1451a37–1451b14, 1449b24–26, 1451b26–29). "It is a matter of coming back to the truth, which lay disguised and impotent under the *automatic functioning* of convention" (Gilman 1963:34). But, whenever these allegedly iconoclastic, trail-blazing theatre artists tried to go back to the "truth," they returned, by way of "heresy," to the logocentric tradition of Aristotle and Plato—sometimes unintentionally. The technique of "transformations," which was traced back to Lewis Carlino, forged an alternative way of playwriting as it was observed in the collaboration of Megan Terry (*Viet Rock*) and Jean-Claude van Itallie (*Serpent*) with the other members of Chaikin's Open Theatre Company (Wagner 1973:100; Weales 1969:244).

The Open Theatre members developed "transformations" into a "playwriting" technique for economic reasons. Their "transformations" justified their inability to afford multiple sets, elaborate costumes, lighting effects, and large casts (M. Smith 1966:13–14; Wagner 1973:81). These "transformations" were based on the many functions and meanings (polysemy) that a theatrical sign could acquire in rehearsal or performance (Honzl 1976:75). For example, the signifying function of a broomstick as "broomstick" could change into "horse," "rifle," "rocket," "witch," depending on how it was used (Lahr 1970:168; Rubin 1967:4). Nonetheless, Schechner saw in "transformations" yet another evidence that theatrical performance—the "original" mode of theatre—took the upper hand over dramatic literature once again. So, he hurried to salute Megan Terry as "one playwright among several who know that action is the soul of drama." She evidently replicated in New York City in 1966 the process by which William Shakespeare, according to Gordon Craig, wrote his plays in London from 1594 to 1612.

> Gordon Craig—madman, genius, failure—suggested that Shakespeare wrote by lifting story-segments from English history chronicles or Italian novellas (and elsewhere) and asking his actors to improvise these scenes. A scribe wrote down what the actors said and Shakespeare went home to rework these crude lines into the iambics of his great plays. The actors gave him what no man working alone could get: a living sense of interaction, irony in depth, different linguistic and gestural patterns, simultaneity. Craig's suggestion has logical, if not historical, merit. (Schechner 1966:8)

For Schechner, this method of playwriting explained the objective, omniscient viewpoint in Shakespeare's plays. Shakespeare was able to stay "out" of his various characters because he was never "in" according to Craig and Schechner. Like a "great transformer," Shakespeare only gathered, rewrote, and re-edited the initial line of action and text created by the actors. Schechner noted that Terry was not Shakespeare but her method of playwriting matched the method which Craig attributed to Shakespeare and that her *Viet Rock* had an Elizabethan scope and tone. Her play was a conglomeration of sources and styles which had a "unity" even though the scenes were not related to "a realistic organic structure" (Schechner 1966:9, 18). The constant revisions put the playwright on the same ground as the actors, and deprived the playtext of its authority by turning it into a "pretext" (Gide's term). Its staging was an act of reconstruction (1966:10).

The performance-text of *Viet Rock* evolved from workshop improvisations and acting exercises partly guided by playwright Terry and partly guided by directors Chaikin and Peter Feldman over a six-month period before it premiered at the Cafe La Mama on 21 May 1966 (Terry 1966:197). During this extended rehearsal (workshop) period, Terry (re)wrote and (re-)edited the "script" making sure that "the emotional imagery held firm" as the other two directors were trying to "finish it, clarifying the movement and line of action." Terry concluded that "together we made the production" (1968:3; 1966:197). The show ran for one week, and it was rescheduled to run for one more week a month later (Pasolli 1970:77). Before the second run, Chaikin and Feldman redirected *Viet Rock* during Terry's absence, opting for a "heavier," "angrier," "Brechtian" tone than Terry's "light irony" (Pasolli 1970:77). When Terry returned, she became upset because she could not distinguish *Viet Rock* from any Brechtian anti-war plays (Wagner 1973:105). She did not want *her* play to turn into an imitation of Brecht.

According to Terry, the "light" ironic tone worked best for the play because it helped the "dark" values surface with greater impact (1966:197). Although this disagreement strained her relationship with the other members of the company, she "managed to get the play back in shape" for its production at Yale University on 12 October 1966 (Pasolli 1970:78–79). Reportedly, Robert Brustein used his influence to change Terry's script (especially the ending which he thought to be sentimental) by bringing her new lines, by coaching the actors, and by undermining her overall authority. "I wanted to take risks in that play," Terry said. "My God, people were losing their very lives. We could risk our vanity, for heaven's sake. Even the Martinique [Theatre] producers got cold feet. A week before they opened, they wanted to bring in Joe Chaikin to redirect the show. I said no" (Wagner 1973:126; Brustein 1969:xii).

Terry had it her way at the Martinique Theatre. But whose vanity was at stake? Harold Clurman, for instance, who saw the show, called it an unintelligent, unoriginal, confused piece of anti-war propaganda (Clurman 1966:587). If, as Clurman believed, a performance-text was an organic whole which resulted from a collective, collaborative effort among playwright, designers, director, actors, spectators, and critics, then all of them shared the blame. Usually, conflicts of opinion reflected conflicts of interest, such as economic, ideological, aesthetic, and sexual. In the case of *Viet Rock*, collaboration ended when communication broke down. Terry was upset because Chaikin and Feldman smothered the artistic effect of "light irony," not because they redirected the show during her absence. From that point on, these "collaborators" used the law as an instrument of coersion rather than as a conflict resolution system. The leading members of the Open Theatre Company castigated the playwright and prohibited her from using the company's name in any future productions of *Viet Rock*. And the playwright used her legal veto to prevent the producers of the Martinique Theatre from inviting Chaikin to redirect her show.

Reportedly, *Viet Rock* uncovered the dirty reality of war by removing the polished rhetoric of the warmongers in American society. It assumed that people were entrapped in a smokescreen of familiar cliches or "word worlds" (Terry's term) and popular mind-sets; and it aspired to make theatregoers see the truth by dropping their linguistic blindfold like a bad habit. Its "authors" believed that if people were "assisted" to think more clearly, they would have taken a necessary first step toward political regeneration (Orwell 1968:128). Ironically, the "authors" of *Viet Rock*, who were "at war" over its appropriate tone of delivery, fell victims to familiar cliches and popular mind-sets when they used the rhetoric and legal framework of traditional theatre in order to justify their artistic functions and actions. The communication breakdown, which resulted in this and other similar cases among the partisans of alternative theatres, hampered theatrical regeneration because it did not resolve some recurrent theatrical conflicts and habits during rehearsals.

One pervasive habit in the theatre has been the use of metaphors to describe the activities of theatre artists. Theatrical production has always operated on popular metaphors—such as the metaphor of the organic whole—for a good reason. Metaphors have helped theatre artists establish, secure, intensify, beautify, and occasionally transform their interactions during rehearsals according to procedural and hierarchical patterns. But the prolonged usage of some metaphors created the illusion that they represented fixed, legitimate, and binding truths. Theatre artists could not deconstruct any dominant metaphors unless they realized that metaphors were unifying tropes with provisional validity and power. Usually, a metaphor remained in place as long as it justified the artistic preferences, beautified the economic interests, and secured the authority of some theatre artists over their colleagues.

For example, the metaphor of the "organic whole" fabricated the impression—which ratified a reciprocal structure—that a theatre company (organization) was an organism whose various employees worked together to accomplish a common vital goal. Any kind of economic or artistic conflict among the employees (organs) would only disrupt their cooperation, destroy the harmony of their aesthetic product, and jeopardize their survival as a common body (corporation). An actor could not question this metaphor without first questioning the validity of two major traditions in the theatre on which this metaphor rested—the Aristotelian and the Hegelian traditions. Aristotle believed that there was an identity between the metaphor and whatever it described (*On Poetics* 1457b 7–35). An actor had to reject Aristotle's view in order to argue that the implied unity between the metaphor (signifier) and reality (referent) was deceptive.

By questioning identity and unity, the three-step dialectical schema of "thesis-antithesis-synthesis," which was introduced by Johann Fichte and was assigned to Georg Hegel by Karl Marx, also came under fire (Kaufmann 1951:459; Mueller 1958:411). Fichte's dialectic resolved the conflict between a "thesis" and an "antithesis" in the totality of a "synthesis." In a similar way, Hegel assumed the existence of a historical origin, a separation through opposition, and a conclusive reconciliation or harmony before, in the next round of conflict, the moving power of human passions produced, once more, unintended results and sudden reversals. Hegel's reversal of the roles between "master" and "servant" occurred when the servant became self-reliant while the master continued to depend on his servant's labor. For Hegel, sooner or later an argument—no matter how logical—was bound to arrive at a contradiction by going against either its initial premises or the selected facts.

According to the popular perception, Hegel endorsed Fichte's dialectic even though Hegel called the schema "thesis-antithesis-synthesis" a "lifeless schema" (*geistloses Schema*) in his preface of *The Phenomenology of Mind* and he condemned it as a cheap trick or tool for producing a monotonous formalism. So, an actor had to reject the popular Fichtean-Hegelian view if he wished to disrupt any new version of totality (synthesis). In fact, the actor had to perform endlessly a disruptive function in order to prevent "closure" from happening in the organic way of the formalists or the mechanical way of the structuralists. It required that an actor examine with suspicion any claims that one could invent new "clearer" systems of thought (neo-Aristotelian, neo-Hegelian, neo-Orwellian, or what-have-you) than the old ones. Some actors began to realize that the "clearer" systems of playwriting, designing, directing and acting depended on as arbitrary, artificial, and idiosyncratic an arrangement of their elements as the "unclear" methods of playwriting, designing, directing, and acting that they sought to replace.

This awareness of the deceptions committed by playwrights, designers, directors, and actors for the sake of intelligibility (coherence) and unity (dominance) undermined the objective status of truth. Truth became relative because it depended on an authoritative desire—which, during rehearsals, usually served the priorities of a director—to either preserve an "old" order of things (playtext) or create a "new" order of things (performance-text). If any claims to truth by an authority source—playwright, designer, director, actor, or critic—amounted to a deception, then an honest actor had to refrain from adding his own version of the "truth" and would only value the process (or method of acting) which helped him show how mistaken were the claims to truth that the various texts and their "authors" made during rehearsals. However, such an actor would eventually put himself in a position of powerlessness because he would dismantle the truth and authority of the methods of acting handed down to him by directors in rehearsal without being able to raise himself to any "new" positions of order or meaning.

If the goal of such an actor or group of actors was to show that the whole (i.e., a performance-text) was in fact a meretricious fabrication of parts which falsified one another when brought together, he or his group could not reassemble the various parts (i.e., rehearsal-texts) into a "complete" performance-text after they had "broken down" the whole (i.e., a playtext) into its constituent parts. The process of disassembling and reassembling a playtext into either an organic whole or a mechanical whole has been a task of formalist and structuralist "script analysis" to date. If actors could not expect to infuse any primary, original, or genuine qualities in their rehearsal-texts either by going back to the playtext or by going forward to the performance-text, where could they turn to? This kind of questioning shook up established practices and encouraged such acting techniques as "transformations." It also turned rehearsals and workshops into a battleground as actors turned playtexts and prompt-copies into rehearsal-texts, and they observed that these "texts" became constructions that lost touch with the texture of the "original" playtext or prompt-copy.

To save themselves and their texts from what was regarded as a process of "disintegration," logocentric directors and actors tried to preserve the disrupted unity of a playtext during rehearsals by claiming that they unraveled the strands that composed it before they reassembled it as a performance-text. Nonetheless, they could not fail to notice that during rehearsals and from rehearsal to rehearsal, their rehearsal-texts never developed or carried any "themes" or "characters" to completion, remaining unfinished, without definite beginnings or ends. They could "glue" or "screw" the various texts together in a "seamless" continuity thanks to the popular metaphors of the theatre as an organic or mechanical whole. However, if the desired unity, which they pursued during rehearsals, only reflected their wishful thinking for coherence and unanimity, then they simply deluded themselves.

Of course, the logocentric views of theatrical production did not deny the existence of opposition, discontinuity, or fragmentation. They only rejected the premise that fragmentation, discontinuity, and opposition preceded unity and harmony. For the formalists, disunity and disharmony resulted from the forces of entropy that, during rehearsals, "dismembered" a playtext into several rehearsal-texts. The words of a playtext functioned as a heavenly origin of meaning that unified the activities of the actors during the trying period of rehearsals. Each actor recalled these words as he or she joined the others in their effort to construct the performance-text. Together they built the performance-text like the descendants of Noah in the Old Testament had built the Tower of Babel in order to reach heaven—the origin of full meaning. The formalists believed that their performance-texts were complete wholes which attained solid meaning and presence in the theatre.

The formalist wholeness, seamlessness, and fullness began to crumble when the early structuralists began to see theatrical production as a (dis)continuous mechanism of conflicting subsystems, functions, or texts. The performance-texts of the late structuralists began to look more like an incomplete Tower of Babel whose builders suffered a communications breakdown when they realized that they spoke in many different languages—the languages of their stage, clan, class, culture, and nation. In order to improve communication and communion, many structuralist projects in the theatre launched a desperate search to find one (ur) language which was shared by all human beings at a deeper, primal or visceral level. Their theatrical explorations and experiments failed to come up with such a language which would bring them in touch with themselves, each other, and the world, securing unanimity in interpretation and stability of meaning.

Although the structuralists challenged and reversed some of the rules of the formalist theatrical game, they continued being rule-bound, this time to the rules of their own game—a condition which deprived innovative actors of their artistic freedom for improvisation and spontaneity according to some critics. When a player sufficiently internalized the rules, he could take them for granted and play with a "freedom" and "abandon" that seemed to ignore the rules. This deceptive sense of artistic freedom in rehearsal and performance was encouraged by Stanislavsky's method of acting, which, according to Peter Brook, turned actors into Pavlovian dogs. However, this kind of skepticism toward established acting methods and rehearsal processes diagnosed the arbitrary and artificial nature of "staged" behavior only to cure it by proposing yet another "genuine" method of acting as a remedy. For these skeptics, theatrical production lost its seriousness as an established economic enterprise, but it retained its "theological" profile, albeit it was now experienced as a secular activity.

The subsidized projects of theatre artists such as Jerzi Grotowski, Peter Brook, Joseph Chaikin, or Julian Beck had a liberating, deconstructive facade whereas, in fact, they merely altered the relationships of the "parts" ("texts") to one another without, necessarily, changing the "machine"—i.e., the economic and artistic structure of logocentric theatrical production. Julian Beck, for instance, viewed the outmoded or "atrophic" language as an obstacle which prevented actors and spectators from directly achieving a state of "real conscious being." For Beck, the difference between "mere" conscious being and "true" conscious being was "the nearness to God" (Beck 1965:7). Likewise, Chaikin tried to find a new "vocabulary" for the actor during workshop rehearsals which would extend beyond verbal expression. The theatre artists, who formed Beck's Living Theatre or Chaikin's Open Theatre, wished to go beyond language into the essence of things and the core of meaning. Unfortunately, their metaphysical explorations mystified rather than clarified the *genesis* of a theatrical language—or of any language.

After the model of Greco-Roman and Renaissance rhetoricians, these theatre artists investigated the propositional (cognitive) value and the affective (emotional) value of meaning. A performance-text was a composition of "languages" designed to produce both a cognitive and an emotional response to the spectators. Some kept the two effects apart and placed greater emphasis either on the cognitive effect (Clurman) or on the emotional effect (Terry). Some others placed an equal emphasis on both effects, favoring a fusion of thought and emotion into a "felt thought" (T.S. Eliot's term). In all cases, a spectator judged a performance-text by his sense of the intensity and quality of its effect on him. Regardless of their emphasis on thought or emotion apart or in unison, they did not investigate the relationship of "felt thought" to theatrical illusion or of primary respondent conditioning to language creation. Instead, they fell into the old schema of investigations which gave the role of verity either to nature (naturalism) or to history (realism). Consequently, their "scientific" or "historical" perspectives constructed patterns of significance which privileged some phenomena at the expense of others in the familiar, traditional way.

CHAPTER TWO

Transactional Analysis

To date, the traditional itinerary of Western theatrical production has followed a fixed pattern: a playtext is transformed into a prompt-copy, which, in turn, through rehearsals, is transformed into a performance-text presented to an audience. During rehearsals, directors, designers, actors, and crews search for the most functional spatiotemporal representation of the dramatic world of a playtext. Rehearsals make concrete the "nonliterary" elements of a prompt-copy, such as sets, props, costumes, lighting, sound, and actors. They aim at developing and maintaining highly predictable behavior and co-ordination among performers and crews during a performance.

Jacques Derrida called this type of theatrical structure "logocentric." In this structure, a playwright can enforce his will and "word" on directors, designers, performers, and crews, reducing them to "interpretive slaves who faithfully execute the providential design of the master" (1978:235). In the United States, for example, the standard contract of the Dramatist's Guild mandates that a playwright should be consulted on changes in the play, on choice of director and the cast. The legal veto of a playwright to control artistic creativity and innovation beyond the playtext has inconvenienced several directors, designers, and performers in many countries over the years.

Back in 1931, Antonin Artaud thought of a way out. He suggested that directors and actors will remain subservient to playwrights only so long as there is a "tacit agreement" that the language of words is superior to the other languages of the stage (1958:105). Artaud's theories helped many directors and actors challenge the logocentric tradition by emphasizing movement and gesture over speech in rehearsal and performance. These directors and actors refused to play the role of midwives and merely deliver lines from the playtext into the performance. They proudly assumed the role of equal parents, and the language of words gave way before the language of paralinguistic and kinetic signs (1958:107).

Artaud, in fact, wanted to change the point of departure in the play-production process: he proposed that rehearsal should assume the function of playwriting (1958:110). Among the directors who upset the pre-eminence of playtexts in the 1960s and 1970s were Peter Brook, Jerzy Grotowski, and Joseph Chaikin. Brook, for example, could not find a play that described the war in Vietnam and life in England in a satisfactory way. Therefore, he proceeded to generate a performance-text through his interaction with the cast (1968:13). The actors improvised on material that the director, the playwright, and they themselves brought into rehearsal. The playwright recorded only what the actors produced and the director approved (1968:17–18). So, the playtext resulted from the rehearsal-texts, and not the rehearsal-texts from a playtext.

Brook and the actors wrote the first part of the performance-text of *US* (Aldwych Theatre 1966) by interacting creatively. "An actor in his interpretation of the word," noted Jovan Hristic, "links it with his movements and his whole body" (1972:353). Hristic, of course, spoke in the context of logocentrism, which views an actor's performance as an act of incarnation of the playwright's words. The performance-text of *US*—except for the last part, which was written by Dennis Cannan—was not an act of incarnation, however. It was based on the actors' improvisation and could be conceived as an act of creation.

This shift from playtext to rehearsal-text creativity shifted attention from the speech-centered playtext of a playwright to the fluid, movement-oriented improvisations of ensemble playwriting. Joseph Chaikin practiced ensemble playwriting in the 1960s and 1970s by allowing (1) the actors to bring provisional texts into rehearsals (workshops) which would help them develop dialogues or monologues and situations, (2) the writers to contribute ideas for stage images and unifying themes, and (3) the musicians to suggest possible directions in which a theme could evolve vocally or instrumentally (Blumenthal 1984:140).

In the course of creating a dozen performance-texts through ensemble playwriting, Chaikin observed that group interaction generated certain patterns such as tension in communication among the participants and permissive or restrictive behavior toward the director, depending on his strong or weak concern for productivity and for meeting deadlines. More analytically, ensemble playwriting strained the traditional working relationship among playwrights, actors, and director because it could not resolve their professional ambitions and personal insecurities decisively or persuasively.

On the one hand, the performers felt vulnerable in their triple role as actors, playwrights, and private people—mainly because ensemble playwriting drew directly on their personal feelings and experiences. Deprived of a fixed playtext that they could interpret from beginning to end, they were also deprived of a sense of direction during rehearsals. "Actors, for example, have sometimes had to generate material for a play whose tone and thrust was not clear to them," wrote Eileen Blumenthal. "One performer noted, a few weeks into the workshop of *Nightwalk* 'I feel like a blind person trying to learn a dance. . . . I can chew on my little corner but I can't see the whole thing'" (1984:143).

On the other hand, the director adopted permissive behavior at the beginning of rehearsals (workshops) and restrictive behavior at the end, postponing casting until the end of the rehearsals. As the opening-night deadline drew nearer, the emphasis shifted from generating new material to pulling the various improvisational pieces together into a complete, coherent performance-text (1984:142). Directorial editing and opening-night deadlines pressured the performers to create as many impressive, well-connected pieces as possible because, despite their hard work, their piece and role in the final product could be curtailed or omitted.

"Chaikin recalls the bitterness in the *Serpent* company," writes Eileen Blumenthal. "When, preparing for performances, he began to weed out various sections and to assign roles to specific people. . . . He cautioned the actors that some decisions could not be *fair* because they were not based on democratic principles but on artistic needs" (1984:144). Were these "artistic needs" dependent on concerns about performance quality and economics? Chaikin, indeed, had considered the role of economics (Blumenthal 1984:38), and his performers had thought about the quality of the "product" that they had prepared for their audiences. For instance, on the day of the opening night of *The Serpent* in Rome, Italy, "one performer exclaimed that the piece was *shit* and a *hoax*" (1984:145).

Finally, the playwrights found themselves in a tug of war between director and performers. Several playwrights felt irritated, undercredited, and amused by the paradox that they were the authors of "authorless" performance-texts! They felt that they were neither an integral part of the group nor independent outsiders providing a finished playtext (1984:146, 147, 148). The only way Chaikin could avoid the tensions between playwrights and performers, if Eileen Blumenthal's account is correct, was "by eliminating either the playwright or the performers" (1984:148). For example, *The Mutation Show* (1971) was created without the real participation of a playwright. Interestingly, Jerzy Grotowski's research at the Polish Theatre Lab is directly relevant to the issue at hand. He investigated, among other things, the new role rehearsal could acquire in the theatrical production. His conclusions can be summed up as follows:

First, the director subordinated and eventually eliminated the playwright, but not the function of "playwriting," which traditionally occurred in the playtext subsystem. Second, the director subordinated and gradually eliminated the designers, but not the function of "designing," which traditionally took place in the prompt-copy subsystem. In this "poor theatre" (1968:19), the performance-text emerged through the rehearsing actor's "autobiography" and "autoperformance," which made the distinction between the actor and the character he impersonated rather fuzzy. Third, rehearsals trespassed into the performance subsystem, and they redefined performances as "events," "happenings," or "holidays." These theatrical events emphasized improvisation and eliminated the traditional distinction between active performers and passive spectators (Findlay 1980:355). Despite their deconstructive pretentions, however, the above displacements remained within the structuralist schema of oppressive reversals. The reintroduction of "new" methods of acting, "new" production styles, and "new" types of theatre did not instigate a "cycle of renewal."

In this and the following two chapters, I will show how different acting methods, which lead to different types of theatrical experience, are different in degree rather than in kind. They vary from one another only by the quantity (degree) of the self-involvement that actors and spectators experience along a continuous scale of intensity rather than by the quality (kind) of verity that, theoretically, they experience in polarized dichotomies commonly drawn between illusion and ecstasy or between realistic theatre and epic theatre. Then, I will demonstrate that the experience of illusion results from the inability of an actor or a spectator to differentiate signifiers from referents during rehearsal or performance when he or she is overwhelmed by intense emotion. This intensity of affect registers the signifieds of referents and the signifieds of signifiers at the subcortical level where both feel or look alike, causing a temporary confusion between reality and make-believe.

I cannot advance the above hypotheses unless I abandon the "spirit" of the formalist approach and I adopt the "jargon" of the structuralist approach. For most formalists, the purpose of theatre criticism was to serve the masterpieces of drama through explanations which would enhance the public's appreciation. This view instilled two perceptions: a critic should interpret playtexts; and the various theories, which made the body of theatre criticism, were only attempts to eliminate methodological errors so as to set playtext analysis on its proper course. When the scientific aspirations of the structuralists took investigation and interpretation from the page to the stage, the formalists felt that structuralism would destroy theatre criticism as a discipline.

What the structuralists destroyed was the formalist definition of criticism, which they did by enlarging their field of inquiry, by forming new sets of theories (hypotheses), by violating previous theories about dramatic literature, theatrical production, and dramatic criticism, and by encouraging a new kind of theatrical practice. Most structuralists tried to explain and control the conditions of theatrical production—i.e., the elusive interaction among designers, directors, and actors and its artistic products—through elaborate diagrams, taxonomies, neologisms, and scientific jargon which occasionally sounded forbidding or pretentious. In "adopting" their jargon temporarily, I will be able to show how they dealt with "the paradox of acting" (Diderot's term) and why they often proposed methods of acting, which flirted with irrationalism, as valid interpretative tools. Then, at my own peril of repeating Genesius' lethal zeal, I will advance a Pavlovian performance theory as an antidote to the Darwinian performance theory that I described in earlier chapters.

The structuralist developments which I described earlier (1) attempted to change the nature of rehearsal as a subsystem in the play-production process and (2) gave those trained in quantitative research in theatre another opportunity to reassess old and new methods used in producing plays. However, there was very little communication or coordination of efforts between those who pushed for a quantitative mode of inquiry and those who practiced a qualitative mode of inquiry—to the loss of both parties. In this context, I feel at ease to postulate that *any* methods of directing and acting that can minimize interactional obstacles and unilateral decisions during rehearsals and that can improve the skills, habits, and attitudes that directors, performers, and crews bring into rehearsal can also improve working conditions and artistic results in the theatre.

An actor's ability for role enactment and a director's communication system can affect both the quantity and the quality of the rehearsal-texts of a theatre company. If different acting methods can indeed lead to different degrees of self-involvement during role enactment and if different types of theatre require different role-acquisition strategies, then we cannot improve any of the above unless we understand the nature of their (dis)similarities. I will therefore proceed by examining two types of interactions in rehearsal: (1) interactions studied by transactional analysis and (2) interactions studied by role research. Transactional analysis examines the interaction between directors and actors in order to understand the real leadership-style properties of the rehearsal process. Role research, on the other hand, is an attempt to understand the ways an actor carries out a role (Hite et al. 1973:11; Miller and Bahs 1974:61; Porter 1975:4).

Then, I will look into several interdisciplinary efforts that harnessed semiotics and psychological aesthetics in order to document and explain the relationship between the sign systems of rehearsal-texts and performance-texts as well as the simultaneous interpretive experiences of actors and spectators. I will first negotiate a way of harnessing psychological aesthetics and semiotic research by equating Umberto Eco's concept of sign systems to Ivan Pavlov's concept of signaling systems before I proceed to examine the nature of theatrical illusion in the experience of actors and spectators. In doing so, I will propose a possible explanation about the emotional and/or congitive aspects of the responses of spectators and actors to the external or internal "signs" (alias "stimuli") in a theatrical situation.

Transactional analysts have observed that a director's communication system influences the type of relationship which develops between director and actors. In turn, this relationship affects the productivity of a cast during rehearsals. For example, the performance of *US* resulted from the teamwork of playwrights, designers, actors, musicians, and technicians under the direction of Peter Brook. They all wanted to make a statement about the Vietnam war, but Brook had no master plan as to how to proceed (1968:12). So, the production team created the circumstances in which such a play could be written (1968:13). Specifically, the production team wanted to illustrate contradicting attitudes in the theatregoers, who as members of the culture-consuming public in England in 1966 abhorred the war. Yet, they watched the conflict escalate on their television sets while they were seated comfortably in their living rooms in London. "We wanted actors to explore every aspect of this contradiction," Brook explained, "so that instead of accusing or condoning an audience, they could be what an actor is always supposed to be, the audience's representative, who is trained and prepared to go farther than a spectator down a path the spectator knows to be his own" (1968:10).

Jerzy Grotowski, director of the Polish Theatre Laboratory, was also invited to London to work with Peter Brook and the actors (Brook 1968:132). The team began to put together into playable units the material which they had accumulated very stumblingly (1968:136). "Preparation for *US* lasted over a year, rehearsals ran for nearly four months" (1968:1). From the standpoint of cost efficiency, the experimental production of *US* was profitless. The rehearsals had no sense of timing or sense of direction. Some randomly selected responses from both artists and spectators testify to that. "We were afraid of making a five-hour show," confessed the playwright (1968:137). "The whole thing is a process, and a process can always go two ways, go into reverse," admitted the director (1968:151). The resulting performances caused equally ambivalent feelings in the team and the audiences: The show "created enormous controversy" (1968:1); "the statement that was eventually made in Aldwych Theatre on 13 October 1966 may not have satisfied all of us" (1968:12). Although this and similar experimental conditions failed to satisfy many people, they inspired a few researchers to formulate hypotheses relevant to the artistic and economic concerns of theatre artists and theatre managers.

For example, Ronald Ruble's study, "Performer Descriptions of Stressed Rehearsal Conditions Created by an Authoritarian and a Libertarian Directing Method," concluded that directing methods created stress when they were incompatible with the perception of an actor about the role of the director (Ruble 1975). Generally, directors strove for a rapid creation of a robust performance-text during the rehearsals, but the results on opening night did not always honor their intentions. How could a researcher help innovative theatre artists eliminate misleading theories and bad habits from their theatrical practices? As a first step to analyzing rehearsal interaction, transactional analysts divided the behavior of a director into permissive behavior and restrictive behavior. Then, they examined how the two different kinds of directorial behavior affected the interaction of the cast as a group (alias "rehearsal atmosphere") and their building of roles or characters (alias "rehearsal task accomplishment").

In order to determine whether a director is using a permissive or a restrictive verbal communication system in rehearsal, Robert Porter developed an Observational System of Rehearsal Interaction (OSRIC), which studied important verbal cues of the communication between director and actors. The influence of a director was defined as "permissive" or "restrictive" when the director's set of verbal behaviors "expanded" or "restricted" the range of the behavior of the actors during rehearsal. Porter's OSRIC recorded the interaction between director and actors every three seconds, and it tabulated a sequence of their verbal communication in a series of numbers which corresponded to OSRIC categories (Porter 1975:8). First, Porter calculated the extent to which the director dominated the discussion during his or her interaction with the actors. Then, Porter computed the interaction ratio which compared the amount of director/actor interaction with the total time that they spent in the rehearsal session. The OSRIC categories and ratio indicated whether the director was using a permissive or a restrictive verbal communication system.

The importance of this distinction is clearly seen in Suzanne Trauth's investigation of permissive vs. restrictive rehearsal communication systems in actor task involvement and rehearsal atmosphere (1980:6). She tested two female directors and four casts three times during rehearsals. Each director used the permissive system of communication with the one cast and the restrictive system with the other. The results suggested that under the permissive communication system casts were more satisfied with the director; were less satisfied with each other in task accomplishment; felt the rehearsal atmosphere was more interesting but less supportive; consumed more rehearsal time in receiving encouragement; and spent more time interacting as a group but with less discipline. On the other hand, under the restrictive communication system, the casts felt that the rehearsal atmosphere was more supportive but less interesting; generated more detailed and better-developed ideas; consumed more rehearsal time in being kept in line, which led to actor resentment and director frustration; and finally, more rehearsal time was spent actually rehearsing the text. So, Trauth's results suggested that restrictive communication systems were more productive in terms of the quantity of work accomplished per rehearsal hour.

Interestingly, a significant number of directors who worked in subsidized theatres rejected both productivity concerns and restrictive communication in their dealings with performers and crews. They claimed that performance-texts were the end result of collective creativity during rehearsals. Grotowski, for instance, required that the participant performers in the production of *Tree of People* (Theatre Lab, Warshaw 1979) rid themselves of all productivity concerns (Findlay 1980:351). However, a close reading of the records of such rehearsals reveals that restrictive habits persisted in several actors and that permissive directors frustrated the actors' desire for quick answers.

Two random examples from the rehearsals of Joseph Chaikin and Peter Brook can illustrate this. One of Joseph Chaikin's performers felt confused during the rehearsals of *Nightwalk* and reported that "it feels like some people are waiting around for someone to tell them what to do" (Blumenthal 1984:143). And when the director did "tell" them, he did not "direct" them. Equally confused were the actors under Peter Brook's direction. Reportedly, Brook sustained a permissive communication system during the rehearsals of both *US* and Shakespeare's *Midsummer Night's Dream* (London 1970). Cast and crews were brought together to share their creative ideas, not to be briefed (Selbourne 1982:19, 29, 33, 47). However, Brook responded to a puzzled actor's question in a mystifying way during a rehearsal session of *US*:

> BROOK: Every group contains the seeds of its own
> destruction.
> ACTOR: Why does this have to be so?
> BROOK: I can't answer that. You must find out how true
> or not it is for yourself. (Brook 1968:147)

Transactional analysts looked further into the relationship between a director's expectations and the work performance of a cast—with regard for the expectations of the spectators. And for a good reason—many spectators, even several "open-minded" ones, expressed their frustration with performance-texts which came out of rehearsals of the above kind. "By itself this play has no meaning, and we cannot call it a play," Jean-Paul Sartre critiqued *US.* "The play ends and the spectator, sent back to his solitude, leaves with a confused despair made up of shock, fury and impotence" (Brook 1968:199). These performance-texts, which were usually created through improvisations and associations during rehearsals, confused and frustrated the expectations of actors and spectators, who subscribed to popular "Aristotelian" definitions according to which a "play" followed a logical, meaningful, progression with a beginning, middle, and end (Marowitz: 1966:153, 156).

Miller and Bahs tested the hypothesis that a director's implicit expectations directly conditioned the performance of a cast (1974:61). Eight volunteer directors were each given a cast of student actors to direct in two scenes. Miller and Bahs led each director to believe that his first-scene cast would perform well and that his second-scene cast would perform poorly. Dialogue, rehearsal time, and props were held constant. The dependent variable was the effective task accomplishment by a cast, and it was measured as "overall scene effectiveness." The performance or task accomplishment of each cast was videotaped and judged by a ten-member panel of theatre professors and advanced graduate students. The results supported the hypothesis that the director's unstated expectations—which were expressed through paralinguistic and kinesic cues—affected the actors' performance.

If the director's expectations about how well or poorly a cast will perform can influence the performance (task accomplishment) of the actors during rehearsal interaction, then the director has a significant role to play in improving rehearsal-text quality and, eventually, performance-text quality. Permissive directors such as

Peter Brook and Jerzi Grotowski (like psychiatrists so-to-speak) investigated the communicative experience of the actors and the spectators who, in a sense, were not in complete contact with the ordinary world during rehearsals or performances. By "briefing" or "interviewing" actors and sometimes spectators, they aimed at a mutual understanding among persons of various social and national origins. They were interested in arriving at an estimate of the meaning and purpose behind the forms of discourse and making directorial goals and interpretations understood by cast and crew.

Successful communication required that the permissive director respected the particular way in which each actor performed and that he was aware of his own directorial preconceptions. For example, Gilbert Lazier tested the traditional belief and practice which claimed that an actor standing on the right area of the stage acquires a "dramatically stronger" position than an actor standing on the left area of the stage. Lazier tried to define the variable "dramatic strength" in observable, quantifiable terms. He decided that one aspect of "dramatic strength" was "attention value," and he measured it with cameras, semantic differentials, and free-response interviews. His measurements of the "dramatic strength" between a downstage-right position and a downstage-left position showed that the alleged difference between the "dramatic strengths" of the two stage areas did not affect the "attention value" of the spectators (Lazier 1963:47). If it did not register in the attention of the spectators, does this mean that the traditional belief is just another myth or that "attention value" is not an aspect of "dramatic strength"?

The slow pace, the methodological flaws, and the uncertain findings about rehearsal interaction of many quantitative research projects have made inquisitive theatre artists discontent and impatient. They would rather pursue the same goals intuitively and faster. The unpopular goal of the structuralists, who adopted a quantitative mode of inquiry for theatre research, has been to arrive at a consensus of rational, verifiable opinion over the process of theatrical production. Indicatively, Lazier's experiment has been waiting to be verified or falsified through replication by other independent researchers for thirty years! Despite their claims to scientific precision in setting up their experiments and in communicating their results, many of these structuralists, such as Lazier, produced studies that were seriously flawed. But they believed that errors could be corrected through independent repetition of experiments if the quantitative mode of inquiry was to generate any knowledge that could approach the "truth" about rehearsal interaction.

The growing skepticism about methods and results, the elusive nature of truth, the limited number of quantitative research projects in theatre, the restricted funding of such projects, and the lack of a widely accepted taxonomic model of theatrical production have delayed the development of a paradigm. Of course, like a model, a paradigm is a metaphor which provides a partial or overall picture of theatrical production as an organic whole, or as a mechanical system, or as what have you. However, there is a crucial difference between models and paradigms. A paradigm is a relatively coherent and consistent set of beliefs which result from a number of *tested* models, providing an updated map of theatrical production. Conversely, a model is an *untested* diagrammatic representation of theatrical production which explains how the system operates logically. The qualitative mode of inquiry has crowded theatre studies with models about theatrical production and its various "parts" since Aristotle. Despite the "scientific" lingo, however, the quantitative mode of inquiry has not developed a paradigm in the field of theatre.

Nonetheless, the models which resulted from a quantitative or qualitative mode of inquiry cannot be slighted because they often resulted from a careful observation of the "experimental" conditions prevalent in rehearsals and performances. Many of these projects articulated their variables and hypotheses in the context of theatrical practice, but they used the models, methods, and techniques of certain disciplines from the humanities and the social sciences. In addition, many a critic argued that the borrowing of methodological tools from other more developed disciplines can increase the scope for obtaining knowledge *about* the theatrical process but not *of* the theatrical process (Clevenger 1965:120). Such critics thought that research in the field of theatre cannot progress unless it gradually develops its own tools adapted to its special subject matter.

For the most part, the structuralists stuck to their logic and to their understanding of the "facts" of theatrical "reality" as observable, mutable entities—trying not to contradict themselves by holding two opposite views at the same time. Ironically, as soon as they forbade themselves from holding conflicting views by rejecting rigid all-or-none and either/or thinking, they thought that the "reality" they described contained contradictory elements—often in binary opposites. They assumed a noncommital posture, and they believed in raising the discussion of the issues involved above personal opinion and into the haven of scientific objectivity. A small portion of their research projects appeared in the journal of *Empirical Research in Theatre* from 1973 to 1984. Once a community of theatregoers and/or theatre artists established a goal (standard), the empiricists felt confident that they could analyze performance conditions, study patterns of (inter)acting, and evaluate whether it would be wiser to modify set goals or to find other ways to achieve them.

But it was precisely these set goals—and their values—that the manifestos and productions of the alternative theatres turned into a bone of contention during rehearsals. Their quasi-deconstructive trends subverted set ideas about the way plays were produced in Western theatre, and they pushed for changes. For example, the formalists, during rehearsals, "reconstructed" the themes and images of a playtext by resolving interpretive difficulties in order to produce as meaningful a performance-text as possible, and they professed that, on opening night, a performance-text became more "intelligible" to a spectator than a playtext to a reader because all the elements appeared well-connected and unified. It was precisely this facile intelligibility of the (dramatic) world that the advocates of some alternative theatres attacked and deconstructed. They showed that to *perform* an interpretation in logocentric theatrical production meant to contrive meanings through closure. Some of their "experimental" productions manifested a higher epistemological sophistication than the "scientific" projects of some empiricists.

CHAPTER THREE

Role Research

Role research studies the available and potential strategies for the acquisition and enactment of roles in the theatre. The acquisition and enactment of a role depends on the capabilities of a person to take a role or to give a role. How an actor will develop depth and breadth in a particular character (role) is related to the way he or she will structure his or her personal system of interpreting and assigning meaning to people and things (Crockett 1965). Of course, actors and spectators differ in the scope and depth of their impressions of people and of things because they differ in the complexity and organization of their cognitive assessments (Delia 1976:152). As cognitive complexity increases in a person, he or she is able to form more differentiated, abstract, and organized impressions of others and has a greater capacity for taking their perspective (Hale and Delia 1976:196, 202; Peevers and Secord 1973:126).

When an actor prepares to perform a character, his ability to take the perspective of that character seems related to his ability to communicate the depth and breadth of that character to his fellow actors and to the spectators. Based on this assumption, Powers, Jorns, and Glenn tested a triple hypothesis: actors with high cognitive complexity *develop* more in-depth characterizations and are *rated* and *rank* significantly higher in performance evaluations than actors of low cognitive complexity. The results obtained from forty-three actors—whose cognitive complexity had been previously assessed with the Role Category Questionnaire (Hale and Delia 1976:201)—confirmed the above hypothesis. The levels of an actor's cognitive complexity seemed to have a differentiated impact on his depth of character portrayal. Powers, Jorns, and Glenn suggested that even if a person's cognitive complexity resists major changes, it is still possible to train him as an actor; to maximize his quota; and to help him acquire perceptual depth in the specific stimulus field created during rehearsal interaction (1980:2, 5).

Richard Boleslavsky expressed a similar thought in the vernacular when he claimed that the "Creature" (an 18-year-old student) could become an actress in just six lessons on concentration, memory of emotion, dramatic action, characterization, observation, and rhythm (1933:16). These lessons would train her body, voice, mind, and, more importantly, her soul because an actress "must have a soul capable of living through any situation demanded by the author" (1933:26). Boleslavsky believed that the physical resources (such as intelligence, talent, beauty, and voice) could not be taught, but a method of acting could. Unless a student acquired a method of acting (technique) and became an "emotion maker," her otherwise impressive physical resources would remain ineffective on stage. The most elemental quality for an actress was her ability to transmit the thoughts, emotions, and words of another person (character) sensibly.

According to Boleslavsky, an actress could transmit these thoughts, emotions, and words by concentrating on the human soul (her own soul first) in order to create a real value, no matter how small, according to her strength. Her deep concentration, through emotional recall, would elicit thoughts and emotions in her soul which were absent earlier. Then, the actress would organize and synchronize her own self with the self of the character. She would substitute the playwright's creation with the "real thing" by creating real emotions and thoughts with the help of her imagination and "affective memory," not by external imitation (1933:35, 41). Like a good playwright who wrote and rewrote a sentence until he found what he wanted, a good actress should try and retry until she found the "right" thought and emotion. The rehearsals would help the actress (1) memorize her (inter)action in accordance with the "character" of the actor who opposes her and (2) build up emotion to a climax in the manner of a tree which grows upward, building sideways resistances, and balance.

Boleslavsky's actress would create the life of a human soul by making the character's soul unique and individual. This soul, like everything else in the world, would partake in a universal rhythm. The soul would transit through three levels to achieve perfection: consciousness, empathic response to external rhythms, and control of the rhythms created by herself and others (1933:77, 117). The universal rhythm would eliminate chaos from the world because, despite any number of disorderly, conflicting actions, *change* sooner or later would show an (orderly) pattern (1933:113). Likewise, the "chaos" that a spectator would observe in a performance-text was in fact artistic rhythm (organized energy) for the same reason: it was composed of the most "orderly and measurable" changes of all the different, disorderly, conflicting elements involved—provided that these changes progressively stimulated the attention of the spectator and led invariably to the final aim of the artist (1933:112). An actress could acquire rhythm by giving herself up freely and entirely to any rhythms she happened to encounter in life.

Eventually, Boleslavsky introduced his student actress to an interesting double standard in order to preserve the sanctity of the playwright's words and the actress' artistic creativity. On the one hand, she could not give an acceptable portrayal of a character's thoughts—which mirrored the rhythm of the playwright's thoughts— unless her delivery observed the rhythm of the character's words (1933:84). If Juliet's words in Shakespeare's *Romeo and Juliet* had the rhythm of the thoughts of a philosopher, an actress who would deliver them with the rhythm that characterizes the thoughts of a teenager would be lost (1933:83). On the other hand, an actress was justified in adjusting the playwright's writing in order to achieve the best results for her own emotional portrayal of the character— and a wise playwright would agree to that because "emotion is God's breath in a part" (1933:84). "Acting is the life of the human soul receiving its birth through art," Boleslavsky claimed (1933:22).

Numerous "methods" of acting have been developed that allegedly facilitate effective character portrayal. Most of them resort to mystifying pronouncements about the art of acting—similar to Boleslavsky's theocratic rehash of Pythagoras and Stanislavsky— reinforcing the logocentric theatrical tradition. These methods of acting range from empathic methods to nonempathic methods. Generally, the empathic methods merge the "self" of an actor with the "self" of a character—that is, an actor understands and identifies with a character's situation, feelings, and motives. Conversely, the nonempathic methods require that an actor understands but detaches himself from a character's situation, feelings, and motives. Understanding remains a stable factor in all methods. Stanislavsky's method of acting provides a prime example of an empathic method. The actor transforms himself into a character through an understanding of the character's textual and subtextual specifications provided by the playwright and of his similar personal experiences (emotion memory). The actor is vested with a *persona* (mask) which is handed down to him by the playwright (playtext) or the director (prompt-copy). So, the illusion, which transforms the dramatic world on stage into a "slice" of life, begins with the actor before it reaches the audience.

Empathic methods would have been reliable only if their main axiom—that the actors who experience true feelings on stage can generate equally true feelings in the spectators in the auditorium—were true. This is not always the case, however. Sometimes actors split their sides with inner intensity, leaving the audience quite apathetic. Conversely, calm actors, who run their daily role routine on stage, sometimes electrify spectators with almost no effort. It seems that under certain conditions the "surface truth" of a nonempathic method can be more effective than the "inner truth" of an empathic method. So, truthfulness in the intensity and authenticity of an actor's personal feelings does not necessarily influence audience response. Artaud warned that "unless that feeling has been shaped into a communicative image, it is a passionate letter without postage" (Marowitz 1966:161). This warning, however, did not discredit an actor's ability to respond to "imaginary stimuli" (Lee Strasberg's term) and to create real thoughts and feelings under imaginary circumstances.

Denis Diderot was the first critic to give a detailed description of a nonempathic method in 1773. But the so-called "nonempathic" methods of acting in the twentieth century—which were introduced by Antonin Artaud, Bertolt Brecht, Richard Schechner, Peter Brook, Joseph Chaikin among many others—were developed in a dialectical opposition to the empathic methods of Konstantin Stanislavsky, Richard Boleslavsky, Lee Strasberg, Uta Hagen, Michael Chekhov, and a host of others. Such dialectical oppositions, however, are deceptive and questionable because they do not explain how or why some "nonempathic" methods instill strong empathic elements. If, indeed, empathic and nonempathic methods have a common denominator, dialectical oppositions of the above kind are invalid and the schematic rhetoric of their advocates is confusing. Nonetheless, historically speaking, oppositions of this kind made clear that different kinds of role-playing lead to different types of theatre—such as Brecht's epic theatre, Brook's holy theatre, Schechner's environmental theatre. In turn, different types of theatre change the role acquisition strategies during rehearsals. Some directors and actors would rather delay blocking to analyze action than block and fix action as soon as possible; they would rather suggest and improvise than order and obey; they would rather stop to intellectualize than act spontaneously based on past experiences; and they would rather perform as the immediacy of each performance directed, not as prescribed by the rehearsals.

The degree of an actor's self-involvement remains a common denominator to all acting methods proposed. Nominally, the nonempathic methods require that an actor's self-involvement take a conscious, critical attitude as it pursues an interplay between his literary "masks" and his real face. Vsevolod Meyerhold's biomechanic method and Brecht's epic method are two cases in point. Both methods insisted that an actor should not allow his own identity to merge with the identity of the character completely. The actor should not permit himself to become totally transformed into the character that he is portraying. "He is not Lear, Harpagon, Schweik; he shows them" (Brecht 1964:137). The dialectical tension between the fictive and the real should be preserved throughout the performance because it allegedly permitted the actor to "demonstrate" rather than "impersonate" the character and his world.

They assumed that if complete empathy was not interrupted, the actor would automatically be carried away and would "lose" himself in the character completely (Brecht 1964:58, 93; Meyerhold 1969:170). Even when an actor's goal was to put an audience into a trance, the actor "must not go into a trance himself" (Brecht 1964:193). Meyerhold, who wished that his actors would affect the emotions of the spectators without resorting to representational methods of acting, invented a grotesque biomechanical method of acting. He thought that grotesque representations subordinate "psychologism to a decorative task," and he gave body language priority over speech (1969:141). Nonetheless, Meyerhold's method turned actors into automatons by subjugating their staged behavior to a sequence of artificial spontaneity. Meyerhold expected the spectators to complete the "stage image" (performance-text) mentally through associations (1969: 199, 250). In the 1930s, Pavlov, if not Stanislavsky, became the departure point for Meyerhold's method of acting, which Meyerhold reduced into a typical structuralist formula: $N = A1 + A2$. The formula expressed the dual status of an actor because an actor ("N") was both the performer ("A1") who conceived an idea, and the instrument ("A2") which executed the idea of "A1."

Meyerhold called this duality the "first I" (i.e., the creative process, imagination) and the "second I" (i.e., the technique, biomechanics). Meyerhold broke down stage movement into "acting cycles" which consisted of three parts: intention, realization, reaction. Robert Leach noticed that Meyerhold drove himself into a contradiction because his "cycle" referred not just to the "second I" (the A2 part), but also involved the "first I" (the A1 part) through the intention.

> In fact, Meyerhold dealt with this confusion by changing the scientific location of his theory to chime now with Pavlov's reflexology and the "acting cycle" became the "playing link." Now, the stimulus (A1 in the previous equation) triggers a reflex action, which is the realization. When the realization is done, it comes to rest prepared for a new intention, and this comprises a state of "excitability" which can provoke the correct reflex action: the "point of excitability" is the period of receptivity and rest. An actor at a "point of excitability" is like a car whose engine is idling: press the accelerator and the car "realizes" the action, it moves forward. If the actor is without this "excitability," he is like a car whose ignition is switched off: press its accelerator, and nothing happens. So biomechanics comes to include the creation of "states of excitability." (Leach 1989:54)

Meyerhold believed that a method of acting should have physical, not psychological, foundations because all psychological states were determined by physiological processes. An actor who had correctly resolved the nature of his state physically could reach a "point of excitability" which was informed by a particular emotion. This "state of excitability" was communicated to the spectators, "gripped" them, and made them share in the actor's performance. The essence of an actor's art was the process of exciting his emotions and the emotions of the spectators (Meyerhold 1969:199, 200).

Another common denominator shared by empathic and nonempathic methods is that they invariably require of an actor to understand the values (psychology or ideology) of both his own mental luggage and the character's during rehearsal interaction. The second requirement was waved by trance methods of acting. Does this mean that a new dichotomy needs to be formed? Jerzi Grotowski's poor theatre, Richard Schechner's environmental theatre, and Peter Brook's holy theatre suggest a negative answer. Grotowski's method of acting dropped the mask (also known as *persona* or character), and it asked the actors to work without a playtext or a prompt-copy in order to develop a performance-text based on autobiographical (i.e., nonliterary) elements. His method favored actor over character and action over memorized speech (*Apocalypsis cum Figuris* 1968). Reportedly, the substitution of speech by movement allowed the actor's direct self-expression. This self-expression was molded by the collective unconscious forces operating during an unstructured rehearsal, and it was incorporated in what gradually emerged as a performance-text.

According to Daniel Cashman, during the making of *Tree of People* at the Polish Theatre Lab, "the intensity and relentlessness of the sound and movement in that confined space verged on being mesmeric" (1979:462). Grotowski's method, which drew on Artaud's method, dictated different specifications for actors in rehearsal than in performance. Whereas empathic and nonempathic methods of acting sustained performances of a predetermined length, trance methods of acting sustained performances of an undetermined length that depended on the power of the trance and on the direct interaction between the actors and the spectators. In some performances of the Balinese theatre, the performers had to be "wrestled out of trance" in order to end the performance (Schechner 1973:18, 24). However, two things cannot escape my attention: (1) the actors in trance were more oblivious to their audience than the actors in empathic performances who performed behind a "fourth" wall, segregating themselves from the spectators; and (2) the trance method of acting followed a "rational" ritual which enabled the actors to reach the state of trance methodically.

Stanislavsky insisted that going to the theatre ought to be like visiting the Prozorov household with the fourth wall removed. Presumably, the various empathic performances concealed the seams which divided the fictive world of the actors from the real world of the spectators. During the various nonempathic performances, the actors took pains to expose the "fact" that the fictive world on stage was of a different conceptual order from the real world in the auditorium through such devises as "alienation" (Brecht's term). Obviously, neither methods of acting seemed satisfactory to the advocates of "environmental theatre" because they removed both the "fourth wall" and the walls surrounding a playhouse. They attempted "to break the hypnotic effect of continuous performance and to unsettle the myth which grows up once a performance has begun a *run*" (Marowitz 1966:166). Environmental performances involved both actors and spectators in role-playing, and they made no attempt to harmonize the feelings of the performers with the alleged feelings of the characters (Schechner 1973:12). Consequently, the old role-acquisition strategies changed once more. But even these new methods of acting failed to escape from the hypnotic or mesmerizing effect.

The "mesmerizing effect," which, in various degrees, has been observed to be a common denominator in theatrical performances sustained by trance, empathic, and nonempathic methods of acting, may become a special means to investigate and affect communication in theatrical production. In all cases, actors and spectators lost their awareness of "acting" or "watching," respectively, as soon as they came under the spell of the "mesmerizing effect." Reportedly, the flight from reality into the world of either illusion or ecstasy allowed actors and spectators to express and watch an "unconscious conflict" overtly in a performance and, paradoxically, to keep this conflict "unconscious." What perplexes me is how and why (1) an actor's responses change when he enters a state of trance, (2) an actor's thought is suspended when his behavior becomes automatic, and (3) an actor's responses can vary from being totally unaffected to being completely affected. Clearly, we cannot improve role-acquisition strategies for both actors and spectators unless we understand the role of the mesmerizing effect as a form of interpersonal (actor-actor or actor-spectator) influence. What conditions cause and sustain the mesmerizing effect in the theatre?

Franz Mesmer excited histrionic crises in his patients. He found that silence, darkness, expectation, and excitement—conditions which are prevalent for actors in a playhouse—encouraged exaggerated behavior in some predisposed persons, especially when these persons were in the presence of a group of people (1799, 1980). It was also assumed that mesmeric phenomena could be explained on the basis of imagination and imitation. As early as the 1840s, James Braid observed that attention, imagination, expectancy, and mental concentration can cause a trance-like state. He also noted two things that are relevant to the issue at hand: (1) physiological changes, such as in respiration, can result by riveting one's attention to an internal idea, an external object, or by overexercising one set of muscles; and (2) trance is a subjective state of mind which occurs when dormant concepts are awakened by dominant one-word concepts or "themes" suggested by the director of the experiment to the person who enacts the hypnotic role (Sarbin and Coe 1972:29, 31). Indicatively, directors, such as Joseph Chaikin, chose their ensembles in part according to their sense of who would get excited by a "theme" that they wished to explore.

Chaikin expected his performers to become "obsessed" and "possessed" by such a theme (Blumenthal 1984:140). The notion of suggestion and autosuggestion was introduced by the Nancy school and was later refined into the concepts of "imitation," "identification," and "role-taking" by social psychologists. More recent studies see trance behavior as a variety in conduct which always begins in a social interaction and, therefore, can be explained by a theory of social behavior, namely, role theory. Role theory recognizes the usefulness of concepts such as believing, imagining, and expecting. It borrows the concept of role from the theatre in order to postulate that human conduct in society adheres to certain "roles" rather than to the "personality" of the people who enact them (Sarbin and Coe 1972:63–64). Role enactment is, of course, observable action whether it takes place in society or in the theatre, on stage (actors), or in the auditorium (spectators).

The quality of role enactment depends on the congruence between self and role, the accuracy of role expectations, the sensitivity of the person to the demands of the role, the mastery of the appropriate role skills by the person, and the influence of the audience. Usually, if one's personality traits are compatible with the role that he or she located, the number of roles she or he may enact diminishes sharply. During the enactment of a role, inadvertently, the actions themselves may cause changes in the same role or bring about new roles. Generally, the more roles are available to a person, the more flexible he or she becomes in social interaction. So, a large repertoire of roles makes it a simpler task to enter a newly assigned role (Sarbin and Coe 1972:69–70). Persons who, like actors, are more adept at taking new roles are also more adept at enacting the hypnotic role (Sarbin and Lim 1963).

Role theory indicates that a person's psychological involvement and physiological involvement in a role vary significantly. Theodore Sarbin and V. Allen suggested eight levels of such involvement in role enactment. Five of these levels are directly relevant to the theatre and to the issue at hand. Schematically speaking, the degree of self-involvement in role enactment can take the following numerical values: casual acting (1/5), ritual acting (2/5), heated acting (3/5), hypnotic acting (4/5), ecstatic acting (5/5). At either extreme of the spectrum, I can also mention the rare occasions of "zero acting" and "bewitched acting" (Figure 12). The conditions and states of awareness from "zero acting" to "bewitched acting" vary, depending on the degree of a person's self-involvement. Zero acting requires a total absence of self-involvement—both psychologically and physiologically. For example, the case of an expired membership to an undesirable theatre association raises no expectation for action and keeps role enactment dormant. Bewitched acting, on the other hand, is the ultimate level of self-involvement in role enactment.

Casual acting requires a minimal degree of self-involvement during role enactment such as that requested of a spectator seated comfortably in the theatre. Richard Schechner, among other directors, observed that, generally, spectators abandoned the passive role enactment of casual acting reluctantly when some performances of the "environmental theatre" requested of them a more active role enactment. Brook, too, noted that shifting oneself totally from one role to another is a superhuman task at any time (Brook 1968:33; Schechner 1973:16). Any methods of acting which build a protective "fourth wall" between actors and spectators, turn the spectators into passive eyewitnesses of a dramatic world. A spectator who talks with the performers or leaves his seat to join the action is immediately "framed" by the other spectators as one of the cast. In environmental theatre, however, such a "framing" can be incorrect. Environmental theatre requires more active role enactment by the spectators so that they can enhance their repertoire of role-taking and self-involvement in role enactment.

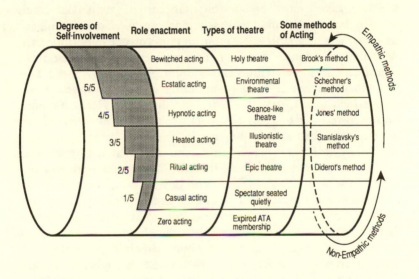

FIGURE 12. Methods of Acting and Degrees of Self-Involvement.

Ritual acting, in turn, calls for low degrees in self-involvement during role enactment. Mlle Clairon (1723–1803) offered a prime example of ritual acting according to Denis Diderot. Like a prostitute in the arms of her client, she did not allow herself to express genuine feelings. Instead, she enacted her role mechanically depicting pleasure, eagerness, etc., but, on self-examination, she reported low self-involvement psychologically and physiologically in the enactment of the assigned role (Diderot 1957:20). Nonetheless, she maintained a degree of consistency in the enactment of the role which engaged more of her self than casual acting. Her acting (diction, intonation, emotional variations, positions, movement, and gestures) was invariably constant from performance to performance. With the precision of a mirror, her memory cooly reflected and reproduced memorized lines and memorized emotions. She did not feel exhausted by repeating a wide range of emotions because she was trained to act from the head, not the heart. Her self-control even allowed her to drop her mask (role), address the audience directly, and then resume her mask (role).

Bertolt Brecht placed this kind of ritual acting into an ideological context in his epic theatre. Brecht's method of acting explored some of the conditions and devices which "estrange" the actor's self from the role that he enacts. Brecht's "alienation" device instructed both actors and spectators how to avoid identifying with theatrical and social roles completely—allowing room for individual freedom and social change. In short, Brecht's "alienation" or "defamiliarization" device, which works best through contrast and parody, introduced the radical idea that role enactment in the theatre, in principle, is not different from role enactment in society. It also raised a serious question about the feasibility of ritual acting, which was praised by Diderot. Brecht was aware that, no matter how hard they tried, his actors were not fully successful in preventing themselves from identifying with the characters that they portrayed during their performances. "So, the most likely result," Brecht concluded, "is that truly rending contradiction between experience and portrayal, empathy and demonstration, justification and criticism" (1964:277).

William Archer expressed a similar skepticism about the feasibility of ritual acting as early as 1888. He submitted that Diderot founded "his doctrine" on slender evidence and that "no man" was entitled to raise his limited experiences about acting into a dogma through armchair philosophizing. Diderot's division between emotional actors (second-rate) and unemotional actors (first-rate) was misleading because, according to Archer, first-rate actors are those who affect their audiences, not those who remain unemotional. Archer's first-rate actors exhibited and reported "many symptoms of acute feeling, some of which are quite involuntary, and are of no direct use in heightening the illusion" (1957:77).

As a good empiricist, Archer wanted to find "the laws" governing the acting of an "average or typical" actor. So, he collected "the views and experiences of actors of the highest order" from self-reports, historical records, and interviews. Then, he compared, classified, studied, and interpreted "as large a circle as possible of individual cases" (1957:76). Archer concluded that some actors maintain their identity under certain conditions, paying lip service to the role through stylized gestures, intoned sentences, and sham effects. However, "the majority of the players" tend to act more effectively when they "play from the heart" than from the head alone—i.e. when they are involved in rather than detached from the emotions and thoughts that they portray.

Heated acting is generally identified with the emotionally involved acting. Heated acting requires a higher degree of self-involvement during role enactment than ritual acting. The actor who takes his role "literally" is the classic example. He temporarily merges his self (identity) with the self (identity) of the character that he impersonates. However, he does not surrender his self to the role totally. In fact, the actor maintains a minimal distance from his role so that he can control his tempo, intensity, and amplitude accordingly. Stanislavsky's method, among other empathic methods, best exemplifies this type of role enactment. The actor knows that everything on stage (sets, props, costumes, makeup, lighting, dramatic action, characters, and so on) is a fake, an imitation, a lie. Nonetheless, the actor says to himself that *if* everything was true, then he would have thought, felt, and (re)acted in this or that way. Based on the "as-if" device, the actor induces in himself genuine emotional, cognitive, and physical responses. The actor can maintain a high level of genuine responses only if he constantly deludes himself by believing that everything on stage—from external actions to internal emotions—is true (1963:354–355). Imaginary stimuli from "within" and from "without" the actor conspire, reinforcing each other through spiraling levels of credibility and authenticity.

> I came to realize that creativeness begins at the moment when
> the magical, *creative "if"* appears in the soul and imagination of
> the actor. Creativeness does not begin while actual reality exists,
> while there is genuine truth which a man naturally cannot but
> believe. Then the creative *if* appears, that is, the imagined truth
> in which the actor believes more sincerely and with greater
> enthusiasm than he would in genuine truth just as a little girl
> believes in the existence of her doll and in everything around
> her. From the moment this *if* appears, the actor passes from the
> plane of actual reality into the plane of another life, a life he
> himself creates and imagines. (Stanislavsky 1963:355)

Stanislavsky would embrace any truth-like conventions of
playwriting, scenography, directing, and acting—realist or
impressionist, conventional or modernist—as long as they were
believable to actors (and spectators) and they helped actors "*recreate
the life of the human spirit of the play and its characters*" (1963:366).
In *The Drama of Life*, Stanislavsky went as far as to eliminate the
material, corporeal, observable means of acting (gestures,
movements, and poses) because he wished to recreate a purely
"unembodied passion." This passion would be born and nourished
by the actor's soul and emotions exclusively, not by any physical
stimuli coming in from his body or from the outside world (1963:359–
360). Since Stanislavsky considered acting as an "embodiment" of
the life of the human spirit, an ideal method of acting would help
an actor not to cause a "break between inner emotion and its physical
incarnation" (1963:399). Indicatively, Stanislavsky called his
exploratory acting sessions, which he held with Gordon Craig and
Leopold Sulerzhitsky, "seances." The metaphysical tone of the above
investigations is more evident in the work of Edmond Jones than
of Stanislavsky.

Edmond Jones called the process of acting "the miracle of
incarnation." Acting was a process of incarnation (1941:31). An actor
who impersonated Hamlet became Hamlet's "host." He invited
Hamlet into himself by lending Hamlet his body, voice, and nerves.
Once the process of incarnation was complete, Hamlet's voice spoke
through the actor who was moved by Hamlet's impulses. "Hamlet
is as real as you and I" (1941:32). Like a medium during a series
of seances, an actor rehearsed and perfected the "art of speaking

with tongues other than one's own" (1941:32–33). However, an actor did not lose his sense of self even though he was "possessed" by a character.

For Jones, it was a "great mystery" to eyewitness how a character developed from the first flashes of contact in the mind of a playwright to the final moment "when the character steps on the stage in full possession of the actor, whose personal self looks on from somewhere in the background" (1941:32). Like a person under hypnosis, an actor went through "a gradual, half-conscious unfolding and flowering of the self into a new personality" (1941:37). Directors and designers should respect this process as sacred and use their designs and directing to "enhance the natural powers" of an actor. The stage belongs to the actors because they, not the director, interpret the play (1941:114). So, like a hypnotist, a director should "call forth" these powers instead of imposing his ideas on an actor.

Hypnotic acting calls for an even higher degree of self-involvement than heated acting. During hypnotic acting, an actor loses his awareness that he is only enacting a role. He no longer behaves "as if" he is in pain, tears, or anger. Instead, he is actually experiencing these emotions or sensations. Some rare moments caused by empathic methods of acting—such as those reported by Antoine, Archer, Jones, or Stanislavsky—provide good examples. Of course, the overt symptoms of hypnotic acting are observable and measurable. The effects of similar kinds of organismic self-involvement during role enactment were measured by galvanic skin response, sphygmomanometer, and verbal self-reports describing the degree of the person's involvement in the hypnotic experience (Hilgard 1969; Sarbin 1956). However, the investigators had no way of determining if the actual experience was indeed similar to the "experience" reported to them by the person who had enacted a hypnotic role (Sarbin and Coe 1972:75–76). The anecdotal reports of actors who slipped in a hypnotic role momentarily suggest that an actor's behavior under hypnotic acting deviates from what is normal in a wakened state, but also that it is conditioned by a specific cultural significance which is based on an actor's grasp of reality and of identity.

Usually, one can slip into a state of hypnosis by listening to the directions of a hypnotist, or to one's heartbeat, or to any other rhythmical sound that entails repetitive movement such as chants, lullabies, and dances. One can also hypnotize himself by performing a task which requires attention but little variation in response (Krippner 1977, 1980). Of course, Brecht objected to "hypnotic tensions" for actors and spectators that develop during a rehearsal or a performance (1964:136). Under a hypnotic state of consciousness, the actor's sensory threshold is lowered, making him extremely receptive to suggestions. The actor is alert, but he shows an absence of continuous alpha waves on the EEG. And he abandons his habitual ways of seeing the world inside and outside his head. He concentrates his attention on a single stimulus (a single emotion, thought, or object) and feels at one with the stimulus without responding to other stimuli. To his credit, Peter Brook, among other theatre artists, was aware of the impossibility of escaping such states of consciousness. "The aim is not how to avoid illusion," Brook commented on Brecht's devise of estrangement. "Everything is illusion, only some things seem more illusory than others" (1969:79). Or, if I may put it in another way, everything is real, only some things seem to be more real than others.

For the mystics, ecstasy describes the experience of one's inner vision of god or of one's union with the divine. Certain physical activities (e.g., trance dance) and certain chemical substances (e.g., hallucinogenic drugs) seem to help one achieve this vision and union. Some mystics prefer dance, and some others use drugs. Many theatre artists used both during the era of the 1960s in order to induce on themselves an ecstatic state of consciousness. If empathic methods of acting can elicit hypnotic states of consciousness, which methods of acting can cause ecstatic states of consciousness? Or, to put it in another way, if realist types of theatre—from socialist realism to bourgeois realism—shrunk, attenuated, and falsified reality by creating only an illusion of reality, then an alternative type of theatre ought to be able to find and present reality (Ionesco 1964:14). Schechner thought that the environmental type of theatre could express reality (i.e., an altered state of consciousness) by inventing a new method of acting and theatrical presentation. "I believe the model is attainable," Schechner wrote. "It's a question of training performers, directors, and audiences to look at theatre not as a reflection or duplication of reality—as secondary reality—but as itself a primary kind of reality" (1973:166).

Alfred Jarry was among the first who had shown a way of tapping "primary" reality. He argued that a comprehensible tale served only to oppress the mind, and he questioned that progress consisted of gradually developing the "embryonic cerebral convolutions" of an audience (1965:84). A theatre artist could not liberate his mind—and subsequently the minds of his spectators— unless he altered his mental activity and the way he perceived reality and his identity. Indeed, after World War II, theatre artists began to attack the coherence of a dramatic world by dismantling the make-believe devices which supported such worlds. They would rather study the interactions among the real actors than among the fictive characters. They would rather strip a staged locale of its "there-and-then" fictive presumtions than disguise the "here-and-now" real presence of a performance space. They would rather encourage the spectators to interrupt and change the course of a contrived plot than encourage the actors to maintain the course of a well-made plot.

Traditional, logocentric plots manipulated the behavior of the actors and the responses of the spectators because they had preselected and prearranged interrelated situations in a time sequence in order to give a certain direction and a sense of causality. The suspense which was achieved through exposition, complication, crisis, climax, and conclusion was criticized because it reinforced an inflexible, authoritarian structure. However, formalist "revolutionaries" of the Brechtian kind discouraged actors and spectators from daring to change the fictive world depicted in their playtexts and prompt-copies. Under such double standards, how could these "revolutionaries" expect the theatregoers to be bold enough to change the real world in a society? So, the structuralist advocates of alternative theatres structured performance-texts which facilitated the active role of the spectators in the outcome of a plot-in-the-making. For example, during a performance of Schechner's *Dionysus in '69*, a group of student spectators from Queens College kidnapped the actor who impersonated Pentheus. In this way, they prevented the sacrifice of Pentheus to Dionysus. The actor impersonating Dionysus protested, accusing the students for coming to the theatre with a plan worked out. "Why not?" the student spectators retorted. "Don't actors plan their actions?" The student spectators dumped the "kidnapped" actor in the street, and the actor refused to return to the theatre to be sacrificed to Dionysus.

In short, this type of theatre eliminated the dividing line between stage (fictive time and space) and auditorium (real time and space) by structuring performance-texts which allowed the spectators to join the action and to contribute to the new direction of the dramatic events.

The Ecstasy Dance during the performance of *Dionysus in '69* made it easy for the spectators to join the performers through singing, clapping, or dancing —as if they were attending a religious service (Schechner 1973:42). Schechner repeatedly observed that the participation of the audience occured precisely at the point where the performance broke down and became a social event (1973:40, 44, 45). In these "social" events, the rhythmical body movement and sounds—such as clapping and inarticulate cries— became the visual and auditory counterpart of the unconscious as it emerged in the fantasies of the participants (1973:131, 167). Although the use of drugs and brainwashing devices are not reported in these social events, the participants (actors and spectators) often followed their revealing associations to the very end "except for physical violence" (1973:132).

For example, a dance of some thirty participants was staged with music in the spacious, dimly lit U.R.I. theatre in 1971. The participants danced for six hours around an altar of fresh fruit and flowers that were spilling from a cornucopia—which was a toilet bowl. They began dancing at midnight and ended their dancing at 6 a.m. when the dance was interrupted. Reportedly, some of them had reached a state of trance, and several others, including Richard Schechner, had an orgie. Schechner himself admitted to having been among the participants who had sex during the "social event." The following day, Schechner defended himself by saying that he was no more responsible than anyone else that night because it was the workshop participants who had made the rules collectively. "And I wasn't the only one to fuck!" he added (1973:103–104). According to Schechner, these kind of ecstatic performances brought the participants close to the theatre of many "primitive" peoples "whose performances have always been an exteriorization of inner states" (1973:194). In a sense, theatre was allegedly returning to its roots—the religious rituals of fertility and dionysiac revelry.

Ecstatic acting requires a complete and extremely intense self-involvement—both psychological and physiological—which suspends voluntary action. Ecstatic acting can damage a person when prolonged. It occurs only in special social or theatrical occasions. Ethnographers have described such experiences that sometimes happen during religious conversions, rock-and-roll concerts, and Balinese type of theatrics. Role enactments of the ecstatic kind are terminated through institutionalized rituals or exhaustion (Hilgard 1965). Ecstatic acting is expressive rather than communicative, releasing individual tensions and providing pleasure. It is primarily meant to remove the ethical, social, and mental inhibitions of the participants by opening up their subconscious and the subliminal dimension of the world. According to their taste, temperament, and tradition, the participants experience ecstasy. This state of consciousness is viewed as a creative spontaneity which brings the participants in touch with the essence of things. This state of consciousness cannot be achieved by the application of rationalism. The ecstatic states of consciousness are not necessarily unpleasant when they occur, although their consequences may be embarrassing or destructive.

Reportedly, ecstatic methods of acting jolted actors and spectators into new insights about their "real" self and the "true" reality (Brook 1968:56). They offered a "profound visceral experience touching off deep reverberations in the audience" (Schechner 1973:173). And they helped the participants experience a satisfaction deeper than that caused by empathic methods of acting. It is said that the ecstatic methods of acting allowed actors and spectators to experience a "nuptial union" with ultimate reality. This sense of contact with the "real thing" resulted from a state of consciousness as the participants surrendered their individual will to the will of the group during a "social" event—cf., Schechner's valid claim that the "workshop" made the rules. Like the psychedelic ("mind-manifesting") drugs, these methods of acting released a vast amount of associations and emotions from the past and present history of an individual actor or spectator. This release offered him or her the pleasure of a direct experience with a sense of "reality." From this sense ensued a feeling that the ego boundaries melted away. This melt-down of the self, reportedly, led to feelings of freedom, creativity, and euphoria.

Ecstatic methods of acting upset the rules of ordinary, everyday life and experience, offering a sense of intoxication—sexual or otherwise. But they did not guarantee that the participants would experience a sense of a mystical union with divinity—i.e., the ultimate reality. A theatre director, who was viewed or viewed himself as a shaman or as a guru, assumed the ability to open up higher, truer states of consciousness which helped actors and spectators transcend reality as it manifested itself though the familiar auditory, visual, tactile, olfactory, and gustatory sensations and signs. The director-guru or shaman would lead his disciples (actors and spectators) on a trip of spiritual growth and self-knowledge through "foreign territories" and would help them experience a direct touch with the ultimate reality. The education of a disciple-actor at the Polish Theatre Lab helped him move ahead by tearing away from his personal and social limitations. According to Jerzi Grotowski, who sought to define what distinguishes theatrical activity from other kinds of performances, this education eliminated the actor's physiological resistance to psychological processes so that the time lapse between inner impulse and outer behavior was reduced to zero (Grotowski 1968:15, 17).

The spontaneity, which resulted from the instant obedience of the body to the commands of the soul, annulled "reasonable," conscious behavior. For Grotowski, a person in an elevated spiritual state—as in the case of tremendous joy—could only use rhythmically articulated signs, beginning to dance and to sing (1968:17–18). At this high level of excitement, the issue was no longer one of degrees of self-involvement during role enactment. The hot issue in Grotowski's method of acting became one of stepping out of theatrical and social roles into a more fulfilling state of being. "What may seem absurd is only the first rung of a much deeper and unified exploration of self" (Lahr 1970:174).

Grotowski's method of elimination and psychic (auto)penetration (*via negativa*) professed to divest the actor of any theatrical "masks" and fixed social roles in order to reach the "innermost core" of his personal and social identity (1968:37, 133). The relationships between director and actor and, in turn, between actor and spectator became a relationship between a shaman and a worshiper. The theatrical event turned into a "live communion" (1968:19). It became an act of revelation or, as Brook put it, a "possibility of salvation" (Brook 1969:59). Actors and spectators were "reborn" into a new state of self-awareness (1968:25, 57). However, Grotowski observed that the "invitation for a rebirth," which he extended to actors and spectators, "often aroused opposition or indignation" among mainstream folks (1968:37). So, Grotowski limited his "chamber theatre" to a small number of actors and spectators with "genuine spiritual needs" (1968:40–42).

Bewitched acting suspends the function of the psychological, physiological, and sociological controls in the actor. This kind of acting may have irreversible effects on the participants. The case of persons who feel themselves to be victims of witchcraft is a good example. The "bewitched" may die a "voodoo death" when she or he takes the role of a moribund person, and the audience (community) reinforces this belief in the "actor" by providing the cues which support this role (Devereux 1939). Peter Brook was particularly fond of "bewitched acting" in the theatre. Brook came to distrust *logos*—in its triple meaning of speech, reason, and order—which was prescribed to directors and actors by the playtexts of the logocentric tradition. Under the influence of Artaud and Grotowski, he moved toward "a theatre, more violent, less rational, more extreme, less verbal, more dangerous" (1969:54). He called this type of theatre "holy" theatre, and he claimed that it had a clearly defined place in the community, responding to a need "that churches can no longer fill" (1969:59–60).

> In Haitian voodoo, all you need to begin a ceremony is a pole and people. You begin to beat the drums and far away in Africa the gods will hear your call. The gods fly in—they circle above your heads, but it is not worth looking up as naturally they are invisible. This is where the pole becomes so vital. Without the pole nothing can link the visible and the invisible worlds. The pole, like the cross, is the junction. Through the wood, earthed, the spirits slide, and now they are ready for the second step in their metamorphosis. Now they need a human vehicle, and they choose one of the participants. A kick, a moan or two, a short paroxysm on the ground and a man is possessed. He gets to his feet, no longer himself, but filled with god. The god now has a form. He is someone who can joke, get drunk, and listen to everyone's complaints. (Brook 1969:64)

The notion that the stage is a place where the invisible can appear had a deep hold in Brook's thoughts (1969:42). He wished to capture in his art the invisible currents which rule human lives (1969:45). And he worked to render the invisible visible through the performer's presence (1969:52). Although he occasionally wondered if "the cult of the invisible" was an "unintelligent" form of theatre, he maintained, in the context of Artaud's theory, that theatre can help people liberate themselves from the roles which trap them in daily life. This "liberating" power would turn theatre into a holy place "in which a greater reality could be found" (1969:54). According to Brook, all religious teaching asserts that this "visible-invisible" cannot be seen automatically unless certain conditions—which relate to particular states of mind or to specific kinds of awareness—are met. So, Brook's "holy" theatre allegedly presents the invisible and offers the conditions which help spectators experience it (1969:56).

In short, the above investigations tried (1) to understand the process of entering and sharing a religious reality and (2) to develop an acting method which would "safely" lead the participants to experience the ultimate reality. Reportedly, some of the nonempathic and empathic methods of acting had the ability to transport actors and spectators into "another" world. For the advocates of a holy theatre, however, helping actors and spectators shift from everyday reality to a fictive reality was not enough. So, they explored the trance methods of acting. The various methods of acting which imposed different states of consciousness on actors and spectators indicated that "reality" had two variables: degree (quantity) and kind (quality). These variables depended on cultural, not biological, codes. Schechner's studies in "human" ethology inadvertently showed that human performances do not share stable systems, which are genetically programed, for the interpretation of signs. Instead of ethosemiotic codes, human performances are based on sociosemiotic codes. Each culture builds its own unstable semiotic systems of meaning which are both incomplete (like the Tower of Babel) or doomed (like the Tower of Pisa).

Presumably, ecstatic acting helped actors and spectators to stand outside their everyday, conventional social roles, but it did not place them into an ultimate reality, nor did it permanently modify their identity. Likewise, hypnotic and heated acting may have helped some actors and spectators to identify completely with a character or a reality, but neither method of acting transported actors and spectators to an ultimate reality or transformed their identity for a long time. If the available testimony is correct, these methods of acting only offered some actors a brief experience of "reincarnation" which did not "last long," but while it lasted, an actor was incapable of distinguishing between himself and the character that he was portraying (Stanislavsky 1948:278; 1963:73). Clearly, a new method of acting was needed to relocate actors to the ultimate reality and to cause their prolonged, if not permanent, identification with the "other" identity for the purpose of "salvation." Salvation requires a shift from the actor's social identity to the identity of the character ("other") which is located in a reality believed to stand higher than any other social or fictive reality. When social reality was devalued, all naturalist methods of acting—which imitated, mirrored, copied, or represented ordinary social reality— were also discredited.

Bewitched acting seemed to offer a method of acting that could help the brave ones attain (realize) the ultimate reality and a prolonged mystical union with the "other" identity. Reportedly, it helped some daredevils enter the ultimate reality by assuming another identity located within the ultimate reality. These "other" identities—which were selected to facilitate identification—extended beyond the conventional "limited" social roles. Scholars, counts, princes, and kings are social roles. But Dr. Faustus, Count Dracula, Prince Hamlet, King Oedipus have become "unreal" archetypal figures of condensed cultural values which often transgress the definition of a dominant social role. This kind of "other" transcendent identity of an archetypal figure was the key to entering the highest reality. Peter Brook's Prometheus and Jerzi Grotowski's Faustus had another dimension which was situated in a universe of meaning beyond society and the empirical world. In their quest for an "invisible" reality, the actors and spectators of a "holy" theatre devalued the empirical world. The enactment of extraordinary identities which were presented as "models" to an ongoing community of theatregoers, suggested that human beings have more than one dimension which lies beyond the narrow definitions of their social roles. As an actor enacted (embodied) the role of an archetypal "other," he lost his identity and he became what he was representing. In this way, the actor presumably could situate himself in the ultimate reality that was inhabited by the "other" identity. What finally defined "salvation" was the actor's transformation of identity through identification with the "right" kind of the "other."

Although the controversial dimension of metaphysical idealism in the various degrees of empathic acting can be dismissed, I must acknowledge, however, that the above "experiments" showed two things: (1) that different methods of role-playing lead to different types of theatre, modifying the traditional structure of play production, and (2) that different types of theatre, in turn, change the strategies for the acquisition of a role. If indeed self-involvement appears in various degrees in all types of role-playing, then acting methods do not fall into sharply separated or polarized types such as those commonly drawn between the realistic theatre and the epic theatre. On the contrary, acting methods vary only by degree along a continuous scale. The self-involvement of actors or spectators during rehearsal or performance may vary from zero acting to bewitched acting. Generally, inquisitive directors or actors soon discovered that each method of acting has its use and that no method was all-embracing. More importantly, however, they realized that spectators not only complete the play-production process, but also have a set of expectations of the "proper" degree of self-involvement required of actors and spectators for every role enactment in each type of theatre. If self-involvement at each level of role enactment appears too little or too much for each type of theatre that they know, spectators may judge role enactment as unconvincing or displeasing.

The reluctance of some spectators to enact a role in the theatre may demonstrate that they have inhibited personalities, but it also proves the capacity of some spectators to detach themselves from the performance of the actors and/or of other spectators. This capacity allows spectators to have considerable control over their own involvement in a theatrical event. For this reason, it becomes imperative for innovative structuralist directors and actors to "rehearse" on the variable "audience response" in order to eliminate unpleasant suprises. It has been a firm theoretical belief of the structuralists that a theatre company could increase its success in "staging" various types of theatre through precision in measuring and in anticipating audience response through "sample" rehearsals or performances.

The various methods of acting, which were employed during rehearsals and performances, could determine the levels of role enactment for both actors and spectators. Stanislavsky, among many others, built a method of acting which actors could turn into a "second nature" only through long, hard work. Exercise and habit were necessary for successful results. One could tell if this method of acting had become a "second nature" with an actor only if the actor acted spontaneously and seemingly naturally, "without his thinking of it" (1963:404, 403). Of course, Stanislavsky was painfully aware of the limited amount of research completed in his day about the "elementary psychophysical and psychological laws" that he described. "There is no information about them," Stanislavsky complained, "no research into them, and no practical exercises based on this research." The actors only learn how a role is played but not how it is organically created (1963:463).

Since the days of Stanislavsky, however, role research, as it has been conducted by formalists and structuralists alike, has not been able to solve a serious problem concerning the interaction between "literary" and "nonliterary" elements on stage. On the one hand, the more an actor's performing situation approaches the nonliterary (real) dimension of performance (as in the case of environmental theatre), the harder it becomes to say that an actor is not experiencing real emotions which result from his role. On the other hand, the more an actor's performing situation approximates the literary (fictive) dimension of performance (as in illusionistic theatre), the harder it becomes again to say that the actor is not experiencing real emotions which result from the illusionary circumstances of the character he portrays. It would seem that the same effect develops at either end of the spectrum. Unless this paradox is resolved in an observable, verifiable way, role research will not advance as a constructive branch of theatre research.

CHAPTER FOUR

A Pavlovian Performance Theory

Maurice Merleau-Ponty concluded his discussion of the "Higher Forms of Behavior: Pavlov's Reflexology and its Postulates" by submitting two major propositions. First, unlike lower responses which are functions of antecedent conditions unfolding in objective time and space, higher responses "do not depend on stimuli, taken materially, but rather on the meaning of the situation" (1967:125). Second, behavior consists of relations that are irreducible to their alleged parts —whether these "parts" are stimuli coming from outside or inside. "The structure of behavior as it presents itself to perceptual experience is neither thing nor consciousness" (1967:127). Is it, then, a sign?

Ivan Pavlov, of course, looked into perceptual behavior as an extension of his theories on respondent conditioning. In theatre studies, however, interdisciplinary research teams, such as the late team of Tinchon and Dietrich at the Institute for Audience Research at the University of Vienna and the controversial team of Schoenmakers and Tan at the Institute for Reception Aesthetics at the University of Amsterdam, sought to describe the audiovisual signs of performance-texts and to explain the emotional and cognitive aspects of spectator response to these signs (Schoenmakers 1982 II:146). Although some of these collaborative research projects are flawed methodologically—especially if they are judged by the standards of contemporary quantitative research in the field of theatre and related disciplines (Gunkle 1985:137)—the intended findings of such teams aspired to help theatre companies increase the affective quality (impact) that performance-texts have on spectators. Interestingly, Umberto Eco argued persuasively enough that "stimuli *cannot* be regarded as signs" (1976:19–20; 241–242). Without first disproving Eco, the above teams carelessly proceeded to harness semiotic research and psychological aesthetics to a common task. My goal here is to refute Eco's point and to investigate the possibility of an interdisciplinary approach to theatrical phenomena.

Wilfried Passow negotiated a way of lifting the barrier between the two disciplines by pairing three types of theatrical experience (visceral, emotional, and cognitive) to Charles Peirce's three kinds of interpretants (immediate, dynamic, and final). Passow suggested that these interpretants have an energetic, emotional, and logical aspect respectively which can, in turn, elicit differentiated responses such as action, feeling, and thought (1982 II: 254). Passow's inspiring negotiations, however, failed on two counts.

First, Passow's negotiations did not establish an equivalence between signs and stimuli. Such an equivalence would allow signs and stimuli to be used interchangeably as interdisciplinary investigations move back and forth from a semiotic, qualitative mode of inquiry to an empirical, quantitative mode of inquiry. Second, Peirce's *interpretant*, which mediates the realization of a sign (Greenlee 1973:34, 62–69; Peirce 1958:1.399), is not necessarily an interpreter—i.e., a spectator. It is rather another sign explaining the previous sign. Peirce's notion of unlimited semiosis—next to Pietr Bogatyrev's notion of theatrical semiosis, which regards theatrical signs as signs of other signs, not as signs of things—frees theatrical signification from the bonds of a referent but also deprives reception aesthetics of an object and a subject for measurement studies.

Ferdinand de Saussure's notion of a sign as a twofold psychological entity comprising a signifier and a signified seems a more appropriate model for bridging the two modes of inquiry. Passow recognized this value of the Saussurean sign because the signified is defined as a mental activity when a listener or a spectator perceives a signifier. This notion of a sign may allow researchers to match signifieds to signifiers and may help them record meaning variations to verbal, paraverbal, and nonverbal signifiers (1982 II:265). It is, indeed, in the context of the Saussurean sign that Ed Tan and Henry Schoenmakers saw psychological aesthetics and theatre semiotics as having each other's point of departure as their goal. For them, theatre semiotics analyzes performance-texts (i.e., signifiers) in terms of general characteristics, which, in turn, determine the spectators' reception processes and results. Psychological aesthetics, on the other hand, analyzes the spectators' reception processes (i.e., signifieds) by isolating subprocesses arising in response to incoming stimuli (but not signs?) from a large variety of performance-texts (Tan 1982 II:158).

Such interdisciplinary approaches as the above promised much too hastily to document and explain the relationship between the sign systems of performance-texts and the interpretive experiences of spectators. Clearly, unless we equate signs with stimuli, we cannot justify this interdisciplinary approach to theatrical phenomena or carry out any worthwhile discussions. Eco is right when he observes that all stimuli do not elicit behavioral responses by convention or have completely predictable effects. Should this, however, deter investigators from equating stimuli with signs?

Both the semiotic (qualitative) mode of inquiry and the empirical (quantitative) mode of inquiry in theatre face an intriguing puzzle concerning the interaction between literary (fictive) and nonliterary (real) elements on stage. The more a spectator's extra-theatrical life approximates the literary (fictive) dimension of a performance-text, the more it appears that he or she experiences real emotions which result from the "slice of life" on stage. Even when the representation is as stylized as in Greek tragedy, the correlation holds. Greek dramatist Phrynichus was fined because his play *The Capture of Miletus* (493 B.C.) brought the Athenian spectators to tears, because most of them had lost relatives during the actual siege of that city (Herodotus 6.21.2). Similarly, the more an actor's performing situation approximates the literary (fictive) dimension of performance (such as in Konstantin Stanislavsky's method of acting), the more it seems that the actor is experiencing real emotions that result from the "as if" circumstances of the character that he or she impersonates (Gunkle 1975:44).

Since the puzzle refers to the experience of both spectators and actors, a solution should address both facets. Presently, quantitative and qualitative studies in psychological aesthetics—depending on their formalist or structuralist orientation—operate on the premise that an "aesthetic" response or experience of a fictive situation either is or is not qualitatively different from a real-life response (Clynes 1977). Two dominant models in the field are available to investigate the puzzle, the psychodynamic and the psychobiological models (Berlyne 1971; Child 1972; Kreitler and Kreitler 1972; Pratt 1961; Valentine 1962). Neither, however, explains, in what ways "aesthetic" responses are similar to real-life responses or, if they are dissimilar, why they can be considered as identical for methodological purposes.

The psychodynamic model embraces approaches of Freudian and Jungian orientation which—generally speaking—examine the influence of "lower" drives on aesthetic content (Grimaud 1976; Holland 1968). If reduced to account for theatrical phenomena, the model holds that the "lower" drives of actors and spectators are gratified temporarily—in the obscure way of *catharsis*, whether Aristotelian or Freudian—through exposure to or participation in the performance. The model focuses on linguistic (cognitive) behavior as a function of four factors: stimulus, psychological profile, drive, and defense. The theories which support this model have changed radically over the years, depending on the degree of emphasis placed upon each of the above four factors in the making (poetic function) and interpreting (hermeneutic function) of playtexts, rehearsal-texts, or performance-texts. The model is limited to merely describing the result (*catharsis*) of an aesthetic experience rather than addressing the process or the causes that trigger it.

The psychobiological model, on the other hand, has grown out of research that suggests the existence of a psychobiological basis for such "higher" drives as curiosity, boredom, and need for novelty (Lindauer 1974). It encompasses two subparadigms: one with a focus on psychological variables, such as expectation (Peckman 1965; Schoenmakers 1982), and the other with an emphasis on physiological variables, such as arousal, which are elicited by three property types in the work of art: signal values, psychophysical properties, and collative properties (Berlyne 1971). Both subparadigms view perception as the assimilation of stimuli to pre-existing internal categories (Sokolov 1963). The psychobiological model illustrates the arousal and "channeling" of actor and spectator "higher" drives, but it does not adequately answer how "higher" drives are gratified or frustrated during a performance. It fails to differentiate the conditioned expectations of spectators or actors between watching or acting in a theatrical performance and eating a chocolate bar during intermission.

In sum, neither model explains how the real elements of a rehearsal-text or a performance-text (unconditioned stimuli) turn into "fictive" elements (conditioned stimuli) and vice versa. This gap in our knowledge justifies the exploratory analysis that I will undertake in this chapter. My purpose is twofold. First, I will try to demonstrate that conditioned stimuli can be regarded as signs. Second, I will investigate what causes referents (i.e., nonliterary elements in performance, such as actors) to become identical with the signifiers (i.e., literary elements, such as characters) in a performer's mind or a spectator's mind and why this "fusion" produces the effect of illusion.

I will follow three steps. I will attempt to equate Umberto Eco's concept of sign systems with Ivan Pavlov's concept of signaling systems. Russian and Czech formalism (Mukařovský 1940; Shklovsky 1919), Russian and European semiotics (Elam 1980; Lotman 1977), and postwar research in the field of Russian respondent conditioning as well as the American learning theory (mediation), all offer avenues justifying this step. Conditioned stimuli share all five requirements that Eco designated as necessary for signs. Therefore, it will be possible to study actor and spectator conditioned responses (signifieds) from an interdisciplinary approach as a next step. Then, I will investigate the nature of theatrical illusion as it relates to the spectator's experience. Theatrical illusion remains a common denominator in many types of theatre. From Walter Gropius' *totaltheater*, which was designed for Erwin Piscator (1927) in order to draw spectators into the fictive world, to the new Ottawa Arts Center, which was designed by Fred Lebensold in order to surround spectators with sound, light, and action even below their feet, theatrical illusion remains a common denominator.

Finally, I will once more examine the nature of theatrical illusion as it seesaws between signifier and referent in the actor's experience. For example, emotional memory stirs the actor to physical action by intensifying "inner and outer stimuli" (Stanislavsky 1936:132–136). Like Pavlov, Stanislavsky explored the "second nature," that is, the artificial spontaneity acquired by habit. The actor rehearses his actions until his emotions appear to be spontaneous (psychophysical events) in the Pavlovian sense of acquired automatisms. I hope that, by equating theatrical signs with conditioned stimuli, I may offer a theory which can explain theatrical illusion in a great variety of performances—from psychophysical events to ideological acts—in a simple and comprehensive way.

For Umberto Eco, semiotics studies everything that can be taken as a sign; a sign is everything that can be taken as significantly substituting for something else; this something else does not necessarily have to exist or actually be somewhere when a sign stands for it. Eco concludes that semiotics, in principle, studies anything that can be used to tell a lie (1979:7). So, Eco argues, stimuli cannot be regarded as signs because in Pavlov's experiment (1) the code does not inform the dog that salivates; instead, it informs the scientist "who knows that to every ring must correspond a salivation" (1979:20) and (2) the bell sound provokes salivation without any other mediation.

Eco's point that the bell sound is a stimulus for the dog independent of any social codes is overstated. Eco fails to distinguish between unconditioned and conditioned stimuli, disregards the rules of first and second signaling system activity, and discards the dog's role as an addressee because he wants to keep sign-function within the confines of cultural anthropology. Don't dogs learn anything while social scientists are "conditioning" themselves? I argue that a sign-function represents the correlation of two functives. Such functives are not by nature semiotic, indeed, outside their correlation. However, insofar as they are correlated, they acquire a semiotic nature—i.e., they can be used to tell a lie. Semioticians know that potential signs become signs only when addressees respond according to—or in avoidance of—sender intentions. Potential signs, therefore, become registered signs (i.e., a code) only if their repeated emissions evoke similar responses. Consequently, the intention/response correlation between social scientists and dogs can be rewritten as a case of expectancy for scientists and a case of conditioning for dogs.

Eco's next point that the bell sound provokes salivation without any other mediation is also debatable. By *mediation,* Eco cannot mean *inference* because he relates inference to symptoms, not to signs. He most likely means a *referent* which mediates between a signifier and its signified. For example, a waiter removes the menu (signifier) before he serves food (referent). In the absence of referents and signifiers, waiters and customers preserve "images" of food (signifieds) in their memories. A concrete referent on the plate mediates between its signifier in the menu and its signified in the mind by reinforcing their abstract correlation.

Similarly, traditional Pavlovian respondent conditioning correlates a conditioned stimulus (bell sound) to an unconditioned stimulus (food powder) blown by an air puff into a dog's mouth to create an expectation in its brain (salivation). Gradually, a stimulus substitution occurs: bell sound (CS) stands for food powder (US), evoking the same response (salivation). Initially, however, salivation was an unconditioned response because it was related to the food powder (US), not to the bell sound (CS). We know that the dog is conditioned when it experiences unnaturally caused salivation (CR) to bell sounds.

The unconditioned stimulus (US) in conditioning theory coincides with the referent in semiotic theory: it evokes a response that results from its natural properties and can be absent when the conditioned stimulus (CS) is present. Normally, a bell sound may induce earache but not salivation. If it induces salivation, it becomes a conditioned stimulus and, thus, capable of lying. It acquires, so-to-speak, a "magic" power that transforms reality, eliciting a subject's natural responses to "deceitful" stimuli.

The conditioned stimulus, on the other hand, meets Eco's five requirements which constitute the attributes of a sign: intentionality, substitution, arbitrariness, convention, and spuriousness. These attributes, which are evident during the conditioning process, become even more apparent during *extinction*. The dog progressively stops salivating to the bell sound when, after many trials with bell sounds alone, it receives no food powder (reinforcement). Obviously, the conditioned stimulus does not share the properties of the unconditioned stimulus; otherwise extinction could not take place. The correlation between conditioned stimuli (signifiers) and conditioned responses (signifieds) is therefore reinforced by the occasional presence of unconditioned stimuli (referents).

In sum, I can equate signs with conditioned stimuli, in theory, so that I can facilitate an interdisciplinary discussion of theatrical phenomena. Pavlov's signaling systems and Eco's sign systems agree that the making or breaking of stimulus and sign connections is an arbitrary, but fundamental, mental activity. Indeed, conditioned stimuli (signifiers) induce responses (signifieds) resembling those of unconditioned stimuli (referents) after they are presented to subjects in an appropriate relationship of time and intensity in the controlled environments of laboratories. Can I also safely argue that the spectators in theatres behave like conditioned dogs or hungry gourmets who—in the absence of the "real thing"—salivate at bell sounds or feel their mouths watering at menu reading?

Under normal conditions dogs do not confuse bell sounds with food powder, and people can easily distinguish between signifiers and their referents—if any. In this way, people can maintain a mental balance between mental images (signifieds) and perceptions of reality, realized in referents and signifiers. The major concern of semiotic theory and conditioning theory has been to understand the nature of the connections in the referent-signifier-signified triangle and in the US-CS-CR triangle, respectively. Both theories try to describe the mechanics and boundaries of the *semiotic action* (Peirce 1958 #5:484) and of the *signaling process*—i.e., the substitution of one sign for another and of one stimulus for another. For example, how flexible or unrestricted is the chain of signs or stimuli that can substitute for one another?

Pavlov divided brain activity into two systems. Our perceptions of the surrounding world are primary (concrete) signals of reality. Words, on the other hand, are secondary (abstract) signals of reality, permitting generalization (1955:590). Freud argued a similar case: the conscious idea comprises a concrete idea plus a verbal idea that corresponds to it. An unconscious idea, on the other hand, is that of the thing alone (1956 4:134). For Piaget, too, the gradual differentiation between signifiers, referents, and signifieds observed in child development, marks the dawn of intelligence (1967:32). What we experience daily during social interaction results, for the most part, from an interpretation of codes such as language, traffic signs, penal codes, and so on. The social interaction of other intelligent species such as dogs, chimpanzees, dolphins, bees, etc., observes its own system of codes, and some of these animals are capable of elementary secondary signaling system activity.

In secondary respondent-conditioning experiments, Pavlov substituted bell sounds (primary conditioned stimuli) for white cards (secondary conditioned stimuli), and he found that the white cards elicited salivation without ever having been connected with food powder (US). Can I also assume that a theatrical experience is a similar case of higher level association which substitutes real-life codes for fictive codes? Since theatregoers are not subject to secondary respondent conditioning in the theatre, such an assumption is unwarranted. However, children and adult audiences alike do occasionally fail to differentiate between reality and fiction, experiencing real emotions to unreal stage situations even though they know performances to be faked reality. What, then, impedes

them from differentiating between literary and nonliterary elements—
i.e, between signifiers and referents? In other words, how willing
is a spectator's willing suspension of disbelief in the theatre?

I cannot extrapolate the findings of experiments on animals
and apply them to people unless the same methods produce similar
responses in both species. Experiments with hallucinogenic drugs
in the 1950s, by inducing disturbed states of consciousness for both
animals and people, helped bridge the gap and draw some analogies.
When animals received a shock (US), they howled (UR). When a
bell sound (CS) substituted for a shock, they lifted a paw (CR).
Under the influence of mescaline, surprisingly, they did not lift a
paw (CR) at the bell sound (CS), but they howled (UR), although
no shock (US) was applied (Bridger 1956:352; Courvoisier 1956:25).
Obviously, hallucinogenic drugs disturbed the CS/UR relationship.
The conditioned stimulus elicited an effect as if it were an
unconditioned stimulus. In semiotic jargon, the signifier appeared
to have the attributes of a referent.

The above observation led Bridger to form the following
hypothesis: if under mescaline a conditioned stimulus assumes some
of the functional properties of an unconditioned stimulus, then a
conditioned response cannot be extinguished easily. Normally, a
conditioned response is extinguished after a number of
nonreinforced trials. But under mescaline, the bell sound (CS) should
acquire the attributes of the electric shock (US/reinforcement), and
the drugged animal should respond to the bell sound, not as a sign
for the shock but as if it were the shock itself. Bridger tested his
hypothesis using two types of conditioned responses: a conditioned
emotional response and a conditioned avoidance response
(1960:426).

In the first case, the animal was shocked on every trial and
showed a great deal of emotional response (fear) to the conditioned
stimulus. In the second case, the animal learned to avoid the shock
and showed little fear to the conditioned stimulus. After the animal
was drugged, however, extinction occurred rapidly for the
conditioned avoidance response only, not for the conditioned
emotional response. This result proved Bridger's hypothesis that
under hallucinogenic drugs the conditioned stimulus assumes the
attributes of the unconditioned stimulus. In theatre, of course,

audiences are not under the influence of hallucinogenic drugs. What then causes signifiers (literary elements) to assume the attributes of referents (nonliterary elements)?

The above behavioral data cannot explain the disturbance of the relationship between signifiers and referents among actors and spectators in the theatre. It is electrophysiological and neuropharmacological experiments that show how hallucinogenic drugs produce this disturbance in the relationship between a conditioned stimulus and an unconditioned stimulus. These experiments indicate that the conditioned stimulus produces a different electrical response (signified) in the neocortex from that produced by the unconditioned stimulus (Gastaut 1958). In the hippocampal region, however, both the conditioned stimulus (signifier) and the unconditioned stimulus (referent) produce the same electrical response (Malcolm 1958). Interestingly, Eco did not draw a clear distinction between the signifieds of signifiers (CR) and the signifieds of referents (UR).

Behavioral, electrophysiological, neuropharmacological, and neurophysiological data indicated that the unconditioned stimulus (referent) and the conditioned stimulus (signifier) are differentiated at the neocortical level but not at the hippocampal level. Strong emotional learning situations and hallucinogenic drugs inhibit neocortical activity and produce hippocampal activity causing confusion between conditioned and unconditioned stimuli. The more emotion is associated with the stimulus, the greater is the hippocampal activity (John 1958:347). Hallucinogenic drugs, such as mescaline and LSD, also inhibit neocortical synapses and, at the same time, activate the hippocampal region (Killam and Killam 1956:35; Marazzi and Hart 1955:365; Purpura 1956:122).

Also, experiments with decorticated animals showed that any condition producing neocortical inhibition shifts the level of thinking from secondary to primary signaling system activity, while any condition that excites hippocampal activity makes it very difficult for subjects to distinguish between conditioned and unconditioned stimuli (Marquis and Hilgard 1937; Wing and Smith 1942; Zeleny and Kadykov 1938). In short, a person's ability to differentiate signifiers (CS) from referents (US) increases or decreases depending on how high or low that person feels an experience is charged emotionally.

Can a spectator's response be compared to a dog's response when harnessed on a seat in a sound-shielded room? I can only argue that *some* portions of some performance-texts produce such strong emotional experiences in their target audiences that they keep *some* spectators "glued" to their seats in relatively sound-shielded playhouses. Can I, then, also argue that the Athenian spectators who watched *The Capture of Miletus* wept because their overflowing emotions prevented them from distinguishing theatrical signs from reality? Aren't there any other explanations? What if the play reminded them of a personal or a family tragedy as, indeed, this was the case?

If I accept the premise that rehearsal-texts and performance-texts work on the emotions of actors and spectators by association, then, can I subsequently sort out primary and secondary signaling system experiences on as rough a basis as life/theatre, which is favored by formalists and structuralists? To what extent the principles of stimulus generalization of animal conditioning can explain theatrical illusion remains to be seen through more research in the field of theatre. In this chapter, I can only suggest a model which may assist interdisciplinary teams to formulate relevant studies. I simply point out that the US/CS substitutions or associations observed in primary signaling system activity are *generalizations by association* due to (1) physical similarity (iconic signs), (2) spatial and temporal contiguity (indexical signs), and (3) identity of effect or function.

Although the connection between signifiers (CS) and referents (US) is an arbitrary one, my notion of a sign or signal and its replicability in labs, societies, or theatres depends on postulating that such a recognition is possible. Generally, semioticians accept any recognition rules based on perception as a given, and they divide signs into a sensory facet (i.e., signifier or referent) and a mental facet (i.e., signified of a signifier or of a referent). If signifiers and referents exist to give access to signifieds, signifiers and referents seem subordinated to the meanings they communicate. Consequently, I cannot account for signifying rehearsal-texts or performance-texts unless I describe the system that makes them possible.

An utterance—be it speech or bell sound—does not "mean" by any inherent properties of its own; it rather "means" through rules of association established between actor and spectators, or Pavlov and his dogs. In the jargon of speech-act theory, the illocutionary force of utterances depends on context rather than on grammatical structure (Austin 1962:8, 26, 52, 119). By "framing" a meaningless speech act or a bell sound, we can make it signify and, in this way, can alter its function. Pavlov's secondary and tertiary respondent-conditioning experiments, as well as experiments with theatrical symbolism, indicate that meaning is context-bound, but context is relatively boundless. Ludwig Wittgenstein's claim that we cannot say "bububu" and mean "if it doesn't rain, I shall go for a walk" (1953:18e) has made it possible to say so and mean so by association.

Clearly, Saussure's notion of a sign and Pavlov's notion of a signal allow us to see performance-texts as a nexus of arbitrary audiovisual signs or conditioned stimuli which "mean" by the differences or similarities that distinguish them from, or associate them with, other signs or conditioned stimuli. Intensity of emotional response, however, registers the signifieds of referents (UR) and the signifieds of signifiers (CR) at the subcortical level where both the unconditioned responses and the conditioned responses "feel or look" alike, causing a temporary *confusion* between reality and make-believe. So, the suspension of disbelief in theatre seems related to the intensity of affect: the more affect a spectator experiences in a situation, the more likely he or she will shift from secondary to primary signaling system activity—i.e., from secondary to primary process thinking.

In this state of emotional imbalance, theoretically speaking, the signifieds of signifiers (i.e., the literary elements on stage, such as characters) and the signifiers of referents (i.e., the nonliterary elements on stage, such as actors) "feel or look" alike at the subcortical level. Illusion, then, is in the mind of an emotionally affected spectator as he or she witnesses "hot" situations such as cases of love/rape, marriage/divorce, success/defeat, suicide/murder, etc., and associates them with his or her personal case history. Such real-life experiences—especially if they are recent in memory— may amuse or distress spectators depending on individual disposition and on the theatrical techniques used for manipulating audience response.

Actors, on the other hand, induce in themselves a state of mind which temporarily makes them behave as the characters that they impersonate. Next to the recognized theories of Denis Diderot, G.H. Lewes, Theodule Ribot, William James, and Lange,

Stanislavsky's psychophysical method of acting was also influenced in the 1930s by Ivan Sechenov's and Ivan Pavlov's neurophysiological research, which placed cerebral reflexes at the center of human behavior (Prokofev 1980 24:465). The method of acting proposed by Stanislavsky accepts an indivisible bond between body and mind, allowing for psychological and physiological acts to influence each other (1936:132–136).

According to Stanislavsky, if thoughts, emotions, and actions arise reflexively by stimulating the senses, then actors can self-induce thoughts and emotions by placing themselves in the appropriate physical context (1936:72, 121, 168). External behavior stimulates reciprocal emotions and thoughts, while emotions and thoughts stimulate reciprocal physical behavior (1949:47). The range of expressive behavior, however, results from the inherited natural and social reflexes of our species. To help an actor seize control over the unconscious reflexes which lie beyond his direct control, Stanislavsky's method of acting lures the involuntary impulses of the subconscious to express themselves by creating spontaneous, adaptive behavior on stage or "motor adjustments" (1936:224). "There is no direct approach to our unconscious," said Stanislavsky. "Therefore we make use of various stimuli that induce a process of living the part" (1936:225). Appropriate physical actions, such as those of an actor drinking wine out of an empty bottle by swallowing his saliva, act on the subconscious to create the inner truth of feeling (1936:132).

Sechenov had observed that physical action stirred muscular memory with a speed and accuracy unmatchable by conscious thought. Stanislavsky came to believe that neuromuscular agility, optimized through gymnastics, would allow actors to respond accurately to the Electrical Conductor for Plays (ECP). ECP was a metronome-like device with two blinking lights attached to the prompter box, dictating an acting rhythm to actors (1949:212). ECP devices allegedly would stimulate appropriate inner feelings in well-trained actors since rhythm and movement constitute a "mechanical stimulus to emotion memory" (1949:236). Pavlov's substitution of an unconditioned response with a conditioned one became Stanislavsky's principle of emotional memory.

To Pavlov, conditioned responses were an "improved" adaptive mechanism, connecting inner function to the environment through the senses. Likewise, Stanislavsky saw that human behavior is conditioned by repetition which reinforces associations that reinstate psychological responses at physical cues. This *artificial spontaneity* of Pavlovian dogs and Stanislavskian actors, which is acquired by repetition, is a process of acquired automatisms. Subsequently, Stanislavsky investigated the associative process of automatization. He experimented by progressively observing how the mental images (signifieds) that an actor induced on himself were manifested as the physical actions of a character (signifiers) by altering the actor's real-life physical actions (referents). Under the principle of physical actions, Stanislavsky's method of acting helps actors on stage to induce on themselves a secondary behavior (role) which is more controllable than their primary behavior in real life.

Rehearsals allow a Stanislavskian actor to build a character by consciously constructing a sequence of automatisms which progressively form a psychophysical sequence of behavior on stage (role). "Life on stage, as well as off it," said Stanislavsky, "consists of an uninterrupted series of objectives and their attainment. They are signals set all along the way of an actor's creative aspirations" (1961:51). However, an actor's stage behavior becomes a conditioned response to the demands of the character that he impersonates. When an actor fixes the sequence through many repetitions, "spontaneity" returns. "The more often he repeated this sequence of so-called physical actions—or, to be more exact, the inner stimuli to action," Stanislavsky observed, "the more his involuntary motions increased" (1961:229). So, repetition in rehearsals makes a role habitual for actors. Habit establishes patterns of thought, emotion, and action, transforming a difficult task into an easy one; and, of course, any task that becomes easy, feels comfortable. "Habit creates second nature, which is a second reality" (1961:62), and the actors, who grow comfortable with their established sequence, cannot conceive of approaching a role otherwise. So, they behave like robots who respond to an inner program and experience an illusion of reflexive vitality.

Altogether, conditioned stimuli could be regarded as signs because they share all five requirements which constitute the attributes of a sign: intentionality, substitution, arbitrariness, convention, and spuriousness. Therefore, an interdisciplinary approach to theatrical phenomena seems to be justified. Concerning the causes that produce the effect of illusion, it would seem that a person's ability to differentiate signifiers (CS) from referents (US) increases or decreases depending on how high or low that person feels an experience is charged emotionally. The intensity of affect in a theatrical experience registers the signifieds of referents (UR) and the signifieds of signifiers (CR) at the subcortical level where both unconditioned responses and conditioned responses feel or look alike, causing a temporary confusion between reality and make-believe to spectators. Actors, on the other hand, who practice Stanislavsky's method of acting induce in themselves a conditioned behavior (role) as they build a character by consciously constructing a sequence of automatisms which progressively form a psychophysical sequence of stage behavior. The artificial spontaneity of Stanislavskian actors, which is acquired by repetition, is a process of acquired automatisms that make actors respond to a "second reality."

Of course, one can argue that spectators may cry during a theatrical performance, not because they fail to distinguish fiction from reality but because other factors are also at play. For example, some spectators may feel more inclined to cry at a tragic event in the theatre rather than in life because tragic events in the real world are rarely as clearly framed as in a fictive world (Langer 1953:310). For this argument, however, the issue is not the actor/spectator interaction but the nature of the "theatrical frame". Ervin Goffman loosely defines the theatrical frame as something less than a benign construction and something more than a simple "keying" for actors and spectators alike. It is the type of the performance (pure, mixed, or impure) that determines the "role" of the actors and the "role" of the spectators.

Pure performances, such as theatrical performances, require that the actors have an audience to entertain. Mixed performances, on the other hand, such as boxing matches or football games, require that the contestants act as if something were at stake beyond the entertainment of their audience; and finally, impure performances, such as surgical or military operations, require that the surgeons or the soldiers in action show no regard for the dramatic elements of their labor. "On-the-spot TV news coverage," writes Goffman, "now offers up the world, including its battles, as work performances" (1974:126). In a similar way the spectator's role depends on the type of performance that he is watching. The theatregoer invariably is cast in an "audience role," according to

Goffman (1974:124). Since the term "role" can describe both theatrical and social activities, Goffman explains that the "audience role" gives theatregoers the license to watch and collaborate in the "unreality" of a theatrical performance. Based on a "syntax of response," the spectator "sympathetically and vicariously participates in the unreal world generated by the dramatic interplay of the scripted characters" (1974:130).

For example, the actor playing Othello acts as if he does not know what the villain will do. Similarly, the actor playing Iago acts as if he can hide his intent from the hero. Naturally, both actors share a full knowledge of Shakespeare's play and of the distribution of this knowledge. But the "actor's role" makes them act as if they are ignorant of each other's motives and of the outcome of the play. The "audience role," in turn, obliges the theatregoer to act as if his own knowledge as well as that of some of the characters is partial and uninformed on the resolution of the conflict. Goffman, however, does not proceed to explain *why* actors and spectators alike induce in themselves this frame of mind. Neither does Elizabeth Burns. "In ordinary life," Burns observes, "the spectator selects the persons and events to which he will pay attention. But for the theatre audience, the selection is of course made by dramatist, producer, and performers. The spectator responds to their sign language and accepts their version of reality" (1972:228). Goffman agrees with Burns that the components of a fictive world are preselected "as what the audience must select out." All audience members have access to the same amount of information provided by the performance, and they assume that all essential information is brought to their attention (Goffman 1974:149). In the "audience role," Goffman reiterates, "we willingly seek out the circumstances in which we can be temporarily deceived or at least kept in the dark, in brief, transformed into collaborators in unreality" (1974:136). And again—it is perfectly obvious to everyone on and off the stage that the characters and their actions are unreal, but it is also true that the audience holds this understanding to one side and in the capacity of onlookers allows its interest and sympathy to respect the apparent ignorance of the characters as to what will come of them and to wait in felt suspense to see how matters will unfold (1974:137).

In sum, Goffman and Burns describe the symptoms but not the causes that make spectator response susceptible to the "unreality" or the "version of reality" of theatrical performances. They do not explain sufficiently *why,* or even *how,* the theatrical (mental or physical) frame transforms some spectators into "collaborators in unreality." Goffman, of course, describes eight transcription practices that render interaction among characters (actors) on stage systematically different from interaction among people in the real world. Goffman details the eight transcription practices or conventions as follows: the stage space arbitrarily separates the fictive world from the real world; the elimination of the fourth wall draws the spectators into the fictive world; the verbal interaction among characters (actors) is designed to help spectators see into the encounter; the characters (actors) take turns in becoming the focus of the interaction; characters (actors) generally respect turns at talking and wait for the audience response (e.g., laughter) to cease before they speak their next line; the character interactions sustain a "disclosive compensation" for the spectators; characters (actors) speak longer and more grandiloquent sentences than real-world people because, in part, actors must project voice and feelings to the audience; and finally, the fictive world, unlike the real world, includes nothing that is insignificant.

Behind these conventions, according to Goffman, lurks the "multiple-channel effect": the senses of a spectator process the information, and, presumably, the brain of a spectator judges the incoming stimuli to be fictive or real. "It is the seeing of the course of these stimuli that allows for a quick identification and definition—a quick framing—of what has occurred" (1974:146). Goffman looks no further into this "quick framing" and closes the issue by finding the spectators' capacity to engross themselves in a transcription that departs radically and systematically from real-world interaction "very remarkable." To his credit, however, Goffman does not simply suggest how interaction in the theatre differs from interaction in real life. He also introduces terms which provide what is needed in order to question the division between real world(s) and fictive worlds. He does not fail to observe that illusion is at work behind this "very remarkable" capacity of the spectators. "An *automatic* and systematic correction is involved," he writes, "and it seems to be made *without* its makers *consciously* appreciating the transformation conventions they have employed" (1974:145).

Nonetheless, Goffman fails to explain *why* they are not *consciously* aware of this *automatic* adjustment. Earlier in this chapter, I proposed the beginning of a possible explanation.

Epilogue

My last word will be a plea. Be a little more careful, I beg you, not to misrepresent me and my friends to the people. We have chosen a difficult, not the easiest way. Have we shirked any discomfort and any sacrifices that were to be made for our theatre? Have we more to sacrifice?

Gordon Craig, *The Theatre Advancing* (1921)

I have heard it said many times during this period that deconstruction was now on the wane, but to judge by what is being published, these comments reflect more wishful thinking than accurate observation: books and articles in the deconstructionist mode continue to appear at an ever increasing rate, and Derrida continues to be cited more than any other theorist.

John Ellis, *Against Deconstruction* (1989)

Deconstruction derives from an ancient form of skepticism which questions all kinds of interpretation. Despite their widely publicized works, neither Jacques Derrida nor Paul de Man are the beginning or the end of deconstruction. Ever since Gorgias wrote his treatise *On Not Being* in Athens in the fifth century B.C., the theory and practice of deconstruction has taken many turns and received many influences as it spread from linguistic community to linguistic community and from discipline to discipline in the Humanities and the (Social) Sciences. In most linguistic communities and disciplines, deconstruction has never been fully Derridean or de Manian. In the field of Theatre Studies, the theory and practice of deconstructors such as Derrida and de Man have remained largely irrelevant and inconsequential to the concerns of most theatre artists and critics.

Those working under deconstruction, like those working under formalism and structuralism, have never been of one mind about their theories and practices. In recent years, several major French deconstructors resisted the influence of the formalist approach, whereas their American counterparts flirted with it. In either case, their controversial writings cannot control the development of deconstruction nor can their "errors" invalidate the work of other deconstructors. The logocentrists who, like my friend, welcomed the collapse of what they perceived as a "united front" among deconstructors have deluded themselves. In the manner of the formalists and the structuralists, some deconstructors formed exclusive "circles" and "schools," but most of them resisted such institutional closures.

Nonetheless, the recent attacks on the inner circle of the Yale deconstructors would make anyone in the theatre who uses deconstruction, reconsider his or her *position* (*stigma* in Greek) while working on the outer fringe. The deconstructors of the "inner circles" tackled some problems that stemmed from the imposition of authority, but they only vaguely explained its power structure. In the field of theatre, the posture of rebellion of many alleged "deconstructors" was assimilated by certain groups of artists and critics who thrived on verbal opposition, and their "rebellion" reinforced rather than subverted what it supposedly opposed.

In the preceding chapters, I showed why theory cannot be separated from practice. Those formalists, structuralists, and quasi-deconstructors who advocated revisionist practices often perpetuated reactionary relationships in theatrical production by imposing either a stifling unity or a hierarchical reversal. Their revulsion for the "poor" quality of the popular productions from Broadway to Hollywood delayed the analysis of the actual relationships in theatrical production and distribution. They would rather predict an irrevocable doom for the commercial theatre and place the future of "quality" theatre in the hands of privileged groups in subsidized theatre companies and research institutions.

Under formalism and structuralism, quite a few of these centers for theatre research operated with a sense of either powerlessness or minimal responsibility for the problems of the "commercial" theatre workers. Some pushed for a unity and some others for a reversal of binary opposites such as subsidized/commercial, inside/outside, Occident/Orient, male/female. However, their exclusion of inharmonious elements and their subordination of undesirable oppositions were political acts which sometimes appeared behind the mask of scholarly impartiality, scientific objectivity, repertory policy, and linguistic neutrality. For the most part, they valued the concept of privileged texts (masterpieces) because it supported the idea of privileged people (masters).

I have used deconstruction as an analytical tool in order to question the notion of fixed meanings, fixed interpretations, and fixed production patterns which have been advocated by some of the old and new masters of the theatre. Now that I have shown how deceptive the rhetoric of change has been and can be, I hope that the readers of this book will yield less easily to the received authoritative and sometimes institutionalized interpretations of these masters. The deconstructive designers, directors, actors, and critics do not substitute their interpretations for the texts that they read. Instead, they create meaning by responding to the injunctions of these texts through their cultural perspectives. Meaning is not the exclusive province of playwright-gods, director-gurus, master designers, expert critics, and erudite scholars who purportedly interpret what an author "truly" meant or what a text "really" means.

Throughout this book, I have argued that deconstruction as an approach is an epistemological practice which prevents the "experts" from producing "new" aesthetic or institutional closures that stabilize existing power relations in theatrical production. I occasionally disrupted the rhetoric of some exclusive, authoritarian and disciplinarian theatre artists, critics, and managers in order to explain how they legitimated their practices. In effect, they perpetuated repression in different forms because neither their reversals nor their unities could generate significant changes. I also exposed the contradictions of several formalist and structuralist projects without imposing a new "masterful" synthesis of my own (even in the very last chapter) which would have allowed "new" relationships of domination to reappropriate the field.

I also subscribed to the premise that there is no final meaning or final interpretation in theatrical production; that there is only a constant, nonlinear deferral of meaning from extra-theatrical texts to playtexts to prompt-copies, to rehearsal-texts, to performance-texts, to critical texts, and so on. This deferral, which is caused by the arbitrary nature of the theatrical signs, keeps their referents at bay, and it allows the various languages (sign systems) to mediate and organize the experience of "reality" in the theatre. The quest to touch an authentic reality beyond or behind the various "languages of the stage" in logocentric theatrical productions stemmed mainly from a desire to overcome the difference between the "I" of the artist (e.g., the actor's presence) and the "I" of the character (e.g., Hamlet's absence) and to restore a unity or a fullness of meaning by meshing memorized speech with live consciousness.

Therefore, it was imperative for formalist and structuralist theatre artists and critics to argue that spoken languages preceded written languages historically as well as during theatrical production—asserting that playwrights and actors have had full control of their written or spoken lines. They conveniently overlooked the fact that for several centuries in most productions the writing of a playtext has preceded its spoken representation on stage and that actors as well as playwrights are not in full control of their lines. For example, it is the written words that control the verbal and other behavior of an actor in performance, who, in a sense, operates as a passive conductor of language (and ideology) without enjoying much creative freedom. An actor's memorized "speech acts" and his other behavioral acts in performance are as much devoid of his actual "presence" (consciousness) as the playtext from the playwright's presence.

This does not mean that the consciousness of a playwright, designer, or actor can stand outside language—any language— during the act of writing, designing, or speaking. Even the (post)structuralist actors who performed "authorless" texts, reportedly discovered that meaning cannot exist outside texts and that everything inside and outside the theatre (and their heads) was a "text." So, their rebellion against the authority of the playwright— the reputed creator and owner of the meanings of the playtext— frustrated any attempt to decipher any playtext. Actors began reading and interpreting playtexts with liberty rather than with fidelity— liberating each text from its "theological" origin of meaning, the playwright-god or the director-guru. As the various texts (playtexts, prompt-copies, rehearsal-texts, performance-texts) acquired plural meanings, the actor-master (of a system of acting, or a technique of acting, or a method of acting) became the theological origin of meaning as he or she strove for authentic emotions and autobiographical texts.

The playwright as a unique genius disappeared, and the playtexts were developed in the "anonymity" of workshops and rehearsals though a collective effort. These texts were identified by a general name (company) rather than by an individual name (playwright). As a result of these changes, the biography of the playwright did not become irrelevant. Simply, it was no longer regarded as more important than the biographies of the other theatre artists who created prompt-copies, rehearsal-texts, and performance-texts. A playwright was as much an ideological product of a historical period as a designer, director, actor, spectator, critic, and historian. The histories of these people were not less significant than the history of a playwright whose play they revived and interpreted. This drive for equality between the past and the present in the vortex of play production created the false impression that some of the early theatre deconstructors valued neither history nor biography.

The denial of the playwright was not a denial of history or fact. The denial of the playwright led to the discovery that there is no fixed point at which the present becomes the past during the production of a historical play; there is no fixed point at which a playtext becomes a performance text, demarcating where a text leaves off and reality begins for designers, actors, or spectators in the theatre; there is no fixed point at which the past becomes present in a revival production of a play. This kind of understanding of the theatrical process turned reality into just another text, and it made the distinction between fact and fiction during the theatrical experience dangerously elusive. This view of theatrical production did not abolish either fact or fiction. It simply asserted that history (reality) is as unpredictable and undecidable as theatre (fiction). Neither one of them is irrelevant to the study of the various texts of theatre—including playtexts.

What is the use of an analytical approach, such as deconstruction, that refuses to transcend conflicts and create a "new" order in the field of theatre? It is useful because it subverts old and new systems of certainty (hierarchies) by eschewing the role of the saviors who stabilize meaning between rival interpretations to promote their own interests. It shows that progress will not necessarily come from projects which extract conflicts from their sociohistorical context and formalize or hypostatize contradiction—in the manner of Peter Brook or Richard Schechner. Nor will progress come from projects which try to save the theatrical texts from the "corrupting" influence of technology—in the manner of Jerzi

Grotowski. Their assumption that the meanings of the theatrical texts are self-referential, depending on who defines them, results from a misunderstanding of the functions of the theatrical sign.

I plead guilty for reducing deconstruction to an analytical approach in this book. As an approach, deconstruction becomes a vigilant activity which mistrusts the epistemological premises and projects of other approaches as much as other approaches—formalism, structuralism, and phenomenology—mistrust the premises and projects of deconstruction. Deconstruction confers a renewed attention to contradictions, ambiguities, and discontinuities in the theatrical texts that other approaches tend to explain away. It shows what happens when a text is read looking for intention, meaning, and representation and what is left out by such readings. Like other approaches, it postulates that what one gets (content) may not be what one sees or hears (form) because the meaning is belied by the rhetorical system that controls it.

Deconstruction differs from other analytical approaches in the way it proceeds to show how a rhetorical structure undermines the meaning that it asserts—exposing how established practices are neither natural nor inevitable. The (re)appearance of deconstruction in the theatre in recent decades was not caused by the crisis in authority and faith—as it is commonly stated. Instead, it was caused by the fact that authority and faith were reinstituted in the field of theatre despite the beguiling radical rhetoric and deregulation politics in the 1960s, 1970s, and 1980s. Deconstruction and the other approaches are not fads which share the thirty-year life spans of academic careers. Formalism has not run its course just because some of its main advocates have retired or have died. Nor is an approach an ideology that claims to explain everything to the satisfaction of its adherents. Approaches are vulnerable to abuse, and, like all other approaches, deconstruction has fallen prey to the power struggle for institutional survival or supremacy in many theatre companies and theatre departments. Among other things, a power struggle entails the promotion of the works of one's friends and the castigation of the works of one's foes.

Of course, the divisions of the signifier from the signified and of the sign from its referent are not comforting thoughts for anyone concerned for one simple reason. If a theatrical experience (coded in signs) is not safely anchored in a sociohistorical reality (referent), then whoever controls the medium of language on the page or the stage can manipulate his readers or his spectators mentally. This can happen because the sense of reality of the reader or the spectator can no longer function as a correcting mirror for the fictive signs. However, the mental manipulation—which postulates a natural and inevitable relationship between the signifier and its signified, between the sign and its referent, between fact and fiction—is equally pernicious and formidable. Deconstruction fosters an analysis of the conditions of totalitarianism in all its forms. But the belief of several poststructuralists in an exclusively linguistic universe leaves much to be desired.

If the reader feels that I have simplified or distorted the very "essence" of deconstruction—assuming that deconstruction has an essence—then perhaps the reader is ready to consult more controversial books on the subject, written by celebrated deconstructors, such as *A World of Difference* by Barbara Johnson, who will give the reader a more complex and confusing definition of deconstruction and its functions.

> Instead of a simple "either/or" structure, deconstruction attempts to elaborate a discourse that says *neither* "either/or," *nor* "both/ and" nor even "neither/nor," while at the same time not totally abandoning these logics either. The very word *deconstruction* is meant to undermine the either/or logic of the opposition "construction/destruction." Deconstruction is both, it is neither, and it reveals the way in which both construction and destruction are themselves not what they appear to be. (Johnson 1987:12–13)

In addition to offering the reader a first encounter with deconstruction in the field of theatre, I also discussed several fundamental notions about theatrical production which have been with us since the Industrial Revolution and the European Enlightenment. Many readers of a text (be it playtext, prompt-copy, rehearsal-text, or performance-text) have dealt with extra-textual "reality" or with whatever lies outside the languages of the stage. However, only few of them investigated how texts exist in the absence of the "real" even though texts do not thereby annihilate "reality." This discussion may inspire some readers to help theatre move in new directions. To date, the pendulum of both academic and nonacademic rationalizations about the art of theatre has been swinging back and forth between a Darwinian performance theory (alias the ethosemiotics of the theatre) and a Pavlovian performance theory (alias the sociosemiotics of the theatre). In applying the deconstructive approach, I offered no signposts for the direction that this movement or (r)evolution should take. I only showed how some (r)evolutionary movements and "new orders" could be questioned and could be taken apart. If some readers think that they cannot endorse *what* I propose in this book unless they know *who* I am or *where* I stand, then I must confess that I am neither a deconstructor nor a logocentrist. My two good friends told me so.

Bibliography

Addington, David. "Art and Science in the Theatre" *Indiana Speech Journal* 10 (1976), 1–8.

Addington, David. "Ego Involvement: Another Approach to Empathy" *Empirical Research in Theatre* (Summer 1981), 22–31.

The Anchor Bible: II Samuel. 9th volume. Tr. & ed. by P. Kyle McCarter, Jr. Garden City, N.Y.: Doubleday, 1984.

Anderson, S. "Generating Computer Animated Movies from a Graphic Console." In *Advanced Computer Graphics: Economics, Techniques, and Applications.* Ed. by Robert Parslow and Richard Green. New York: Plenum Press, 1971, 717–722.

Antoine, André. *Mes souvenirs sur le Théâtre-Libre.* Paris: Fayard, 1921.

Appia, Adolphe. *Die Musik und die Inscenierung.* Munich: Bruckmann, 1899.

Appia, Adolphe. "La mise en scène du drame wagnérien" (1895). In *Oeuvres complètes.* Ed. by Marie Bablet-Hahn. Berne: Societe Suisse du théâtre, 1983, I:261–283.

Archer, William. *Masks or Faces?* (1888). In *The Paradox of Acting by Denis Diderot and Masks or Faces? by William Archer.* Ed. by Eric Bentley. New York: Hill and Wang, 1957, pp. 75–228.

Aristotle. *Aristotle on the Art of Poetry.* Tr. by Ingram Bywater. Oxford: Clarendon Press, 1920.

Aristotle. *Aristotle on the Art of Poetry: An Amplified Version with Supplementary Illustrations for Students of English.* Tr. by Lane Cooper. Boston: Ginn, 1913.

Aristotle. *Aristotle's Poetics.* Tr. by Kenneth Telford. Lanham: University Press of America, 1961.

Aristotle. *Aristotle Poetics.* Tr. by Gerald Else. Ann Arbor: University of Michigan Press, 1967.

Aristotle. *The Poetics of Aristotle.* Tr. by Stephen Halliwell. London: Duckworth, 1987.

Aristotle. *Aristotle's Theory of Poetry and Fine Art with a Critical Text and Translation of the Poetics*. Tr. by Samuel Butcher. 2nd ed. London: Macmillan, 1898.

Aristotle. *Aristotle's Theory of Poetry and Fine Art with a Critical Text and Translation of the Poetics—with a Prefatory Essay "Aristotelian Literary Criticism" by John Gassner*. 4th ed. New York: Dover Publications, 1951.

Aronson, Arnold. "Design and the Next Wave" *Theatre Design and Technology* 22:1 (1986), 6–15.

Aronson, Boris. *Stage Design As Visual Metaphor*. Ed. by Frank Rich. Katonah, N.Y.: Katonah Gallery, 1989.

Artaud, Antonin, *The Theatre and Its Double*. Tr. Mary Richards. New York: Grove Press, 1958.

Atkins, Douglas, "Dehellenizing Literary Criticism" *College English* 41 (1980), 769–779.

Austin, John. *How to Do Things with Words*. Cambridge: Harvard University Press, 1962.

Barba, Eugenio. *Beyond the Floating Islands*. New York: PAJ Publications, 1986.

Barba, Eugenio. "Theatre Anthropology." Tr. by Richard Fowler. *Drama Review* 26:2 (1982), 5–32.

Barba, Eugenio. "Words or Presence" *Drama Review* 16:1 (1972), 47–54.

Barthes, Roland. "The Death of the Author" (1968). In *Image, Music, Text*. Tr. by Stephen Heath. New York: Noonday Press, 1977, pp. 142–148.

Barthes, Roland. "Diderot, Brecht, Eisenstein" *Screen* 15:2 (1974), 33–39.

Barthes, Roland. *Elements of Semiology*. Tr. by Annette Lavers and Colin Smith. London: Hill and Wang, 1968.

Barthes, Roland. *On Racine*. Tr. by Richard Howard. New York: Hill and Wang, 1964; Octagon Books, 1977.

Batten, L.W. "Helkath Hazzurim, 2 Samuel 2, 12–16" *Zeitschrift für die alttestamentliche Wissenschaft* 26 (1906), 90–94.

Battison, Robin, and I. King Jordan. "Cross Cultural Communication with Foreign Signers: Fact and Fancy" *Sign Language Studies* 10 (1976), 53–68.

Beck, Julian. "Storming the Barricades." In *The Brig: A Concept for Theatre or Film*. By Kenneth Brown. New York: Hill and Wang, 1965, pp. 1–35.

Benesh, Rudolf, and Joan Benesh. *An Introduction to Benesh Movement Notation: Dance*. Brooklyn: Dance Horizons, 1969.

Bennett, Tony. *Formalism and Marxism*. London: Methuen, 1979.

Berberich, Junko. "Some Observations on Movement in Nō" *Asian Theatre Journal* 1:2 (1984), 207–216.

Berger, Joseph, M. Hamit Fisek, Robert Norman, and Morris Zelditch, Jr. *Status Characteristics and Social Interaction: An Expectation-states Approach*. New York: Elsevier, 1977.

Berlyne, D.E. *Aesthetics and Psychobiology*. New York: Appleton-Century-Crofts, 1971.

Berke, Bradley. "A Generative View of Mimesis" *Poetics* 7 (1978), 45–61.

Biblia Germanica: Faksimilierte Ausgabe der Lutherbibel von 1545. Ed. by Wilhelm Hoffmann. Stuttgart: Omnitypie Gesellschaft Nachf. Leopold Zechnall & Wurttembergische Bibelanstalt, 1967.

Biblia Sacra: Vulgate Editionis, Sixti V & Clementis VIII, Pont. Max. auctoritate recognita. Editio nova. Juxta editionem parisiensem Antonij Vitre. Antverpiae: Joannes Baptista Verdussen, via vulgo Cammerstraet, MDCCXV.

Birdwhistell, Ray. *Kinesics and Content*. Harmondsworth: Penguin, 1971.

Block, Anita. *The Changing World in Plays and Theatre*. Boston: Little, Brown, 1939.

Blumenthal, Eileen. *Joseph Chaikin: Exploring the Boundaries of Theatre*. Cambridge: Cambridge University Press, 1984.

Boleslavsky, Richard. *Acting: The First Six Lessons*. New York: Theatre Artists, 1933.

Bolkestein, Hendrik. "De Cultuurhistoricus en zijn stof." In *Nederlandsche Philologen-congres*. Leyden: Handelingen van het Zeventiende, 1937.

Boman, Thorlief. *Hebrew Thought Compared with Greek*. Tr. by J. Moreau. London: SCM Press, 1960.

Bordewijk-Knotter, J. "Empiric Audience Research: Its Relevance and Applicability." In *Das Theater und sein Publikum*. Wein: Österreichische Akademie der Wissenschaften, 1977, pp. 388–396.

Braid, James. *Braid on Hypnotism: Neurypnology*. Ed. by Arthur Waite. London: George Redway, 1899; rpt. New York: Julian Press, 1960.

Brandstelter, A. "Funktion und Leistung grammatischer Einfachstrukturen: Anmerkungen zur Syntax der Filmtexte" *Sprache im technischen zeitalter* 13–15 (1965), 1082–1090.

Brecht, Bertolt. "Alienation Effects in Chinese Acting." In *Brecht on Theatre*. Ed. and Tr. by John Willett, London: Hill and Wang, 1964, pp. 91–99.

Brecht, Bertolt. *Brecht on Theatre: The Development of an Aesthetic.* Ed. and Tr. by John Willett. London: Methuen, 1964.

Brewster, Ben. "From Shklovsky to Brecht: A Reply" *Screen* 15:2 (1974), 82–102.

Bridger, Wagner, and W. Horsley Gantt. "The Effects of Mescaline on Differentiated Conditioned Reflexes" *American Journal of Psychiatry* 113 (1956), 352–360.

Bridger, William. "Signal Systems and the Development of Cognitive Functions." In *Central Nervous System and Behavior*. Ed. by Mary Brazier. New York: Josiah Macy, Jr., Foundation, 1960, pp. 425–456.

Brook, Peter. *The Empty Space*. New York: Atheneum, 1968.

Brook, Peter. "The Holy Theatre." In *The Empty Space*. New York: Atheneum, 1968, pp. 42–64.

Brook, Peter. "Penetrating the Surface" *Parabola: The Magazine of Myth and Tradition* 13:2 (1988), 57–59.

Brook, Peter. *Shifting Point: 1946–1987.* New York: Harper & Row, 1987.

Brook, Peter. *US.* London: Calder and Boyars, 1968.

Brooker, Peter. *Bertolt Brecht: Dialectics, Poetry, Politics.* London: Croom Helm, 1988.

Brunetière, Ferdinand. "Le naturalisme au XVIIe siècle: conference faite a la Sorbonne" (1883). In *Études critiques sur l'histoire de la litterature française*. 9 vols. Paris: Librairie Hachette, 1888–1925; 1888, I:305–336.

Brustein, Robert. "Introduction: The Third Theatre Revisited" *The Third Theatre*. New York: Alfred Knopf, 1969, pp. xi-xx.

Budde, Karl. *Die Bücher Samuel.* Tubingen: Mohr, 1902.

Burian, Jarka. *The Scenography of Josef Svoboda.* Middletown, Conn.: Wesleyan University Press, 1971.

Burns, Elizabeth. *Theatricality: A Study of Convention in the Theatre and in Social Life.* London: Longman, 1972.

Burton, Deidre. *Dialogue and Discourse: A Sociolinguistic Approach to Modern Drama Dialogue and Naturally Occuring Conversation.* London: Routledge & Kegan Paul, 1980.

Burzynski, Tadeusz, and Zbigniew Osinski. *Grotowski's Laboratory.* Tr. by Boleslaw Taborski. Warsaw: Interpress Publishers, 1979.

Cain, William. "Deconstruction in America" *College English* 41:4 (1979), 367–382.

Calvert, Thomas, John Chapman, and Aftab Patla. "Aspects of the Kinematic Simulation of Human Movement" *IEEE Computer Graphics & Applications* 2:9 (1982), 41–50.

Carlson, Marvin. *Theatre Semiotics: Signs of Life.* Bloomington: Indiana University Press, 1990.

Cashman, Daniel. "Grotowski: His Twentieth Anniversary" *Theatre Journal* 31:4 (1979), 460–466.

Chaikin, Joseph. *The Presence of the Actor.* New York: Atheneum, 1972.

Child, Irvin. "Esthetics" *Annual Review of Psychology* 23 (1972), 669–694.

Christiansen, Broder. *Philosophie der Kunst.* Hanau: Clauss & Feddersen, 1909.

Clevenger, Theodore. "Behavioral Research in Theatre" *Educational Theatre Journal* 17 (May 1965), 118–121.

Clevenger, Theodore, Margaret Clark, and Gil Lazier. "Stability of Factor Structure in Smith's Semantic Differential for Theatre Concepts" *Quarterly Journal of Speech* 52:3 (1967), 241–247.

Clevenger, Theodore, and John Tolch. "The Reliability of Judgments of Acting Performance" *Educational Theatre Journal* 14 (1962), 318–323.

Clifford, James, ed. *Writing Culture.* Berkeley: University of California Press, 1986.

Clurman, Harold. *The Divine Pastime: Theatre Essays.* New York: Macmillan, 1974.

Clurman, Harold. *The Fervent Years: The Story of the Group Theatre and the Thirties* (1945). New York: Harcourt Brace Jovanovich, 1975.

Clurman, Harold. *Ibsen.* New York: Macmillan, 1977.

Clurman, Harold. *Lies Like Truth.* New York: Macmillan, 1958.

Clurman, Harold. *The Naked Image: Observations on the Modern Theatre* (1958). 2nd enhanced printing. New York: Macmillan, 1967.

Clurman, Harold. "Theatre" *Nation* CCIII 11–28–1966, pp. 586–588.

Clurman, Harold, ed. *Famous American Plays of the 1930s.* New York: Dell, 1968.

Clurman, Harold, ed. *Famous American Plays of the 1960s.* New York: Dell, 1972.

Clurman, Harold, ed. *Nine Plays of the Modern Theatre.* New York: Grove Press, 1981.

Clynes, Manfred. *Sentics: The Touch of Emotions.* Garden City, N.Y.: Anchor Press, 1977.

Cobin, Martin. "Text, Subtext, Antitext: The Relation of Verbal and Nonverbal Communication in the Production of Shakespeare" *Maske und Kothurn* 29 (1983), 152–160.

Cohen, Robert, and John Harrop. *Creative Play Direction.* Englewood Cliffs, N.J.: Prentice-Hall, 1974.

Constantinidis, Stratos. "Feedback in Play Production" *Kodikas/Code: Ars Semiotica, An International Journal of Semiotics* 7:1–2 (1984), 63–88.

Constantinidis, Stratos. "Is Theatre Under Deconstruction?" *Journal of Dramatic Theory and Criticism* 4:1 (1989), 31–52.

Cornford, Francis. *The Origin of Attic Comedy.* London: Edward Arnold, 1914.

Craig, Gordon. *Craig on Theatre.* Ed. by Michael Walton. London: Methuen, 1983.

Craig, Gordon. *On the Art of Theatre.* London: Heinemann, 1911.

Crockett, Walter. "Cognitive Complexity and Impression Formation." In *Process in Experimental Personality Research.* Ed. by Brendan Maher. New York: Academic Press, 1965, II:47–90.

Courvoisier, Simone. "Pharmacodynamic Basis for the Use of Chloropromazine in Psychiatry" *Journal of Clinical and Experimental Psychopathology* 17 (1956), 25–37.

Culler, Jonathan. *Structuralist Poetics: Structuralism, Linguistics, and the Study of Literature.* London: Routledge & Kegan Paul, 1975.

D'Amico, Silvio. *La crisi del Teatro.* Roma: Polemiche, 1931.

Darwin, Charles. *The Expression of the Emotions in Man and Animals.* London: John Murray, 1872.

Darwin, Charles. *On the Origin of Species by Means of Natural Selection; or, the Preservation of Favoured Races in the Struggle for Life.* London: John Murray, 1859.

Delia, Jesse. "Change of Meaning Processes in Impression Formation" *Speech Monographs* 43:2 (1976), 142–157.

Derrida, Jacques. "Force and Signification." In *Writing and Difference.* Ed. and Tr. by Alan Bass. Chicago: University of Chicago Press, 1978, pp. 3–30.

Derrida, Jacques. "Limited Inc abc..." *Glyph* 2 (1977), 162–254.

Derrida, Jacques. *Of Grammatology.* Tr. by Gayatri Chakravorty Spivak. Baltimore: Johns Hopkins University Press, 1976.

Derrida, Jacques. *Positions.* Tr. by Alan Bass. Chicago: University of Chicago Press, 1981.

Derrida, Jacques. "Structure, Sign, and Play in the Discourse of the Human Sciences." In *The Structuralist Controversy.* Ed. by Richard Macksey and Eugenio Donato. Baltimore: Johns Hopkins University Press, 1970, pp. 247–265.

Derrida, Jacques. "Structure, Sign, and Play in the Discourse of the Human Sciences." In *Writing and Difference.* Tr. by Alan Bass. Chicago: University of Chicago Press, 1978, pp. 278–293.

Derrida, Jacques. "The Theatre of Cruelty and the Closure of Representation." In *Writing and Difference.* Tr. by Alan Bass, Chicago: University of Chicago Press, 1978, pp. 232–250.

Derrida, Jacques. "White Mythology: Metaphor in the Text of Philosophy" *New Literary History* 6 (1974), 5–74.

Devereux, G. "Social and Cultural Implications of Incest among the Mojave" *Psychoanalytic Quarterly* 8 (1939), 510–533.

Diderot, Denis. *The Paradox of Acting.* In *The Paradox of Acting by Denis Diderot and Masks of Faces? by William Archer.* Ed. by Eric Bentley. New York: Hill and Wang, 1957, pp. 11–71.

Dooley, Marrianne. "Anthropometric Modeling Programs: A Survey" *IEEE Computer Graphics & Applications* 2:9 (1982), 17–25.

Dumas, Alexandre, *fils.* "L'entrangere: Preface." (1879) In *Théâtre complet avec préfaces inédites de Alexandre Dumas fils.* 7 vols. Paris: Calmann Levy, 1898–1899; 1898, VI:173–225.

Durham, Weldon. "At Issue—Conference 1990" *ATHE News* 3:5 (1989), 1.

Eco, Umberto. *A Theory of Semiotics.* Bloomington: Indiana University Press, 1976.

Elam, Keir. *The Semiotics of Theatre and Drama.* London: Methuen, 1980.

Ellis, John. *Against Deconstruction.* Princeton: Princeton University Press, 1989.

Ellis, John. "Wittgensteinian Thinking in Theory of Criticism" *New Literary History* 12 (1981), 347–452.

Erbe, Berit. "Theatrical Codes" *Maske und Kothurn* 29 (1983), 307–310.

Erlich, Victor. *Russian Formalism: History-Doctrine.* 4th ed. The Hague: Mouton, 1980.

Esslin, Martin. *Brecht: The Man and His Work.* Rev. ed. Garden City, N.Y.: Anchor Books, 1971.

Findlay, Robert. "Grotowski's Cultural Explorations Bordering on Art, Especially Theatre" *Theatre Journal* 32:3 (1980), 349–356.

The First Germanic Bible: Translated from the Greek by the Gothic Bishop Wulfila in the Fourth Century and Other Remains of the Gothic Language. Ed. by G. Balg. Milwaukee: Germania Publishers, 1891.

Fischer, Michael. *Does Deconstruction Make Any Difference? Poststructuralism and the Defense of Poetry in Modern Criticism.* Bloomington: Indiana University Press, 1985.

Fish, Stanley. *Is There a Text in This Class?* Cambridge: Harvard University Press, 1980.

Foucault, Michel. *The Order of Things: An Archaeology of the Human Sciences.* Tr. by A.S. London. New York: Random House, 1970.

Foucault, Michel. "What is an Author?" In *Textual Strategies: Perspectives in Post-Structuralist Criticism.* Ed. by J.V. Harari. Ithaca, N.Y.: Cornell University Press, 1979, pp. 141–169.

Freud, Sigmund. "The Unconscious." In *Collected Works.* Ed. by James Strachey, et al. London: Hogarth Press, 1956.

Gallaway, Marian. *The Director in the Theatre.* New York: Macmillan, 1963.

Gardner, Helen. "The Historical Approach." In *The Business of Criticism.* Oxford: Oxford University Press, 1959, pp. 24–51.

Garfinkel, Harold. *Studies in Ethnomethodology.* Englewood Cliffs, N.J.: Prentice-Hall, 1967.

Gastaut, Henri. "Some Aspects of the Neurophysiological Basis of Conditioned Reflexes and Behavior." In *Neurological Basis of Behavior*. Ed. by Gordon Wolstenholme and Cecilia O'Connor. London: Ciba Foundation, 1958, pp. 255–272.

Gellius, Aulus. *Noctes Atticae*. 2 vols. Ed. by P.K. Marshall. Oxford: Oxford University Press, 1968.

The Geneva Bible: A Fascimile of the 1560 edition. Madison: University of Wisconsin Press, 1969.

Gibson, M. "Peter Brook on Africa" *Drama Review* 17 (1973), 37–51.

Gilman, Richard. "The Drama Is Coming Now" *TDR* 7:4 (1963), 27–42.

Glück, J.J. "Reviling and Monomachy as Battle-Preludes in Ancient Warfare" *Acta Classica* 7 (1964), 25–31.

Goffman, Erwin. *Frame Analysis: An Essay on the Organization of Experience*. Cambridge: Harvard University Press, 1974.

Gombrich, E.H. *The Sense of Order: A Study in the Psychology of Decorative Art*. Ithaca: Cornell University Press, 1979.

Goodall, Jan. *In the Shadow of Man*. New York: Dell, 1972.

Gorelik, Mordecai. *New Theatres for Old*. New York: E.P. Dutton, 1962.

Gray, Ronald. *Brecht the Dramatist*. Cambridge: Cambridge University Press, 1976.

Green, William. "Reinterpreting *Macbeth* through the Director's Employment of Nonverbal Devices" *Maske und Kothurn* 29 (1983), 161–167.

Greenfield, Patricia, and Joshua Smith. *The Structure of Communication in Early Language Development*. New York: Academic Press, 1976.

Greenlee, Douglas. *Peirce's Concept of Sign*. The Hague: Mouton, 1973.

Grimaud, Michel. "Recent Trends in Psychoanalysis: A Survey with Emphasis on Psychological Criticism in English Literature and Related Areas" *Substance* 13 (1976), 136–162.

Groos, Karl. *The Play of Animals*. Tr. by Elizabeth Baldwin. New York: D. Appleton, 1898.

Groos, Karl. *The Play of Man*. Tr. by Elizabeth Baldwin. New York: D. Appleton, 1901.

Gross, Robert. *Words Heard and Overheard: The Main Text in Contemporary Drama*. New York: Garland Publishing, 1990.

Gross, Roger. *Understanding Playscripts: Theory and Method*. Bowling Green, Ohio: Bowling Green University Press, 1974.

Grotowski, Jerzi. *Towards a Poor Theatre.* Ed. by Eugenio Barba. Holstebro: Christian Christensen, 1968.

Guardini, Romano. *Vom Geist der Liturgie.* Freiburg im Breisgau, Berlin: Herder, 1918.

Gunkle, George. "Addendum on Quantitative Research in Theatre" *Kodikas/ Code: Ars Semeiotica* 8:1/2 (1985), 137–141.

Gunkle, George. "Emotion, Language, and Acting" *Empirical Research in Theatre* 1 (1975), 41–49.

Haberman, David. *Acting as a Way of Salvation: A Study of Raganuga Bhakti Sadhana.* New York: Oxford University Press, 1988.

Hale, Claudia, and Jesse Delia. "Cognitive Complexity and Social Perspective Taking" *Speech Monographs* 43:3 (1976), 195–203.

Hall, Lawrence, ed. "Critical Approaches and Methods." In *A Grammar of Literary Criticism: Essays in Definition of Vocabulary, Concepts, and Aims.* New York: Macmillan, 1965, pp. 435–533.

Handke, Peter. *Offending the Audience.* In *Kaspar and Other Plays.* Tr. by Michael Roloff. New York: Farrar, Straus and Giroux, 1969, pp. 1–32.

Hanson, Allen, and Edward Riseman, eds. *Computer Vision Systems.* New York: Academic Press, 1978.

Harrison, Jane. *Themis: A Study of the Social Origins of Greek Religion.* 2nd rev. ed. Cambridge: Cambridge University Press, 1927.

Havemeyer, Loomis. *The Drama of Savage Peoples.* New Haven: Yale University Press, 1916.

Hawkes, Terence. *Structuralism and Semiotics.* London: Methuen, 1977.

Heath, Stephen. "Lessons from Brecht" *Screen* 15:2 (1974), 103–128.

Hegel, Georg. *Aesthetics: Lectures on Fine Art.* Tr. by T. Knox, 2 vols. Oxford: Clarendon Press, 1975.

Hegel, Georg. *The Phenomenology of Mind.* Tr. by J. Baillie. 2nd rev. ed. London: George Allen & Unwin, 1931.

Heilpern, John. *Conference of the Birds: The Story of Peter Brook in Africa.* Indianapolis: Bobbs-Merrill, 1978.

Herbison-Evans, Don. "Rapid Raster Ellipsoid Shading" *Computer Graphics* 13:4 (1980), 355–361.

Herbison-Evans, Don. "Real-time Animation of Human Figure Drawings with Hidden Lines Omitted" *IEEE Computer Graphics & Applications* 2:9 (1982), 27–33.

Herrick, Marvin. *The Fusion of Horatian and Aristotelian Literary Criticism 1531–1555.* Urbana: University of Illinois Press, 1946.

Hertzberg, Hans. *I and II Samuel: A Commentary.* Tr. by J. Bowden. Philadelphia: Westminster Press, 1964.

Hess-Lüttich, Ernest. "Towards a Semiotics of Discourse in Drama" *Kodikas/ Code: Ars Semeiotica* 6:3/4 (1983), 187–201.

Hilgard, E. "Altered States of Awareness" *Journal of Nervous and Mental Diseases* 149 (1969), 68–79.

Hilgard, E. *Hypnotic Susceptibility.* New York: Harcourt, Brace and World, 1965.

Hingley, Ronald. *Chekhov.* London: Allen & Unwin, 1950.

Hite, Roger, Jackie Czerepinski, and Dean Anderson. "Transactional Analysis: A New Perspective for the Theatre" *Empirical Research in Theatre* (Summer 1973), 1–17.

Holland, Norman. *The Dynamics of Literary Response.* New York: Oxford University Press, 1968.

The Holy Scriptures according to the Masoretic Text: Genesis to II Kings: Hebrew-English Edition. Vol. 1. Philadelphia: Jewish Publication Society of America, 1955.

Honzl, Jindrich. "Dynamics of the Sign in the Theatre." In *Semiotics of Art.* Ed. by Ladislav Matejka and Irwin Titunic. Cambridge: MIT Press, 1976, pp. 74–93.

Hoover, Majorie. "Brecht's Soviet Connection, Tretiakov" *Brecht Heute/ Brecht Today* 3 (1973), 39–56.

Hornby, Richard. *Drama, Metadrama, and Perception.* Lewisburg, Penn.: Bucknell University Press, 1986.

Hornby, Richard. *Script into Performance: a Structuralist View of Play Production.* Austin: University of Texas Press, 1977.

Hristic, Jovan. "On the Interpretation of Drama" *New Literary History* 3:2 (1972) 345–354.

Huizinga, Johan. *Homo Ludens: Versuch einer Bestimmung des Spieleleme der Kultur.* Basel: Akademische Verlagsanstalt Pantheon, 194

Huizinga, Johan. *Homo Ludens: A Study of the Play Element in Culture.* Tr. by R. F. Hull. London: Routledge & Kegan Paul, 1949; rpt. Boston: Beacon Press, 1955.

Hutchinson, Ann. *Labanotation or Kinetography Laban: The System of Analyzing and Recording Movement.* New York: Theatre Arts Books, 1970.

Immoos, Thomas. "The Birth of Non-verbal Theatre in Shinto Ritual" *Maske und Kothurn* 29 (1983), 301–306.

Inden, Ronald. "Orientalist Constructions of India" *Modern Asian Studies* 20:3 (1986), 401–446.

Ingarden, Roman. "The Functions of Language in the Theatre." In *The Literary Work of Art: An Investigation on the Borderlines of Ontology, Logic, and Theory of Literature, with an Appendix on the Functions of Language in the Theatre.* Tr. by George Grabowicz. Evanston, Ill.: Northwestern University Press, 1973, pp. 377–396.

Ionesco, Eugene. "Experience of the Theatre." In *Notes and Counter-Notes.* Tr. by Donald Watson. London: John Calder, 1964, pp. 13–35.

Jakobson, Roman. "The Dominant" (1935). Tr. by Herbert Eagle. In *Readings in Russian Poetics: Formalist and Structuralist Views.* Ed. by Ladislav Matejka and Krystyna Pomorska. Cambridge: MIT Press, 1971, pp. 82–87.

Jakobson, Roman. "Linguistics and Poetics." In *Style in Language.* Ed. by Thomas Sebeok. New York: MIT Press, 1960, 350–377.

Jakobson, Roman. "Two Aspects of Language and Two Types of Aphasic Disturbances." In *Selected Writings.* 2nd expanded ed. The Hague: Mouton, 1971, II:239–259.

Jameson, Fredric. *The Prison House of Language: A Critical Account of Structuralism and Russian Formalism.* Princeton: Princeton University Press, 1972.

Jansen, Steen. "Esquisse d'une theorie de la forme dramatique" *Languages* 12 (December 1968), 71–93.

Jarry, Alfred. "Theatre Questions." Tr. by Barbara Wright. In *Selected Works of Alfred Jarry.* Ed. by Roger Shattuck and Simon Taylor. New York: Grove Press, 1965, pp. 82–85.

hn, E. "Electrophysiological Correlates of Avoidance Conditioning in the Cat." In *Central Nervous System and Behavior.* Ed. by Mary Brazier. New York: Josiah Macy, Jr., Foundation, 1958, pp. 334–347.

Johnson, Barbara. *A World of Difference*. Baltimore: Johns Hopkins University Press, 1987.

Jones, Robert Edmond. *The Dramatic Imagination: Reflections and Speculations on the Art of Theatre*. New York: Theatre Arts Books, 1941.

Jones, Robert Edmond. *Drawings for the Theatre*. New York: Theatre Arts Books, 1925.

Jordan, King, and Robbin Battison. "A Referential Communication Experiment with Foreign Sign Languages" *Sign Language Studies* 10 (1976), 69–80.

Kaufmann, Walter. "The Hegel Myth and Its Method" *Philosophical Review* LX (1951), 459–486.

Kernodle, George. "Wagner, Appia and the Idea of Musical Design" *Educational Theatre Journal* 6:3 (1954), 223–230.

Killam, Keith, and Eva Killam. "The Action of Lysergic Acid Diethylamide on Central Afferent and Limbic Pathways in the Cat" *Journal of Pharmacology and Experimental Therapeutics* 116 (1956), 35–36.

Kirby, Ernest. *Ur-Drama: The Origins of Theatre*. New York: New York University Press, 1975.

Klostermann, August. *Die Bücher Samuelis und der Konige*. Nordlingen, Ger.: Beck, 1887.

Kreitler, Hans, and Shulamith Kreitler. *Psychology of the Arts*. Durham, N.C.: Duke University Press, 1972.

Krieger, Murray. *Poetic Presence and Illusion: Essays in Critical History and Theory*. Baltimore, Johns Hopkins University Press, 1979.

Krippner, Stanley. *Drug-related Altered States of Consciousness*. Meerut, India: Anu Prakashan, 1977.

Krippner, Stanley. *Human Possibilities: Mind Exploration in the USSR and Eastern Europe*. Garden City, N.Y.: Anchor Press/Doubleday, 1980.

Lahr, John. "The Open Theatre's *Serpent*." In *Up Against the Fourth Wall: Essays on Modern Theatre*. New York: Grove Press, 1970, pp. 158–174.

Lang, Franciscus. "Dissertatio de actione scenica cum figuris eandem explicantibus, A Discourse on Stage Movement" (1727). Tr. by Dean Regenos. In Franz Lang and the Jesuit Stage by Ronald Engle. University of Illinois: Ph.D. thesis, 1968, pp. 78–195.

Langer, Susanne. *Feeling and Form: A Theory of Art.* New York: Charles Scribner, 1953.

Lazier, Gilbert. An Experimental Study of the Attention-value of Certain Areas of the Stage. University of Pittsburgh: M.A. thesis, 1963.

Leach, Robert. *Vsevolod Meyerhold.* Cambridge: Cambridge University Press, 1989.

Lessing, Gotthold. *Hamburg Dramaturgy.* Tr. by Helen Zimmern. New York: Dover Publications, 1962.

Lessing, Gotthold. *Laocoon: An Essay on the Limits of Painting and Poetry.* Tr. by Edward McCormick. Baltimore: Johns Hopkins University Press, 1984.

Lessing, Gotthold. "Un Friedrich Nicolai: Hamburg, 26 Mai 1769." In *Gotthold Ephraim Lessings sämtliche schriften.* Ed. by Karl Lachmann and Franz Muncker. 23 vols. Stuttgart: G.J. Goschen, 1886–1924; Leipzig, 1904, XVII:289–292.

Levi-Strauss, Claude. *The Raw and the Cooked.* Vol. 1. Tr. by J. and D. Weightman. New York: Harper & Row, 1969.

Lindauer, Martin. *The Psychological Study of Literature.* Chicago: Nelson-Hall, 1975.

Lippit, Ronald, and Ralph White. *Autocracy and Democracy.* New York: Harper, 1960.

Loizos, Caroline. "Play Behaviour in Higher Primates: A Review." In *Primate Ethology.* Ed. by Desmond Morris. Chicago: Aldine Publishing, 1967, pp. 176–218.

Lorenz, Konrad. *On Aggression.* Tr. by Marjorie Kerr Wilson. New York: Harcourt, Brace and World, 1966.

Lotman, Yurii. "The Structure of the Narrative Text." In *Soviet Semiotics.* Ed. by Daniel Lucid. Baltimore: Johns Hopkins University Press, 1977, pp. 193–197.

Lucian. "Menippus ē Nekyomanteia." In *Lucian.* 8 vols. Tr. by A.M. Harmon. London: William Heinemann, 1925, IV:71–109.

Lucian. "Zeus Tragōidos." In *Lucian.* 8 vols. Tr. by A.M. Harmon. Cambridge: Harvard University Press, 1953, II:89–169.

MacCabe, Colin. "Realism and the Cinema: Notes on Some Brechtian Theses" *Screen* 15:2 (1974), 7–27.

Macgowan, Kenneth. *The Theatre of Tomorrow.* New York: Boni and Liveright, 1921.

McKane, William. *I and II Samuel: The Way to the Throne.* London: SCM, 1963.

Malcolm, J.L. "The Electrical Activity of Cortical Neurones in Relation to Behavior, as Studied with Microelectrodes in Unrestrained Cats." In *Neurological Basis of Behavior.* Ed. by Gordon Wolstenholme and Cecilia O'Connor. London: Ciba Foundation, 1958, pp. 295–302.

Mallarmé, Stéphane. "Richard Wagner, rêverie d'un poète français" *Revue wagnerienne* 1 (1885), 195–200.

Marazzi, Amedeo, and E. Ross Hart. "Relationship of Hallucinogens to Andrenergic Cerebral Neurohumors" *Science* 121 (1955), 365–367.

Marowitz, Charles. "Notes on the Theatre of Cruelty" *Tulane Drama Review* 11:2 (1966), 152–172.

Marquis, Donald, and Ernest Hilgard. "Conditioned Responses to Light in Monkeys After Removal of the Occipital Lobes" *Brain* 60 (1937), 1–12.

Marranca, Bonnie, and Gautam Dasgupta. "The Drama in American Letters" *Performing Arts Journal* 7:1 (1983), 4–6.

May, Herbert, and Bruce Metzger, eds. *The Oxford Annotated Bible with the Apocrypha.* New York: Oxford University Press, 1965.

Mehrabian, Albert, and H. Reed. "Some Determinants of Communication Accuracy" *Psychological Bulletin* 70 (1968), 365–381.

Merleau-Ponty, Maurice. "Higher Forms of Behavior: Pavlov's Reflexology and Its Postulates." In *The Structure of Behavior.* Tr. by Alden Fisher. Boston: Beacon Press, 1967, pp. 52–128.

Mesmer, Franz. *Memoir of F.A. Mesmer, Doctor of Medicine, On His Discoveries* (1799). Tr. by Jerome Eden. Mount Vernon, N.Y.: Eden Press, 1957.

Mesmer, Franz. *Mesmerism: A Translation of the Original Scientific and Medical Writings of F.A. Mesmer.* Ed. and tr. by George Bloch. Los Altos, Calif.: W. Kaufman, 1980.

Meyerhold, Vsevolod. *Meyerhold on Theatre.* Ed. and tr. by Edward Braun. New York: Hill and Wang, 1969.

Milhous, Judith, and Robert Hume. *Producible Interpretation: Eight English Plays 1675–1707.* Carbondale: Southern Illinois University Press, 1985.

Miller, Keith, and Clarence Bahs. "Director Expectancy and Actor Effectiveness" *Empirical Research in Theatre* (Summer 1974), 60–64.

Mitchell, Stanley. "From Shklovsky to Brecht: Some Preliminary Remarks Towards a History of the Politicisation of Russian Formalism" *Screen* 15:2 (1974), 74–81.

Moore, Sonia. *The Stanislavski System: The Professional Training of an Actor.* New York: Viking Press, 1974.

Moussinac, Leon. *La decoration théâtrale.* Paris: Rieder, 1922.

Mueller, Gustav. "The Hegel Legend of 'Thesis-Antithesis-Synthesis'" *Journal of the History of Ideas* 19:3 (1958), 411–414.

Mukarovsky, Jan. "Art as Semiotic Fact." In *Semiotics of Art: Prague School Contributions.* Ed. by Ladislav Matejka and Irwin Titunik. Cambridge: MIT Press, 1976, pp. 3–9.

Mukařovský, Jan. "On Structuralism" (1946). In *Structure, Sign, and Function: Selected Essays by Jan Mukarovsky.* Tr. and ed. by John Burbank and Peter Steiner. New Haven: Yale University Press, 1978, pp. 3–16.

Myers, Terry, John Laver, and John Anerson, eds. *The Cognitive Representation of Speech.* Amsterdam: North-Holland Publishing, 1981.

Nietzsche, Friedrich. *The Birth of Tragedy and The Case of Wagner.* Tr. by Walter Kaufmann. New York: Vintage Books, 1967.

The NIV Interlinear Hebrew-English Old Testament: Joshua to 2 Kings. Vol. 2. Ed. by John Kohlenberger III. Grand Rapids, Mich.: Zondervan, 1980.

Nowell, Lucy, Frank Silberstein, John Carr, Gary Gaiser, Leon Brauner, and Adel Migid. "Promotion and Tenure Evaluation of the Theatrical Design and Technology Faculty: Issues and Recommended Guidelines" *Theatre Design and Technology* 23:3 (1987), supplement, 1–15.

The Old Testament in Syriac according to the Peshitta Version: Samuel. Ed. by P.A.H. der Boer. Leiden: Brill, 1978.

Orwell, George. "Politics and the English Language." In *The Collected Essays, Journalism and Letters: 1945–1950.* 4 vols. Ed. by Sonia Orwell and Ian Angus. New York: Harcourt, Brace and World, 1968, IV:127–140.

Osgood, Charles, and Thomas Sebeok, eds. *Psycholinguistics: A Survey of Theory and Research Methods and Problems.* Bloomington: Indiana University Press, 1965.

Pagnini, Marcello "Per una semiologia de teatro classico" *Strumenti critici* 12 (1970), 122–140.

Parslow, Robert, and Richard Green, eds. *Advanced Computer Graphics.* London: Plenum Press, 1971.

Parslow, Robert, Roger Prowse, and Richard Green, eds. *Computer Graphics: Techniques and Applications.* London: Plenum Press, 1969.

Pasolli, Robert. *A Book on Open Theatre.* New York: Bobbs-Merrill, 1970.

Passow, Wilfried. "Affekt und Wirkung: Peirces Interpretantenbegriff im Dienste empirischer Theatersemiotik am Beispiel des *Mandragola* von Niccolo Machiavelli." In *Theatre Semiotics,* vol. II of *Multimedial Communication.* Ed. by Ernest Hess-Lüttich. Tubingen, Ger.: Narr, 1982, pp. 254–267.

Pavis, Patrice. *Languages of the Stage.* New York: Performing Arts Journal Publications, 1982.

Pavlov, Ivan. *Activity of the Cerebral Cortex.* Tr. by G. Anrep. London: Oxford University Press: Humphrey Milford., 1927.

Pavlov, Ivan. *Selected Works.* Tr. by S. Belsky. Ed. by J. Gibbons. Moscow: Foreign Language Publishing House, 1955.

Peckham, Morse. *Man's Rage for Chaos: Biology, Behavior, and the Arts.* Philadelphia: Chilton Books, 1965.

Peckham, Morse. "Perceptual and Semiotic Discontinuity in Art" *Poetics* 7 (1978), 217–230.

Peevers, Barbara, and Paul Secord. "Developmental Changes in the Attribution of Descriptive Concepts to Persons" *Journal of Personality and Social Psychology* 27:1 (1973), 120–128.

Peirce, Charles. *Collected Papers.* Cambridge: Harvard University Press, 1958.

Performance Group. *Dionysus in '69.* Ed. by Richard Schechner. New York: Farrar, Straus and Giroux, 1970.

Piaget, Jean. *Language and Thoughts of the Child.* 3rd ed. New York: Humanities Press, 1967.

Pirandello, Luigi. *Six Characters in Search of an Author.* Tr. by John Linstrum. London: Eyre Methuen, 1979.

Plato. *Apology.* In *The Collected Dialogues of Plato, Including the Letters.* Ed. by Edith Hamilton and Huntington Cairns. Princeton: Princeton University Press, 1963, pp. 3–26.

Plato. *Ion.* In *The Collected Dialogues of Plato, Including the Letters.* Ed. by Edith Hamilton and Huntington Cairns. Princeton: Princeton University Press, 1963, pp. 215–228.

Plato. *Laws.* In *The Collected Dialogues of Plato, Including the Letters.* Ed. by Edith Hamilton and Huntington Cairns. Princeton: Princeton University Press, 1963, pp. 1225–1513.

Plato. *Letter VII.* In *The Collected Dialogues of Plato, Including the Letters.* Ed. by Edith Hamilton and Huntington Cairns. Princeton: Princeton University Press, 1963, pp. 1574–1598.

Plato. *Phaedrus.* Tr. by R. Hackforth. In *The Collected Dialogues of Plato, Including the Letters.* Ed. by Edith Hamilton and Huntington Cairns. Princeton: Princeton University Press, 1963, pp. 475–525.

Plato. *Republic.* Tr. by Paul Shorey. In *The Collected Dialogues of Plato, Including the Letters.* Ed. by Edith Hamilton and Huntington Cairns. Princeton: Princeton University Press, 1963, pp. 575–844.

Plato. *Timaeus.* Tr. by Benjamin Jowett. In *The Collected Dialogues of Plato, Including the Letters.* Ed. by Edith Hamilton and Huntington Cairns. Princeton: Princeton University Press, 1963, pp. 1151–1211.

Plotinus. "Enneados A, Logos S, peri tou kalou/Ennead Primae, Liber VI, De Pulchritudine." In *Plotinou Apanta/Plotini Opera Omnia.* Ed. by Daniel Wyttenbach and G. Moser. 3 vols. Oxford: Academic Press, 1835, I:97–115.

Plotinus. "First Ennead, Book Sixth." In *Complete Works.* Tr. by Kenneth Guthrie. 4 vols. Alpine: Platonist Press, 1919, I:40–55.

Plutarch. "Demosthenes." In *Plutarch's Lives.* 11 vols. Tr. by Bernadotte Perrin. London: William Heinemann, 1971, VII:1–79.

Plutarch. "Symposiakōn Problēmatōn Biblia O'." In vol. VIII (612b-697c) of *Plutarch's Moralia.* Ed. by E. Warmington. Tr. by Paul Clement and Herbert Hoffleit. London: William Heinemann, 1949.

Porter, Robert. "Analyzing Rehearsal Interaction" *Empirical Research in Theatre* (Summer 1975), 1–31.

Powers, William, David Jorns, and Robert Glenn. "The Effects of Cognitive Complexity on Characterization Depth and Performance" *Empirical Research in Theatre* 6 (1980), 1–5.

Poyatos, Fernando. "Interactive Functions and Limitations of Verbal and Nonverbal Behaviors in Natural Conversation" *Semiotica,* 30:3/4 (1980), 211–244.

Poyatos, Fernando. "Nonverbal Communication in the Theatre: The Playwright-Actor-Spectator Relationship." In *Theatre Semiotics*, vol. II of *Multimedial Communication* Ed. by Ernest Hess-Lüttich. Tubingen: Narr, 1982, pp. 75–94.

Pratt, C. "Aesthetics" *Annual Review of Psychology* 12 (1961), 71–92.

Prokofev, V. "Stanislavsky Method." In *Great Soviet Encyclopedia: A Translation of the Third Edition of Bol'shaia Sovetskaia Entsiklopediia.* 31 vols (1973–1983). Ed. by A. Prokhorov. New York: Macmillan, 1980, 24:464–465.

Purpura, Dominick. "Electrophysiological Analysis of Psychotogenic Drug Action" *Archives of Neurology and Psychiatry* 75 (1956), 122–143.

Rapp, Uri. "Simulation and Imagination: Mimesis as Play" *Maske und Kothurn* 28:2 (1982), 67–86.

Riccoboni, François. *L'Art du théâtre.* Paris: 1750; rpt. Genf 1971.

Riccoboni, Louis. *Réflexions historiques et critiques sur les différents théâtres de l'Europe.* Paris: 1738; rpt. Bologna, 1969.

Ricoeur, Paul. *The Rule of Metaphor.* Toronto: University of Toronto Press, 1977.

Ridgeway, William. *The Dramas and Dramatic Dances of Non-European Races in Special Reference to the Origin of Greek Tragedy.* Cambridge: Cambridge University Press, 1915.

Riess, Curt. "The Catastrophe of Modern Theatre: On 'Negative Culture'" *Encounter* (London) April 1990, pp. 66–69.

Riffaterre, Michael. *Text Production.* Tr. by Terese Lyons. New York: Columbia University Press, 1983.

Rimmon-Kenan, Shlomith. *Narrative Fiction: Contemporary Poetics.* London: Methuen, 1983.

Roach, Joseph. *The Player's Passion: Studies in the Science of Acting.* Newark: University of Delaware Press, 1985.

Roose-Evans, James. *Directing a Play.* New York: Theatre Arts Books, 1968.

Ross, Duncan. "Towards an Organic Approach to Actor Training" *Educational Theatre Journal* 20:2A (1968), 225–268.

Rouche, Jacques. *L'art théâtral moderne.* Paris: Librairie Bloud & Gay, 1924.

Rubin, Don. "The Avant-Garde of Yesterday and Today Seen in the Plays of Cummings and Terry" *New Haven Register Features* 9–10–1967, p. 4.

Ruble, Ronald. Performer Descriptions of Stressed Rehearsal Conditions Created by an Authoritarian and a Libertarian Directing Method. Bowling Green State University: Ph.D. dissertation, 1975.

Ruesch, Jurgen. *Semiotic Approaches to Human Relations.* The Hague: Mouton, 1972.

Ruesch, Jurgen, and Gregory Bateson. *Communication: The Social Matrix of Psychiatry.* New York: Norton, 1951.

Ruesch, Jurgen, and Weldon Kees. *Nonverbal Communication: Notes on the Visual Perception of Human Relations.* Berkeley: University of California Press, 1956.

Said, Edward. *Covering Islam: How the Media and the Experts Determine How We See the Rest of the World.* New York: Pantheon Books, 1981.

Said, Edward. *Orientalism.* New York: Pantheon Books, 1978.

Salmon, Eric. *Is Theatre Still Dying?* Westport: Greenwood Press, 1985.

Sarbin, Theodore. "Physiological Effects of Hypnotic Stimulation." In *Hypnosis and Its Therapeutic Applications.* Ed. by R. Dorcus. New York: McGraw-Hill, 1956.

Sarbin, Theodore. "Role Theory." In *Handbook of Social Psychology.* Ed. by Gardner Lindsey. Cambridge: Addison-Wesley, 1954, pp. 223–258.

Sarbin, Theodore, and V. Allen. "Role Theory." In *Handbook of Social Psychology.* Ed. by G. Lindsey and E. Aronson. Reading, Mass.: Addison-Wesley, 1968.

Sarbin, Theodore, and William Coe. *Hypnosis: A Social Psychological Analysis of Influence Communication.* New York: Holt, Rinehart and Winston, 1972.

Sarbin, Theodore, and D. Lim. "Some Evidence in Support of the Role Taking Hypothesis in Hypnosis" *International Journal of Clinical and Experimental Hypnosis* 11 (1963), 98–103.

Saussure, Ferdinand de. *Course in General Linguistics.* Ed. by Charles Bally and Albert Sechehaye. Tr. by Wade Baskin. New York: Philosophical Library, 1959.

Saussure, Ferdinand de. *Course in General Linguistics.* Ed. by Charles Bally and Albert Sechehaye. Tr. by Roy Harris. London: Gerald Duckworth, 1983.

Savage, G., and J. Officer. "CHOREO: An Interactive Computer Model for Dance" *International Journal of Man-Machine Studies* 10 (1978), 1–8.

Schechner, Richard. "Approaches." In *Performance Theory.* Rev. and exp. ed. New York: Routledge, 1988, pp. 1–34.

Schechner, Richard. "Drama, Script, Theatre, Performance" *Drama Review* 17:3 (1973), 5–36.

Schechner, Richard. "Drama, Script, Theatre, and Performance." In *Essays on Performance Theory, 1970–1976.* New York: Drama Book Specialists, 1977, pp. 36–62.

Schechner, Richard. "Drama, Script, Theatre, and Performance." In *Performance Theory.* Rev. and exp. ed. New York: Routledge, 1988, pp. 68–105.

Schechner, Richard. *Environmental Theater.* New York: Hawthorn, 1973.

Schechner, Richard. "Ethology and Theatre." In *Performance Theory.* Rev. and exp. ed. New York: Routledge, 1988, pp. 207–250.

Schechner, Richard. "Exit Thirties, Enter Sixties." In *Stanislavski and America.* Ed. by Erika Munk. New York: Hill and Wang, 1966, pp. 13–23.

Schechner, Richard. "An Interview with Joseph Chaikin" *TDR* 13:3 (1969), 141–144.

Schechner, Richard. "Performance and the Social Sciences" *Drama Review* 17:3 (1973), 3–4.

Schechner, Richard. "The Playwright as Wrighter." In *Four Plays by Megan Terry.* New York: Simon & Schuster, 1966, pp. 7–18.

Scheflen, Albert, and Alice Scheflen. *Body Language and the Social Order: Communication as Behavioral Control.* Englewood Cliffs, N.J.: Prentice-Hall, 1973.

Schickel, Richard. "In Computerland with TRON: Disney's Video Adventure is a Vision of the Movies' Future" *Time* 120:1 (1982), 62–65.

Schlieben-Lange, B. "La Cantatrice Chauve: Ein Lehrstuck in gelungener Kommunikation?" In *Literatur und Konversation: Sprachsoziologie und Pragmatik in der Literaturwissenschaft.* Ed. by Ernest Hess-Lüttich. Wiesbaden: Athenaion, 1980, pp. 239–257.

Schneidau, Herbert. *Sacred Discontent: The Bible and the Western Tradition.* Berkeley: University of California Press, 1976.

Schoenmakers, Henry. "The Tacit Majority in the Theatre." In *Theatre Semiotics*, vol. II of *Multimedial Communication*. Ed. by Ernest Hess-Lüttich. Tubingen: Narr, 1982, pp. 108–155.

Scott, Wilbur, ed. *Five Approaches of Literary Criticism.* New York: Collier Books, 1962.

Searle, John. *Speech Acts: An Essay in the Philosophy of Language.* London: Cambridge University Press, 1969.

Segal, M. "Studies in the Books of Samuel II: The Composition of the Book" *Jewish Quarterly Review* 8 (1917–1918), 75–100.

Selbourne, David. *The Making of A Midsummer Night's Dream: An Eyewitness Account of Peter Brook's Production from First Rehearsal to First Night.* London: Methuen, 1982.

Septuaginta. Ed. by Alfred Rahlfs. (1935) 5th ed. Stuttgart: Privileg. Wurtt. Bibelanstalt, 1952.

Shakespeare, William. *Macbeth.* Ed. by Kenneth Muir. London: Methuen, 1964.

Shklovsky, Viktor. "Art as Technique" (1917). In *Russian Formalist Criticism: Four Essays.* Tr. by Lee Lemon and Marion Reis. Lincoln: University of Nebraska Press, 1965, pp. 3–24.

Shannon, Claude, and Warren Weaver. *The Mathematical Theory of Communication.* Urbana: University of Illinois Press, 1964.

Shaw, Bernard. "Preface." In *Three Plays by Brieux.* New York: Brentano's, 1911, pp. xxii-xxvii.

Shepard, Sam. *The Tooth of Crime and Geography of a Horse Dreamer: Two Plays.* London: Faber and Faber, 1974.

Shepard, Sam. "Visualization, Language and the Inner Library" *Drama Review* 21:4 (1977), 49–58.

Simonov, P.V. "The Method of K.S. Stanislavsky and the Physiology of Emotion." In *Stanislavsky Today.* Ed. by Sonia Moore. New York: American Center for Stanislavski Theatre Art, 1973.

Simonson, Lee. *The Stage Is Set.* New York: Harcourt, Brace, 1932.

Smith, Anthony. *Orghast at Persepolis: An International Experiment in Theatre Directed by Peter Brook and Written by Ted Hughes.* New York: Viking Press, 1972.

Smith, Michael. "Introduction." In *Eight Plays from Off-Off Broadway*. Ed. by Nick Orzel and Michael Smith. New York: Bobbs-Merrill, 1966, pp. 1–16.

Sokolov, Evgenii. *Perception and the Conditioned Reflex*. Tr. by Stefan Waydenfeld. New York: Pergamon Press, 1963.

Spillner, B. "Pragmatische Analyse Kommunikativ komplexer Gesprächssituationen in den Komodien Molieres." In *Literatur und Konversation: Sprachsoziologie und Pragmatik in der Literaturwissenschaft*. Ed. by Ernest Hess-Lüttich. Wiesbaden: Athenaion, 1980, pp. 279–308.

Stambusky, Alan. "American College and University Play Production: 1963–1964" *Educational Theatre Journal* (May 1965), 122–127.

Stanislavsky, Konstantin. *An Actor Prepares*. Tr. by Elizabeth Hapgood. New York: Theatre Arts Books, 1936; rpt. 1948.

Stanislavsky, Konstantin. *Building a Character*. Tr. by Elizabeth Hapgood. New York: Theatre Arts Books, 1949.

Stanislavsky, Konstantin. *Creating a Role*. Tr. by Elizabeth Hapgood. New York: Theatre Arts Books, 1961.

Stanislavsky, Konstantin. *My Life in Art*. Tr. by G. Ivanov-Mumjiev. Moscow: Foreign Languages Publishing House, 1963.

Stanislavsky, Constantin. *My Life in Art*. Tr. by J.J. Robbins. Cleveland: World Publishing, 1948.

Stokoe, William. *Semiotics and Human Sign Languages*. The Hague: Mouton, 1972.

Stokoe, William. "Sign Language Structure: An Outline of the Visual Communication Systems of the American Deaf" *Studies in Linguistics: Occasional Papers 8*, 1960.

Styan, J.L. *Drama, Stage, and Audience*. Cambridge: Cambridge University Press, 1975.

Styan, J.L. *Shakespeare's Stagecraft*. Cambridge: Cambridge University Press, 1967.

Sukenik, Yigael. "Let the Young Men, I Pray Thee, Arise and Play before Us" *Journal of the Palestine Oriental Society* 21 (1948), 110–116.

Sullivan, Harry. *The Fusion of Psychiatry and Social Science*. New York: Norton, 1964.

Tan, Ed. "Cognitive Processes in Reception." In *Theatre Semiotics*, vol. II of *Multimedial Communication*. Ed. by Ernest Hess-Lüttich. Tubingen: Narr, 1982, pp. 156–203.

Terry, Megan. "Introduction to *Viet Rock*" *TDR* 11:1 (1966), 197.

Terry, Megan. *Viet Rock (A Folk War Movie)*. In *Viet Rock and Other Plays*. New York: Simon & Schuster, 1966, pp. 19–110.

Terry, Megan. "Who Says Only Words Make Great Drama?" *New York Times* 11–10–1968, sec. 2, pp. 1, 3.

Thenius, Otto. *Die Bücher Samuels*. 3rd ed. Leipsig: Max Lohr, 1898.

Trauth, Suzanne. "Effects of Director's System of Communication on Actor Inventiveness and Rehearsal Atmosphere" *Empirical Research in Theatre* (1980), 6–16.

Trilling, Ossia. "Playing with Words at Persepolis" *Theatre Quarterly* 2:5 (1972), 33–40.

Ubersfeld, Anne. *Lire le théâtre*. Paris: Editions sociales, 1977.

Unruh, Delbert. "Action Design" *Theatre Design and Technology* 23:1 (1987), 6–13.

Unruh, Delbert. "Composition in Light" *Theatre Design and Technology* 38 (1974), 17–22.

Valentine, Charles. *The Experimental Psychology of Beauty*. London: Methuen, 1962.

Vaux, Roland de. *The Bible and the Ancient Near East*. Tr. by Damian McHugh. Garden City: Doubleday, 1971.

Vega, Lope de. *Lo fingido verdadero/Acting is Believing*. Tr. by Michael McGaha. San Antonio: Trinity University Press, 1986.

Veltrusky, Jiri. "Dramatic Text as a Component of Theatre." In *Semiotics of Art*. Ed. by L. Matejka and J.R. Titunic. Cambridge: MIT Press, 1976, pp. 94–117.

Wagner, Phyllis. *Megan Terry: Political Playwright*. Ann Arbor: University Microfilms, 1973.

Wardle, Irving. "Actors at their New Exercise" *The Times* (London) 7–19–1968, p. 13, cl. 3.

Weales, Gerald. *The Jumping-Off Place: American Drama in the 1960's*. New York: Macmillan, 1969.

ellhausen, Julius. *Der Text der Bücher Samuelis untersucht*. Gottingen: Vandenhoeck und Ruprecht, 1871.

Wilkinson, Andrew. "A Psychological Approach to *Julius Caesar*" *Review of English Literature* 7 (1966), 65–78.

Wimsatt, William, and Monroe Beardsley. *The Verbal Icon: Studies in the Meaning of Poetry.* Lexington: University of Kentucky Press, 1954.

Wing, Kempton, and Karl Smith. "The Role of the Optic Cortex in the Dog in the Determination of the Functional Properties of Conditioned Reactions to Light" *Journal of Experimental Psychology* 31 (1962), 478–496.

Wittgenstein, Ludwig. *Philosophical Investigations.* Tr. by G. Anscombe. Oxford: Basil Blackwell, 1953.

Woodward, James, and Suzan De Santis. "Two to One It Happens: Dynamic Phonology in Two Sign Languages" *Sign Language Studies* 17 (1977), 329–346.

Zarrilli, Phillip. "For Whom Is the Invisible Not Visible? Reflections on Representation in the Work of Eugenio Barba" *TDR* 32:1 (1988), 95–106.

Zeleny, G., and B. Kadykov. "Contribution to the Study of Conditioned Reflexes in the Dog After Cortical Extirpation" *Psychological Abstracts* 12 No. 5829, 1938.

Zola, Emile. "Therese Raquin: Preface" (1873). In *Theatre: Therese Raquin; les Heritiers Rabourdin; et le Bouton de Rose.* Paris: Eugene Fasquelle, 1914, pp. 3–16.

Name Index

Subject Index